DATE DUE

KNOWLEDGE
and the
WEALTH *of* NATIONS

ALSO BY DAVID WARSH

The Idea of Economic Complexity
(1984)

Economic Principals:
Masters and Mavericks of Modern Economics
(1993)

KNOWLEDGE

and the

WEALTH *of* NATIONS

A Story of Economic Discovery

DAVID WARSH

W. W. NORTON & COMPANY

New York · London

For information about permission to reproduce selections from this book, write to Permissions,
W. W. Norton & Company, Inc., 500 Fifth Avenue, New York, NY 10110

Manufacturing by The Haddon Craftsmen, Inc.
Book design by Charlotte Staub
Production manager: Anna Oler

Library of Congress Cataloging-in-Publication Data

Warsh, David.
Knowledge and the wealth of nations : a story of economic discovery / David Warsh. — 1st ed.
p. cm.
Includes bibliographical references and index.
ISBN-13: 978-0-393-05996-0 (hardcover)
ISBN-10: 0-393-05996-0 (hardcover)
1. Economics—Research—United States. 2. Economics—Study and teaching—United States.
3. Economics—United States—History. 4. Economists—United States. I. Title.
HB74.8.W37 2006
330.0973—dc22

2005033677

W. W. Norton & Company, Inc., 500 Fifth Avenue, New York, N.Y. 10110
www.wwnorton.com

W. W. Norton & Company Ltd., Castle House, 75/76 Wells Street, London W1T 3QT

3 4 5 6 7 8 9 0

To the memory of

E. LAWRENCE (LAURY) MINARD III,
1950–2001

The construction of a model, or of any theory for that matter (or the writing of a novel, a short story or a play) consists of snatching from the enormous and complex mass of facts called reality a few simple, easily-managed key points which, when put together in some cunning way, become for certain purposes a substitute for reality itself.

—Evsey Domar, *Essays in the Theory of Economic Growth*

Truth emerges more readily from error than from confusion.

—Francis Bacon, *Novum Organum*

CONTENTS

PART TWO

PREFACE

This book tells the story of a single technical paper in economics—the events leading up to its publication in 1990 and some subsequent changes in our understanding of the world. My subsidiary aim is to convey something about how economics is done today in universities, for it is there, not in central banks or government offices or Wall Street firms, that the most important work takes place.

Between 1979 and 1994 a remarkable exchange unfolded among economists in hard-to-read technical journals concerning economic growth: what it is, what makes it happen, how we share it, how we measure it, what it costs us, and why it is worth having. Such was the sense of novelty that emerged from this exchange—of learning how to understand something for the first time, to write it down in such a way as to perpetuate the understanding of it, of *discovery*, in other words—that this literature quickly became known as "new growth theory." Many persons made contributions. A new generation rose to prominence in the field. Yet the issues themselves and the manner of their resolution remain unfamiliar to a wider audience.

I am an economic journalist, for many years a newspaperman, not an economist or a historian of economic thought. My mathematics is rudimentary, but my English is good, my skepticism fluent, and my background knowledge of economics fairly extensive from having followed the field for many years. The book is written from an outsider's point of view—an appreciative outsider, but one who hasn't altogether surrendered his skepticism. In other words, I am a civilian and a believer in civilian control.

Why focus on a single skein of work? Progress in economics these last thirty years has been rapid. Its scope has broadened and its generality increased. There are a great many stories to report. The new growth story first caught my eye because I was interested in specialization and the growth of knowledge. I've come to see it since, however, as a *representative* story—an illustration of how mathematics became the working language of modern economics, of why its practitioners deem their formal methods to have been such a success.

The new growth story shows how economic discovery occurs—in intense intellectual competition among small groups of researchers working in rival universities. From this competition emerge occasional transformations in understandings of the world, reflecting simultaneously the cumulative work of generations *and* the border-crossing journeys of research partners or, perhaps, a single person. Gradually these transformations make their way outward, like ripples spreading from a pebble thrown on a pond, until what originally was *their* understanding becomes *our* understanding as well.

Even today a majority of economists may not have made up their minds about what happened to their subject during the 1980s and early 1990s, in the subdiscipline of their field that is concerned with growth and development. Specialists tend to keep their heads down, after all. Nor have all the parties to the argument capitulated. Some readers may prefer to skip the backstory in this book and go directly to the various guides and textbooks that are beginning to appear.* They will be missing altogether a good story (and an important lesson) in their haste.

Many of the more public events in this story I covered as they occurred, often in meetings in stuffy hotel rooms on sunny days and in the conversation afterwards—a strange kind of news indeed. It is

---

* Elhanan Helpman's *The Mystery of Economic Growth* is the most illuminating of these summaries; Charles I. Jones's *Introduction to Economic Growth*, the best of the texts. David Landes's *The Wealth and Poverty of Nations: Why Some Are So Rich and Some So Poor* is a brilliant, entertaining, but largely atheoretical world tour of the issues.

humbling to look back and see how slowly the significance of these developments dawned on me, and how much longer it took me to put it into words on paper. But then, if it had been obvious, it wouldn't be news.

I talked to many people along the way. Almost all of them talked back, with varying degrees of candor. My thanks to all. Economists are a good lot, and they like a yarn as well as the next person. Only toward the end did I realize how much they were interested in keeping secret. Economists have their foibles too.

INTRODUCTION

O ne of the oldest chestnuts in the inventory of our common sense is this: Give a man a fish, and you feed him for a day. Teach a man how to fish, and you feed him for a lifetime. To which it now must be added, invent a better method of fishing, or of farming fish, selling fish, changing fish (through genetic engineering), or preventing overfishing in the sea, and you feed a great many people, because these methods can be copied virtually without cost and spread around the world. Of course, depending on the circumstances, your invention can make *you* rich as well. New ideas, more than savings or investment or even education, are the keys to prosperity, both to private fortunes, large and small, and to the wealth of nations—to economic growth, in other words, with its incalculable benefits for all. In the background are the intricate rules of the game that we summarize as the rule of law—and politics.

Yet it was not until October 1990 when a thirty-six-year-old University of Chicago economist named Paul Romer published a mathematical model of economic growth in a mainstream journal that the economics of knowledge at last came into focus, after more than two centuries of informal and uneasy presence in the background. The title of the paper was at once deceptively simple and intimidating: "Endogenous Technological Change."

The thirty-two-page article in the *Journal of Political Economy* observed all the ordinary conventions of scientific writing: passive

voice, mathematical analysis, modest claims. There were careful citations of earlier work in the same tradition, especially the paper
which it sought to supplant and on which it sought to build, "A Contribution to the Theory of Economic Growth," published in 1956 by
Robert Solow.

The first paragraph contained a sentence that was initially more
puzzling than not: "The distinguishing feature of . . . technology as
an input is that it is neither a conventional good nor a public good;
it is a nonrival, partially excludable good. . . ."

And thereupon hangs a tale. For that particular sentence, written
more than fifteen years ago and still not widely understood, initiated
a far-reaching conceptual rearrangement in economics. It did so by
augmenting the familiar distinction between "public" goods, supplied by governments, and "private" goods, supplied by market participants, with a second opposition, between "rival" and "nonrival"
goods—between goods whose corporeality makes possible their
absolute possession and limited sharing (an ice-cream cone, a house,
a job, a Treasury bond) and goods whose essence can be written
down and stored in a computer as a string of bits and shared equally
by many persons at the same time practically without limit (a holy
book, a language, the calculus, the principles of design of a bicycle).
Inevitably, most goods must consist of at least a little of each. In
between these extremes lie myriad interesting possibilities.

A designer dress. The operating system software in a personal
computer. A jazz concert. A Beatles recording. The design of a new
computer chip. The coded signal from a communications satellite. A
map of the human genome. The molecular structure of a new
drug—and the secrets of its efficient manufacture. A genetically
altered seed—and the series of manipulations that produced it. A
Picasso painting, both the canvas itself with its brushstrokes and lay-
ers of paint, and its myriad reproductions. A "Baby on Board" sign
in an auto window. The text of the book you are reading now. The
equation on page 24. All these are nonrival goods because they can
be copied or shared and used by many people at the same time. Most
are partially *excludable* as well, meaning that access to them can in
some degree be controlled, at least in principle. Rival goods are

objects and nonrival goods are *ideas*—"atoms" and "bits," in a catchy phrase borrowed from computing, where ideas are expressed in strings of binary bits; or "convexities" and "nonconvexities," in the more austere language of mathematics.

By itself the concept of nonrivalry wasn't altogether new to economics. For more than a century public finance specialists had used a series of often confusing terms to explain the source of "market failure"—to describe the underlying commonality of, say, national defense or streetlights, a new bridge or the warning provided by a lighthouse. Nonrivalry took its place among them in the 1960s. It was by marrying nonrivalry to the concept of excludability, and applying the distinction where it had not been employed before, that Romer cast a new light on the ubiquitous role of ideas in the economics of everyday life—meaning trade secrets, formulas, trademarks, algorithms, mechanisms, patents, scientific laws, designs, maps, recipes, procedures, business methods, copyrights, bootleg copies; collectively, that is, the economics of *knowledge*. He illuminated an inescapable tension between creating incentives for the production of *new* ideas and maintaining incentives for the efficient distribution and use of *existing* knowledge—the social choice that creates what we call intellectual property.

Managing the tension between these ends—furthering the growth of knowledge while ensuring that its benefits are widely shared—is a responsibility of government every bit as important as monetary and fiscal policy. If the intricate system of incentives to create new ideas is underdeveloped, society suffers from the general lack of progress (most of all, the poor). So, too, if those incentives are too lavish or too closely held.

Grasp that, and you understand the punch line of the story that this book has to tell. Chances are that intuitively you understood it well enough already

But with the publication of "Endogenous Technological Change," Romer won a race of sorts, a race within the community of university-based research economists to make sense of the process of globalization at the end of the twentieth century, and to say something practical and new about how to encourage economic development in places where it had failed to occur. That there had been a race at all was apparent only to a relative handful of persons, those offering competing explanations of events. That there might exist a "right answer" to the riddle of economic growth, or even that a riddle existed at all, was denied by many people and probably doubted by most.

Yet within a few years the issues attending the post–World War II growth in the wealth of nations had been clarified and, if not resolved, at least reframed in the formal language of technical economics. The basic choices had become clearer than before. The contribution of the growth of knowledge had been broached in a way that permitted its analysis. A new emphasis had been placed on the role of institutions. And a secure role finally was assigned to that long-neglected figure (at least in economics classrooms), the enterpreneur.

"Romer '90" (to use the article's citation shorthand) doesn't fit our conception of a classic, to be placed on the shelf alongside the works of other great worldly philosophers. But it *is*—for reasons that are relatively easy to explain.

CONSIDER THE BASIC building blocks of economic theory—the familiar "factors of production." They are described in the first chapter of almost any elementary economics text. For three centuries these most fundamental analytic categories of economics were land, labor, and capital. Land was shorthand for the productive capacities of the earth itself, its pastures and forests and rivers and oceans and mines. Labor, for the diverse efforts, talents, and simple motive power of working men and women. Capital, for the equipment that they employed and the structures in which they work and live, not just the goods themselves, but financial assets of all sorts representing command over these goods and the services of labor. These categories had been worked out during the seventeenth century, when the expanding global economy gave birth to modern capitalism. They referred to familiar, everyday things and seemed to leave nothing out. They enabled economists to argue about who should produce what goods and for whom, about work relationships, about the determinants of the size of the human population, about which responsibilities properly belonged to government and which were best left to markets.

From the beginning, some circumstances in the human condition were simply taken for granted. The extent of knowledge was one. Human nature itself, expressed as tastes and preferences, was another. These were "givens," not necessarily thought to be unchanging, but considered to be determined by noneconomic forces—a simplifying custom in technical economics that went back at least to the nineteenth century and John Stuart Mill. These background conditions were, in modern parlance, treated as being *exogenous* to the economic system. They lay outside the model, treated as a "black box" whose detailed internal workings were to be willfully ignored. Exogenous to her concerns is what the waitress means when she says, "It's not my table."

Certain loose ends arose as a result of this way of dividing up the world, especially a well-known family of troublesome effects that were filed under the heading of "increasing returns" to scale. Decreasing returns to additional investment were a familiar topic in economics. After all, even the richest vein of coal plays out. The first barrel of fertilizer does wonders for a plot of land; the tenth only burns the crops. Decreasing or diminishing returns simply mean that you pick the low-hanging fruit first, and that you collect less fruit for the same amount of effort over time. It means that your costs slowly rise.

Increasing returns are just the opposite. They set in when the same amount of work or sacrifice produces an *increasing* quantity of goods or, to turn the definition on its head, when your average costs fall and keep falling with the number of articles produced. Pins are the example usually given, after a famous passage by Adam Smith about the gains from specialization. But Smith's story of falling costs seemed to be only about the benefits of the subdivision of tasks. Obviously there were limits to that, too.

Throughout the nineteenth century, increasing returns were considered to have to do mainly with the output of machines—the printing press, the mechanical loom, the steam engine. Gradually it was recognized that increasing returns were present any time there was little or no additional cost to adding a customer to a network—railroads, electricity, telephones, for example. Increasing returns (falling costs) in these and other industries were so destructive of the ordinary forces of competition that such businesses soon were declared to be not just monopolies but "natural monopolies," markets whose fundamental properties led inexorably to a single producer of goods with no close substitutes, and whose conduct in the absence of competitive forces necessarily would have to be overseen by government.

Economists who came after Adam Smith never were very comfortable with the phenomenon of increasing returns, of steadily falling costs. It ran counter to their most basic intuition—that scarcity was the fundamental problem, that the human race was forever running out of something, whether land, or food, or coal, or clean air. Falling costs violated this understanding, and they were much less consistent than rising costs with the mathematical tools that they employed to describe and analyze the effects of competition. Monopolies were understood to be exceptions to the rule. Situations in which producers were free to set their prices, rather than have them set by competitive forces, were special cases of "market failure," to be mentioned in footnotes, left out of the argument altogether, while economists focused on competition.

So the problem of increasing returns was put aside for some later date. Economists finessed it, introducing concepts that seemed to make the contradictions disappear—the convenient assumption, for example, that overall returns to scale might generally be neither increasing nor decreasing but *constant*, that effort and output forever would increase only in direct proportion to one another. In establishing this assumption as a mostly unconscious mental habit, growing formalization played a central role.

With the addition of each new wave of technique, from literary economics to syllogism in the eighteenth century, from syllogism to calculus in the nineteenth, from calculus to set theory and topology in the twentieth, the status of increasing returns became more problematic and obscure, especially after the triumph in the 1950s of formal models of the economy as a whole.

IN THE LATE 1970s and early 1980s, the situation began to change. The developments in growth theory with which this book is concerned unfolded mainly in Cambridge, Massachusetts, and Chicago, very far indeed from the controversies over "supply-side economics" that garnered headlines in New York City and Washington, D.C. in those days. A handful of graduate students at the University of Chicago, the Massachusetts Institute of Technology, Harvard University, and Princeton University discovered for themselves that the blind spot in the vocabulary and analytic framework of economics, once small, had with the passage of time (and increased abstraction) become enormous. They set out to make formal models of the phenomena that led to increasing returns. And in fairly short order they succeeded.

For a time these matters were no more earthshaking than conversations among the young economists and their teachers, their spouses, friends, and competitors. Excitement slowly spread throughout the discipline. New ideas about subjects such as novelty, variety, and market power were mapped into the tapestry of economic thought—first in the subfield of industrial organization, then in trade, then in growth, then back into industrial organization. New models were applied to policies for population, education, science, entrepreneurship, trade, antitrust, and cities, not to mention the familiar macroeconomic concerns of monetary and fiscal policy. These studies meshed with the new emphasis on political economy. They turned rapidly to the political and economic institutions that accommodate change—arrangements that were themselves a kind of knowledge. For a few years in the early 1990s, almost everybody in economics had something to say about the new ideas regarding increasing returns.

These developments, which would otherwise remain quite obscure, have the advantage of having been a deeply human drama as well, in which present-day heroes in certain ways personify the generations of modern economics—Robert Solow born in 1924, Robert Lucas born in 1937, and Paul Romer born in 1955. The story of how knowledge was left out of economics for so long—and why, in some quarters, it is *still* met with a reluctant reception—makes a pretty good yarn by itself.

For the significance of "Endogenous Technological Change" becomes clear as soon as soon as the paper's key equations are translated into everyday language. Romer's 1990 paper divided up the economic world along lines different from earlier ones. Overnight for those who were involved in actually making the intellectual revolution, more slowly for all the rest of us, the traditional "factors of production" were redefined. The fundamental categories of economic analysis ceased to be, as they had been for two hundred years, land, labor, and capital. This most elementary classification was supplanted by people, ideas, and things.

People, ideas, and things. This phrase isn't in the textbooks yet. It isn't widespread in the literature. But once the economics of knowledge was recognized as differing in crucial respects (nonrival, partially excludable goods!) from the traditional economics of people (human beings with all their know-how, skills, and strengths) and things (traditional forms of capital, from natural resources to stocks and bonds), the matter was settled. The field had changed. The familiar principle of scarcity had been augmented by the important principle of abundance.

Technical change and the growth of knowledge had become *endogenous*—within the vocabulary and province of economics to explain. A certain amount of commotion was the result. To see it, however, you have to know where to look.

PART
I

The Discipline

"THE MEETINGS," as its initiates usually call the annual conventions of the Allied Social Science Associations, the agenda dominated by the American Economic Association (AEA), unfold each year like an urban Brigadoon, their location forever shifting among convention cities. On the first weekend after New Year's Day, economists who are members of the AEA and various hangers-on gather in a big hotel—in several big hotels—to give talks, learn about the newest ideas, hear ventilated the latest controversies, interview job seekers (or troll for job offers themselves, and just schmooze). Something like 8,000 persons attend, depending on the city; around 12,000 AEA members stay home, content to make their intellectual capital serve for another year. (They can skim the best papers when short versions are published in May.) Perhaps another 18,000 professional economists don't bother with membership in the society. The Meetings are where economics is ceremonially performed by its adherents; they are the capital of a law-governed republic of ideas.

The program listings make a 400-page book. Yet everybody seems to know just what to do; conversations in one city are resumed more or less where they were left off in another the year before. Great intrigues are plotted behind the scenes beforehand, then unfold in public with barely a clue as to the identity of the mugger and the muggee. Rank and privilege are all clearly understood by the initiates: there are very few disruptions, except for the occasional quack. Always there are a handful of outsiders. Every year a few journalists attend for the first time. Everything is open-ended, forward-looking; no conversation ever seems to end. Two and a half days of intensive talks of one sort or another, and then the meeting-goers are gone.

The AEA is, if not the most senior body of those who consider themselves scientific economists, at least the most visible forum in which they convene. Included are the people who win the Nobel Prizes, write the textbooks, coin the vocabulary, staff the president's Council of Economic Advisers, advise central bankers and Wall Street, frame the understanding with which we discuss the issues of the present day. Above all, here are the people who teach the subject to the next generation in colleges and universities. Indeed, the overwhelming majority of the association's roughly 18,000 members are professors. With the exception of four scholars from the Brookings Institution, three ex-economists turned university presidents, and an economist from the Institute for Advanced Study at Princeton, the AEA hasn't been headed by anyone other than a university professor since it was founded in 1885. (Paul Douglas, a University of Chicago professor, served as president the year before he was elected to the U.S. Senate from the state of Illinois.) Nor has the AEA been headed by anyone who was not a U.S. citizen, the three who were born in Canada included.

There are many ways an economist can make a mark other than as a researcher/teacher: run a company, lead a university, make a lot of money, administer a foundation, be a central banker, become a policy maven, a measurement economist, a powerful adviser, or even a politician. At least until recently—perhaps still—those who make their living in financial markets made a sharp distinction between academic economists and *markets men* (and women), meaning those whose instincts have been honed more by practical experience than by research and teaching. So significant a figure as Paul Volcker disparaged economic book-learning, even though (or perhaps because) he received a master's degree at Harvard in the early 1950s. His successor, Alan Greenspan, completed his New York University Ph.D., but only twenty-seven years after leaving school, having first served a term as chairman of the president's Council of Economic Advisers. The National Association of Business Economists, which meets in the autumn, caters to more practical analysts working mostly for financial and industrial firms; the Academy of Management, for business school professors and consultants, meets every summer. And of course the overwhelming majority of participants in markets—executives, money managers, traders, accountants, lawyers, practitioners of all sorts—are not economists at all.

Some very good economists have gone to work on Wall Street in recent years, and a few remain active in the AEA, even though their primary focus has become making money instead of creating a widely shared understanding of it. But the significance of the Meetings is that, at its highest levels, economics is a science practiced and overseen by a professoriate, like astronomy, chemistry, physics, and molecular biology. It has been increasingly so ever since Adam Smith, who was, after all, the first economist to be based in a university (the University of Glasgow). This deeply structured community of self-selecting peers is the uppermost stratum of the world of technical economics.

It says "American" on the program, but for the past half century, the Meetings have also served the de facto world organization, because it is in America that the discussion of economics is most liquid and deep—just as are its financial markets. Beneath the umbrella of the American Social Science Association, itself the relic of nineteenth-century battles among reformers, religious leaders, historians, and economists that produced the AEA, there exists a loose hierarchy of lesser professional economic societies, more than fifty of them, of which the AEA is the most important. (The American Historical Association long ago set up housekeeping on its own.) The more specialized societies are organized along both geographical and functional lines—the Western, Eastern, Southern, and Midwest Associations; the Finance Association; the Public Choice Society; the Union of Radical Political Economists; and so on—all operate with the informal understanding that players who do well devising explanations that are persuasive to one group will want to present their material in the next higher venue until it is accepted or rejected by all.

The elite Econometric Society has much more of an international flavor than the AEA. It was organized in the 1930s, explicitly along global lines: half its members reside outside the United States, it deliberately selects its presidents from rotating regions, and it has regular annual or biennial meetings on every continent and a world congress every five years. Its membership has two classes. Anyone is free to join, but fellows of the society are nominated by existing fellows, occasionally even before they are thirty-five years old. The fellowship itself then votes, and nearly two-thirds of all nominations are defeated on the first try. The result is a self-consciously international society of the crème de la crème of technical economists (580 fellows, 141 of them "inactive," meaning mostly old, 4,910 members at the end of 2004) that deliberately does not seek the public eye. Yet even though its intellectual level is pitched much higher, the Econometric Society in fact functions one notch below the AEA in terms of public recognition, for it is the AEA that self-consciously aims to be the big tent, the forum to which all serious developments eventually must be brought for examination, comparison, and collision, the math translated back to verbal formulation before the results are reported to the waiting public. Balkanization among professional specialties is forever a threat. And in recent years the European Economic Association has greatly improved its standing. But even so there has been no serious challenge to the AEA's hegemony.

Why does America dominate? Because it is by far the world's broadest, deepest market for what economics has to offer—everything from cutting-edge research to routine instruction to mechanism design, strategic analysis, and prognostication. The financial markets alone account for thousands of jobs for economists. The major banks and Wall Street firms have become founts of serious research. Mainly through the National Science Foundation, the U.S. government spends several hundred million dollars annually training economists and sponsoring pure economic research. The opportunity to specialize, to burrow deep, to test wits against others of similar ambition, is greatest in the country's research universities (though its colleges are home to many active scholars, too).

If you look at the list of AEA presidents in the last few years, a composite picture emerges of all the various ways there are to make a living. There is Arnold Harberger, whose marriage to a Chilean woman foreshadowed the establishment of a strong and durable connection between Chilean technocrats and the University of Chicago, a tie that in turn by a series of infinitely small ripples eventually changed the practice of development economics around the world. Amartya Sen, who rose from a small Bengali village to become master of Trinity College, Cambridge, by dint of asking penetrating questions about the nature of wealth and poverty. Victor Fuchs, who started out studying the economics of the retail fur trade, only to become one of the profession's premier students of health care economics. Zvi Griliches, a Lithuanian survivor of the Holocaust who zeroed in on the significance of hybrid corn and focused attention on corporate research and development. William Vickrey, a brilliant Canadian eccentric, far ahead of his time, who had been all but forgotten by the profession—until his former students lobbied for his election as president of the association and argued successfully for a Nobel Prize (he died three days after it was announced). Thomas Schelling, the pioneering strategist who made game theory serve everyday economics for thirty years. Gerard Debreu, an austere Frenchman who codified mathematical economics while the Berkeley "free speech" movement unfolded outside his window. Indeed, go back far enough and you'll find John Kenneth Galbraith, a literary economist who criticized the profession in a succession of widely read books—and who is said to have won his presidency only after the immediate past president, Milton Friedman, angered the nominating committee (of which he was a member) by asserting that Galbraith "wasn't an economist at all."

Moreover, many of those who most profoundly affect economics never go to the convention, at least not until they have reached the point of universal recognition. Like any science, economics reserves its highest honors to those who operate in the realm of original research in such a way as to change professionals' minds. Thus a small corps of foreign honorary members of the AEA (it is limited to forty) provides a way of recognizing the most distinguished thinkers in other lands—fourteen from the United Kingdom, six from France, four each from Israel, Germany, and Japan; two Indians, and single representatives from Australia, Belgium, Hungary, Spain, Sweden, and Switzerland as of 2004. Senior figures who are not expected to be called upon to be president, but whose contribution is judged quite remarkable nonetheless, are named distinguished fellows of the association, at the rate of two a year, a consolation prize. At the very pinnacle of the profession, at least in terms of prestige among *outsiders*, are the Nobel laureates.

The Nobel award for economics is a recent invention. It is reserved for people who have been able to make some dramatic change in the tapestry, the vision of the field as seen by all economists. These thinkers often are not drawn from the same pool as the clubbable leaders of the association. (Academic diplomats make the best presidents.) There are overlaps, of course: Paul Samuelson and Milton Friedman were prizewinners and good presidents. Yet some Nobel laureates are persons who have worked in isolation from one another, interacting intensely with small groups of other specialists, but otherwise fairly aloof from civic affairs. There are even those who may not come to the Meetings until they are honored; a few never come at all. What these thinkers have in common is a very deep understanding of rules and ideas that govern debate in what they view as a republic of ideas. They are persons who, one way or another, have changed what it is that economists are able to see.

CHAPTER TWO

"It Tells You Where to Carve the Joints"

THE 400-PAGE PROGRAM of the Meetings is overwhelming, not so much the range of topics—from money and banking to health and environmental economics—but rather the bewildering array of mathematical and econometric tools employed in their discussion. Dynamic programming and matrix algebra. Markov processes and Euler equations. Nonparametric covariance estimation for space-time random fields. Even when economists are talking about familiar topics—self-confidence, say, or identity—their discussion is likely to be couched in terms of hyperbolic discounting and subject to probabilistic interpretation. Hundreds of sessions, dozens of topics, myriad points of view. Sometimes it seems no one economist could comprehend, or even subscribe to, it all.

Underneath, however, the social fabric of the Meetings is the very picture of normal science. Large numbers of people are occupied filling in details, elucidating puzzles, solving problems, creating tools, demonstrating applications. To the participants this is the exciting stuff with which careers are built. To outsiders much of the Meetings is boring.

When big doings are at hand, however, when the system of belief is under stress, you can see people choosing up sides, though not necessarily in the public sessions. To discover the institutions through whose workings technical economics changes from year to year, it is necessary to go behind the scenes, to the social occasions where much of the convention's real business is done. The very existence of these is easy to miss, though listings appear in the front and the back of the 400-page book. The easiest place to discover them is the exhibition hall. It is here that the real money is made, with the first of several powerful institutions that concern us—textbooks.

Publishing is the operating arm of economics. Many books are on display in the exhibition hall, but the talk centers mainly on "adoptions"—which textbooks are being assigned in colleges, junior colleges, and universities in the coming year. At more than $130 a copy (plus as much as another $25 or so for "supplementals," meaning workbooks, study guides, batteries of tests, and so on that are used at many colleges), economics textbooks, at least the successful ones, are among the most lucrative of all publishing investments. No wonder every year sees the publication of new texts by economists seeking to impose a slightly different vision on their field.

Every once in a while a famous economist will wander into the hall and cut a swath through it: the reaction to celebrities is no different at an economics fair from that in any other business. Publishing officials manning the booths and bystanders stop talking and orient themselves to the star. If you pause for a moment to wonder where big shots are in the long hours between their appearances in the exhibition hall or on the dais, you will discover that they are down in the basement or off in hotel suites, interviewing the young economists who have entered the job market, most of them for the first time: the best people of one generation, looking for the best people of the next.

The job market is the culmination of an intense process that begins one day each spring when a new crop of applicants to the graduate schools around the world find out whether they've been accepted. How many apply? Perhaps 10,000 annually, to something like 400 programs, ranging from Harvard and the University of Chicago to the Tel Aviv University, Moscow's Plekhanov Institute of National Economy, and the Delhi School of Economics. How many enroll? Fewer than a quarter of that. How many finish? Not even most—the system churns out plenty of master's degrees and ABDs abound (students who have completed all but their dissertation). Around 850 new Ph.D.'s have graduated annually from U.S. universities for the last few years—perhaps about as many again in other universities around the world. In contrast, some 15,000 physicians are minted annually in the United States. Around 4,400 dentists. More than 6,600 Ph.D. engineers. Nearly 40,000 lawyers. And about 120,000 M.B.A.'s.

Yet the professorships and government appointments for which the best young economists eventually will compete are in many ways comparable to and even a bit more rewarding than the situations of top doctors and lawyers, despite a considerable pay gap. A few young economists' salaries have reached $200,000 and up in universities and three times as much in some business schools. There can be a great deal of outside income—a proprietary software program, a consulting relationship, board memberships, expert witness fees. And, of course, there are always possibilities in the financial markets.

In economics, as in basketball, it is relatively easy to tell who has major-league potential. A walk-on genius turns up occasionally, to be sure. And every year a few prospects apply to economics rather than to some other field at the last moment. But in general most of the top candidates in each entering class have been identified by their colleges, from the courses that they take, as early as their junior year. Often these are more in mathematics than in economics, for mathematics is the language in which the basic business of economics is conducted, and proficiency in it must be acquired at an early age. So graduate programs compete among themselves to lure these students.

Faculties promise the most personal attention, the best teaching, the greatest support, the quickest and least disruptive paths to senior appointments. The very best students are awarded National Science Foundation grants and scholarships to cover their tuition bills and living expenses, as much as $50,000 a year, on the basis of their math Graduate Record Exams and letters of recommendation.

What makes a good student? It takes more than mathematics. Just because acolytes learn the intricacies of formal reasoning doesn't mean that they necessarily will have anything to say. But then, neither does background knowledge of specifics seem to have to do with it. Apt pupils come from all walks of life, and one of the best young economists of recent years lived in the former Soviet Union until he was sixteen. Scientific temperament is a plus ("desire to seek, patience to doubt, fondness to meditate, slowness to assert, readiness to reconsider, carefulness to dispose and set in order," was how Sir Francis Bacon described it long ago). But the essential gift among those who will have an impact is an aptitude for "thinking economically," for translating every problem into one that can be addressed by means of the discipline's standard kit of tools, devising new tools as required.

The first year is commonly described as a kind of a boot camp, in which recruits are drilled relentlessly in the use of the techniques and tools they must master in order to begin, ever so tentatively, their professional careers. The best schools don't even bother with a text. Instead, there are lectures and assigned readings, followed by endless sets of problem to be worked out. Students often compare the process to learning to speak a new language fluently. There are papers to be written, examinations to be taken to establish competence in broad fields, and, all the while, the students' endless conversation among themselves. Two years of courses are enough for students to master the basic tools of economics and the consensus that is the cutting edge of a particular specialty. Then comes a third year of seminars and topics courses in which it is said that students, having received the dogma, must learn to think for themselves. Then a thesis. Five years in all; six, perhaps, four for a few. When the thesis is nearly complete, the newly minted Ph.D.'s enter a job market that resembles a professional sports draft, one in which each year's entrants are well advertised to potential employers in advance. Every year a few sure-fire stars join the league, many journey persons, the usual collection of utility players and dark horses. Some will go to work in industry or government without ever teaching. Only a handful from each graduating class will eventually enter the research hall of fame. But nearly all will enjoy a full career.

The third institution at the Meetings you are less likely to find on your own. It is the cocktail parties that are given in the evenings by the various university departments for their alumni and friends. In principle, you are welcome without an invitation, but you may feel a little odd. If the shorthand of the corridors is somewhat telegraphic, the talk at the cocktail parties is even more abbreviated. Much is left out because it is already known. These are, after all, people who have been to the same boot camp. They entered the job market in different eras, went forward, changed the dogma—or failed to change it. Surprises occur. The facile kid gets stuck; the quiet one grows graceful. Completely unremembered faces return as peers or, more likely, take up secure positions in the provinces. People come together, briefly relive old glories of the early years, then go on to dinner in quite different combinations.

The best departments—those of MIT, Harvard, Chicago, Princeton, Berkeley, Stanford—remain on top, year after year. Yet change is forever under way. Departments are like so many major-league sports teams, not just hiring entry-level economists but also making offers to stars in other departments—sometimes flurries of offers—in effect, free-agent signings. Somehow the very top of the pole is forever up for grabs. For example, rich Princeton University has made offers to nearly twenty top people around the world. If all were suddenly accepted, Princeton might suddenly be considered the best department in the world. But there are powerful counterforces, too. Those who are raided raid back.

There are perhaps a dozen candidates for the next five spots in the pecking order—Yale, Cambridge, Oxford, the London School of Economics, Northwestern University, Boston University, New York University, the University of Pennsylvania, and the University of Michigan among them. Beyond that second tier are many other departments in good universities at which it is possible to do top-quality research. A circular interdependence is the rule: the best universities are the ones that get the best students; they in turn attract the best teacher/researchers; add mixture as before. But there are plenty of good students, enough to support well over 100 Ph.D. programs in the United States alone, of which forty or fifty are considered pretty good.

The final destination on our tour, and in many ways the most important, we will find only if we linger in the corridors after the cocktail parties break up, and meeting-goers stream out into the night to restaurants around the town. Throughout the hotels' public floors, rooms have been put aside for smaller dinners. These are the editor/referee dinners of the journals, the most nearly invisible and most exclusive of our institutions—here there is no sneaking in. It is at these dinners where departmental loyalties symbolically are divided, where economics' ambition to be a true republic of ideas takes over from its more parochial concerns and institutional loyalties.

The journal article is the basic vehicle of a career in economics, just as it is in any other scientific field worthy of the name. Journals, as someone has said, were invented (in the late seventeenth century) to publish fragments. The idea is to limit claims narrowly to what can be said with absolute certainty; to map them carefully into the tapestry of what is already known; to use citations sparingly to reward prior work and indicate where the new material fits in. Journal articles may be used to announce new discoveries, to comment on or criticize the discoveries of others, to synthesize and seek to build consensus about what is known. The subtlety of the form is very great. Above all, however, each new contribution to the literature must be honest and original. These standards are enforced through the tradition of refereeing.

Refereeing in economics (or any science) is not much different from what it is in sports, though the etiquette is more delicate. In economics the referees don't wear striped shirts, the job is usually done sitting down, and nobody does it full-time. The main difference is that scientific refereeing is performed *anonymously*. As the historian of science John Ziman says, "The mere fact that an author has a Ph.D.—or is even a distinguished professor—does not ensure that he is free from bias, folly, error, or even mild insanity." So journal editors depend upon the advice of panels of friendly experts to read submissions and recommend their acceptance or rejection. The manuscript to be reviewed arrives in the referee's mailbox with no name or affiliation. A recommendation is arrived at and explained and returned, also anonymously. Referees, of course, may instantly recognize the distinctive stamp of a colleague's work, just as authors often are aware of their referees' identities. It is in the nature of the virtual communities of experts scattered around the world by which cutting-edge research is performed—"invisible colleges," Sir Robert Boyle dubbed them 350 years ago—that everybody in a particular subdiscipline knows everyone else. But the arm's-length façade is maintained. Then the editor decides to accept or reject—and hopes that the published article will not be criticized or, worse, ignored.

It is this mechanism, which ensures that published research meets community standards of plausibility and honesty, that permits economists to utter the most strangely powerful words in all the vocabulary of science, "The profession thinks . . ." A useful definition has it that "economics is what economists do." But this is mainly for the benefit of outsiders. What economists are *trying* to do among themselves is pin things down, achieve consensus. Following Norman Campbell's famous formulation of scientific aims, economics is "the study of those judgments [about certain phenomena] concerning which universal agreement can be obtained"—first from referees and eventually from the rest of us.

Notice something interesting, which will turn out to be important. Money has no place in this refereeing system. Yet most top economists spend a significant fraction of their time at the task. Journal editors assemble networks of researchers who have reputations for being the smartest or fairest persons on the edges of their fields or, ideally, both. These referees agree to read all new submissions and recommend for or against their publication. Often they suggest changes—or insist on them. Editors judge referees by their turnaround time, the degree of their constructive engagement with authors, and their wisdom. The good behavior of referees is reinforced by the fact they, too, are scientists. Their own papers will be submitted to other referees. Elaborate pains are taken to assure that success in economics, as in any science, is independent of wealth, prestige, or connections. These efforts are not always successful. A good deal of back-scratching and favor trading takes place. Still, the peer-selected meritocracy that is professional economics stands in sharp contrast to the social system of commerce and industry, where top-down orders are the rule and making money is the prime directive.

Indeed, refereeing is perhaps the single most effective way to demonstrate good citizenship and to assess character. Journal editors are selected from those who serve most successfully as referees. So are the officers of professional associations, such as the AEA. Only a few referees prove to be downright dishonest. They may press submitters for inappropriate citations of their own work, or even engage in "front-running"—trying to quickly incorporate into articles of their own the freshest and most penetrating insights they glean from the work they have been asked to review. But even the best referees can censor ideas that deserve to be heard. In fact, the most common failing is the tendency to attach too much weight to received opinion. Most pathbreaking contributions—not many, *most*—are rejected several times before they finally find a home.

That's why there is not just one journal of economics but many, with overlapping interests. The "big four" mainstream journals, publishing work of the broadest interest, are the *Journal of Political Economy*, the *Quarterly Journal of Economics*, the *American Economic Review*, and *Econometrica*. The *Economic Journal*, the flagship of economics in the United Kingdom for more than a century, always will have a sentimental place in the firmament as well, but it is now regarded as being well off the chase. A second echelon exists, and a third and a fourth. Start-ups, such as the *Journal of Economic Theory*, occupy an important place in the production of the scientific literature; they can light up the sky for a time by taking the winning side in doctrinal disputes, eventually forcing others to imitate and conform. The sense of hierarchy, however—among departments, among journals—is always present.

Now LET US VISIT a particular set of meetings—the convention of the American Economic Association that was held in San Francisco in January 1996. Remember, our interest here is how a particular paper published in 1990, "Endogenous Technological Change," precipitated some changes, first in the language of economics and thereafter in the wider world. For the purposes of our story, the San

Francisco meetings were unusually interesting. It was there that the new ideas were presented to a general audience for the first time.

Those who attend each year's Meetings are taking part in an intricately choreographed ritual that, for all its imperfections, serves to survey, summarize, and put the stamp of social recognition on some portion of what is deemed to be the best formal work done by members of the profession in the year or three years or five before. I say three or five because there is something "rolling" about the procedure; there can be no attempt to have everything on the program every year, and, besides, three to five years is about the length of time it takes to get a new contribution thought through and tested and ready to show. I say formal because the papers presented at the Meetings are only a certain part of technical economics. The hardest work, real economics, is done elsewhere, alone or in intense collaborations. The work presented at the Meetings almost always has a long pre-history as part of an individual's research agenda.

The contributions that are reported may have begun in a moment of inspiration. But before they can make their way to the Meetings, models must be carefully spelled out, evidence assembled, drafts written—long hours spent at the computer—before initial submissions can be sent and posted to the community as "working papers" by first-draft publishers such as the National Bureau of Economic Research or the Social Science Research Network; then presented, first at home and later at other institutions; and, in due course, submitted to journals. Not all papers are published by the journal to which they are first submitted; not all papers are published, period. But those that are headed for important journals ordinarily are subject to a continual wash of informal appraisal and debate, carried on in an endless series of emails, lunchroom conversations, telephone calls and seminar participation, conferences, project meetings, and summer camps. Only when a skein of work has achieved a certain degree of recognition as being *significant* in relation to all the rest of the stream of published research is it considered eligible for recognition at the Meetings. Then the wait for an invitation begins.

The assignment of the president-elect is to organize Meetings that will showcase the most interesting work across all fields. No one per-

son can possibly have well-informed opinions about the eighteen or
so subdisciplines into which economics is divided by the AEA. So for
that purpose the new president appoints a program committee. Its
members organize a majority of the invited sessions. The president
herself chooses three or four panels. The program of the Meetings
only looks passive and impersonal. Inevitably the program bears a
strong element of personality.

The 1996 San Francisco meetings, for example, were organized by
a Stanford University economist named Anne Krueger. Like every
president, she had her story. As adviser to the government of Turkey,
she had been a contributor to the renaissance of market liberalism in
the 1970s on strictly analytic grounds, at a time when relatively
heavy regulation of many aspects of economic life had been taken
for granted by most economists. There were many other significant
contributors to what in the early 1980s came to be known as the new
political economy. They included many distinguished names, and to
enumerate even the best known among them is to risk sounding like
Homer's Catalog of Ships.* By the early 1990s the mood of perestroika was universal, and it was time to begin handing out honors.
Krueger had succeeded greatly in a world that until recently had
been populated almost entirely by men. It was appropriate that
someone from the new political economy community should get the
nod. That year it was Krueger.

The incoming president confronts a blank agenda that looks like

---

* For example, how many on this short list of heavy hitters in the perestroika move-
ment do you know? Rudiger Dornbusch, Paul Joskow, Richard Schmalensee, and
Jagdish Bhagwati at MIT (later Columbia); Milton Friedman, George Stigler, Ronald
Coase, Sam Peltzman, D. Gale Johnson, and Arnold Harberger at Chicago; John Meyer
and Martin Feldstein at Harvard; Assar Lindbeck at Stockholm University, Hollis
Chenery at the World Bank; Reuven Brenner at McGill; Peter Bauer at the London
School of Economics; Mancur Olson and Julian Simon at the University of Maryland;
and James Buchanan and Gordon Tullock at Virginia Polytechnic Institute; not to
mention policy advisers such as Paul Craig Roberts, Alan Walters, Domingo Cavallo,
Václav Klaus, and Grigory Yavlinsky. Stigler, Chenery, Olson, and Simon died in the
1990s and Dornbusch in 2002, but most of the other professors on this impressionis-
tic list either were or could be appropriate association presidents. All made important
contributions to the worldwide turn toward markets, and there were many, many
more.

a Yahtzee scorecard. There are a certain numbers of regular functions to be arranged. In San Francisco in 1996 a luncheon would be given for John Nash, winner of the Nobel Prize the year before. The mathematical genius had been confined to the sidelines for thirty years by schizophrenia, but he grinned sheepishly in the San Francisco limelight. Another luncheon featured Stephen Ross of Yale University, the generalizer of the capital asset pricing model. A scholar had to be invited to give the Meetings' most important address (the Ely Lecture); Krueger chose Martin Feldstein, who used the occasion to call for the privatization of the U.S. Social Security system, striking evidence of the sea change in expert opinion that was taking place. The outgoing president had to be introduced; the health economist Victor Fuchs gave a jaunty address. A distinguished fellow of the association was to be named and presented. Walter Oi of the University of Rochester almost perfectly exemplified the charm of economics as a discipline in which pure thought may be as valuable as a computer or a scientific instrument, for the Chicago-trained Oi had made contributions to several fields over thirty years, culminating in service to the commission that helped create the all-volunteer U.S. Army— despite his having been completely blind.

The biggest draw in San Francisco turned out to be a fifty-four-year-old economist named McCloskey, a conservative former University of Chicago professor, president of the Economic History Association and member of the AEA executive committee, who during the autumn had undertaken a change of gender. Donald had become Deirdre. (Many of these events spilled over into public view; McCloskey's absorbing book about her metamorphosis was published in 1999 as *Crossing*.) Another drama was unfolding behind the scenes: Graciela Chichilnisky was suing a colleague, for allegedly having misappropriated her ideas. Chichilnisky still had some of the glamour that got her in *Vogue* magazine in the mid-1970s, when she was the well-publicized young Argentine genius with twin Ph.D.'s from Berkeley in math and economics. The halls were abuzz with gossip about her lawsuit. Within a matter of weeks Chichilnisky's charges would be embarrassingly withdrawn, amid indications that she had fabricated her evidence. The most startling event of the meetings was the ambush of David Card. Card had been awarded the John Bates Clark Medal, given every two years to the American economist who is judged by a panel of his peers to have made the greatest contribution by the age of forty. Card was handsome, rich, and winsome. But he had coauthored a controversial book about experiences with the minimum-wage law that had angered the more conservative of his fellow labor economists. In a session just before the award, a group of Chicagoans on the dais jumped him with scathing critiques of his statistical methods. So on what otherwise would have been one of the happiest afternoons of his life, Card was rendered momentarily speechless. Nothing further was said at the time, but the incident would be long remembered.

With so many interesting people engaged in such various goings-on, it was easy to overlook the events at the San Francisco meetings that in time would have the greatest effect on the discipline. The more visible of these were to be found in a session devoted to recent developments among economists concerned with economic growth—its theory and its history. Like most of the other discussions, Session 53 of the Meetings was held in a windowless room.

THE CROWD THAT GATHERS at 2:30 P.M. on Friday, January 5, 1996, in Plaza Ballroom B of the San Francisco Hilton is big enough to fill the long, narrow room and pack the back with standees, but not so large as to spill into the hall outside. "New Growth Theory and Economic History: Match or Mismatch?" meets on schedule with perhaps two hundred people in the audience. A couple of dozen journalists attend; they know that something is up. There is the usual quota of young kids just starting out. Expectations are high.

As we have seen, there are many ways to view a session. This one has brought together two groups who usually don't have much to say to one another: economic historians and leading theorists of economic growth. There is a picturesque quality to the occasion, for a dozen years earlier at the 1984 Meetings in Dallas a similar session had been organized by the historians to consider the "total darkness" that was said to exist at the intersection of theory and history *wie es eigentlich gewesen* (as it really was). In 1984 the theorists were defensive. The historians argued persuasively that theorists had selected only those problems that could be answered easily, giving rise to an elegant but sterile formalism that had left a vast array of disturbing considerations said to lie just "outside" of economics, exogenous to its models.

But the 1984 session had taken place on the eve of a revolution. Barely a year later the University of Chicago professor Robert Lucas reminded his colleagues of a riddle known loosely as "the problem of increasing returns" and, in a famous lecture, placed it at the center of the great policy questions of the 1980s. A great debate had ensued. Most of the macroeconomists of the rising generation had taken part. Factions had raised competing (and confusing) banners. Neo-Schumpetrian Economics. The New Economics of Imperfect Competition. The New Economics of Technical Change. The Increasing Returns Revolution. New Growth Theory. Or, most simply and obscurely, Endogenous Growth.

Whatever else, this particular intersection is no longer dark. For a decade the corner where theory meets history has been illuminated by battlefield flares and muzzle flashes. Yet the San Francisco session is hardly one of emotion recollected in tranquillity.

The historians and new growth theorists talk at cross-purposes. Joel Mokyr, author of *The Lever of Riches: Technological Creativity and Economic Progress*, is in the chair. He is the foremost of the new generation of economic historians who are working on the problem of technical change. He has a lively interest in identifying the most important element in growth, and he has organized a panel to permit listeners to assess some of the new work. From London the historian Nicholas Crafts has sent a paper called "The First Industrial Revolution: A Guided Tour for Growth Economists." Crafts is the proprietor of what is known among economic historians as the Crafts-Harley view of England's industrial revolution, to wit, that there *was* no industrial revolution, that the "take-off" into sustained growth of the eighteenth century was an illusion, and that the "years of miracles" (in a famous phrase) should be seen as a matter of misleading index numbers. Crafts's paper casts a cold eye upon on the recent new growth theory, which is to say the work associated with

Paul Romer. His tone is gingerly, skeptical of the new claims, reluctant even to confront them directly. The new emphasis on market size seems to be misplaced, he says. The evidence from history is "less than compelling." If there has been a theoretical revolution, it is hard to tell it from the historian's response to new growth theory.

Now it is Paul Romer's turn. He is the one the journalists are here to see. His reputation is as among the most mathematical of the new generation. He is also seen as the foremost young standard-bearer of the new style of University of Chicago argumentation, with all its latest high-tech rigmarole: infinite-horizon planning models, dynamic programming, competitive equilibria reduced to maximization problems for a single representative consumer, rational expectations, and all that. Yet more than any other, it is Romer who has put the new ideas about growth and knowledge and market power on the table. His 1983 dissertation was characterized by formidably difficult mathematics. The 1986 paper he carved out of it, "Increasing Returns and Long-Run Growth," remained difficult and austere. The 1990 version, "Endogenous Technological Change," contained simpler math, thanks in large part to Robert Lucas, as well as a striking new formulation of the problem by Romer. That new formulation amounted to a bombshell, at least in the tight community of growth theorists, insofar as it placed him in opposition not only to his teacher Lucas but to the entire Chicago tradition of taking perfect competition as its most fundamental assumption.

Romer has been insistent all along about the power of mathematical methods. They state problems more clearly and solve them with greater clarity and persuasive power than any other method, he asserts—including field trips to factories, or sifting through great quantities of data. He describes the process. The evidence of the senses is where the theorist must begin, moving then to verbal description, to theorizing, and up to formal math in a steadily ascending arc of ever greater generality—and then back down again from high abstraction to verbal formulation and the evidence of the real world. This last step checks the math, he says. It is the only part of the process for which we needn't take the theorist's word (though, of course, by now many other theorists have become involved as well). But then, Romer also has often warned that logic and evidence "have a power that transcends the wishes, beliefs and preferences of the people who use them. When you start up the trajectory towards abstraction, you don't know exactly where you will come back down." He himself has found his politics altered by what he discovered in his equations—from acolyte of Milton Friedman in his freshman year in college to, as a professor, advocate of some new forms of government intervention.

Six years have passed since Romer first presented his most important paper. The issues have been thoroughly examined by the little community of growth theorists. Now in San Francisco he is trying to close the loop, to describe his model in simple terms, to compare it to alternative explanations, to turn its key equations back into English. His title is "Why Indeed in America? Theory, History and the Origins of Modern Economic Growth."

He begins with a defense of formal methods. Every time a new piece of mathematical formalism is introduced, he says, the same objections are raised. Some people complain "these equations are so simplistic and the world is so complicated." Others claim that equations "don't tell us anything new." For example, he says, economists at least since Adam Smith have understood that total output—Y, as economists abbreviate it in their equations—depends on the quantity of physical capital and labor effort expended. Yet when in the 1950s a group of economists at MIT expressed this relationship mathematically as an aggregate production function, a group of English economists kicked up a terrific row. Nevertheless, the idea of production function—a mathematical statement of the relationship between inputs and outputs—had quickly become accepted around the world as an invaluable shortcut for measuring productivity.

When, a few years later, economists at the University of Chicago introduced a series of new equations aimed at capturing individuals' accumulation of experience and education as a variable they called H, this time it was the MIT economists (and others) who objected. Yet "human capital" as a gauge of personal productive capacities had become a standard tool. Now in the 1990s, Romer says, economists were arguing that knowledge was a key output of the economy and that its production is systematically related to the resources committed to its pursuit. That the growth of knowledge depends on the number and quality of scientists producing new knowledge and on its prior stock was not exactly a shocking proposition. Yet expressed mathematically as $dA/dt = G(H,A)$, the new theory once again was encountering the usual objections. This time the resistance was coming from both Chicago and MIT! (Cambridge, England, has long since been left behind.)

Such objections miss the point, says Romer. It is true that the introduction of mathematical language often seems to cause a neglect of important issues. Modelers focus on the issues that are easy to formalize, and defer the more difficult issues for a later day, even though they may be recognized as being quite important. History suggests that as the math accumulates, its scope expands and the important questions do not go away. "The sensible approach is not to shut down the development of formal theory, but to tolerate a division of labor in which natural language and formal theorizing continue in parallel. Specialists in each camp can address those issues in which they have a comparative advantage and periodically compare notes."

The appearance of new variables usually reflected an improved understanding of the economy as a whole. A good theory sizes up the overall system, then identifies certain points at which it can be broken down into a natural collection of subsystems that interact in a meaningful way. It tells us how to "carve a system at the joints." To illustrate, Romer borrows the familiar example of the steam engine. A famously bad explanation offered by an engineer in the mid-nineteenth century ascribed its motion to a *"force locomotif"* (in a similar way Aristotle had attributed the fall of stones to their "inner nature"). A more satisfying explanation says Romer, divides the steam engine into component parts—firebox, boiler, steam governor, and so on—in order to account for the working of the locomotive overall. "What theories do for us is take all the complicated information we have about the world and organize it into this kind of a hierarchical structure," he says. By removing ambiguity and stressing logical consistency, math makes clarity easier to achieve.

Next Romer describes the controversy in present-day economics. The "old" growth theory associated with Robert Solow explains economic growth through the interaction of two kinds of factors, he says. There are conventional economic inputs. And there is "exogenous" technology, improving at a steady rate "outside" the system. At the next level of decomposition, conventional economic inputs are divided into physical capital, labor, and human capital, but technology is still considered a force apart. So far so good, says Romer, "because technology does differ from all other inputs," in that technology can be employed by any number of persons at the same time. For reasons of convenience, however, old growth theory maps the dichotomy between technology and conventional economic inputs directly on the traditional distinction between universally available public goods and entirely private goods. For the purposes of the analysis, technology is viewed as being essentially a public good, freely available to anyone who wants some. The government provides it, through universities. It is to be thought of as being like ham radio, available to anyone who wants to tune in, in one famous analogy; like "manna from heaven," in another. In old growth theory no further distinctions can be made. To speak of "intellectual property" in its terms would be as striking a contradiction as if one were to seek to describe a "private public good." Untangling this paradox is what Romer's work is all about.

New growth theory divides the world along different lines—into "instructions" and "materials," Romer says. In the short interval between his talk in San Francisco and its appearance in print a few months later, his vocabulary will change slightly: "instructions" will become "ideas" and "materials" will become "things." Materials can be thought of as goods with mass or energy (electricity, for instance), Romer explains. Instructions are goods that can be stored as a bit string of computer code: software, content, databases, that sort of thing. The catchy distinction between atoms and bits is being made elsewhere, by others, in speeches and magazine articles instead of mathematical papers.

This day Romer offers a more homely illustration. When we make dinner, he says, the materials we use are "our pots and pans (our capital), our human capital (our brains) and our raw materials (the ingredients). . . . The recipes stored as text are our instructions." The key distinction, he says, is no longer between public and private but between rival and nonrival goods—that is, between items that can be consumed by one person at a time and those that can be employed simultaneously by any number. In many industries, the most important assets are more like recipes or instruction sets than anything else—computer software, pharmaceuticals, musical recordings.

In new growth theory, says Romer, "Technological Change" is no longer the *"force locomotif"* of economics. "With materials and instructions, you can give a simple answer that shows how economic growth works. Humans use non-rival instructions together with rival goods (like pots, pans or machine tools) to transform other rival goods, rearranging them into new configurations that are more valuable than the old ones. We rearrange steel rod into ball bearings or sheet steel into grinding machines that make ball bearings." Often people can exclude others for a time from using a particular set of potentially nonrival instructions. They can keep it secret, or have a patent—a possibility that is excluded by old growth theory's public-good approach. The hope of appropriating some part of a stream of earnings from an invention is enough to animate a constant search for new ideas. The ultimate impossibility of excluding others from copying and improving new ideas is enough to guarantee a steady stream of growth.

These ideas, as old as Adam Smith, have been neglected, Romer avers, yet they are absolutely central to economics. Since an idea can be copied and used over and over, its value increases in proportion to the quantity of the rival materials it can be used to transform: the larger the market, the greater the payoff to a new idea. More widgets can be sold in a big city than in a small town, more in a big country than in a small one. Indeed, that more than any other is the reason the United States long ago surpassed Great Britain in income growth. "Scale effect should no longer be treated the way a growth accountant such as [Edward] Denison did, as a kind of afterthought that had something to do with plant size," Romer concludes. "They should be treated the way Adam Smith did, as one of the fundamental aspects of our economic world that must be addressed right from the start."

The audience stirs uncomfortably. People have not heard these ideas before. Ordinarily the authority to whom readers are exhorted to return in order to regain their bearings is John Maynard Keynes, not Adam Smith.

The next speaker is Martin Weitzman of Harvard University. Romer is cool, fortyish, laid-back, California; but Weitzman is hot, fiftyish, excited, Brooklyn. If Romer is difficult to grasp all at once, Weitzman is all but unfathomable. He was one of the first to anticipate how general the discussion of increasing returns was becoming when, in 1982, he invoked increasing returns to explain why the unemployed couldn't simply go into business for themselves. Now he is trying to mediate between the old growth theory and the new: his topic is hybridization as a suitable metaphor for the growth of knowledge. Economic growth will continue as long as there are different strains of knowledge to cross. He has given this talk before, at the summer meeting of the economic fluctuations group at the National Bureau of Economic Research. In fact, because of the continuing stream of this sort of work, the project has been renamed "fluctuations and growth." But Weitzman's mathematics is unfamiliar—combinatorics instead of programming—and the talk of evolutionary biology leaves the bright young people cold. The economist is met by uncomprehending stares. It does not dim his enthusiasm. "Holy smokes, Marty," says his discussant Robert Solow afterwards. "You were like Savonarola in there." Weitzman replies, "It's like a revolution!" But the young people are not similarly struck. Who in the world is Savonarola?

There is no ambush, no counterattack, no controversy, no debate. The meeting ends on a flat note. The economists stream out of the hotel, out of San Francisco, to fly into a snowstorm, to convene again next year in New Orleans. The reporters do not race for the phones. The new ideas have not yet found the proper path to widespread understanding. The natural resistance to them is great. The stakes are high. The tip-off is the invocation of the name of Adam Smith.

CHAPTER THREE

What Is a Model?
How Does It Work?

FEW PH.D. ECONOMISTS today read Adam Smith—any more than modern physicists learn their stuff from Isaac Newton. Instead, graduate students rely on textbooks to tell them what has been learned since Smith set forth his views in *The Wealth of Nations* in 1776. There is nothing surprising about this; it is the way that science is supposed to work. As Alfred North Whitehead said, a science that hesitates to forget its founders is lost.

There are times, however, when scientists themselves may feel lost, when the explanations they have learned from textbooks do not hang together as they should. Then scientists, at least the best of them, experience the quiet torment described as "crisis." Then their standard operating procedure may be to retrace their steps, return to their first assumptions, in order to understand where things got off the track.

That was what Romer did, after he completed his first, tentative model of the economics of ideas in December 1986. He went back to the classics, to see how a phenomenon as obvious to the untutored eye as the growth of knowledge had been handled systematically by earlier generations of economists. He then sketched the antecedents of his model in a "working paper," published informally by his department.

As developments unfolded, many others did the same, none more clearly than the Nobel laureate James Buchanan, who had been backed into increasing returns by an intuition that the advent of the Protestant work ethic must have had general economic effects (more work and less leisure would broaden the market for goods, he reasoned). When the significance of the new work on trade and growth became clear to him, Buchanan combed the literature of two centuries to produce a "reader" reflecting the history of the controversy (including two articles of his own). *The Return to Increasing Returns* appeared in 1994.

But Buchanan's reader was designed for graduate students. Romer's comments eventually were filed away in a highly technical conference volume. And the new textbooks on economic growth that had begun to appear cut straight to the new ideas. There had been no attempt to explain to a general audience where the new ideas came from, or why they matter.

If we, too, revisit the classics, it will be easier for us to understand why a series of simplifications and shortcuts taken long ago suddenly have become important in the present day. As with most things in economics, the story begins with *The Wealth of Nations*.

ONE OF THE THINGS that set Adam Smith apart from all other writers on economics was his formidable power of concentration. As a result, stories about his absentmindedness abound. How he walked out for air in his nightshirt and didn't stop for fifteen miles. How he thrust a slice of bread and butter into a teapot, poured in, waited, poured out—and complained of the quality of the tea. His friend Alexander Carlyle said, "He was the most absent man in Company that I ever saw, moving his lips and talking to himself and Smiling, in the midst of large Company's. If you awakened him from his Reverie, and made him attend the Subject of Conversation, he immediately began a Harangue and never stopped till he told you all he knew about it, with the utmost Philosophical Ingenuity." Presumably all the while he was silent he was thinking, thinking, tracing through the long chains of causation.

He was born in 1723, into a connected and well-to-do Scottish family in Kirkcaldy, a little town across the Firth of Forth from Edinburgh. His father died just before he was born; he was raised by an adoring mother whose own father had been a rich landowner and member of Parliament. Much sometimes is made of the fact that as a baby he was kidnapped by gypsies. They left him in the next town down the road; he would have made a very poor gypsy, it was said.

From the beginning, Smith was the beneficiary of a good education. At fourteen he was sent to the University of Glasgow, where the tradition of experimental demonstration was strong. Aristotelian physics was fading. The new "mechanical philosophy" was in the air. No longer was it sufficient to explain the fall of stones or the rise of sparks by saying that it was "in their nature." Now it was necessary to show the how and why. Smith became acquainted with air pumps, barometers, and other paraphernalia of the "new Pneumaticks." He learned, too, about Isaac Newton's amazing "doctrine of bodies," as physics then was called. At seventeen he won a scholarship to Oxford University, where he stayed for six years.

Smith hated Oxford. There are several colorful passages in *The Wealth of Nations* in which he attacks the tenure system for having destroyed professors' incentives to learn, or teach, or even meet their students. Oxford's pampered colleges were thoroughly insulated from the winds of change. They "chose to remain, for a very long time, the sanctuaries in which exploded systems and obsolete prejudices found shelter and protection, after they had been hunted out of every other corner of the world," he wrote.

When he wrote of "exploded systems and obsolete prejudices," Smith probably had in mind Aristotelian physics. It was still taught at Oxford when he arrived in 1740, more than half a century after Newton published his *Principia*. But then, he just could as well have been thinking about the discovery of the circulation of the blood. That had a famously slow reception at Oxford, too.

A SMALL DIGRESSION is in order here, to consider what constitutes a satisfying explanation and how it is achieved. This is, after all, a book about how one system of thought replaces another. So let us consider a short history of one of the very first really powerful mathematical models. What is a model? How does it work?

William Harvey was born in 1578, a rough contemporary of

Shakespeare (b. 1564). He was determined to become a physician, so, after Cambridge, he traveled to Padua as a medical student to study under the leading anatomist of the day, Fabricius ab Aquapendente, whose skill at drawing was legendary. Close observation and description was the way in which physiology was investigated and understood.

The heart was conceived of by physicians and anatomists in those days, as it had been since the time of the physician Galen (first century A.D.), as resembling a furnace, or even the sun itself. The major organ of the body was thought to be the liver. It was there that food was turned into blood, which then seeped to the heart and lungs. The heart's warmth drew the blood to its chambers, where it could be heated before being condensed in the lungs, a little like the morning dew. In this way it combined with the vital spirits of the air.

As a native of Kent, Harvey knew something about pumps, for a fascination with their operation was sweeping mining circles in those days, thanks to recent discoveries of the mechanics of the invisible "ocean of air." At some point Harvey concluded that the heart's obvious heat was a secondary matter, that the muscle must serve as a pump rather than as a furnace or lamp, and that therefore blood must flow through the body in a circular path.

In his book *On the Motion of the Heart and the Blood,* he set out to prove his case. First Harvey measured the capacity of an average human heart. It was two ounces of blood, more or less. He asked his readers to suppose that half that much were driven into the lungs by each contraction, or even an eighth. He figured that the heart beats a thousand times in thirty minutes. Both these estimates were very low, according to what we now know. But that conservatism was central to Harvey's method. Even on the least generous assumptions, he showed that the heart pumps more blood into the arteries in half an hour—well over two gallons—than the entire body contains. Where else could it go but around in a circle? "A truly beautiful argument," says the historian of science Charles Coulston Gillispie. "Absolutely appropriate facts are arranged with perfect art. It would be almost as difficult to withhold assent from his demonstrations as from a geometric theorem."

But did Harvey's calculations convince all thoughtful observers at the time? Hardly! The trouble was that there was no obvious avenue by which blood could return to the heart. In all the 1,500 years since Galen had firmly established the furnace model of the heart, careful observation had shown that the vascular system resembled the branches of a tree, or the tributaries of a coastal wetland. Harvey's brash assumption that an invisible set of tiny pipes connected the arteries to the veins persuaded few, at least among the older physiologists. Indeed, they were infuriated by a model whose few simple assumptions brushed aside everything that they had struggled so laboriously to understand.

Only with the invention of the microscope, some thirty years later, was the existence of the capillaries firmly established, exactly as Harvey had predicted. Even then, members of the old community found it difficult to convert to the new views. But those who came to the matter then without any prior training were instantly and completely persuaded. Gradually the new generation replaced the old. (In the twentieth century, the physicist Max Planck summed up this familiar process: "Science advances funeral by funeral.")

Harvey's calculations amounted to one of the first mathematical models in history—perhaps the very first to enjoy widespread success in the English-speaking world. It remains one of the most powerful today, even though its if-then statement involved little more than a couple of multiplications. In was a giant step forward for formal reasoning. Adam Smith apparently never told this story in his various public lectures, though it seems unlikely that he was unaware of it. Not until 1906, when Sir William Osler made the reluctant reception of Harvey's discovery the subject of a famous London lecture entitled "The Growth of Truth as Illustrated in the Discovery of the Circulation of the Blood," did it become a standard scientific cautionary tale.

Besides, while at Oxford, Adam Smith had prepared a cautionary tale of his own.

WHEN HE RETURNED to Edinburgh from Oxford, Smith was invited to give a series of talks—public lectures first on rhetoric, then on the history of philosophy, and finally on jurisprudence. It is thanks to these lectures that we know something about Smith's views of what constitutes a satisfying explanation. One lecture in particular, "The History of Astronomy," affords a glimpse of what the otherwise modest Smith himself set out to do. Even today his account of astronomy is fun to read: a boyishly thrilling account of the growth of knowledge from ignorance to understanding.

He began with the Greeks. Imperfect as their understanding of the cosmos seemed by the standards of the eighteenth century, their physics still supplied its scholars with more coherence with which to think about the phenomena of the heavens than the "pusillanimous superstition" that had prevailed before Aristotle and Ptolemy, Smith wrote. Narrating the now familiar succession of Copernicus, Tycho Brahe, Galileo, Kepler, and Isaac Newton, Smith described the manner in which modern celestial mechanics had replaced the older Aristotelian learning by offering more satisfying explanations of various prominent puzzles (the retrograde motion of the planets, the behavior of weights dropped from the masts of moving ships, and so on), until eventually there emerged in the mind of Newton a surpassingly successful creation: "the discovery of an immense chain of the most important and sublime truths, all connected together by one capital fact [gravity], of which we have daily experience."

What we look for in an explanation, said Smith, is "a connecting principle" between apparently unrelated events. Science is a search for the "invisible chains which bind together all these discordant objects" with the precision of a physical mechanism, because "systems in many respects resemble machines." The trick of achieving an explanation, therefore, is to create a mental model, an "imaginary machine" of ever greater power and suitability, until all the causes and effects in question are worked out and mystery is dispelled. "Who wonders at the machinery of the opera house who has once been admitted behind the scenes?" Even so, he gibed, the old Aristotelian system was still being taught to undergraduates at Oxford and other backwaters of the English crown.

The enemy of good theory is promiscuous analogizing, Smith stated, the work of thinkers who endeavor to explain one thing in terms of another. The Pythagoreans, for instance, explained all things by the properties of numbers. Physicians were forever making extended parallels between physiology and the "body politic" (for example, William Petty wrote, "Money is the Fat of the Body-politick, whereof too much doth often hinder its agility, as too little makes it sick . . ."). Really good explanations are virtually seamless, Smith wrote. "There is no break, no stop, no gap, no interval." Ideas should "float through the mind of their own accord."

Moreover, a successful explanation has to be capable of persuading not just practitioners but the general public as well. Otherwise, experts have too many incentives to pretend to know more than they do. Chemistry is a good example, still stuck in deserved obscurity, Smith said, because it hasn't yet penetrated the mysteries of its field. Remember, Smith was writing in the 1750s, when chemists explained fire by the presence in all flammable substances of the elusive substance "phlogiston." Those chemists might all call each other "Doctor," but to those outside the field, their explanations lacked the ring of truth. "Salts, sulphurs and mercuries, acids and alkalis, are principles which can smooth things out only to those who live about the furnace." In other words, if it cannot be said in plain language, said Smith, it probably is not right.

The three lecture series were a great success, and Smith was called to Glasgow University in 1751, elected to the chair of logic. This made him history's first academic economist. In this, too, he set the pattern for the field. His first book, a meditation on human temperament that he called The Theory of Moral Sentiments, was published eight years later. Today we would call it a psychology primer. (Its first sentence affords a good glimpse of its author: "How selfish soever man may be supposed, there are certainly some principles in his nature which interest him in the fortunes of others, and render their happiness necessary to him, though he derives nothing except the pleasure of seeing it." Later in the book he adds, "The chief part of human happiness arises from the consciousness of being beloved.") Even in Glasgow, however, teaching only reinforced the lessons he had learned at Oxford about the nest-feathering tendencies of tenured scholars. So when the duke of Buccleuch offered to double his professor's pay to serve as his tutor and live in France,

Smith jumped. And in 1764, in Toulouse, he began a second book, "in order to pass away the time."

WHAT A BOOK! *An Inquiry into the Nature and Causes of the Wealth of Nations* is one of a handful of economic classics that is actually fun to read, even now. It possesses epic sweep—950 pages—and yet, if you make allowances for a certain stateliness of language, it reads as much like a present-day business magazine as like an eighteenth-century treatise on political economy. It starts with a disquisition on the advantages of the division of labor. Then comes a history of money, followed by an exposition of the familiar categories of economic analysis: prices, wages, profits, interest, rent of the land. And then a long digression on the price of silver, or what today we would call a history of inflation. In the second book is to be found a discussion of national income accounting and theory of capital accumulation. (There is actually an early model concealed here, of what economists have come to call the circular flow. They mean the two-way circulation, of money on the one hand and of goods and services on the other, among the various "factors of production," landlords, farmers, and manufacturers. Richard Cantillon, a fabulous Irish-born adventurer who is credited with having estimated the first real national income accounts, made the concept clear in the early years of the eighteenth century. The French court physician François Quesnay rendered it at least theoretically measurable—and the talk of all Paris in the 1760s—with his *tableau économique*, a zigzag diagram designed to serve as a blueprint for measuring the flows of income among various sectors of the French economy. Now Smith effortlessly assimilated the concept of national income accounts into his scheme. Today the circular flow can be found explained in the first chapter of any introductory economics text.)

The third book of *Wealth* contains a fascinating history of Europe since the fall of Rome. The fourth book presents a long attack on government attempts to regulate trade to achieve certain ends, the "system of mercantilism," as it was known. Smith opposed such doctrines with arguments in favor of free trade at every turn—all in all, as powerful a brief for competition, as opposed to "the wisdom of the politician," as has ever been written. Finally, there is a fifth book that amounts to a manual of public finance. All of this was couched in prose as well designed and neatly balanced as the mechanism of a good watch, with shrewd insights, bons mots scattered throughout. The book was taken up and celebrated around the world.

And yet the work is not merely a stylish masterpiece. If it were only that, it would be in the same class as Edward Gibbon's *Decline and Fall of the Roman Empire*, which also appeared on the list of the publisher William Strahan that autumn of 1776—and which outsold *Wealth* by a large margin for a time. The *Decline and Fall* is still read (though perhaps more often for its footnotes than in its entirety). It is a badge of culture, with relatively little measurable impact on the academic history of the Roman Empire as the craft is practiced today.

Wealth, on the other hand, is scarcely ever read by students. Within fifty years the first of a long series of textbooks of economic principles had replaced it. Fifty years more and the chief means of amending the consensus had become an article in a scholarly journal. Yet the influence of *The Wealth of Nations* on our daily lives is as if it had been passed into law; in effect, it has been accorded the status of law, by the universal consensus that formed around its underlying framework for the analysis of markets.

That is to say that *Wealth* possesses those qualities that collectively have been known, ever since Thomas Kuhn published *The Structure of Scientific Revolutions* in 1962, as a paradigm, meaning what we have before we have a theory. That is, *Wealth* provides "a problem set, a tool box, an authoritative ordering of the phenomena it set out to explain." The book contains not a single chart, few enough numbers, and no diagrams, but so penetrating was its reasoning that it launched a science. Like Aristotle's *Physica*, Ptolemy's *Almagest*, Newton's *Principia* and *Opticks*, Harvey's *Motion*, Franklin's *Electricity*, Lavoisier's *Chemistry*, and Lyell's *Geology*, and Darwin's *Origin of Species*, Smith's *Wealth of Nations* taught mankind to take the foundations of its subject for granted—to see markets in a certain way.

Through bifocals, it turns out.

CHAPTER FOUR

The Invisible Hand and the Pin Factory

Ask an economist what *The Wealth of Nations* is about, and chances are he or she will answer "competition." Inquire further, and you'll learn that the book's publication marked the discovery of "the Invisible Hand"—that is, of the great self-organizing interdependency of prices and quantities that we know today as the price system. But there is a second deep insight in the book as well, having to do with the relationship between scale and specialization, one that is usually overlooked—and that is crucial to our story.

That so famous a work should contain two powerful propositions is not surprising. What is surprising—and what requires some explanation—is that the significance of the second idea could have been eclipsed for so long, especially since Smith considered it so fundamental that he placed it first in the book. The problem is that the propositions seem to be contradictory. The Invisible Hand and the Pin Factory: these are the bifocals of Adam Smith.

Smith wrote *Wealth* with a view to explaining England's rise to global prominence. He sought to identify policies that would promote rather than retard prosperity. William Petty a hundred years earlier had been preoccupied with the economic miracle of the Low

Countries, Holland and the Netherlands (two different counties in those days), which seemed much more prosperous than England. In 1723, when Smith was born, it still was legitimate to wonder who were richer, the English or the Dutch. But by 1776 England had long since surpassed its rivals as the richest and fastest-growing nation in Europe.

In England there was meat on laborers' tables, not just bread. There was flatware, not just a spoon. The island kingdom was in the midst of a great consumer boom—the world's first, since the Dutch Republic had become more wealthy than diversified. In terms of pins, or tea, or calico, or tableware, or woolen goods and leather shoes, everyday English people were the richest in the world. "Everything presented an aspect of . . . plenty," wrote a Russian visitor in the 1780s. "No one object from Dover to London reminded me of poverty."

It certainly wasn't climate that had made England rich, Smith wrote, nor the quality of its soil or the extent of its territory. About these there was little to boast. Nor was it a matter of every English citizen's beavering away in "productive" labor, for in poor countries virtually everybody worked, he noted, while in rich countries—especially England—many persons didn't work at all. Smith's thesis is stated in the book's very first sentence: "The greatest improvement in the productive powers of labour, and the greater part of the skill, dexterity, and judgment with which it is any where directed, or applied, seem to have been the effects of the division of labour."

On this point—that specialization is the key to wealth—Smith could not have been clearer (or so one might have thought).

The division of labor was ubiquitous in England, but it was not always obvious. In some large-scale enterprises different contributors to the final product were scattered all over the world. So Smith began his book with one of the most famous illustrations in history: a visit to a modern pin factory. There the process could be seen all under one roof, and its arithmetic worked out. A worker unschooled in the pin business, with no access to its special machines, would be lucky to turn out a single pin a day.

But in a modern factory, Smith relates,

One man draws out the wire, another straights it, a third cuts it, a fourth points it, a fifth grinds it at the top for receiving the head; to make the head requires two or three distinct operations; to put it on, is a peculiar business, to whiten the pins is another; it is even a trade by itself to put them into the paper; and the important business of making a pin is, in this manner, divided into about eighteen distinct operations, which, in some manufactories, are all performed by distinct hands, though in others the same man will sometimes perform two or three of them.

In this way, Smith calculated, ten or fifteen men can between themselves make enormous quantities of pins: twelve pounds or so in a day. There may be 4,000 pins to a pound; therefore ten men can make 48,000 pins a day, or nearly 5,000 pins apiece. Every two weeks, a million pins.

Lest the world quickly be covered with pins, Smith introduces a new topic in chapter 2: a proposition about the mechanism by which the division of labor is governed. It is the willingness to buy and sell. "Nobody ever saw a dog make a fair and deliberate exchange of one bone for another with another dog," Smith writes, but humans do it all the time. The wish to better our condition is universal, a desire that "comes with us from the womb and never leaves us till we go into the grave." This self-interested "propensity to truck, barter, and exchange" is the force that makes the system go. "It is not from the benevolence of the butcher, the brewer, or the baker, that we expect our dinner, but from their regard to their own interest. We address ourselves, not to their humanity but to their self-love, and never talk to them of our own necessities but of their advantages."

How, then, to sell a million pins? Smith's answer was encapsulated neatly in the title of chapter 3—"The Division of Labour Is Limited by the Extent of the Market." That means that the degree to which you may specialize depends on how much of your product you can sell, on the *scale* of your business, because you must cover your fixed costs (whatever they are) and have at least a little left over.

To Smith, this matter of scale—of the extent of the market—had to do mainly with transportation costs. The distribution of people over the landscape he takes pretty much for granted. In the Scottish

Highlands, where villages were few and far between, "every farmer must be butcher, baker and brewer for his own family." A man would have to go to a city before he could expect to make a living as, say, a porter. No little village can support a pin factory, and only in a very biggest cities can be found that new class of citizens "whose trade it is not to do anything but to observe everything; and who, on that account, are often capable of combining together the powers of the most distinct and dissimilar objects"—inventors, in other words. So specialization is a matter of geography: where there is a river or a port, a city grows. There can be little or no commerce of any kind between the distant parts of the world without the sea. "What goods could bear the expence of land-carriage between London and Calcutta?"

These first three chapters and the plan of the book provided the whole kernel of what we would call today a theory of growth. Much stress has been laid over the years on the significance of the description of the pin factory. In fact Smith never visited one. Apparently he based his account on an article in an encyclopedia. Never mind that Smith was widely traveled and sharply observant everywhere he went. His failure to expend much shoe-leather in this case has occasionally been cited to discredit him. Such cavils entirely miss the point.

Adam Smith may sound a lot like Aristotle, smoothly descriptive, almost journalistic, rarely offering so much as a number, much less a mathematical equation. But we remember him precisely because he rejected so forcefully the Aristotelian tradition of mere classification of phenomena in favor of the mechanical philosophy—the description of how and why various elements interact within a system. Underneath the elegant prose, he is continually abstracting away the complicating detail, building and refining his mental models. The division of labor is limited by the extent of the market: wealth depends on specialization, and specialization depends on scale. Bigger nations with better-developed transportation networks will have more specialization and therefore be richer than smaller ones lacking rivers and roads, and nations with easy access to the sea will do best of all. That is the take-home message of the first three chapters of *The Wealth of Nations*. It is not as tight an argument as, say, William Harvey's demonstration of the circulation of the blood 150 years before, but it is similarly illuminating.

An even more remarkable "imaginary machine" was to follow.

NEXT IN *The Wealth of Nations* come some housekeeping details. In the fourth chapter Smith describes the role of money and tells something of its history and significance. Shells, cod, tobacco, and sugar served in their day, he says; in one Scottish village they still use iron nails. But coins have generally come to be preferred to all other possibilities, though in some places they are beginning to use paper notes. In chapter 5 he describes the existence of a great system of relative prices (one beaver for two deer and so on) and then propounds the difference between real price and money price. ("The real price of every thing . . . is the toil and trouble of acquiring it.") In chapter 6, he enumerates "the component parts of the price of commodities" that had earlier been codified by Cantillon: namely rent, wages, and profit, these distinctions being the returns to the familiar three factors of production that were land, labor, and capital (or "stock," as Smith still sometimes calls the last).*

Only in chapter 7, "Of the Natural and Market Price of Commodities," does Adam Smith sketch for the first time how it all hangs together. Here it is that, for most persons, the light comes on. In all markets for all things, he states, there is a "natural rate" of wages, profits, and rent, regulated by the willingness of buyers and sellers to exchange at different rates for different things. From this "natural" price, market price sometimes departs: there may be a famine, or a blockade, or a sudden abundance of oranges. "A publick mourning raises the price of black cloth," he writes. But either the cause of the

---

* Because it is so essential to the understanding of what follows, the key passage here is worth quoting at some length: "The whole annual produce of the land and labour of every country, or what comes to the same thing, the whole price of that annual produce, naturally divides itself . . . into three parts; the rent of land, the wages of labour, and the profits of stock; and constitutes a revenue to three different orders of people; to those who live by rent, to those who live by wages, and to those who live by profit. These are the three great, original and constituent orders of every civilized society, from whose revenue that of every other order is ultimately derived."

perturbance is temporary, in which cases the price quickly falls again; or else a complicated concatenation of changes will set in. If oranges are too expensive, consumers will switch to apples or do without, sea captains will import more citrus, orange growers in Seville will plant more trees—and sooner or later the price will return to its natural level.

What makes the system work, of course, is *competition*. All that is necessary for it to function smoothly is that everyone should be free to enter and leave the market, and change trades as often as he pleases—"perfect liberty," Smith calls it. Intelligent self-interest will take care of the rest. Where competition is free, Smith writes (later in the book), "the rivalship of competitors, who are all endeavoring to justle one another out of employment, obliges every man to endeavour to execute his work with a certain degree of exactness." People will seek to sell whatever they can at the highest price the market will bear, and buy at the lowest, and somehow it will all balance out over time.

Here is the first real glimpse of what it since has come to mean to "think like an economist": to see the world as a vast system of interdependent and essentially self-regulating markets in which prices constitute an automatic feedback mechanism coordinating the allocation of resources—land, labor, and capital—among competing uses. The description of counterbalancing competition among buyers and sellers is barely more than a vision. The words "supply" and "demand" scarcely appear. Smith employs the word "equilibrium" only once in the entire book, though "balance" and "counterbalance" appear frequently enough. Certainly the concept of equilibrium was a familiar one to scientists and practical men alike; water sought its own level, a lever balanced on a pivot when weights were equal, Newton had demonstrated equilibrium of forces in the heavens.

In all Smith's discussion of competition, there is no rhetorical device quite so tight as the Pin Factory, with its message so succinct that it can be expressed in a chapter heading, as if it were a theorem that already had been proved. Instead, there is his lengthy word picture of a great system regulated through negative feedback and, of course, an evocative metaphor—"an invisible hand." The phrase appears only once in the book, and then almost as an afterthought, toward the middle.

Some people have concluded that the counterbalancing equilibrium has much to do with Newtonian gravitation—that it is "nothing more" than a mechanical principle applied to human affairs. And it is true that Smith himself sometimes equated the force of self-interest with the principle of gravity. Among the equations economists today employ to describe Smith's "center of repose and continuance" are some originally written by Sir William Rowan Hamilton in 1843 to describe the manner in which sun and planets and moons exert force on one another in such a way as to render the solar system a stable and well-understood whole. Yet the idea of counterbalance and negative feedback surely is independent of the circumstances in which it is described. The rest of the celestial metaphor was left behind long ago. Smith's word picture evoked a mental model of astonishing generality.

Much in Smith's account remained to be worked out by others: the interdependence of all prices and quantities that today we call general equilibrium; subjective value and the importance of substitution "at the margin" (the decision point at which apples are preferred to oranges). The key concept of opportunity cost is not spelled out—"this or that, you can't do both." The various assumptions have been identified and elaborated. Assume a Scotsman in every man (as Walter Bagehot, a famous editor of London's *Economist*, later put it), and let the countervailing forces have their play. Yet all these concepts are implicit in chapter 7. Scholars say many of the same elements can be found in the work of Sir James Steuart, who published a lengthy treatise nine years before *Wealth*. But who remembers Jamie Steuart now? It was for having described the connecting principle of negative feedback that Adam Smith won his fame. Even though he wrote no mathematics, thus did Adam Smith put economics on a trajectory of abstraction and model building.

Smith was the first to acknowledge that there can be many imperfections in the competitive process. He mentions them right away.

Merchants must be free to change their business as often as they please for the system to work perfectly, and often they are not. Secrets can keep prices artificially high; secrets in manufacturing last longer than secrets in trade. Certain geographical advantages—those enjoyed by the vineyards of Bordeaux, for example—can keep prices above natural levels for centuries at a time. Official monopolies, licensing requirements, trade unions, regulations of all sorts also raise prices artificially and keep them high, at least for a time. But hardly any commodity can be offered for very long below its natural price, Smith says. All manner of interesting departures from the norm may exist, but they are secondary to the great interdependence of the whole. The natural price is "the central price, to which the prices of all commodities are continually gravitating. . . . [W]hatever may be the obstacles which hinder them from settling in this center of repose and continuance, they are constantly tending towards it."

Smith's "system of natural liberty" had enormous political significance. Markets thus understood will, for the most part, be self-regulating; hence the "let-alone" doctrine, *laissez-faire*. A steady growth of specialization will take place, "not the result of any human wisdom, which foresaw and intended the wealth to which it gives rise," but rather the result of myriad little undertakings of self-interested individuals, inventors, adventurers, entrepreneurs, usually in competition with one another. Hence the great metaphor: "As every individual, therefore, endeavours . . . to employ his capital . . . so . . . that its produce may be of the greatest value. . . . He generally, indeed, neither intends to promote the public interest, nor knows how much he is promoting it. . . . [H]e intends only his own gain, and he is in this . . . led by an invisible hand to promote an end which was no part of his intention. . . . By pursuing his own interest he frequently promotes that of the society more effectually than when he really intends to promote it."

Smith was no simpleton with respect to businessmen. He understood better than most that there will be continual attempts to interfere with the free play of the market. "People of the same trade seldom meet together, but the conversation ends in a conspiracy against the public, or in some diversion to raise prices." Collusion for a time can make it so. In these situations, government has certain responsibilities to act.

But the Scottish philosopher reserved his greatest scorn for the habitual attempts of governments to substitute guiding human hands for market forces. His long experience with politicians, royals, and those Oxford professors had bred an abiding skepticism regarding the fine intentions of the Great and Good. "In the great chess board of human society, every single piece has a principle of motion of its own altogether different from that which the legislature might choose to impress upon it," he wrote in *The Moral Sentiments*. Mainly what is required for rapid economic growth is (as Smith himself put it as a young man) "peace, low taxes and a tolerable administration of justice." Thus one can think of Adam Smith as the ultimate consumer advocate—vigilant watchdog against the businessmen and bureaucrats who can be expected routinely to conspire (and sometimes succeed) against the public's interest. *The Wealth of Nations* book was published in 1776, the same year as the American Declaration of Independence. It was a great success. No less a figure than Gibbon described Smith as the philosopher who "for his own glory and for the benefit of mankind had enlightened the world by the most profound and systematic treatise on the great objects of trade and Revenue which had been published in any Age or any Country."

Smith's subsequent years were mostly pleasant. He was rewarded with an appointment as a commissioner of customs in Scotland, much as Sir Isaac Newton had been made master of the London Mint. He lived in Edinburgh with his aging mother, saw his friends, revised his great work, and took an active interest in the American colonies' struggles against the crown. Toward the end of *The Wealth of Nations*, he had written, "To prohibit a great people . . . from making all that they can of every part of their own produce, or from employing their stock and industry in the way that they judge most advantageous to themselves, is a manifest violation of the most sacred rights of mankind."

So what's the problem? There is one, and though at first glance it seems innocuous enough, it turns out to have posed an enormous challenge to the economists who came after Smith. Let us return to the pinmaker, the one whose division of labor is limited by the extent of the market.

Suppose the pinmaker gets into the market early, expands, specializes in pinmaking by investing in new equipment and pinmaking R&D. He develops better steel, more attractive packaging, more efficient distribution channels. The bigger his market, the greater the specialization of this sort he can afford. He replaces workers with machines. The greater the specialization, the more efficient his production, the lower the price at which he can afford to sell his pins. The lower the price, the more pins he sells, and the more he sells, the higher his profits: a greater return for the same effort, hence increasing returns to scale. The economics of the pin factory seem to be that, thanks to the advantages of falling costs, whoever starts out first in the market will run everybody else out of the pin business. Does that mean that big business is natural? That monopolies are inevitable? Desirable? If scale economies are so important, how do small firms manage to exist at all? How do we get the sort of competition essential to the Invisible Hand? These questions, which seem so pressing today, are unexplored in *Wealth*.

The problem is that the two fundamental theorems of Adam Smith lead off in quite different and ultimately contradictory directions. The Pin Factory is about falling costs and *increasing* returns. The Invisible Hand is about rising costs and *decreasing* returns. Which is the more important principle? When Paul Romer read back over the literature, he found that one of his teachers had seen the dilemma perfectly clearly as a young man. In 1951 George Stigler had written, "Either the division of labor is limited by the extent of the market, and, characteristically, industries are monopolized; or industries are characteristically competitive, and the [Invisible Hand] theorem is false or of little significance." According to Stigler, they cannot both be true.

These are the bifocals of Adam Smith. Through one lens, specialization (as in the Pin Factory) leads to the tendency we describe as monopolization. The rich get richer; the winner takes all; and the world gets pins, though perhaps not enough to satisfy its need for them. Through the other lens, the situation we describe as "perfect competition" prevails. The Invisible Hand presides over the situation among pinmakers (and all others). No manufacturer is able to achieve the upper hand. As soon as one raises his prices, someone else undercuts him and price returns to its "natural" level. There are exactly as many pins as people are willing to pay for.

No one perceived the contradiction at the time. But then, it was only pins.

CHAPTER FIVE

How the Dismal Science Got Its Name

THE WEALTH OF NATIONS appeared in 1776, at the very beginning of the cascade of events we now call the industrial revolution. Adam Smith wrote much about the disturbances that would culminate in the American War of Independence. But about the series of inventions that were beginning to transform English life, he seemed to have almost nothing to say.

Water-powered looms don't appear in *Wealth*. Neither do steam engines, gas lighting, or even the revolution in the marketing and mass production of dinnerware contrived by Josiah Wedgwood, even though Wedgwood was Smith's good friend. Many economic historians have concluded therefore that, despite his focus on the Pin Factory, Adam Smith was blind to the causes and consequences of industrialization.

By 1815, however, evidence of the transformation was everywhere. A mania for canal building had come and gone during the 1790s. Turnpikes now connected English cities. Cotton was spun in urban mills. Such was the demand for wool that vast lands were fenced in and crofters driven off their farms to make room for sheep. Steel furnaces and coke ovens belched flames. The outlines of the factory system had emerged. As the English historian T. S. Ashton later wrote, "Chimney stacks rose to dwarf the ancient spires."

Thus, when the next generation of economists undertook to "correct the errors" in Smith, there could be no ignoring the effects of the many new technologies—especially considering the head start that his analysis of the Pin Factory had given them.

Or so, at least, you might expect. What happened next is the key to the whole story.

THE 1790S WERE dangerous times for optimists. Smith died in 1790, still thinking the fall of the Bastille was a hopeful sign. But then the French Revolution boiled over, touching off a struggle between England and France that would last a quarter of a century. Its skirmishes extended to the farthest corners of the earth. In England the enthusiasm for political economy faded. Adam Smith's ideas came to be viewed in ruling circles as downright subversive of the established order.

War brought privation, and privation brought unrest. England's wars with France began in 1792 and continued with little interruption through 1799, when Napoleon took control. He produced a revolution of his own, at least for the rest of Europe. The theaters of war already extended from Egypt and Syria to Switzerland, Italy, and Holland. Napoleon expanded them. By 1803 he was preparing to invade England with an army of 100,000 French soldiers. Turned back by the British navy, he gradually set his sights on Russia instead.

All the while, the English population mysteriously had begun to grow. After nearly two centuries of relative stability, it doubled to an estimated ten million persons over the twenty years 1780–1800, provoking new sorts of crises. A nation that had always fed itself became an importer of grain. Bread prices soared to unheard-of levels. Next, the importation of grain was banned to guarantee British farmers the high prices necessary to bring more land into cultivation. Poverty and misery increased dramatically, especially in the swollen cities. There were mutinies and riots and summonses to revolution. Military crisis precipitated financial panic—or rather a series of panics.

By 1800 no major treatise on economics had appeared in the quarter century since Smith put down his pen. There were, however, plenty of commentators on Smith's views, on both sides of the

English Channel. Today we would call them political philosophers, savants, and popularizers. They ranged from practical men such as Benjamin Franklin and Edmund Burke, to reformers such as William Godwin, whose writings on the evils of government and the perfectibility of man attracted a wide following in England. None was more sanguine than the Marquis de Condorcet (1743–1794), a French mathematician and philosopher of distinction who had entered politics and became president of the legislative assembly during the early stages of the French Revolution.

Condorcet was a serious commentator, but, as the revolution reached its terror phase, he was running out of time. He set down in ideas in the hastily conceived *Sketch for a Historical Picture of the Progress of the Human Race.* He was well aware that the population of France and that of England were growing rapidly, but he was not particularly worried by it. He emphasized the transformative powers of science. "Not only will the same amount of ground support more people," he wrote, "but everyone will have less work to do, will produce more, and satisfy his wants more fully." Even life expectancy will increase. Before long, he argued, population growth would slow with the increasing wealth.

But such cheerful assertions of the tendency to progress increasingly fell upon deaf ears. It didn't help that, shortly after he completed his paean to scientific progress, Condorcet was murdered by revolutionaries in France, poisoned in his jail cell. In due course even Adam Smith himself was impugned. By the time that Napoleon was finally defeated at Waterloo in 1815, nearly half of all those living in England and Europe had never known peace, and most had known famine and disease.

It was against this background that David Ricardo and T. R. Malthus rose to prominence, sober commentators on the changing scene, in touch with history's darker tendencies.

MALTHUS TOLD the simpler story, at least at first, and he was first to begin. Born in 1766, he was ten years old when *The Wealth of Nations* was published. He formed his views over breakfast arguing with his well-to-do father about the cheerful optimism of Godwin and Condorcet, to which his father subscribed. As early as 1798 he set the tone of the debate with his first published work: *An Essay on the Principle of Population, As It Affects the Future Improvement of Society, with Remarks on the Speculations of Mr. Godwin, M. Condorcet, and Other Writers.*

The year in which these opinions were published was one of unrest in England bordering on panic. The enclosures of privately owned land were accelerating in the countryside, peasants being driven off their land to make way for sheep. The city of London, in which 200,000 persons had lived in Shakespeare's time, had 900,000 inhabitants in 1800. Most of the new residents were wretchedly poor.

No wonder, then, that Malthus reacted with withering scorn to the various popularizers of doctrines associated with Adam Smith. Malthus's *Essay* marked a sharp departure from simple journalism. (He had graduated a few years before with honors in mathematics from Cambridge University.) Its central argument, on which all the rest depends, is set out in a famous table comparing geometric and arithmetic rates of growth.

To make its logic inescapable requires only two strong assumptions, he wrote: first, "that the passion between the sexes is necessary"; second, that fertility "will remain nearly in its present state" no matter what else changed (Condorcet and many of Smith's other disciples had predicted that the birthrate would decline with wealth).

Year	1	25	50	75	100	125	150	175	200	225
Population	1	2	4	8	16	32	64	128	256	512
Food supply	1	2	3	4	5	6	7	8	9	10

This is Malthus's basic model. Its implication is as forceful as William Harvey's elementary calculation of the quantity of blood pumped in a single hour. On its logic "the power of population" would quickly outweigh "the power in the earth to produce subsistence for man"—no ifs, ands, or buts. He was adamant on the futility of reform. "No fancied equality, no agrarian regulations in their utmost extent," could stave off the collision, even for as much as a century. Condorcet's pleasant vision of a society in which all members should have plenty to eat and time to spare was a logical impossibility. Malthus added many subtleties in a second edition of his *Essay* a few years later, but the emphasis on biological carrying capacity remained. He became known as Population Malthus, father of demography.

And though he moderated his views somewhat in the ensuing years, he never lost his contempt for those who believed that social conditions could be ameliorated. "A writer may tell me that he thinks man may ultimately become an ostrich," he wrote. "But before he can expect to bring any reasonable person over to his opinion, he ought to show that the necks of mankind had been gradually elongating; that the lips have grown harder and more prominent; that the legs and feet are daily altering their shape; and that hair is beginning to change into stubs of feathers."

David Ricardo came to the topic just about the same time, but from a different angle—from the direction of banking policy and war finance. His progenitors, Sephardic Jews, had been expelled from Spain at the end of the fifteenth century, had moved first to Italy, then to the Netherlands, finally to England in the mid-nineteenth century, not long before he was born in 1772. Following his father's trade, Ricardo made his living as a stockbroker, later as a dealer in government securities. And in 1798, the year Malthus published his *Essay*, Ricardo took his wife and children to Bath, to recover from the death of a child. There he picked up a copy of *The Wealth of Nations* at a lending library. As he read through it with growing excitement, he, too, became convinced that ultimately Smith's optimism would prove to be mistaken.

Whereas Malthus had focused mainly on the exploding population, Ricardo zeroed in on a different aspect of the conflict. Watching the grain fields climb the hills, Ricardo decided that the real problem must be the ongoing conflict among the three economic classes that had been identified by Adam Smith: land, labor, and capital. It was not the farmers who would get rich, as ever worse land was put in cultivation. They would pay out all their profits in wages to workers. The workers in turn would spend all they earned on food. Only landowners would grow wealthy. Society would stagnate in the end.

Soon thereafter he wrote the first of a series of letters to a newspaper about the causes of wartime inflation. James Mill introduced him to Malthus, and the two men became members of a group that met regularly in London to talk about economic matters.

RICARDO AND MALTHUS had discovered the principle of diminishing returns—the idea that, after a certain point, each succeeding increment of effort might produce less output. The first barrel of fertilizer does a lot, but the tenth only burns the crops. The same must be true of seed or water or time spent weeding. There must come a point at which nothing more can be obtained from adding an hour to the workday, or another worker in the field, or another row of seeds, or another tool, or an extra dose of plant food.

Remember, agriculture and mining were the dominant economic activities of the day. The insight was very great. The impulse to apply it universally was even greater. The idea had tremendous intuitive appeal. The two men believed that humankind always would be coming up against its limits—running out of food, in Malthus's view; running out of land on which to grow food, according to Ricardo. Either way, the central tendency of human history would be a descent into poverty for the vast majority of the human race from which there could be no escape.

Ricardo was well aware of the existence of a new and rising class of industrial capitalists. He recognized that they were jostling for position with landlords and workers. But he became increasingly convinced that industrialization would be a short-lived phenomenon. The rate of profit in manufacturing industries had to follow the rate of profit in farming. The fledgling revolution in industrial goods would be snuffed out because no one would be willing to invest in products for which there would be no market. Accumulation would cease. This state of affairs, in which agricultural production had reached its maximum and economic evolution had ground to a halt, would come to be known as the stationary state. For Ricardo, it could only be delayed, not avoided.

By 1813 Malthus and Ricardo were writing letters back and forth, arguing about the effects of high tariffs on imported grain designed to protect the profits of English farmers and maintain the island's self-sufficiency. Malthus believed that the protection was necessary, even desirable, for the maintenance of English institutions. Ricardo supported free trade because he believed it could postpone the inevitable a little while longer—long enough, perhaps, for his grandchildren to live out their lives before the fall. The two thinkers became friends, rivals, commentators on each other's work. When the wars were over, they published dueling treatises on political economy—Ricardo in 1817, Malthus four years later.

It was Ricardo's book that became economics' first real textbook, in the modern sense.

FROM ITS VERY FIRST sentence, *Principles of Political Economy and Taxation* differed from *The Wealth of Nations*. Whereas Smith had sought to explain the *growth* of wealth, Ricardo declared that the economist's proper task was to explain its *distribution* among the three great classes of society: workers, capitalists, landowners. Phrases such as "the science of political economy" and "the laws of political economy" occur in his work but appear nowhere in Smith's.

Otherwise, the architecture is much the same as that of *The Wealth of Nations*. As the intellectual historian Denis P. O'Brien has noted, Ricardo used remarkably few sources besides Smith; criticism was his natural style. Smith's discussion of the Pin Factory is shrunk into a single line in the chapter on wages in order to dismiss it. It is true that the tendency of the prices of manufactured goods is to fall, writes Ricardo, because knowledge is increasing.* Then he returns to arguing that it doesn't matter, since the price of food and labor is going up.

* "The natural price of all commodities, excepting raw produce and labour, has a tendency to fall, in the progress of wealth and population; for though, on one hand, they are enhanced in real value, from the rise in the natural price of the raw material of which they are made, this is more than counterbalanced by the improvements in machinery, by the better division and distribution of labour, and by the increasing skill, both in science and art, of the producers."

The essence of Ricardo's method was to imagine the entire economy as a single giant farm, producing only a single output—"corn," meaning any sort of agricultural good—with inputs of labor and land. Everything else, including the Pin Factory, was assumed away. The idea was to identify the relationships among a few economic aggregates and reason through to sweeping conclusions. For example:

> Thus, taking the former very imperfect basis as the grounds of my calculation, it would appear that when corn was at £20 per quarter, the whole net income of the country would belong to the landlords, for then the same quantity of labour that was originally necessary to produce 180 quarters, would be necessary to produce 36; since £20:£4::180:36. The farmer then, who produced 180 quarters, (if any such there were, for the old and new capital employed on the land would be so blended, that it could in no way be distinguished,) would sell the

the value of	180	qrs. at £20 per qr. or	£3600
	144 qrs. {	to the landlord for rent being the difference between 36 and 180 qrs. }	2880
	36 qrs.		720
the value of	36 qrs. to labourers ten in number		720

leaving nothing whatever for profit.

If this, then that: Ricardo's terse chains of reasoning are easily recognized today as an early economic model. Economists have called it the "corn models" ever since. "My object has been to simplify the subject," he wrote. His syllogisms turned out to be far more persuasive than Malthus's "principle of population" in professional circles, even though his friend was far better known to the English public as Population Malthus. The corn models were easy to calculate and therefore unsurpassed for arguing—a long step beyond Smith's "imaginary machines," in that their magnitudes could be measured and tested against the real world. They seemed to include all the relevant variables. And they were designed to predict explicitly the future course of events, not just to illustrate particular tendencies.

Ricardo and Malthus—or at least their most enthusiastic followers—felt as though Newtonian laws had been glimpsed. Ricardo wrote to a friend, "I confess that these these truths appear to me as demonstrable as any of the truths of geometry, and I am only astonished that I should so long have failed to see them." Malthus wrote that the calculus would prove to be an indispensable tool, for in economic problems there always was "a point where a certain effect is at the greatest, while on either side of this point it gradually diminishes"—precisely the purpose for which the calculus had been invented.

The new models produced insights that were not intuitively obvious. The most conspicuous was in the theory of foreign trade. The principle of comparative advantage held that it paid for nations to make the most of their geographical and climatological endowments through specialization and trade. There were endless arguments about wine and wool. Economists always won.

This aspiration to precision and certainty was consistent with the temper of the times in the early nineteenth century. Such certainty had formed no part of Smith's ambition. One of the things that makes *The Wealth of Nations* a masterwork is that it tolerates a certain amount of ambiguity—the tension between the Invisible Hand and the Pin Factory, for example; or the sense that, thanks to science, there were no fixed logical limits to growth. But Ricardo had friends doing geology in Scotland and chemistry in Paris. Malthus had studied math. Not for them the literary approach. At a certain point Ricardo wrote to his friend,

> Political economy you think is an enquiry into the nature and causes of wealth—I think it should be called an enquiry into the laws which determine the division of the produce of industry among the classes who concur in its formation. No law can be laid down respecting the quantity, but a tolerably correct one can be laid down respecting proportions. Every day I am more satisfied the former enquiry is vain and delusive, and the latter is the only true object of the science.

THE GIFT OF ABSTRACTION was real enough. But for the strength of their new convictions about diminishing returns, the early economists paid a heavy price.

Outsiders complained that Ricardo and his followers didn't seem to feel any need for verification of their premises; that for them, internal consistency was enough; that inconvenient facts were simply ignored. A logical conclusion from plausible premises was taken to be correct, no matter what the data said. Later this tendency to premature certainty would be described as the Ricardian vice. But justified as such criticisms were, they often missed the deeper point—the fierce joy at internal cohesion, the sense that such formal methods were the way to the future.

Professional societies were springing up everywhere in those days. Botanists formed one in 1788, surgeons in 1800, geologists in 1820, astronomers in 1820, statisticians in 1834. Public support for the new "savants" of economics was very great. A political economy club was organized in London in 1821, with ambitions to become a scientific society.* By 1825 the first university chair in economics had been created at Oxford.

There followed a deluge of books, pamphlets, and magazine articles. Enthusiasm spread to polite society. Maria Edgeworth, a popular novelist, wrote her sister, "It has now become high fashion among blue ladies to talk Political Economy." With the end of the war, Ricardo had made a comfortable fortune. In 1819 he entered politics as "*the* representative of *the* science."

Almost as an afterthought, Ricardo added a chapter about machinery to the third edition of his *Principles*, in 1823. It is elusive and distracted. Improvements in technology and agriculture may check the "gravitation" of profits toward the zero state for a time, he wrote. But whatever tendency to falling costs thus created will be limited and weak. New inventions will lead only to more people. Any

---

* From the very first meeting, Malthus was deemed to be in error. The paper he presented on that occasion was entitled "Can There Be a General Glut of Commodities?" His answer—Yes!—was dismissed as incorrect.

increase in the living standards of ordinary people will be temporary at best. "That the opinion entertained by the labouring classes, that the employment of machinery is detrimental to their interests, is not founded upon prejudice or error, but is conformable to the correct principles of political economy. . . ."

A friend in Parliament wondered from what planet Ricardo had recently arrived.

So POWERFUL was the logic of their new tools—Ricardo's corn model, Malthus's table comparing geometric and arithmetic growth rates—that economists lost interest in countervailing tendencies, despite the evidence all around. What they could not easily depict in terms of their newfound near-geometric proofs, they now studiously ignored. That is, they rendered it "exogenous"—though at the beginning of the nineteenth century, they did not choose exactly this word to describe the curious narrowing of the subject that now took place.

Strange as it seems, the subject of specialization simply disappeared from economics with the entry of Ricardo and Malthus, even though Adam Smith had begun his book with it. The phrase "division of labor" appears only three times in Ricardo's *Principles of Political Economy*, and then only to dismiss its significance to the argument of the book, and only once in the first edition of Malthus's *Essay* (and seven more times, inconsequentially, in the sixth edition).

The economist Paul Krugman devised a simple parable a few years ago to explain this "hollowing out" that sometimes occurs when scientists first adopt formal methods. His story had to do with the disappearance of certain features from maps of Africa that were prepared during a few key decades during the eighteenth century.

Maps themselves were an old story even then, Krugman wrote in a little book called *Development, Geography, and Economic Theory*. Arab traders had kept track of its Mediterranean shore from the twelfth century on. And from the time the Portuguese began sailing south, in the fifteenth century, maps of Africa had been more or less complete. They presented not just the coastline but a reasonably full account of the major details of the continent's interior——the relative position of Timbuktu, for example, or the presence of a mighty river flowing west to east several hundred miles north of the coast of the Bight of Benin.

The trouble was that the old maps were not entirely dependable. Distances were foreshortened or exaggerated. Not all the depicted features of the continent's interior were real. Sometimes the Nile was shown to have its headwaters in a giant lake. In other cases the domain of a tribe of one-eyed men was reported, or a people whose mouths were in their stomachs.

Then, in the early eighteenth century, newly published maps began emptying out. New scientific methods for mapping were beginning to make their appearance—methods of measuring latitude and, soon thereafter, longitude. Before that watershed, mapmakers had been happy to consult travelers to the interior of the continent and to incorporate in maps the features that their informants described. Now they raised the bar of what was considered to be reliable evidence. "Only features of the landscape that had been visited by reliable informants equipped with sextants and compasses now qualified," wrote Krugman. And so the detailed old maps were replaced for a time by the concept of "darkest Africa."

The interval didn't last very long. By the beginning of the nineteenth century, formal methods of measurement would permit the details to be filled in with a certainty and precision possible in no other way. (Mapping the source of the Nile River was part of the purpose of the journey on which the missionary/physician David Livingstone became lost in 1866 only to be "found" by the *New York Herald* reporter Henry Stanley.) But for a few decades there had been "an extended period in which improved technique actually led to some loss of knowledge."*

Something of the sort happened occasionally to economics, according to Krugman. "Economics understandably and inevitably follows the line of least mathematical resistance," he observed—the

* Evidence of this fascinating flow and ebb and flow of knowledge can be seen in *Afrika auf Karten des 12. bis 18. Jahrhunderts*, a beautiful collection of seventy-seven old maps from the collection of the Staatsbibliothek of Berlin, edited by Egon Klemp and published in Leipzig in 1968.

equivalent of first mapping a continent from its coast. Because universal diminishing returns were both intuitively appealing and easy to express mathematically, economists concentrated on their implications. They ignored countervailing forces that were far less easy to describe.

Thus preoccupied with shortages, and guided by primitive models whose great advantage was that they could be written down, Ricardo and Malthus sent the mainstream of the profession off on a lengthy detour. The next part of the story—seven chapters, in all—has to do with how economists traveled on their long journey, the various artifices they developed along the way, and how, in the late 1970s, they at last began to regain their bearings.

CHAPTER SIX

The Underground River

THE IDEA THAT perpetual shortages were the inescapable fate of humankind didn't persuade very many people for very long in the early nineteenth century, at least not beyond the small circle who were members of the Political Economy Club. Even for them, backing away from the inevitable running-out orthodoxy soon became a way of life. The debate about what could be expected in the future broadened out once again. Charles Dickens, the novelist, and Ralph Waldo Emerson, the essayist, soon became far more widely interpreters of English-language economics than David Ricardo or T. R. Malthus.

True, England itself seemed to totter on the brink of revolution for a few tense years after Napoleon was finally defeated in 1815. But then a broad and lasting peace took hold. England and the Continent settled down to a period of unmistakably rising prosperity. Railroads were built, canals dug, steamships launched, telegraph cables strung. By 1830 England was feeding itself once again.

A few prominent economists continued to work in the tradition of Pin Factory economics. These were no longer cheerful visionaries like Condorcet and Godwin but rather practical, empirical scholars possessed of a historical bent. They included Charles Babbage, who maintained in *Economy of Machinery and Manufactures* (1833) that industrialization, not competition, was the new century's most salient fact. Or the French engineers Augustine Cournot and Jules Dupuit, who virtually invented mathematical microeconomics in the 1830s, working through on their own the economics of monopolies, roads and bridges. A Scottish economist, J. R. McCulloch, put the problem with Ricardo and his disciples most clearly: "He lays it down as a general principle, or rather axiom, that, supposing agricultural skill to remain the same, additional labour employed on the land will, speaking generally, yield less return. But though this proposition be undoubtedly true, it is at the same time quite as true that agricultural skill never remains the same for the smallest portion of time. . . ." The worst lands in his day, wrote McCulloch, yielded more than has the best lands two hundred years before.

But these dissenters never quite succeeded in raising the banner of specialization and the growth of knowledge as a central concern of economics. Instead, the prestige of mainstream economics—Invisible Hand economics—grew steadily, even though its dire predictions failed to pan out, surely one of history's more interesting examples of cognitive dissonance. Ricardo and Malthus were "scientific," and that was good; Adam Smith was "literary," and that was not.

So the Political Economy Club flourished in London. Bank reviews appeared, precursors of today's economics journals. The British Association for the Advancement of Science established its Section F, for Economics and Statistics. Popularizers found vast audiences—including the London *Economist*, founded in 1843 to espouse the new doctrines of free trade. Heterodox economists such as Babbage and McCulloch were consigned to the fringe. And by 1840 fascination with industrialization and its attendant falling costs—with "increasing returns," as the phenomenon would be described by economists—had become pretty much a circumscribed topic. The economics of the Pin Factory had become "an underground river," as Kenneth Arrow described it many years later, "springing to the surface only every few decades."

At which point, a radical journalist turned philosophical economist named Karl Marx entered upon the scene. Here was a heterodox economist whom the profession could not ignore.

So much has been said and done over the years in the name of Karl Marx that probably the best way to understand his role in history is as a religious leader whose followers often carried guns. He was a close contemporary of Mary Baker Eddy, fifteen years younger than Brigham Young, the product of a strong religious background himself, born in 1818 into a distinguished family of rabbis in the old German city of Trier. His father had renounced Judaism to become a disciple of Voltaire and Rousseau, and Marx himself dabbled in anti-Semitism all his life. Yet his work had a powerful prophetic dimension. It produced, as the historian and biographer of Marx, Frank Manuel, has noted, "an amazingly fast conversion of millions of human beings to a new spiritual world belief."

In the beginning, however, Karl Marx was an economist. He was a natural academician who had studied at the universities in Bonn and Berlin, before moving in 1843 to Paris, where he met Friedrich Engels, the son of a wealthy textile manufacturer who quickly became Marx's best friend. Together they wrote *The Communist Manifesto*, whereupon Marx's career as a political leader commenced. He was chased out of town to Brussels, but not before he signed a contract for a two-volume work to be called *Critique of Politics and Political Economy*. In 1849 Marx and his family finally found a home in London. There he read the classical economists, including Adam Smith, sitting in the British Museum day after day. For our purposes, the way to understand Marx the economist is as a close student of David Ricardo, albeit one who was anxious to turn the master on his head. Marx loved Ricardo for his precision, his aspirations to science, his axiomatic proofs. He was Ricardo's student in all respects but one. Marx took continuing growth as his starting point, instead of assuming it away.

Otherwise, Marx bought wholeheartedly into Ricardo's idea of a three-way struggle for supremacy. He embraced the logic of immiseration, too, though with a twist. Reflecting the continental tradition, he re-labeled the familiar "factors of production" as "classes." So instead of the factor "land," there were the owners of land, aristocrats of the feudal order. Instead of "capital," there was the bourgeoisie. Marx argued that these newcomers were in the process of displacing the aristocrats in the course of a nearly invisible capitalist revolution whose beginning he traced to events two or three centuries before. And instead of "labor," there was the hapless "proletariat."

Already in *The Communist Manifesto* he had summed up the situation more succinctly than any comparable economics text of his day:

> The bourgeoisie, during its rule of scarce one hundred years, has created more massive and more colossal productive forces than have all preceding generations together. Subjection of Nature's forces to man, machinery, application of chemistry to industry and agriculture, steam navigation, railways, electric telegraphs, clearing of whole continents for cultivation, canalization of rivers, whole populations conjured out of the ground—what earlier century had even a presentiment that such productive forces slumbered in the lap of social labor?

Technology was the genius of the rising capitalist class. The bourgeoisie would continue to squeeze all possible profit out of the current arrangement. Its members were psychologically conditioned to do so. Eventually they, and not the landlords, would wind up with all the chips. At that point, however, the proletariat would rise up and turn the tables. Its members would expropriate "the means of production" through political revolution, and thereafter everything would be jake.

It was at this point in the argument that the arm-waving began in earnest. What would life be like after the revolution? Afterwards, Marx said in one famous aside, the division of labor would all but disappear, and a man might fish in the morning, hunt in the afternoon, rear cattle in the evening, "or criticize the dinner," just as he desires, "without ever becoming hunter, fisherman, shepherd or critic." If that sounds like a description of middle-class retirement living in the industrial democracies today, surely it is an accident.

For the next thirty-five years Marx produced a continuous stream of newspaper articles, pamphlets, essays, and, of course, the three volumes of *Capital*. His fundamental disagreements with the English economists became more and more obscure. Ricardo had believed that growth would cease because of the scarcity of natural resources. Marx believed it would continue because of the growth of knowledge. That was about as much common ground as can be discerned.

This is no place to go into Marx's contributions. Some of the political reforms that he propounded in the *Manifesto* do not sound particularly shocking by the standards of the present day: public schools, central banking, graduated income tax, nationalization of key industries. Others turned out to be terrible ideas: no private ownership of land, no right of inheritance. He gave the world the term "capitalism," which came into use in the 1860s. It seems to me that the use of the word "revolution," to connote a change of division of labor, traces to him as well. Many shrewd insights are scattered throughout his enormous book.

At his most lucid, Marx sought to redefine economics as a "critical history of technology"—unfortunately, in a footnote in *Capital*. Otherwise the language is obscure and, sometimes, absurd. Many of his detailed arguments are principles that, as Smith had written a hundred years before, "can smooth things out only to those who live about the furnace." Yet economic growth is Marx's problem on every page. The problem he inherited from Ricardo, distribution among the classes, over which so much ink has been spilled, is everywhere of secondary importance.

So, the image of Marx that lingers is the one described by his son-in-law, Paul Lafargue—as the painter in a Balzac story that Marx was known to admire ("The Unknown Masterpiece"): "A talented painter tries again and again to limn the picture which has formed itself in his brain; touches and retouches his canvas incessantly; to produce at last nothing more than a shapeless mass of colors; which nevertheless to his prejudiced eye seems a perfect reproduction of the reality in his own mind."

BY 1848 CLASSICAL ECONOMICS was overdue for a reformulation. It wasn't just the threat to its authority posed by outside challengers such as Marx. Nor were the mobs in the streets of Paris and other European capitals sufficient reason to explain the shake-up. The internal contradictions were piling up, becoming unmistakable to economists themselves. No longer was it possible to pretend that David Ricardo had pronounced the last word on manufacturing.

So an English economist named John Start Mill undertook to restate the vision that had been so persuasive in *The Wealth of Nations*—subject, of course, to the various "scientific improvements" that Ricardo had made. Mill's father, James, had been Ricardo's great friend. His son's task would be to square the highly visible results of the industrial revolution with the intuitively obvious logic of diminishing returns.

Like Smith and Marx, Mill took growth as his starting point in *Principles of Political Economy* (1848). Nevertheless, Ricardo had been Britain's "greatest political economist," Mill asserted, and his "pure theory" was basically Ricardian. "The real limits to production" would be determined by "the limited quantity and limited productiveness of land," he wrote. But he also identified a tendency of "increasing returns," meaning rising profits in certain industries thanks to falling costs.* He set this tendency out in opposition to the "general law" of diminishing returns in agriculture. Then he split the difference. Diminishing returns remained economics' "most important principle," wrote Mill in chapter 12. But in chapter 13 it turned out that the anticipated slowdown of growth could be suspended or temporarily controlled "by whatever adds to the general power of mankind over nature."

Thus Mill didn't ignore technical progress altogether. But he didn't try explain it, either—at least not in economic terms. He simply assumed that it would continue for at least a while longer and otherwise left it out of his story. The crucial passage is tucked away

---

* Adam Smith had tucked away a similar distinction between increasing and decreasing returns in his "Digression concerning the Variations in the Value of Silver during the Course of the Four Last Centuries." Ricardo, too, in his chapter on wages, had quietly taken note of the effect of the growth of knowledge. For most goods, he wrote, the rising cost of increasingly scarce raw materials would be more "than counterbalanced by the improvements in machinery, by the better division and distribution of labor, and by the increasing skill, both in science and in art, of the producers." But by chapter 20, "Of Value and Riches," Ricardo was arguing that knowledge might increase wealth but still would not improve things for the worker, because value depended on labor alone.

in the "preliminary remarks" that begin the book: "In so far as the economical condition of nations turns on the state of physical knowledge, it is a subject for the physical sciences and the arts founded on them. Political economy concerns itself only with the psychological and institutional causes of growth."

This is the formal beginning of the economists' it's-not-my-table tradition of exogenous growth. The division of labor has all but vanished. It has become a single department of what the author describes as "a more fundamental principle," the principle of "cooperation." Cooperation occurs whenever workers help one another in the performance of their tasks, whether simple or complex. It is a principle a little too general, perhaps, to be helpful. In specialization's place was a black box that Mill called "productiveness." (Today we would say "productivity.") We'll be all right, Mill declared, as long as productiveness increases. The growth of technological knowledge had become a force in economics, but productiveness was an *exogenous* force. "Not my table," said the economist.

Mill took another idea from Adam Smith and gave it a modern treatment—the idea of the "stationary state"—a country that had finally reached "the full complement of riches which the nature of its laws and institutions permits it to acquire." Holland had long been mentioned as a possible specimen of a nation that had become about as rich as it was going to get. It seemed to "take a little off" as frequently as it "put a little on," and thus remained more or less in the same place with every passing year, growing neither richer nor poorer. Ricardo, as usual, made the concept more precise. The stationary state (he did not use the term) had reached the point at which there was just enough profit possibility left to make it worthwhile to go on accumulating. Let rents rise past that point, and the inevitable decline would begin, a dismal prospect. With Mill, however, the arrival of the steady state was to be desired rather than feared. Everybody would have enough money. All could relax and enjoy the beauty of nature and the arts.

Such conceptions of societal "adulthood" came easily to theorists in the mid-nineteenth century. So much in nature seemed to follow the pattern of a pronounced "S" curve. A slow gestation giving way to rapid alterations in youth, followed by a lengthy and substantially unchanging adulthood, followed by decline and eventual death, seemed to be a nearly universal pattern among living things. The notion that someday the growth in productivity would come to a halt became deeply embedded in economics with Mill. The concept of a steady state would continue to turn up in mathematical form for more than a century, an assumed condition of adulthood on which economies of all nations, of all shapes and sizes, would relatively quickly converge.

Economists were happy to have Mill's *Principles.* The book was a timely rejoinder to *The Communist Manifesto.* It gave a good commonsensical explanation of why the industrial revolution didn't mean Ricardo had been wrong—increasing returns had trumped decreasing returns, but only for a while. Decreasing returns would triumph in the end. It put a brighter face on the population problem and the subsistence wage in particular. And even though it was written in strong, clear English, it gave a good account of the underlying mathematical nature of the Ricardian system and even extended it a little.

"Happily," Mill wrote, "there is nothing in the laws of value for the present writer or any future to clear up; the theory of the subject is complete." No wonder, then, that Mill lost interest in the subject. He went on to become the patron saint of Victorian liberalism, a feminist, environmentalist, and social democrat who was at least a hundred years ahead of his time. He revised his text only once, in 1852 (others updated it a total of seven times in his lifetime). He considered that he had done all that was required.

As IT HAPPENED, economics was on the verge of its second great escalation in the degree of its theoretical abstraction and mathematical expression (Ricardo/Mathus represented the first, of course). As early as the 1830s interest was growing among the engineers in France in the clarity of mathematical reasoning. By the 1840s it had spread to Germany. By the 1860s it was in full flower, all over Europe. *Principles of Political Economy* continued to be the bible of civil religion in the British Empire well into the 1880s and beyond, but as an economist, John Stuart Mill was instantly obsolete—a literary theorist in the dawn of mathematical economics.

The new economics stemmed from the recognition that the prices of things must be subjective, that they arose from goods' relationship to human needs. Since Smith, economists had thought that value must be inherent in the goods themselves. It seemed to have something to do with the amount of labor required to produce and distribute it. But this view presented irresolvable paradoxes. Why, for example, were diamonds expensive whereas water was cheap? In this new psychological view, diamonds were expensive not because men dug in the earth for them; rather, men dug for them because they knew they would fetch a good price.

The real key was the insight that it was not the total quantity of goods that mattered, but rather the additional increment. This was the method that would become known as marginalism. The name on which economists gradually settled for the elusive quality of pleasure giving was "utility." Utility was a way of generalizing the principle of diminishing returns. From there it is only a short step to supposing that every commodity can be made to serve many different uses, that every undifferentiated need may be satisfied by myriad competing commodities.

Another bite of ice cream or a cigar? A cigar or save the same sum of money for a new shirt? Or another pearl on the string? Consumers would see to it that the last dollar spent on any one good would equal the last dollar spent on any other. It was this tendency to adjust the last atom of expenditure to make the greatest contribution to total utility that turned the exercise into a maximization problem—of exactly the sort that astronomers, architects, and engineers were accustomed to solving as a problem of "statics," as the branch of physics dealing with forces and masses in equilibrium was then called—and opened the way to the application of the calculus to the everyday business of life. Here's the way William Stanley Jevons excitedly put it in 1871: "The nature of Wealth and Value is explained by the consideration of indefinitely small amounts of pleasure and pain, just as the theory of Statics is made to rest upon the inequality of indefinitely small amounts of energy." This same idea was hit upon nearly simultaneously by thinkers all over Europe—by Hermann Heinrich Gossen in Germany, Carl Menger in Vienna, Léon Walras in Lausanne.

Every kid who has ever passed high school algebra must have some feeling for the pleasures of this kind of thing: the way in which careful thought can translate the messy detail of a word problem into the precise shorthand language of a system of mathematical equations. The new means of describing the problem with differential calculus as a matter of optimization subject to constraint soon rendered the verbal corn model obsolete. Literary economists didn't like being shoved aside, of course. Mill, for instance, wrote, "Jevons is a man of some ability, but he seems to me to have a mania for . . . a notation implying the existence of greater precision in the data than the question admits of." But it was Jevons who won the day, with arguments such as this: "The ratio of exchange between any two commodities will be the reciprocal of the ratio of the final [marginal] degrees of utility of the quantities of commodity available for consumption after the exchange is completed."

The possibilities of marginalism were given their fullest statement by the French economist Walras—"the Ricardo of the calculus era," as he has been called. He was born in 1834 and prepared extensively for the Ecole Polytechnique, reading Descartes, Newton, Lagrange, and Cournot. Twice he failed to gain admittance to France's top school, but he slept with a copy of Louis Poinsot's *Eléments de statique* by his bed for decades, and, after a galvanizing walk one day in 1858 with his father (himself an amateur economist), Walras resolved to do for economics what engineers already had done for various intricate physical systems—that is, construct a model of economic general equilibrium from among the relevant interdependent variables.

English marginalists, including Jevons, were content to talk about the market for two goods. Walras wanted to talk about everything at once. His method of describing the interdependence of "the system of exchange" could, at least in principle, handle infinitely many simultaneous equations, with an equal number of unknowns, he maintained. Change one price or one budget constraint or one utility function, and the repercussions could then be traced throughout the system—much the same hope as Quesnay had had for his *tableau économique* (and, for that matter, Marx for his laborious calculations of "surplus value"). This program of establishing "general" interdependence of prices and quantities was viewed as impractical by most economists in England—too ambitious for the present state of the art. Retorted Walras, "If one wants to harvest quickly, one must plant carrots and salad. If one has the ambition to plant oaks, one must have the sense to tell one's self, my grandchildren will owe me this shade."

The marginalists felt they were running away from Ricardo, and in a certain sense they were, for no longer did they require his discredited labor theory of value, with its futile distinction between value and wealth. They now had subjective utility to work with. At a deeper level, however, they were embracing Ricardo more closely than ever, for the mathematics of their scheme depended critically on the assumption of diminishing returns. Underneath, the mathematics of individual optimization described only the Invisible Hand of perfect competition—still regularly compared to the law of gravity. Sometimes the equilibrium concept was illustrated by tabletop models in which water flows until it reaches a uniform level. In these demonstrations, increasing returns were as implausible as water running uphill.

Economists took the policy implications of their models very seriously indeed. More than ever, it seemed apparent that scarcity sooner or later was going to bring all economic growth to a halt. Jevons gained fame in England in the 1860s by explaining how the looming exhaustion of British coal mines would probably mean the end of improvements in its wealth and power. (Oil was discovered in Pennsylvania four years later.) And after Jevons died, in 1882, his study was discovered to be filled from top to bottom with stacks of scrap paper. Soon enough England would be running out of paper, too. He didn't want to be caught without.

CHAPTER SEVEN

Spillovers and
Other Accommodations

BY 1890 ENGLAND BORE little resemblance to the nation that had tottered on the brink in its war with Napoleon seventy-five years before. The gloomy certitudes of Ricardo and Malthus seemed seriously out of touch. So did the arguments between Marx and Mill. The island kingdom had become far more prosperous than its ancient rival France, though a unified new power, Germany, had recently appeared, and the United States had begun its rise to prominence.

Everywhere there were giant factories: not just dye works, steel mills, and meatpacking plants but great new systems of railroads, steamships, telephones, and electric lights as well. The new industries all flirted with monopolization. Those who owned the factories were richer than ever before. The biggest surprise was the emergence of a large new middle class. To be sure, whole neighborhoods in London still lived in abject poverty, but it was a poverty of a different kind from that of a century earlier. The poor had more shelter, heat, light, food, and clothing, not less—thanks, apparently, to the appearance of new industries.

This was the phenomenon that we now describe as economic growth. In 1890 the term had yet to enter the language. In those days economists talked about increases in the net national dividend. Faithful followers of Ricardo considered these increases to be transient, soon to be reversed. Others viewed the gains as permanent, the fruits of an unanticipated industrial revolution. One thing was clear to the best economists. John Stuart Mill's not-my-table approach was inadequate to the facts. It would be necessary to give this growth an economic explanation.

So in 1890 a master economist again stepped forward to explain how the industrialization of the preceding century had come about. This time it was no gentleman philosopher who took up the challenge but rather Alfred Marshall, professor of political economy at Cambridge University. To a surprising extent, he succeeded. In explaining how specialization and competition coexisted in the modern world, Marshall remanufactured the bifocals of Adam Smith so artfully that the line could no longer be seen.

All that was required was a little sleight of hand. You can't understand what happened to economics in the twentieth century without knowing something about *external* increasing returns—about "externalities," as Marshall's invention was quickly dubbed.

THE MORE OBVIOUS innovation in Marshall's *Principles of Economics* was the vocabulary of supply and demand, and the diagrammatic apparatus that supports it. It is queer to think that these most familiar of all economic concepts ever required an introduction, but Mill scarcely mentioned them, and the earliest marginalists had been too preoccupied with working out the meaning of utility to give much thought to expressing the underlying unity of their vision. It was in Marshall's hands that the opposing forces became a universal framework with an answer to every question, small and great.

Did price depend on the cost of production? Or on the craving of the person who paid the price? Marshall declared that the answer was both. Supply and demand, production and consumption, the utility gained and the cost of production—all mattered in different degrees at different times, and it was no easier to say which was the more important than to say which scissors blade did the cutting. The little diagrams of intersecting supply curves and demand curves made the nature of the relationship clearer than words could do, and more easily than mathematical symbols could. "The argument in the text is never dependent on them," wrote Marshall, and, if need be, they could be dispensed with altogether, "but experience seems to show that they give a firmer grasp of many important principles than can be got without their aid; and that there are many problems of pure theory, which no one who has once learnt to use diagrams will willingly handle in any other way."

Marshall's authority stemmed partly from his brilliant economic intuition and partly from the understated elegance of his prose. ("Political economy or economics is a study of mankind in the ordinary business of life," the book begins.) But his decision to take a literary/diagrammatic approach instead of a mathematical one entailed an important intellectual sacrifice. The economics of his text would not be the grand project that Walras had conceived—to show how, in a system of *general* equilibrium, the price of tea depended on everything else under the sun—wages in China, the size of the crop in Assam, the price of coal in Singapore and of coffee in Brazil, demand in Birmingham. Marshall adopted a strategy of compromise, a method he described as *partial* equilibrium—which considered just a couple of things at a time. That's all the more the little supply-demand diagrams in the footnotes could do: illustrate the interdependence of *particular* markets: tea versus coffee, or tea and lemons. The trick was simply to assume that all the rest would remain more or less the same, said Marshall—ceteris paribus, in the Latin phrase.

The tome he called his "book of curves" might be a halfway measure, but to emphasize that his text was on a higher analytic plane than what had gone before, he described his subject as *Economics* instead of *Political Economy*. For underneath the diagrams Marshall had built *Principles* on algebra, not geometry. He understood full well that his diagrams did not deliver on economists' loftiest ambitions of an entirely mathematical treatment of the issue. When the great mathematician Lagrange had supplanted the geometrical proofs of Isaac Newton's *Principia* a century before with his own *Analytical Mechanics*, he had written proudly in the preface, "No figures can be found in this work, only algebraic operations." Following Lagrange, Walras, too, had dreamed of replacing Quesnay's cumbersome diagram (the *tableau économique*) with a model of the entire economy expressed as a system of equations. Marshall understood the superiority of a strictly mathematical approach, so in note 21 of his mathematical appendix he sketched a handful of equations designed to describe a fully interdependent global model—an approach that he noted would offer a "bird's-eye view" of the economy as a whole. He wrote to a friend, "My whole life has been and will be given to presenting in realistic form as much as I can of my note 21." But in *Principles* he carefully laid out his arguments in words; he supported them with geometry. The algebra remained tucked away in the appendix.

Nor did it escape Marshall, and many others who were writing at the time, that the mathematics seemed to offer an answer to a question that had preoccupied economists since Ricardo denied that it could exist—a systematic account of why people received what they did in a competitive economy. How did owners of machinery earn their tall silk hats? Why did farm land cost much, and city land cost more, and desert land cost little or nothing at all? Why were railroad conductors paid more than physicians? How did the Invisible Hand allocate portions of the total product among producers?

This answer, too, apparently depended on what each contributed at "the margin" to the other's work. To one of Marshall's contemporaries, the evangelical American economist John Bates Clark, the marginalist insight promised nothing less than "a Scientific Law of Wages." The market acted as a giant calculator, giving to capital and labor alike precisely the share that each could add to the interdependent efficiency of the other. The appearance of trusts and unions would only enhance the effect. "Labor is robbed by capital in the same way that capital is robbed by labor, and no other; for the returns of each agent are fixed in identically the same manner." Moreover, this chain of reasoning could be put more clearly in mathematics than in words (where, in truth, it was none too clear), given that the calculus was rapidly becoming the lingua franca, for talking about the relative growth of various quantities toward a maximum. The Swedish economist Knut Wicksell put the same idea this way in 1890: "If the total output of production is interpreted as a real (continuous) function of the cooperating factors . . . then efficiency clearly requires that each factor be used to such an extent that the loss of a small portion of it reduces the resulting output by just so much as the share of output going to that portion."

This mathematical description of the relationship between inputs and total output—a fancy way of describing the yield of a given quantity of ingredients (the "cooperating factors"), as in a recipe— became known as the production function. Many assumptions were concealed in the math, to be teased out over the years, as production functions became ever more central to economics. For the purposes of our story, none is more interesting than the supposition that increasing all inputs by a given amount would increase the output in the same proportion. Such a straightforward relationship, it was quickly pointed out, had been described 150 years before by the great Swiss mathematician Leonhard Euler in a very general way as "linear," or "homogenous in degree one." Euler's theorem now became part of the economists' standard toolkit, part of a tidy mathematical package whose largely unobserved side effect was to neatly average out instances of increasing and decreasing returns. To double output whenever inputs doubled meant assuming generally *constant* returns to scale. The resulting edifice doctrine soon was labeled marginal productivity theory.

Today the chapters on costs and firms in competitive markets are the heart of any introductory economics text. That is where you learn that, in a world of competing firms, the marginal product of every factor is said to be equal to the price it commands in the market. A firm can be expected to hire another worker, or purchase another ton of steel for manufacturing purposes, only insofar as it expects that it will cover its cost and add to its income. Under perfect competition, each factor will be paid its marginal product, and the whole thing will work out perfectly: there will be nothing left over in the end. One prominent Victorian economist deeply interested in the new formalism (Francis Ysidro Edgeworth, author of *Mathematical Psychics*) groused that marginal productivity theory left no room for entrepreneurs.

About all his rigorous logic, Marshall remained ambivalent for many years. On the one hand, he consistently preferred to use the new mathematical methods. (To a friend, he wrote of John Stuart Mill, "I agree with you that he is literary and therefore full of error. But I think he and Ricardo contain the kernel of truth.") But he also feared the power of more abstract reasoning to mislead investigators. The mathematical method's "limitations are constantly overlooked," he wrote, "especially by those who approach it from an abstract point of view, that there is a definite danger in throwing it into definite form at all." He set out his philosophy in a letter to his friend and former student Arthur Bowley in March 1901:

(1) Use mathematics as a shorthand language rather than as an engine of inquiry;
(2) Keep to them till you have done;
(3) Translate into English;
(4) Then illustrate by examples that are important in real life;
(5) Burn the mathematics
(6) If you can't succeed in (4) burn (3).
    This last I did often.

A violation of rule (4) that especially exasperated Marshall was the way in which so fine a thinker as the French mathematician Augustin Cournot had been seduced by his algebra. Cournot had in 1838 produced the first argument that falling costs/increasing returns might lead to monopoly. He had made little attempt to describe counterforces that might prevent such an outcome. In a footnote Marshall complained of those who "follow their mathematics boldly, but apparently without noticing that their premises lead inevitably to the conclusion that, whatever firm first gets a good start will obtain a monopoly of the whole business of its trade in its district."

It was the paradox of the Pin Factory. The underground river had burst to the surface again. Those "externalities" would be required to contain it.

FALLING COSTS were even more obvious to Marshall than they had been to Mill. That living standards had been rising for most of the century, even for the poor, was hard to square with the iron logic of diminishing returns. Thanks to marginalism, economists had a more precise way of stating the meaning of the conundrum. Increasing returns were present whenever the *marginal* cost of each new article—the cost of each pin—was lower than the *average* cost of all the pins. Given the elaborate system of equations that described the Marshallian system, everything should sooner or later become *more* expensive to produce, not less expensive, or else whichever firm had the lowest costs of production would take over the whole market for, say, pins. So what was going on?

To deal with increasing returns, then, Marshall decided that there must be *two* sources of falling costs, *two* kinds of increasing returns. Both were associated with the scale of production—that is, with the size of the market. The "internal economies," as Marshall called the first sort, were simply the familiar economics of the Pin Factory. They were "dependent on the size of individual houses of business engaged in it, on their organizations and the efficiency of their management." The "external economies," the second sort, were dependent, he said, on "the general development of the industry" as a whole. Internal economies were familiar enough to Marshall's readers, but external economies, or *externalities*, as they quickly became known, were a breakthrough, an economic "discovery." They were perhaps the single most important feature to differentiate his account from that of Mill, since, as we will see, they were the device that rendered "productiveness" internal to his system.

A certain poetry crept into Marshall's account as he described those internal economies whose benefits were captured by individual firms.

> An able man, assisted perhaps by some strokes of good fortune, gets a firm footing in the trade, he works hard and lives sparely, his own capital grows fast and the credit that enables him to borrow more capital grows even faster; he collects around him subordinates of more than ordinary zeal and ability; as his business increases they rise with him, they trust him and he trusts them, each of them devotes himself with energy to just that work for which he is especially fitted, so that no high ability is wasted on easy work, and no difficult work is trusted to unskillful hands. Corresponding to this steadily increas-

ing economy of skill, the growth of his business brings with it similar economies of specialized machines and plant of all kinds; every improved process is quickly adopted and made the basis of further improvements; success brings credit and credit brings success; credit and success help to retain old customers and bring new ones; the increase of his trade give him great advantages in buying; his goods advertise one another, and thus diminish his difficulty in finding a vent for them. The increase in the scale of his business increases rapidly the advantages which he has over his competitors, and lowers the price at which he can afford to sell.

These sources of falling costs are precisely those advantages that we sum up today as "economies of scale." They involve spreading overhead and fixed capital costs over ever greater output and so lead to increasing returns. Marshall's account of the rise of a great business house sounds like the story of Rockefeller, or Carnegie, or Gillette, or Nobel in his day—or Bill Gates in our own. His chapter on the tendency to automation ("machinery takes over sooner or later all monotonous work in manufacture") could have been written yesterday. It would be another twenty-five years before most economists learned to speak reflexively of "mass production"; twenty years after that before the next buzzword of "R&D"; and still longer before the modern management techniques associated with, say, Wal-Mart were firmly identified as a source of internal economies as well. But they are all present here, implicit in Marshall's account of the "specialized machines" and "improved processes."

So why would a businessman blessed with increasing returns—a manufacturer, say, of pins—not take over his market completely? He might, said Marshall, at least for a time. He and one or two others could carve up between them the whole branch of industry in which they were engaged.

Then, too, some modern activities seemed to possess a tendency to monopoly by the very nature of the technologies they employed. Railroads were a good example of these "natural monopolies," because the costs of setting up the business are so great that a single company ordinarily can provide service to the entire market for a lower cost than can two or more firms. (Railroaders often learned this lesson the hard way, building parallel lines and finding one soon going out of business.) In fact, Marshall wrote, in modern transportation industries "the law of increasing returns operates almost unopposed." Government regulation would be required to provide discipline in such industries where competition was unlikely to be maintained. But surely the pin business required no such day-to-day regulation. That was the whole point of the Invisible Hand, after all.

Strong counterforces militated against increasing returns in normally competitive industries—meaning most of them, Marshall wrote. Sheer mortality was one. The founder of the Pin Factory would retire; without a great second-act manager, the business would likely be destroyed by the very forces that enabled it to rise in the first place.

But, just in case, to ensure that competition otherwise would be preserved overall in his system, Marshall incorporated benefits that would be freely available to all—*external* increasing returns, he called them. Such returns derived from the *scale* of the industry. Sometimes they were described as "neighborhood effects." This second source of falling costs was shortened to "externalities" and quickly translated as "spillovers," with no loss of meaning. External economies were benefits (or costs) that came without money changing hands. They were to be had simply by getting up in the morning.

Again, the serene Victorian prose:

> When an industry has thus chosen a locality for itself, it is likely to stay there long: so great are the advantages which people following the same skilled trade get from near neighborhood to one another. The mysteries of the trade become no mysteries; but are as it were in the air, and children learn many of them unconsciously. Good work is rightly appreciated, inventions and improvements in machinery, in processes and the general organization of the business have their merits promptly discussed: if one man starts a new idea, it is taken up with others and combined with suggestions of their own; and thus it becomes the source of further new ideas. And presently subsidiary trades grow up in the neighborhood, supplying it with implements and materials, organizing its traffic, and in many ways conducing to the economy of its material.

Marshall didn't inquire too deeply into exactly how this spillover process might work to loosen a monopolist's control, though, as an immensely practical man, he certainly had his ideas. Presumably, if you wanted to know a rival's secrets, you could buy his product and take it apart to see how it worked. Or hire his assistant. Or visit his factory and secretly memorize the plans. You could capitalize on opportunities your competitor created but didn't recognize, deliberately searching for weaknesses in his business plan. Pure brainpower would lead to substitutes—staples for pins, railroads for canals. Or you could simply read the newspapers and trade journals. It was enough for Marshall to stipulate that the good ideas of one man inevitably would be taken over and built upon by others, for "the most important improvements in method seldom remain secret for long after they have passed from the experimental stage." These "neighborhood" effects had to do less with spatial propinquity than with scale. They depended not on the firm itself but on "the general development of an industry." The more extensive the virtual neighborhood, the more external economies freely available to all. He may have been writing about his experience with the cotton industry, but he could have been describing the steel industry, or shipbuilding or banking, or, for that matter, Silicon Valley.

The externalities concept was an instant success. For the unpaid side effects of economic activity were, in fact, everywhere to be observed in the everyday world. They were sometimes good and sometimes bad. Secrets that were hard to keep often seemed the least of them. A dam eliminates flooding of farmers' fields whether or not they pay for it. That's a good externality. But it also damages the fishermen's catch. That's bad—an "external *dis*economy." A farmer rents bees to pollinate his orchard, and they pollinate his neighbor's trees as well. The presence of a brewery in town requires that more police be hired. The cigarette vendor sends soaring the dry-cleaning bills of nonsmokers and necessitates an extra wing on the local hospital. But the school that teaches Latin also trains workers who will be more productive. How convenient it was to have a catchall term for all these benefits and costs not captured in a price.

In the years after World War II, it was unpriced *costs* that took center stage. Bad spillovers such as resource depletion, pollution, and congestion became known as "the problems of the common"—the externalities that come into play when a valuable resource belongs to everyone and no one, a pasture, say, from which each person has reason to take as much food as possible for his animals and no person has reason to create more pasture by clearing land, since other persons will capture the gains. Largely overlooked in those days was the role of good externalities in Marshall's scheme—those freely available *benefits* that assured that ultimately there always would be someone ready and willing and able to contest a given business, thanks to the "something" in the air.

The important thing to remember is that spillovers were the *unpaid* side effects of economic activity. They were not captured in a price. They didn't have to be written down in the demanding calculus of marginal productivity; indeed, they *couldn't* be written down. They were not inputs. They required no compensation. They played no part in the geometry of price. Therefore, they required no description. This convenient feature of Marshall's analysis may not have been apparent to most of his readers, but certainly it was understood by the mathematician himself. Spillovers kept Marshall's system intact. They were a clever device to reconcile increasing returns with the assumption of Invisible Hand perfect competition and still make the mathematics come out right.

Marshall recognized that there were certain loose ends to his analysis. At one point he echoed John Stuart Mill: "Knowledge is our most powerful engine of production; it enables us to subdue nature and force her to satisfy our wants." At another juncture he wrote, "The distinction between public and private property in knowledge and organization is of great and growing importance: in some respects of more importance than that between public and private property in material things; and partly for that reason it seems best sometimes to reckon Organization apart as a distinct agent of production." He promised a full examination at "a much later stage in our inquiry." But hints and glimpses of many potentially disruptive problems remained buried in Marshall's footnotes and asides.

In the conclusion to the section of *Principles* devoted to the factors of production, Marshall summed up the tension between increasing and decreasing returns, between the Invisible Hand and the Pin Factory, with another powerful analogy. Such firms, he wrote, were like the great trees of a forest. "Sooner or later, age tells on them all."

> But here we may read a lesson from the young trees of the forest as they struggle upwards through the benumbing shade of their older rivals. Many succumb on the way, and a few only survive; those few become stronger with every year, they get a larger share of light and air with every increase of their height, and at last in their turn they tower above their neighbours, and seem as though they would grow on for ever, and for ever become stronger as they grow. But they do not. One tree will last longer in full vigour and attain a greater size than another; but sooner or later age tells on them all. Though the taller ones have a better access to light and air than their rivals, they gradually lose vitality; and one after another they give place to others, which, though of less material strength, have on their side the vigour of youth.

The concept of externalities slipped smoothly into the literature. Once again, economics was considered by its leading practitioners to be pretty nearly complete. So tight was its logic that his treatment of the system of marginal analysis was regularly compared to the achievements of classical astronomy or to the table of atomic weights in chemistry. In 1908 Marshall stepped down from his professorship. He never completed his second volume, never returned to the topic of knowledge as an agent of production, never quite surrendered his doubts about marginal productivity theory, though he did make up his mind about mathematics: "Ere another generation has passed, its dominion over that limited but important field of economic inquiry to which it is appropriate will probably be no longer in dispute." He died in 1924.

And when, two years later, economists gathered at the University of Chicago to mark the 150th anniversary of the publication of *The Wealth of Nations*, it was the marginalist analysis of value and distribution, elaborated by Marshall, that they celebrated implicitly, not Smith's contribution. And as for his ideas about how national product was shared among capital, labor, and land, an up-and-coming Chicago professor named Paul Douglas told the meeting that it might be better to pass over them in "discreet silence" in favor of subjects such as the division of labor, "where his realistic talents enabled him to appear at greater advantage."

DESPITE THE ATMOSPHERE of self-congratulation, several young economists in the 1920s recognized that something was not quite right with the Marshallian system—in particular, with its treatment of increasing returns. For one thing, the seeming gift of "external economies" turned out to be something of a Trojan Horse. Marshall's handpicked successor as professor at Cambridge, A. C. Pigou, now argued that externalities were so pervasive and substantial that government ought to subsidize those industries exhibiting falling costs (manufacturing businesses) and tax those with rising costs (agriculture and mining)—a wide-open invitation to government management of the economy. Could this really have been what Adam Smith was all about? There had to be an inconsistency somewhere.

Thus a considerable controversy over "the laws of return" bubbled in the economic journals on both sides of the Atlantic throughout the second half of the 1920s. In Cambridge the professor of economic history, John Clapham, impishly complained that his more theoretical colleague had failed to give concrete examples of external increasing returns. Without effects that could be clearly seen and measured, wasn't the category simply an "empty economic box"? In Chicago the economist Frank Knight asserted that, as a matter of logical consistency, one man's spillover must become another man's internal economy. And Piero Sraffa, a dashing refugee from Fascist Italy who had come to Cambridge to study with John Maynard Keynes, observed that the costs of almost *all* manufactured consumer goods were falling. Could this all possibly be the result of spillovers? In fact, wrote Sraffa, increasing returns were the "one dark spot which disturbs the harmony of the whole."

It was a curious man named Allyn Young who most nearly put his finger on the problem. This Ohio-born economist is little remembered today, but in the 1920s he was considered to be one of the leading economists in the world. Born in 1876, seven years before John Maynard Keynes and Joseph Schumpeter, Young caught the new wave of marginalism at the flood and rode it to success, even as he preached the limitations of the new methods. He moved from university to university in the first years of the new century, an itinerant professor, teaching the new economics wherever he went. While at Stanford, Young hired a shaggy young iconoclast named Thorstein Veblen, a refugee from the University of Chicago. At Cornell he taught Frank Knight; at the University of Michigan, Edward Chamberlin—later the two would be at the opposite poles of the ongoing debate about the nature of competition.

In 1920 Young was called to Harvard. He regularly commuted from Cambridge to Manhattan to advise the New York Federal Reserve Bank governor Ben Strong, in the days when the New York chief ran the Fed. And when the London School of Economics hired him away from Harvard in 1926, he became the first American to be invited back to teach in England, and the highest-paid economics professor in the United Kingdom to boot. Immediately after he arrived, he was elected head of the British Association's economics and statistics Section F. His presidential address, which he delivered in Edinburgh, he titled "Increasing Returns and Economic Progress." The year was 1928.

Straight off, Young told his audience that he would have nothing to say about "alluring but highly technical" debates in which Cambridge economists were then engaged. Not for him their geometry and the fancy algebra of marginal productivity theory. He wanted to talk about the division of labor instead, that old chestnut of Adam Smith's—specifically, Smith's dictum that the ability to specialize was limited by the extent of the market. "That theorem, I have always thought, is one of the most illuminating and fruitful generalisations which can be found anywhere in the whole literature of economics." Yet the principle had become all but forgotten.

Why? Perhaps, Young ventured, Smith himself had somehow missed the point when he described specialization in the Pin Factory as consisting entirely of the subdivision of the same old tasks. Instead, wasn't the division of labor mainly about using the knowledge gained thereby to undertake new and different tasks? Maybe pinmakers found new applications for their pins. Maybe they created tools and dies that turned out to be useful to those engaged in the manufacture of other kinds of goods. You wouldn't make a hammer to drive a single nail, said Young. But maybe once you yourself had use for such a tool, driving many nails, you could sell it to others for other purposes. Maybe other manufacturers in other industries brought new machines to the pinmakers. In this way, industries themselves might grow more differentiated, in which case "the progressive division and specialisation of industries is an essential part of the process by which increasing returns are realised." Scale would be the important aspect.

Three great stories of the 1920s illuminated Young's remarks. He assumed that his listeners knew about them from the newspapers. One was Henry Ford's automotive success, exemplified by the great new plant at River Rouge, in Dearborn. Another was Lenin's daring attempt to transform the backward economy of the Soviet Union into a modern one, known as the New Economic Policy. The third was America's success in surpassing Great Britain as an economic power. In each case it was the connection between scale and specialization that explained success or failure, Young said.

Henry Ford could single-mindedly pursue mass production because the potential market for his mass-produced vehicles was so large. Lenin, on the other hand, would have a hard time effecting an "Aladdin-like" transformation of Soviet industry, not for lack of a large potential market (Russia was huge), but because he was not taking fully into account the costs of creating the necessary subsidiary industries and inculcating new habits. And America's growing economic superiority arose from its huge internal market. Not even the extensive trade within the British Commonwealth could overcome the advantages of geographical proximity, excellent transportation networks, and the large population that American manufacturers enjoyed.

Alas, Young was unable to do more than put his thoughts into words—somewhat difficult words at that. For instance, he retained the Austrian term "roundaboutness," meaning machine-driven specialization, to describe the increasing division of labor. He spoke of qualitative change, disequilibrium, increasing complexity, "cumulative causation"—all code words for processes not yet fully understood. Even today people who know what he was driving at, who have carefully worked through the logic of his address for themselves, have difficulty sorting out the wheat from the chaff.

"Increasing Returns and Economic Progress" evoked a wave of admiration in the profession. It was a vigorous dissent from the conventional wisdom of its day. It persuaded a handful of young economists to rethink their convictions, among them Young's teaching assistant in London, a young Hungarian émigré named Nicholas Kaldor. Otherwise it had little effect. It was another example of Kenneth Arrow's underground river, bursting to the surface, attracting startled attention, then disappearing again. It wasn't that Young was wrong; it was that he was literary. His talk appeared at the very moment that economics was taking a broad new turn toward higher degrees of abstraction and generality.

The Edinburgh address was Young's last chance to influence profession opinion. Having decided to return to Harvard, he boarded a ship and died of influenza, in the epidemic in 1929, at age fifty-three. In October stock markets crashed around the world, ending the grand boom of the 1920s.

CHAPTER EIGHT

The Keynesian Revolution and the Modern Movement

IN RETROSPECT the watershed in technical economics in the twentieth century is easy enough to discern. In 1930, England was the center of world economics, as it had been for 150 years. Europeans flocked to London eager to discuss the Great Depression. There they were met with incomprehension by the aging keepers of the Marshallian tradition. The leading authorities of the profession, mostly Oxbridge dons, were locked in a hard-to-fathom controversy about increasing and decreasing returns. Politicians were caught up in a host of old arguments about the desirability of free trade and other laissez-faire policies. Forward motion in the field itself seemed to have all but halted, while unemployment topped 25 percent in the United Kingdom and other industrial democracies.

By 1945 economics was booming again, optimistic, many-pathed, vibrant—and headquartered in America. Before the watershed, economists wrote a literary style, seldom mentioned numbers, and propounded theories. Afterwards, they wrote mathematics, thought probabilistically, measured everything. And instead of propounding theories, they built models.

What happened? The Great Depression, of course. And John Maynard Keynes. The story as it usually is told is that a "Keynesian revolution" occurred starting around 1935, just in time to unlock the mysteries of the forces that had created the unprecedented world-wide slump—and save industrial capitalism from the fate of central planning.

Keynes had discovered "macroeconomics," it was said. It was a strange world where supply wasn't necessarily met by demand, were saving wasn't necessarily good and borrowing wasn't necessarily bad, a realm as oddly different from the everyday world of "microeconomics," of thrift and comparison shopping, as the world of Einstein was said to be from that of Newton.

Meanwhile, the flower of a generation of scientists, led by Albert Einstein himself, had been chased out of Europe by the Nazis. The preponderance of these refugees settled in America, causing centers of gravity of many fields to shift to the New World, including that of economics. There the Keynesian blueprint served as the basis for the great prosperity of the postwar world—and for the eventual victory of the West over the nations that had chosen communism.

And something like this certainly did occur. But already in the 1920s and early 1930s a great wave of new scientific thinking was sweeping through technical economics, raising economists' ambitions and putting new tools in their hands. Call this the Modern program—a shared determination to supplant the ambiguities of verbal reasoning with more rigorous methods. These founders were born around the turn of the twentieth century. They were imbued with a broad optimism about the possibilities of science that was characteristic of those days.

Some wanted to build statistical thinking into economic theory for the purpose of analyzing data drawn from the real world. Others were more interested in practical problems of planning. Still others were determined to construct a purely formal scheme of mathematical analysis of human interaction, starting from a handful of basic axioms. And some envisaged a science of strategic behavior. The shared hallmark of all these skeins was a preference for mathematical methods and formal logic: the Modern movement emerged in contradistinction to economics' long-standing literary tradition. The shared excitement after 1945 had to do as much with tool building for these new pursuits as with more familiar "Keynesian economics."

One conviction shared by all serious Modernists emerged only slowly. It was that the division of the field into microeconomics and macroeconomics as broached by Keynes, however useful it might have been in the beginning, would be unacceptable if it were to continue for any length of time. The first order of scientific business, in other words, was to build foundations for understanding macroeconomic phenomena, such as the failure of prices to adjust to changing conditions, on explanations of the microeconomic behavior of individuals. Economics would have to present a unified account of economic behavior from the bottom up if it were to be persuasive.

With the exception of the polymath John von Neumann (who nowadays may be as widely remembered for his work on game theory as for his contributions to the mathematics of quantum mechanics and machine computing), the pioneers of economics' Modern program are little remembered outside the profession. Nobody better exemplified the new style than Francis Plumpton Ramsey, a prodigy better known as Frank, who in the 1920s was tearing up Cambridge, England.

THE EXTENT OF THE FERMENT among the young in Cambridge in those days may be gleaned from a letter that the twenty-year-old wrote to his friend Wittgenstein in 1923 (and which the Ramsey scholar Peter Newman has retrieved):

> I have not been doing much towards reconstructing mathematics; partly because I have been reading miscellaneous things, a little Relativity and a little Kant, and Frege. . . . But I am awfully idle; and most of my energy has been absorbed since January by an unhappy passion for a married woman, which produced such psychological disorder, that I nearly resorted to psychoanalysis, and should probably have gone at Christmas to live in Vienna for nine months and be analyzed, had I not suddenly got better a fortnight ago, since when I have been happy and done a fair amount of work. I think I have solved all problems about finite integers, except such as are connected with the axiom of efficiency, but I may well be wrong.

Ramsey was born in 1903, the same year as Von Neumann. That made him twenty years younger than his friend and tutor John

Maynard Keynes. By the early 1920s it was clear that Ramsey was far better equipped mathematically than his tutor for the challenges that lay ahead. He published just three papers in economics, each said to be of fundamental importance. The one of greatest relevance to our story, "A Mathematical Theory of Saving," appeared in the *Economic Journal* of 1928, in the pages immediately following Allyn Young's presidential address "Increasing Returns and Economic Progress."

Perhaps never has the difference between a great mainstream contribution and an underground classic been more clear. Whereas Young eschewed mathematics altogether, Ramsey turned to the rarely used and somewhat forbidding calculus of variations as a means of deciding how much of its income a nation should save in order to obtain the greatest possible satisfaction over time. Using a model in which labor and capital combined to create a stream of output ("jam," in his friend John Maynard Keynes's famous phrase), part of which was consumed ("jam today") and part was saved ("jam tomorrow") on the way to the steady state of "bliss," Ramsey propounded a somewhat complicated but mathematically precise answer: a wise planner should peg jam consumption to the rate of interest: having more when it fell, eating less when it rose.

Had he lived, Ramsey might have become one of the great economists of the twentieth century. For even though "A Mathematical Theory of Savings" was not revived until the 1950s, by Robert Solow, it was the Englishman Ramsey, not the American Allyn Young, whose methods and insights were taken up and carried to the New World, part of the Modern movement. But Ramsey died of complications arising from jaundice at the age of twenty-six, in 1930, barely a year after Young succumbed to influenza.

The Modern program in economics made its unlikely landfall in America during the 1930s, high on the slopes of the Rocky Mountains. Alfred Cowles, a well-fixed Cincinnati stockbroker, was astonished that forecasters had done so poorly in anticipating the October crash of 1929, much less the ensuing depression, deeper and more persistent than any that had come before. In the belief that someone, somewhere, must be on the right track, Cowles resolved to find the best students of the next generation. His search took him to Irving Fisher at Yale, his old college professor.

Alfred Cowles's significance for economics was mainly symbolic. It lay in who he was: a well-heeled practitioner turning decisively to experts for advice. His grandfather had founded the *Chicago Tribune*; he was connected to the McCormick reaper fortune; he had plenty of money: he was interested in financing promising work. He symbolized the growing recognition by most business experts that the twentieth-century economy had become complex beyond their ability to grasp it with familiar methods of intuition and hobby investigation. Cowles was remarkable in that he turned not to the various amateurs who populated the landscape of the early 1930s but to the research wing of university economics.

Fisher put Cowles in touch with a group of European and American thinkers, who were then organizing a new international society dedicated to the advancement of economic theory in its relation to statistics and mathematics—the Econometric Society, it would be called. Later the word "econometrics" came to have a very specific connotation—a self-consciously empirical approach to economics that blended theory, measurement, and statistical techniques. Then it meant little more than modern. The new body would have two kinds of members—a relatively large society of general members, and a very small corps of fellows elected to it by other fellows—the economists' economists. The society was to be meritocratic, rigorous, intense.

The first group of twenty-nine fellows included mainly the already famous men who had organized the society—the Americans Fisher, Wesley Clair Mitchell, and Harold Hotelling, the Norwegian Ragnar Frisch, the Dutchman Jan Tinbergen, the Austrian Joseph Schumpeter, the Englishman John Maynard Keynes, the Frenchman Jacques Rueff, and, though none knew whether he was alive or dead, the Russian Nikolai Kondratieff (he died six years later in a Soviet labor camp). Not included was the Hungarian Von Neumann, who was still thought of as being only a physicist, although he already had begun to think seriously about economics. Passed over in the next selection, the first real election, were several whose names would become very familiar to followers of economics—John Hicks, Piero Sraffa, Friedrich von Hayek, Oskar Morgenstern, and Wassily Leontief. Deeply offended, Sraffa asked for his membership dues to be returned.

Cowles agreed to bankroll the society's new journal, *Econometrica*.* He created an organization, the Cowles Commission, to encourage the new-style work as well. To manage it, he hired Charles Roos, a Cornell University professor who had grown frustrated as research director for the National Recovery Administration, and installed him at Colorado College, near Cowles's vacation ranch. And every summer for the next few years, the Cowles Commission brought leading mathematical economists from around the world to a summer institute at the college. So the most visible expression of the formal modern style of economics took root in the 1930s in the shadow of Pike's Peak.

For several years a steady stream of leading thinkers stopped in Cambridge or New York, then trooped to Colorado to attend this intellectual summer camp. There and in the seminar rooms and dining halls of the great universities occurred animated (and animating) conversations about what economics would look like in the coming years. The economists were a very lively bunch. They talked about economic policy; about the excitement of developments in mathematics and in physics taking place in Europe; about the relations between the sciences; about what would be necessary to create a truly scientific economics. But whatever they talked about at meals in Colorado, after dinner they must have occasionally stopped talking and simply listened. For like almost everyone else in the industrial world in the 1930s, the economists at the Cowles Commission listened to radio. It was radio that brought the news from turbulent Europe, the music from New York. And, at least at Cowles, virtually everyone understood that the story of radio constituted an astonishing demonstration of the power of the axiomatic method to deliver

* A second new journal emphasizing formal methods, the *Review of Economics Studies*, also appeared in 1933, published by a group of young British and American economists in London. The wellsprings of the Modern movement in economics were to be found in many places.

the goods. This wonderful invention had been plucked out of thin air by a couple of mathematical equations.

To UNDERSTAND WHY the history of electricity might have been not only interesting but compelling to the economists who composed the Modern movement, you have only to remember that the physics of electromagnetism was barely older than their own science of economics. When Adam Smith was writing *The Wealth of Nations* in the eighteenth century, the phenomenon was still an utter mystery, the connection with magnetism unobserved. Benjamin Franklin—Smith's near-contemporary—was cheerfully flying kites with Leyden jars attached in thunderstorms.

But then Franklin wrote up his experiments in a series of papers collected and published in 1751 as *Experiments and Observations on Electricity*. In that book he introduced much of the language still employed to discuss the subject—battery, conductor, condenser, charge, shock, electrician, and so on. And thereafter the study of electricity quickly coalesced into purposeful investigation. It had become a discipline, with its own special community of investigators. And starting in 1820, its understanding of the phenomena evolved with great rapidity, thanks to a generation of experimental scientists who worked mainly at the laboratory bench.

In London, Humphrey Davy formulated the field of electrochemistry. His pupil Michael Faraday built a primitive generator to transform mechanical energy into electricity—a magneto, he called it. Within a few decades practical inventors were everywhere, developing more sophisticated generators, lighthouse arc lights, lightbulbs, power plants, transmission lines, and all the rest. At the same time academic physicists described various aspects of electrical behavior. There were Coulomb's laws of electric and magnetic force, Ampere's law, Faraday's law of induction, Ohm's law of resistance—all adduced from various experiments, each separate from the others. Meanwhile, practical leadership remained with inventors.

In 1864 a Scottish physicist named James Clerk Maxwell achieved one of the most remarkable insights in the history of science. Three years earlier he had published a design for a mechanical model of what he called the electromagnetic field, a wooden board to which was fastened a series of spinning wheels and idle wheels, designed to represent physical forces. Now he put aside the physical model he had built to check his own understanding, and instead summarized his results with a few straightforward equations describing the fundamental relations among light, electricity, and magnetism. Talk about parsimony! Maxwell's equations not only unified all the previously disparate laws. They went far beyond, suggesting the existence of a whole spectrum of energy, most of it undetected by the human senses. For the next few years physicists argued about whether this radiation actually existed. Many physicists were critical of the axiomatic approach and the fancy new mathematics supported by it.

The tenor of the discussion changed abruptly when Maxwell's findings were confirmed. In 1888 a young German graduate student, Heinrich Hertz, steeped in Maxwell's theories, contrived an ingenious test. At one end of a room he set up a couple of brass knobs each connected to an induction coil and separated by a gap across which sparks could leap—an "electrical oscillator," he called it. At the other end of a room, he placed a "detector loop," an antenna with two similar brass knobs also separated by a tiny gap. When leaping sparks in the oscillator (the transmitter) sent sparks leaping out of thin air in the detector (the receiver) across the room, in exactly the manner and *at the speed* (that of light) implied by Maxwell's equations, Hertz had demonstrated, to the satisfaction of virtually all those knowledgeable about the issue, the existence of the predicted electromagnetic waves. These were similar to heat and light but otherwise completely invisible to the naked eye. Once he had measured the length of the waves, Hertz had produced "as decisive an experimental victory as any in the history of science," as the historian C. C. Gillispie described it later. A mysterious continent of wireless energy had been discovered by a physicist with the courage to put away his wooden board covered with metal wheels in favor of his mathematics, and confirmed by an experimentalist following his logic.

Maxwell's equations led in many different directions—toward relativity theory and quantum mechanics in one, toward a cornucopia of practical applications in another. Wireless telegraphy was developed and subsequently radio. X-rays were discovered, quantum theory developed, the atom split, transistors and semiconductors invented. Maxwell, Hertz, and other physicists were leading would-be inventors and industrial scientists to depend more heavily upon a base of scientific understanding.

While the lofty abstractions of science were turning out to have practical applications, pure mathematics, too, was making unexpected contributions. For example, mathematicians at the frontiers of their subject in the early 1920s, interested in solving equations with infinitely many unknowns, were working on what they called the theory of function "spaces," including one of an infinite number of dimensions—pretty clearly a case of abstraction for abstraction's sake. Then, in 1927, young John von Neumann showed how just such a formalism might be the right tool with which to resolve the apparent contradictions in the two competing empirical theories of newly discovered quantum mechanics—Schrödinger's wave equation and Heisenberg's matrix mechanics. Von Neumann called it Hilbert space, after his teacher, the great German mathematician David Hilbert. Among his countless other contributions at the beginning of the twentieth century, Hilbert had developed the concept taking advantage of the strange connection between geometry and algebra that had been recognized since the seventeenth century, when Descartes pioneered the graphing of equations. Before long it would prove useful to economists.

By the 1920s engineering schools around the world were adding basic science and math departments to their faculties. Professors were beginning to consult regularly to industry. This was by no means a strictly linear process, in which inventions were handed down from above. Thomas Edison and others like him still used their understanding of what he called "packed down science" to achieve remarkable results. But with Maxwell *theory* finally moved ahead of *practice*, at least in physics—thanks to the axiomatic approach.

Small wonder, then, that the young economists who drew up the blueprints for the Modern program in the 1920s and 1930s hoped to follow suit. The same passion that had led Frank Ramsey to read relativity theory, psychoanalysis, and integer theory prompted some of his brightest contemporaries to adopt the axiomatic approach. The idea was to follow in the footsteps of the great Euclid, who had written down the axioms of geometry. Start with a few simple postulates accepted as true, for which no proof is required. Add some definitions. Build on these, showing how each new theorem is the logical outgrowth of some previously proved proposition, checking constantly to make sure that the facts of the model correspond to the facts of the world, until all the salient facts of an entire field have been brought into logical axiomatic form. At that point it was to be expected that new discoveries would begin to emerge, just as they had for William Harvey and James Clerk Maxwell. In 1892 Irving Fisher built a hydraulic machine complete with pumps, floats, pipes, and wheels to illustrate the principle of general equilibrium in economics—the interdependence of one fact with every other. By the late 1920s that seemed merely quaint.* Economics, at least at its leading edge, was beginning to be written entirely in mathematics now. Economists, too, had thrown away the wooden board.

Cowles's summer camp was just a beachhead. In Europe there was a sense of time running out. The great migration of intellectuals to America had begun, first from Soviet Russia in the 1920s and then from Nazi Germany in the 1930s and the countries that it subsequently conquered. A few of the European refugees who were interested in social science went to research institutes, such as the Rockefeller Institute (now Rockefeller University) in Manhattan and the famous new Institute for Advanced Study, at Princeton, which played host to both Einstein and Von Neumann. Here these giants were supposed to pursue their investigations free of real-world entanglements, such as teaching duties. But the vast majority of émigrés went to university departments of economics. (The New School for Social Research in New York, founded by a group of professors who in 1919 broke away from Columbia University, became a home

---

* Fisher built a second version of his model as late as 1925, though mainly for rhetorical purposes.

to many.) Economics was becoming professionalized. Economists increasingly wrote only for each other, in more and more specialized journals. The Modern movement trembled on the brink.

Before mathematics could become the lingua franca of economics, however, an English economist would write one last chapter—in inimitable, commanding prose.

EVEN TODAY John Maynard Keynes bulks so large that it is hard to imagine a time when he wasn't the most famous economist of the twentieth century. But in 1929 he was just one among many, and by no means considered to be the deepest or the best. He was an authority on currency matters in the City (as the financial district of London is known). His government service made him widely sought after for his policy views. But around Cambridge he was better known for managing his college's finances than for his teaching.

Not that Keynes was inconspicuous—ever. To begin with, he was (like his friend Frank Ramsey) the much favored son of a Cambridge don: Keynes's economist father was a colleague of Alfred Marshall; his cheerful mother, the daughter of a well-known minister. After studying math and classics at Eton, young Maynard became Marshall's star pupil. Like many Cambridge undergraduates of those days, he fell under the spell of the philosopher G. E. Moore, joined the secret society known as the Apostles, and spent a good deal of energy on homosexual affairs. Keynes never took an economics degree. He sat for the civil service exam instead.

He clerked in the India office, worked for the Treasury during World War I, and joined the British mission to the Paris Peace Conference in 1919. *The Economic Consequences of the Peace*, his bitter denunciation of the treaty's terms, made him famous at the age of thirty-six, and for the next quarter century he was at the center of English public affairs. He became embedded in the literary group known as the Bloomsbury set, wrote a treatise on probability, and married the Russian ballerina Lydia Lopokova in a society wedding in 1925. He was a talented speculator, making one fortune, losing it, and soon making another. He was consulted by the Treasury. To cap it, tall and elegantly tailored, he cut a striking figure wherever he went.

For all that, as he approached the age of fifty, Keynes was trapped behind the thought leaders of his generation. His 1930 *Treatise on Money* had been indifferently received. Arthur Cecil Pigou, six years his senior, was "the Prof" at Cambridge—the only outright "professor" allowed under the English system. Younger colleagues, including Dennis Robertson and Hubert Henderson, were better known. The flamboyant Austrian Joseph Schumpeter was teaching in London; another, younger arrival, Friedrich von Hayek, was the straw that stirred the drink. As Keynes entered the decade of the 1930s, he was just another economist. Ten years later, however, he was widely regarded as having solved the mystery of the business cycle.

Capitalism had been troubled by periodic banking panics at least since 1837, but the event that began on Black Tuesday in October 1929 was the worst episode by far. Fortunes were lost and bankruptcies declared, but far more alarming was the underutilization of resources. Unemployment increased until it was nearly 25 percent of the labor force in the United States and Europe. The volume of production itself fell by a third during the 1930s; its monetary value, by a half. And new investment all but stopped. There were ripples throughout the world. The critic Edmund Wilson compared it to an earthquake. Economics itself was under siege. Was it the collapse of capitalism that Marx had forecast?

The crash catapulted Keynes to prominence. At first there was only a preanalytic vision that he described as "the great wooly thing" in his head—a conviction that seemed to contradict what he had been taught as an undergraduate. Gradually the insight grew in clarity until it became a book, *The General Theory of Employment, Interest and Money*, presented chapter by chapter to a group of acolytes in Cambridge known to its members as "the Circus," then to an excited seminar of fellow teachers and students conducted midway between Cambridge and London. At the heart of *The General Theory* was the notion of a generalized glut—the possibility that, given what had been produced, consumers might be unwilling to buy it back, and that a depression might arise and prevail indefinitely, until something was *done*. In other words, the balance-redressing tendency of the Invisible Hand could fail.

In fact, this was the very possibility against which Malthus had warned at the first meeting of the Political Economy Club 120 years before and which had been quickly dismissed by the followers of Ricardo, who believed that supply would automatically call forth demand. But Malthus had been right and Ricardo wrong, Keynes wrote. Economics' smug complacency was misplaced. Modern industrial economies possessed tendencies to stall at high levels of unemployment. Inadequate aggregate demand, not overaccumulation, was the great threat.

Implicit in the diagnosis was a new solution: government should fill the gap in aggregate demand, borrowing in order to spend money it didn't have. If the government could "prime the pump," move the economy towards full employment, it would soon go there by itself. (Alternatively, Keynes said, "We have magneto [generator] trouble [as in a car]. How, then, can we start up again?") But whereas public debate continued with homely analogies, economists now fashioned a complicated new vocabulary with which to discuss the causes of the crash and subsequent depression among themselves.

The frank recognition that the market couldn't necessarily always be depended upon to get things right was highly subversive of the received wisdom. It raised the possibility of "multiple equilibria." Instead of the single, general, dependable, best-possible equilibrium of supply and demand that the Invisible Hand was supposed to produce, a high-unemployment equilibrium was possible as well. The economy could become "stuck," far from its full-employment equilibrium. A new mechanism was identified to account for this possibility—wage rigidity, or "sticky" wages that employers and employees were unwilling to adjust. Psychological factors became newly important—labeled "liquidity preference" and the "propensity to consume," to be restated as the "consumption function." Amid the sparkling prose, in place of the usual diagrams in *The General Theory*, were a few scattered equations, just enough to introduce Keynes's readers to a new style of argument. But there were many other strands of argument in the book, not all of them consistent with one another. Although it had a sprinkling of equations, the book was far more literary than not.

With this, Keynes was said to have invented macroeconomics, to have begun to unlock the secrets of the workings of the economy as a whole, particularly its systemwide pathologies of unemployment, underemployment, and even the business cycle itself. Others in Europe had been working along the same lines: the Polish economist Michal Kalecki, the Norwegian Frisch, the Dutchman Tinbergen. But it was Keynes who made the greatest impression. Even his archrival, "the Prof," Pigou, eventually agreed: "Nobody before [him] so far as I know, had brought all the relevant factors, real and monetary, together in a single formal scheme, through which their interplay could be coherently investigated."

Moreover, Keynes was a fabulous publicist for his own ideas. There was the portentous title he chose for his book, "The *General Theory*," perhaps to remind the reader of Albert Einstein, whose general theory of relativity had revolutionized physics a dozen years before. (Never mind Keynes's habit of collecting first editions and manuscripts of Isaac Newton!) There was his famous letter to George Bernard Shaw: "I believe myself to be writing a book on economic theory which will largely revolutionize—not, I suppose, all at once, but in the course of the next ten years—the way the world thinks about economic problems."

What Keynes did *not* address in *The General Theory*, even in passing, was the controversy that had preoccupied Cambridge for the preceding decade or so, namely, the tension between increasing and decreasing returns and the contribution of the former to economic growth. There was nothing about externalities in the book, nothing about whether increasing returns would continue to trump classical diminishing returns. To Keynes the depression seemed to have little to do with the running-out forebodings that had worried Ricardo. He was not worried that generally diminishing returns had yet set in. The depression did not reflect a shortage of productive capacity; it was the opposite. The problem was stabilization of the business cycle, not economic growth.

In fact, Keynes had set out his ideas about growth a few years earlier in a talk he called "Economic Possibilities for Our Grandchildren." In its published form, the essay is basically a literary formulation of his pupil and good friend Frank Ramsey's model of optimal savings. Another hundred years or so, he ventured, was all that would be required for humankind to attain its steady state. What worried him was the possibility that, before the economy could reach its ultimate destination, it would go off the road and into a ditch.

For these were desperate times. Unemployment in England in 1936 was still nearly 25 percent. The purges in the Soviet Union were beginning. In the turmoil of the Great Depression, Keynes understood that people wanted action. Lorie Tarshis, a Canadian economist and an early convert who wrote the first Keynesian textbook, described it this way: "What Keynes supplied was hope: hope that prosperity could be restored and maintained without the support of prison camps, executions and bestial interrogations. In those years many of us felt that by following Keynes . . . each one of us could become a doctor to the whole world."

WITH THE APPEARANCE of *The General Theory*, cutting-edge economists could be classified as belonging to one of two broad camps. Some of them became policy-oriented Keynesians. Others remained Moderns or were recruited to the movement. Very few economists exemplified one pure point of view or the other, of course; almost everyone operated with some particular blend of motives. The differences had to do not so much with politics, liberal or conservative, as with orientation to the problems and possibilities at hand. It was a matter, first and foremost, of different research strategies, flowing from different temperaments, expectations, and ambitions.

In *Pasteur's Quadrant: Basic Science and Technological Innovation*, the political scientist Donald Stokes distinguished between two very different motives that led investigators to undertake scientific research: considerations of usefulness and the quest for fundamental understanding. Then he drew a matrix that looked like this. The upper-left cell he named for Niels Bohr, the Danish physicist whose youthful quest for a model of atomic structure he described as "a pure voyage of discovery," undertaken with no thought of practical applicability. The lower-right cell he designated the tradition of the great

Research is inspired by:

Considerations of Use?

		No	Yes
	Yes	Pure Basic (Bohr)	Use-inspired Basic (Pasteur)
Quest for Fundamental Understanding?			
	No		Pure Applied (Edison)

American inventor Thomas Edison—"research that is guided solely by applied goals without seeking a more general understanding of the phenomena of a scientific field." The lower-left quadrant wasn't really empty, Stokes wrote; it belonged to careful observers with great curiosity about *particular* phenomena. It could as easily belong to the birdwatchers who contributed their observations of species' incidence, markings, and migratory patterns that went into *Peterson's Guide to the Birds of North America* as to the legendary astronomer Tycho Brahe, who recorded the data that Johannes Kepler needed to establish that the orbits of the planets were elliptical.

To Stokes the highest payoff from social investing in science seemed to come from the *fourth* quadrant, the upper-right cell in which he described as "use-inspired basic research" the work that seeks to expand the frontiers of knowledge in connection with a pressing problem. This cell he named for Louis Pasteur, the progenitor of germ theory who developed many fundamental public health technologies as well. But Stokes was quick to add that there was nothing reliably linear about the process. The purest blue-sky basic research sometimes quickly produced highly practical results and vice versa, and every science blended far more tones and voices than any symphony. There was no hard-and-fast "right" approach, except to listen to the scientists themselves.

For Stokes, John Maynard Keynes, at least his "major" work,

belongs in Pasteur's quadrant. For our purposes, however, it is Paul Samuelson (whom we will meet in the next chapter) who probably better exemplifies use-inspired basic research in economics, while Keynes (and, later, Milton Friedman) may be better understood in terms of economics' vigorous tradition of applied research. Keynes was more concerned, that is, with achieving practical results than with mapping into the more general understanding of their science.

Immediately attracted to the Keynesian tradition were practically motivated men who were determined to get the economy *working* again. They usually (but not always) had strong political feelings. They thought of themselves as research economists, to be sure. Their primary motivation, though, was to unlock and harness and tame and channel the powerful forces of the business cycle for the benefit of humankind, like so many science-based *engineers* (if they were Americans), or to diagnose and prescribe and cure its maladies as if they were *doctors* (if they were British). That is to say, economists operating in the Keynesian tradition shared a practical, clinical, action-oriented philosophy of research. They viewed economics first and foremost as *useful* knowledge.

Modernists, on the other hand, were much more likely in private to compare their enterprise to the new quantum physics or the nascent molecular biology. They saw the task of economic understanding as an end in itself—sometimes, especially when they were mathematical economists, as being no more practical than creating *beauty*, "beauty" being an oft-used word in mathematics. They emphasized rigor instead of relevance not because they were uninterested in the problems of the world but because they were convinced that deep and solid foundations would be necessary if the knowledge they created was to be really reliable. In the 1930s, 1940s, and 1950s, they were more likely to be associated with the Cowles Commission and the RAND Corporation than with, say, the Brookings Institution or the National Bureau of Economic Research.

Before very long, the policy-oriented engineering/doctor economists in America split into two groups, Keynesians and counter-Keynesians. (Left behind in Cambridge, England, was a third group of radical Keynesians, for whom Karl Marx gradually became a more compelling figure. They were increasingly ignored.) The American Keynesians were generally slightly left of center; they retained the banner. The American counter-Keynesians re-interpreted themselves as monetarists. The Keynesians favored policies that tended to depend on action by the government; monetarists generally favored laissez-faire policies and sought to impose constraints on governments through various rules. However much they disagreed about the various mechanisms in question, though, the Keynesians and monetarists shared a sense of urgency and mission. Not so the Moderns, who worked on matters considered more abstruse. Eventually the population of basic science-oriented economists of the Modern movement grew until it, too, experienced the same kind of split along political lines. Its members then distinguished among themselves between Saltwater and Freshwater schools, so called because of the regions of the country where their research centers were to be found. And in a sense all the controversy went back to Keynes, whose discovery of the paradox of thrift had sparked a conversation that lasted for seventy-five years.

As a clinician, John Maynard Keynes was superb. He understood markets. He understood politics. He understood psychology. As an economic detective, he had no peer—except, perhaps, Sherlock Holmes. As a scientific economist, however, he was a bit of a windbag, more Harley Street physician depending on his intuition to reach an inspiring diagnosis* than a plodding theorist intent on setting out his analysis in unemotional terms to be certain he was correct—a man in a hurry, more concerned with persuading politicians to act than with addressing the doubts of his fellow economists. In his determination to reach the widest possible audience, Keynes had set up the Marshallian orthodoxy as a straw man. By declaring himself in opposition to "the classics," he overemphasized the originality of his work. He severed his links with the rest of the discipline.

---

* In a wonderful moment of false humility, Keynes wrote at the end of *The General Theory*, "If economists could manage to get themselves thought of as humble, competent people on a level with dentists, that would be splendid." In fact, Keynes's macroeconomics probably has more in common with Sigmund Freud's psychoanalysis—a brilliant heuristic, a durable mental map of an otherwise mysterious terrain.

(There was, for example, only one Marshallian diagram in the entire book.) These links now had to be rebuilt.

In 1937 Keynes acquired an interpreter, a sympathetic leader of the Modern movement willing and able to translate Keynes's insights into terms that Classicals and Moderns alike would understand. John Hicks was everything that Keynes was not: self-effacing (at least on the surface), Oxford-trained, London-based, mathematical, and, above all, *young*. At fifty-three, Keynes, like his rival Joseph Schumpeter, was an eminent Edwardian; Hicks, at thirty-three, was a child of the new century (his 1904 birth year placed him, along with Von Neumann and Ramsey, among the older members of the generation that made up the Modern movement). He was a professor at the London School of Economics and the author of *Value and Capital*, a pathbreaking mathematical treatment of everything-at-once general equilibrium models that would appear in 1939, the most persuasive version yet of the bird's-eye view of which Marshall had dreamed and Walras had described. Moreover, Hicks had reached the same conclusions as Keynes, more or less independently—that markets might indeed become "stuck."

Almost as an afterthought, Hicks wrote a paper called "Mr. Keynes and the Classics." With a pair of Marshallian diagrams and a couple of algebraic equations, Hicks recast Keynes's wordy message in terms of a simple model of the relationship between income, interest, savings, and investment—the "aggregate supply" of goods, and the "aggregate demand" for them, in the form of money. Now, suddenly, a lightbulb came on for the profession. (Similar models were presented at the same meetings of the Econometric Society that year by Roy Harrod and James Meade, but Hicks's apparatus won hands down.) Translated into familiar terms, expressed as variables that could be measured and communicated and perhaps even manipulated, Keynes's message spread like wildfire among the young. "Economists more easily penetrated the thickets of Keynes' prose," Paul Samuelson himself later wrote. "Indeed, until the appearance of the mathematical models of [it] there is reason to believe that Keynes himself did not truly understand his analysis."

Thus it fell to Hicks to build the bridge between the camps—the

Classicals of the older generation and the rising radical English Keynesians of the new. He moved to Cambridge from London in 1935. His attempt at mediation didn't work; the gap between the young would-be revolutionaries and the conservators of Marshallian tradition was too great, and, besides, neither faction in the proud old university was much interested in the analytic style of the Modern movement, of which he was a prime exemplar. So in 1937 Hicks packed up and left Cambridge for Manchester, where he spent the war teaching undergraduates—all the while being carefully read by graduate students in the United States.

That same year Keynes had a massive heart attack. It left him weakened and somewhat disengaged. Though he continued to advise on international finance and economic policy at the topmost levels until his death in 1946, scientific leadership already had passed to the next generation. In Germany and Italy and elsewhere, the exodus long since had begun. In America lay economics' future. In England was its past, although Hicks (who moved to Oxford after the war) remained influential because he was so clear and insistent.

On one point Hicks was especially firm. The new everything-at-once analysis that he had pioneered would not accommodate much in the way of increasing returns, at least not in its present state. The Pin Factory was out of bounds. His treatise *Value and Capital* was built on the assumption of perfect competition. If it is to be abandoned, then, Hicks wrote, "the threatened wreckage is that of the greater part of general equilibrium theory."

CHAPTER NINE

"Mathematics Is a Language"

IN THE LATE 1930S the center of gravity of technical economics shifted from England to the United States. No ceremonial barge conveyed sacred texts. There was no announcement in the newspapers. Yet with the arrival of countless European refugees, the debates about the field's frontiers that had been taking place mainly in London, Vienna, and Berlin were relocated to the New World—the kernel of the Keynesian revolution to Cambridge, Massachusetts, the more diffuse agenda of the Modern program, briefly but symbolically, to the Rocky Mountains. During the next ten years the two traditions, economic engineering and economic science, mixed and mingled until they became difficult to tell apart.

One economist, more than any other, personified *both* the Keynesian revolution and the Modern movement, as well as the tension between means and ends that lay at their heart. Paul Samuelson was only twenty years old when he arrived as a graduate student at Harvard University in the autumn of 1935, fresh from having learned economics at the University of Chicago.

Over the next decade Samuelson codified much of the new axiomatic approach in a mathematical handbook called *Foundations of Economic Analysis.* Then he introduced the new approach to college freshmen in the enormously influential text *Economics*, emphasizing the Keynesian contribution with its distinction between microeconomics and macroeconomics. With this split-level approach to his readers—*Foundations* for economists, *Economics* for the rest—Samuelson's texts quickly supplanted Alfred Marshall's *Principles of Economics* as the standard exposition of technical economics. Before long the public would know it simply as "the new economics." Always in principle and often in fact, it was an enormous improvement on the old.

For the purposes of our story, however, what happened next had less to do with what was gained than with what was lost. Another hollowing out of economics now took place, as the Modern movement and the Keynesian revolution changed economists' ideas about which questions on their long-term agenda were most pressing and at the same time had answers within reach. For the opportunity that had brought Samuelson to Massachusetts in the first place had nothing to do with mathematical economics or Keynesian macroeconomics. These had yet to arrive. Despite the deepening depression, the excitement in economics in the United States in the early 1930s still had to do with increasing returns.

The man who drew Samuelson to Harvard was Edward Chamberlin. He seemed to have a more promising handle on the topic of economic growth than anyone else, thanks to a doctrine he called monopolistic competition. In England a similar doctrine had been developed by a young woman named Joan Robinson. She called it imperfect competition. But it was Chamberlin who had the most to say about the phenomenon that had been the hallmark of the Roaring Twenties—the steady stream of new products and new methods. After all, you couldn't go out in the street without seeing brand names plastered on new products: Chevrolet automobiles (with General Motors financing), Kelvinator refrigerators, RCA radio programs, Standard Oil, Quaker Oats, Gillette razors. What were so many new things doing in a world of diminishing returns and perfect competition?

BEFORE MEETING CHAMBERLIN, however, we must return to the itinerant professor Allyn Young, the man we met talking in Edinburgh about increasing returns and progress. The story of monopolistic competition goes back to him. As early as 1908 Young had zeroed in on the centrality of trademarks, brand names, and advertising in the modern age. In a textbook he wrote, "A clever device, coupled with excellence and advertising, may have very high value. The purchaser of oysters, for example, may feel that when he buys oysters of a particular 'brand' (trademark), he is getting oysters, plus something else; or in other words, not merely an oyster such as others sell, but a particular excellence which can nowhere else be surely had. It is merely this 'plus something else' that is a monopoly." Trademarks gave control not over oysters but over the name. It was the property of the seller; no one else could use it.

This is an especially clear early appearance in the economic literature of the idea of intellectual property in its full modern sense. It can be argued that there is nothing here that wasn't implied in Marshall. (Nor is it very different from what can be found in less precise form in the books—*The Theory of the Leisure Class, The Engineers and the Price System*—of Thorstein Veblen, a colorful critic of economics who lived from 1857 until 1929, and whose views have been communicated to a wide audience through the works of John Kenneth Galbraith.) In his next edition Young zeroed in on "selling expenses" as the budget heading under which these costs ordinarily were booked: "Put in a very general but roughly accurate way, these expenses are incurred, not in producing things people want, but inducing people to want the particular things the entrepreneur has for sale."

Selling expenses would be an issue only in a firm whose output was sufficiently large and/or isolated from the competition of close substitutes to permit it to choose where to set the price at which it will sell its products—take the Pin Factory, for example. In a perfectly competitive market for pins, no firm could affect the market price. Each firm could sell however many pins it produced at the market rate, and not a penny more, for if it attempted to raise its price, its competitors would get the business. There could be no "selling expenses" of pins if the Invisible Hand was truly at work.

But suppose the Pin Factory is not facing a market price? Here it may be helpful to remind ourselves of the taxonomy of costs that economists had identified to discuss these matters—the heart of those elementary chapters on production that are part of any elementary text. To begin with there are the *fixed costs* of going into the pinmaking business. These have to do with the time it takes to set up the business, the machines and matériel that must be purchased before the first pin can be sold—the minimum outlay, in other words, to begin manufacturing. (*Opportunity cost* is what you missed by not doing some other thing.) *Variable costs* are those that rise and fall with the numbers of pins you make—the cost of labor and materials. *Average costs* are what the name implies, total costs (fixed and variable costs added up) divided by the total number of pins you have made. *Marginal cost* is the cost of producing the most recent pin, the incremental pin.

At first the manufacturer sells as many pins as he can make, at whatever price people are willing to pay for them. Others enter the market, but the first pinmaker has a good head start. He may not yet have much influence on the industry price for pins. As he sells more pins, however, he begins to realize internal economies. He purchases wire in bulk at the cheapest possible price, invests in new pinmaking machinery, hires engineers to invent still more efficient methods of making pins, buys advertising, hires salesmen, enters contests (Gold Medal, Paris Pin Exposition!), pays off bureaucrats (to certify that his pins meet *official* standards), contracts with retailers for shelf space to display his pins. Eventually, after a long series of battles, he puts most other pinmakers out of business.

The interesting question is, What happens next?

CHAMBERLIN WAS BORN and raised in Iowa City, Iowa. That meant he knew a lot more about railroads than about pins. That was to his advantage, for railroads were rapidly replacing the Pin Factory in economists' imagination as an example of increasing returns. For Adam Smith, rivers and harbors were the key determinants of potential market size. By the early twentieth century, however, railroads were changing the landscape, if not rearranging it altogether, connecting the old markets that had sprung up along waterways and creating new ones. With railroads, whoever got there first had a critical advantage. Even when competition existed, when a parallel rail line was in place, railroads' advantage over water transport was so great that firms could pretty well set prices where they pleased. The increasing returns for which pin companies had to strive came all but automatically to trains.

Railroads, in other words, were a natural monopoly. A monopolist is someone for whose goods there are no close substitutes (yet). He *makes* his price, sets it where he thinks it will yield the greatest revenue, instead of *taking* whatever price others offer in the market. He is, at least momentarily, free of the discipline of the Invisible Hand. Even though his prices are likely to be falling—think of pins—the monopolist will generally supply fewer of them than people want, and at higher prices than if other manufacturers were able to enter the market. He will go home early on Wednesdays and take long vacations. As the saying goes, the chief reward of monopoly is a quiet life.

Before long the practical problem came to be recognized as one of getting the most profit out of a line of track. That meant charging different prices to different customers—employing price *discrimination*, as the practice quickly became known. Today we take it for granted that the person sitting next to us on an airplane might have paid a lot more or a lot less than we did for a ticket. In those days, however, there was something astonishing about the realization that if railroads charged only the average price, all those shippers and travelers for whom a ride would be worth something, but not as much as the average, would stay home. And the railroads themselves would lose out on the still higher prices that many riders and shippers would be *willing* to pay if the railroad charged all that their particular traffic would bear. Copper and coal were the examples usually given: with much higher value and smaller bulk than coal, the owners of copper surely should be willing to pay more to get to market.

What Chamberlin realized was that *any* seller who had a market mostly to himself could sell not at a market price that just covers his marginal cost of production but rather at whatever combination of quantity and price he thought would afford him the greatest profit. If customers felt they *had* to have a particular product, they'd pay more. It was a short jump from railroads to goods whose differences were largely contrived by their manufacturers: toothpaste, or tobacco, or automobiles, for example. Successful differentiation—by characteristics, by trademark, by advertising, by location—was the essence of successful marketing.

Chamberlin became convinced that some such element of monopoly was virtually always present, because firms either dominated the market for their product or shared dominance with a few big rivals with whom they ordinarily would successfully collude to carve up the market, at least for long periods of time. Perhaps the Pin Factory owner was more like the railroad owner than had been surmised. Falling average costs, after all, is the very definition of increasing returns.

He called his approach *monopolistic competition*. To many the opposition of the two words seemed a big mistake. Wasn't the phrase a contradiction in terms, an oxymoron? Yet neither force excluded the other, said Chamberlin, and more often than not both were required to give an intelligible account of prices. The "something extra" in a successfully differentiated product was the monopoly; its usefulness as a commodity also helped set its price. In England, Joan Robinson came up with what appeared to be more or less the same analysis in her book *The Economics of Imperfect Competition*. Yet the theories were significantly different. Robinson was trying to hang on to as much of the economics of Marshall as she could. Chamberlin was interested in the product itself as a variable to be manipulated. Moreover, he asserted that some degree of monopoly would be *necessary* if a business was ever going to cover its fixed costs. Otherwise, the Invisible Hand of competition would shave the margin between cost of production and selling price to zero.

The resistance to the new framework was fierce. When Chamberlin sought to analyze oligopoly, meaning industries with only a few large competitors, in terms of monopolistic competition, in the *Quarterly Journal of Economics* in 1929, the editor (Harvard's Frank Taussig) banned the term on the grounds that theory had shown that there could be no such thing as an industry with only a few sell-ers. Frank Knight, Allyn Young's other great pupil, invented an elab-orate framework in order to explain why competition among oyster sellers, too, or Buick dealers, for that matter, was perfect after all. He wound up at the University of Chicago, elaborating the meaning of perfect competition. And Nicholas Kaldor, who had been Allyn Young's last teaching assistant at the London School of Economics, suggested treating the study of all increasing returns/economies of scale under the heading of "indivisibility," further obscuring the matter.

What exactly was an indivisibility? It was something *lumpy*, a bot-tleneck of sorts: a commodity that was not to be had beneath a cer-tain size. A bridge from one side of a river to the other. The *two* steel rails required to form a railroad track from one city to another, rather than just one. The trip to the store one had to make in order to buy a candy bar as an armful of groceries. The entrepreneurial flair necessary to create a dominant firm. Anything, in short, that would confer a monopoly position, however fleeting. A crucial strut of perfect competition was the assumption that there were infinitely many possessors of every traded commodity; that way no individual could influence the market price of anything. There would be no troublesome increasing returns; indeed, no firms would be necessary to organize production: instead, interplay play of economic forces would reign free. By the mid-1950s this discussion had degenerated into one about the divisibility of human labor. A hundred half men equal to fifty whole men? A hundred ant men equally to one laborer? No wonder the discussion of the significance of indivisibilities even-tually shut down. But we will encounter this elusive concept again!

Unfortunately for Chamberlin, his book on monopolistic compe-tition appeared at the worst possible time. New algebra was sweep-ing the profession; he offered geometry. Unemployment was 25 percent in the autumn of 1935; he offered insights into advertising. As Joan Robinson said, nobody was interested in the determinants of the price of tea. Robinson at least was wrapped up in Keynesian analysis; Chamberlin offered no credible prescription to end the Great Depression.

The underground river had surfaced again, this time in plain view. But the circumstances were too dire in 1933 for anyone to care.

THE BIG INFLUENCES on Paul Samuelson when he arrived at Harvard turned out to be not Chamberlin but rather a refugee from the Russian revolution named Wassily Leontief and a mathematical physicist named Edwin Bidwell Wilson. Leontief (born in 1906) was only nine years older than Samuelson, but he had grown up in St. Petersburg and studied in Berlin. There, in an article called "The Balance of the Russian Economy," he had created the most tractable model yet of the circular flow of goods and services. He called it an input-output table. He had also cocked an ear to the excitement over the latest mathematical techniques, the new discoveries in quantum mechanics, and the tools being developed to solve equations with fabulously many variables.

Wilson was an even more imposing figure, a protégé of the great Yale thermodynamicist Willard Gibbs and, at fifty-six, a man determined to hold economists' feet to the fire of science. To Wilson that meant, among other things, a new level of mathematical rigor in the description of economic phenomena. Like most other Moderns, he maintained that mathematics, by emphasizing the consistency of the explanation, scouring it for breaks or gaps in the chains of reasoning, would force theorists to think clearly. At one point in the late 1920s, Wilson tried to persuade the American Association for the Advancement of Science to mount an effort from the outside in which scientists from other fields would be temporarily seconded to "put economics on a sound footing."

The son of a pharmacist, Paul Samuelson was born in 1915 in Gary, Indiana, and grew up in Chicago. He graduated from the University of Chicago in 1935, having won every available undergraduate award. He received a graduate school fellowship from the newly created Social Science Research Council, and chose Harvard over Columbia. He arrived in Cambridge expecting to find a white church on a village green. Instead, he discovered a grimy little industrial city across the Charles River from Boston, one that nevertheless was home to the most important center of learning in North America.

(Cambridge is an interesting place. For a time after the *Arbella* arrived in 1630 to found the Massachusetts Bay Colony and establish Boston and three other settlements, the little community of religious dissenters on the Charles River had the most densely educated populace on earth. Most of them were graduates of Cambridge University. In 1636 they founded Harvard College and two years later changed the name of their little settlement from Newtowne to Cambridge. The religious community at Plymouth—the old colony, sixty miles to the south—had no such pretensions. The emotional and intellectual links between the New World Cambridge and the old Cambridge remained fairly tight ever after. Harvard was about to celebrate its three hundredth anniversary when Samuelson arrived.)

The thermodynamicist Wilson taught a seminar on mathematical economics that autumn of 1935, an outgrowth of his attempt to reform the field. Only four students enrolled—Abram Bergson, Sidney Alexander, Joseph Schumpeter and Samuelson. Samuelson immediately began translating into math the economics he had brought with him from Chicago. "A student who studied only one science would be less likely to recognize what belonged to logic rather than to the nature of things," he recalled later. "One of the most joyful moments of my life was when I was led by E. B. Wilson's exposition of Gibbsian thermodynamics to infer an eternal truth that was independent of its physics or economics exemplification."

What truth? Nothing was drearier than listening to an economist or retired engineer trying to force analogies between physics and economics, Samuelson said. But it turned out that, starting from a maxim known as Le Chatelier's principle, which at one level could be stated simply as "Squeeze a balloon and its volume will contract," it was possible to work out mathematical formulation that would apply just as well to a profit-maximizing firm trying to decide what inputs to buy as to the balloon. "Pressure and volume, or for that matter absolute temperature and entropy, have to each other the same conjugate or dualistic relation that the wage rate does to labor, or the land rent does to acres of land." Moreover, thanks to the generality of the math, the story would work just as well for a problem with ninety-nine variables as for a problem with two! The Le Chatelier principle turned out to have myriad economic applications, all involving the formulation of a maximum—mathematical "black magic" permitting precise solutions to complicated problems.

Suddenly Samuelson was operating across a broad front, applying the calculus to obtain maximum or minimum values for variables of one sort or another in production economics, consumer behavior, international trade, public finance, and income analysis, seeking the formal similarities that underlay each, much as Marshall fifty years before had unified the various theories of profit, interest, and rent in a single general theory of individual optimization. "I was like a fisher for trout in a virginal Canadian brook," Samuelson recalled of those years. "You had only to cast your line and the fish jumped to meet your hook." He sent papers out to editors; they came back marked, "Please shorten and make less mathematical." To do both was impossible, he joked, and neither was optimal. The quality of the papers that the editors rejected was, he later wrote, "if anything, a bit better than the rest."

In these circumstances the significance of Keynes's *General Theory* dawned on Samuelson only slowly. Indeed, he didn't think much when the first copies of *The General Theory* arrived in early 1936.

> My rebellion against its pretensions would have been complete except for an uneasy realization that I did not at all understand what it was about. And I think that I am giving away no secrets when I solemnly aver—upon the basis of vivid personal reflection—that no one else in Cambridge, Mass., really knew what it was about for some 12 to 18 months after its publication. Then the first mathematical models appeared, and gradually, against heavy resistance, the realization grew that Keynes' concept of effective demand—of aggregate buying power, willingly exercised or not—was not a fad but part of the wave of the future.

It was Alvin Hansen who did the heavy work of spelling out the implications of the Keynesian thesis. His fiscal policy seminar at Harvard became the hotbed of the new American macroeconomics. As Samuelson has recalled, the fifty-year-old South Dakota native was an unlikely revolutionary. But with Cambridge banks earning ⅜ of a percent on their loans, graduate students like Samuelson couldn't persuade them to bother to accept deposits. The Federal Reserve had eased, but the United States offered a nearly perfect example of a liquidity trap. Hansen's students understood the futility of "pushing on a string."

With the war rapidly approaching, Samuelson set out to pull together his papers in a thesis. His plan was to demonstrate the underlying unity of the Modern approach and Keynesian theory—to create a "general theory of general theories," as he described it forty-five years later. Already he had concluded that he and the various Europeans were barking up the same tree. His goal was the same as Hicks's: a fully dynamic general equilibrium statement of all the entities in the economic universe. *Foundations of Analytical Economics* was written at fever pitch from mid-1940 to January 1941, as World War II closed in. The dissertation's debt to the Modern movement was apparent in Samuelson's choice of title. Classicals wrote about *principles*. Moderns sought *foundations*. Seven years later the thesis appeared in book form, as *Foundations of Economic Analysis*.

You don't have to look very hard at *Foundations* to see that it is a manifesto. "Mathematics is a language," declared the frontispiece—a quotation from Willard Gibbs (all four words of what was said to have been the longest speech that the physicist ever made). Whereas Marshall had confined his math to the appendix, Samuelson now wrote page after page of equations. ("I have come to feel that Marshall's dictum that 'it seems doubtful whether anyone spends his time well in reading lengthy translations of economic doctrines into mathematics that have not been made himself' should be exactly reversed," he wrote in the introduction.) And whereas Marshall had put the quest for general equilibrium on the back burner in favor of the method of one thing at a time, and ceteris paribus for the rest, Samuelson now returned the idea of interdependence, at least in principle.

But instead of the unstructured, unnumbered, and perhaps insoluble series of equations that Walras had envisaged, Samuelson created a system strongly influenced by the new macroeconomics. He identified the same few key variables as had Keynes—saving, investment, consumption, government expenditure—and spelled out their relation to one another. No longer was it sufficient to say that everything depended on everything else. Now it was necessary to break the economic world into subsystems and demonstrate how the big spending categories depended on one another.

In retrospect it is apparent that Samuelson himself belonged fully to neither the Modern program nor the Keynesian revolution. He had a foot in both camps, and the tension between them was never quite resolved in him. Only in 1944 was he elected a fellow of the Econometric Society, by which time it was clear he was in the forefront of developments.* He remained a midway figure all his life, continually mediating between the old and the new, between lofty scientific goals and pressing engineering concerns. Skeptical of fads, he insisted on the durability of the progress that had been made. He was, above all, a man of contagious enthusiasm.

Long before it appeared in 1947, *Foundations* had begun converting the leaders of the next generation of economists to a new style of doing economics in the language of mathematics. His influence on them could scarcely have been greater. "Here was a graduate student in his twenties reorganizing all of economics in four or five chapters right before your eyes, and let Marshall, Hicks, Friedman, and everyone else get out of the way!" wrote Robert Lucas many years later, describing the confident and exhilarating tone of the book. In a brilliant metaphor, Lucas captured the effect of *Foundations* and the enthusiasm of its author on the postwar generation of students of economics around the world: "Samuelson was the Julia Child of economics, somehow teaching you the basics and giving you the feeling of becoming the insider in a complex culture at the same time." Instead of French cooking, economists now learned to express themselves mathematically.

WITH THE COMPLETION of his thesis in 1941, Samuelson picked up and moved down the river—to MIT, or Tech, as it was called at the

---

* A leader in every field, that is, *except* the statistical and empirical tool-building program that eventually became known as econometrics.

time. Harvard had been reluctant to promote him swiftly, perhaps even more out of professional resentment of his mathematical tendencies than as a result of the anti-Semitism that lingered in American universities on the eve of World War II. MIT made a better offer, which Harvard failed to match. He spent the war at Lincoln Labs, the military research arm of MIT, compiling ballistics tables. He had little to do with the group at Cowles. Toward the end of the war, he was lent to the Science Secretariat to write drafts, along with a few others, for Vannevar Bush's famous manifesto, *Science, the Endless Frontier*. What emerged, he has written, was "beyond [his] fondest hopes: a National Science Foundation (inclusive of the social sciences) and a vastly expanded National Institutes of Health, rather than a nominated plan to give every US county its population quota of dollar subsidies for research."

Ahead lay Samuelson's various triumphs: the broad synthesis of economic doctrines over which he presided, the eighteen editions of his college text, his role as an informal adviser to President John Kennedy and the rest of the New Frontier, his Nobel Prize in 1970, his deep interest in the workings of financial markets, culminating in the remarkable financial success of the Commodities Corporation, founded by his students, in which he was a founding and longtime investor.

Behind him at Harvard erupted a series of battles that cost the great old university its leadership in economics. The resistance to mathematics continued. Although Harvard University Press was compelled by prior agreement to publish *Foundations*, because Samuelson's dissertation had won the economics department's prize for best thesis, Chairman Harold Burbank ordered the laboriously hand-set plates (with their thousands of equations) destroyed after a single printing of 1,500 copies. That meant no revisions were possible for the next thirty-five years. Then, too, the Veritas Society, a group of alumni dedicated to opposing Keynesian influences, waged a witch hunt against the department. Harvard's legendary complacency took its toll as well.

Also left behind at Harvard was Edward Chamberlin. He was now attacked from both ends of the spectrum—by some for failing to give a mathematical account of his subject, by others for departing from the idea of perfect competition. The questions he had raised were consigned to courses on industrial organization, or banished to business schools, where barriers to exit and entry and strategic differentiation became lively topics. And instead of making common cause, Chamberlin and Robinson turned their insights into a rivalry, a long-running Punch and Judy show, battling with each other and the rest of the profession. Chamberlin died in 1967 and Robinson in 1983, neither having made much of a dent, at least not on the Modern movement.

ONE OTHER figure traversing the landscape of the 1930s and 1940s must be mentioned. The name of Joseph Schumpeter has become a kind of a code word for nonmathematical theories of increasing returns, monopoly new goods, and economic growth, more so than Edward Chamberlin. As a specimen of the phrasemaker's art, "creative destruction" ranks second only to "the Invisible Hand." Yet, as a young man in Vienna, Schumpeter had been in the vanguard of the Modern program. His very first paper, "On the Mathematical Methods in Theoretical Economics" (1906), had been a forceful brief for the general equilibrium equations of Leon Walras.

Schumpeter's early fame rested on a book, *Theory of Economic Development*, published in German in 1912, when he was twenty-nine. Even then he had zeroed in on technical change as the essence of growth, and on the entrepreneur as the mainspring. "It is . . . the producer who as a rule initiates economic change, and consumers are educated by him if necessary; they are, as it were, taught to want new things." This was, after all, the Age of McCormick, of Rockefeller, Bayer, Edison, Swift, Carnegie, Duke, and Alfred Nobel. Years afterward, economic historians were still fleshing out case studies of Schumpeter's main points. The story of the rise of the railroads became the classic example.

Railroads supplanted man-made canals as the dominant transportation system of industrial economies in the nineteenth century not just because they were technologically superior, although they clearly were, but because the canal owners made it easy for them. Waterway proprietors routinely conspired among themselves to keep transport prices high and, in doing so, provided a golden opportunity. Not only were railways cheaper to build and run than canals; they didn't freeze in winter. So railroad entrepreneurs were welcomed as liberators, delivering shippers from the canal owners' "insolent hold." The railroad men bankrolled advances in steam technology and metallurgy in turn, which led to many other advances. Coal miners, rail manufacturers, and steam engine factories gained; mule breeders and bargemen lost out. This was the essence of what Schumpeter later termed creative destruction. The competition between similar firms in a particular industry, the kind of competition that preoccupied most economists, was trivial, he insisted. It was the competition between old technologies and disruptive new ones that counted.

But Schumpeter didn't even try to describe his system mathematically. There was little explicit analysis of increasing returns—of the particular mechanisms that led to change over time, even though change over time was, as with Marx's, his theory's most salient characteristic. (That is, it was *dynamic*, emphasizing change, rather than *static*, emphasizing equilibrium.) This much they shared with Alfred Marshall, though spillovers and neighborhood effects played no part in their account. Schumpeter's bad fortune, like that of Keynes and Chamberlin, was to have been born at the wrong time—both he and Keynes in 1883. Schumpeter admired math, taught it, and understood what it could do, but, as Abram Bergson said, he could not manipulate and do fresh things. (He never did any econometrics either, though he was a founder and early president of the Econometric Society.) He complained to a friend, "I sometimes feel like Moses must have felt when he beheld the Promised Land and knew that he would not be allowed to enter."

Schumpeter arrived to teach in Cambridge, Massachusetts, in 1932, just as attention was swinging rapidly to his rival Keynes—a turn of events that he greatly resented. He lost credibility by opining that the Great Depression was the result of a fifty-year cycle of too much science and that growth therefore soon would resume. His colleague Leontief replaced him in 1935 as the professor in the mathematical economics course. When Schumpeter's two-volume study of business cycles was finally published in 1939, it could scarcely have seemed less relevant, given the prominence of Keynes's new ideas. Students described "Schumpy" as hopelessly old-fashioned— "someone who could say 'marginal utility' in 17 languages" but nothing more. Worse yet, he was suspected of harboring pro-German sympathies.

Sidelined, disappointed, resentful, Schumpeter spent the war years in Cambridge, out of touch with other centers of learning, an orphan at the feast of mathematical progress. He pumped himself up to write a gloomy meditation on the centrality of Karl Marx. For the most part *Capitalism, Socialism, and Democracy* is an awkward book, wordy and weary, preoccupied with the history of European socialism. Can capitalism survive? "No, I do not think it can." "[E]ntrepreneurs and capitalists—in fact the whole stratum that accepts the bourgeois scheme of life—will eventually cease to function."

Yet the chapter "Creative Destruction" is a classic of the tradition of the underground river. For in reiterating the themes of his 1912 book, Schumpeter nailed, verbally, many of the key mechanisms by which economic growth takes place: the appearance of new goods, new markets, new methods of production and transportation, new forms of industrial organization, usually in clusters and usually as sudden bursts of activity, punctuating long periods of comparative quiet and leading to dramatic improvements in living standards. Ignoring this kind of change in economics is like playing "Hamlet without the Danish prince," he wrote. Yet the growth of knowledge was almost completely ignored by textbooks that taught the new doctrines of marginalism. Regarding the old fear, now accentuated by wartime shortages, that the human race soon would be running out of food and natural resources, Schumpeter wrote, "It is one of the safest predictions that in the calculable future we shall live in an *embarras de richesse* of both foodstuffs and raw materials, giving all the rein to expansion of total output that we shall know what to do with."

By packaging his growth theory in a literary book, disjointed and somewhat grandiose, Schumpeter almost guaranteed that he would be ignored by the young economists who were attracted by the action-oriented *General Theory* and the promise of the formal methods of the Modern movement. *Capitalism, Socialism, and Democracy* found a respectful audience among business executives, policy makers, and intellectuals. Literary economists rallied to its banner. But even as his fame grew among civilians, Schumpeter's influence faded. He published a little book on rudimentary mathematics for economists and statisticians ("From creeping to crawling," his students joked). He helped found the Research Center for Entrepreneurial Studies at Harvard. He began an enormous history of economic thought. And then, in 1950, he died. Like Chamberlin and Robinson, Schumpeter became another literary theorist who was swept away.

YEARS LATER, by which time it had become difficult to think of another way to celebrate a man who had receive nearly every honor his contemporaries had to give, Paul Samuelson's admirers conceived one more, a particularly pleasing one: a banquet whose centerpiece was a dish of revenge, served, as the old aphorism held, well chilled. Harvard University Press offered to publish finally, with great ceremony, a second edition of *Foundations* on its thirty-fifth anniversary, as a way of making amends for the indignity of having destroyed the plates at the dawn of the age of mathematical economics. Its equations now were generated by computer, its plates now laser printed. A new introduction gave Samuelson an opportunity to survey all the extensive developments in mathematical economics since 1947.

At one point he took note of the hollowing out that had occurred after *Foundations* appeared and the Cowles group had gone to work. "More can be less. Much of mathematical economics in the 1950s gained in elegance over poor old . . . Edward Chamberlin. But the fine garments sometimes achieved fit only by chopping off some real arms and legs." The next wave of mathematical techniques had produced remarkable advances, he wrote. "But they seduced economists away from the phenomena of increasing returns to scale and . . . technology that lie at the heart of oligopoly problems and many real-world maximizing assignments."

It was vintage Samuelson: honest, unsentimental, opaque ("Easy victories over a science's wrong opponents are hollow victories—at least almost always"), and as close to a mea culpa as he would come. Chamberlin might have been right about what he had to say. But he had chosen the wrong language with which to say it. Whoever would make sense of "monopolistic competition" would have to write it in formal math.

CHAPTER TEN

When Economics Went High-Tech

WITH THE ENTRY of America into World War II in 1941, technical economics was drafted into wartime service and extensively reorganized. In many centers around the country, teams of economists rolled up their sleeves and went to work.

In Cambridge, Massachusetts, Paul Samuelson worked on radar and mathematical fire control for MIT's Lincoln Laboratories, revising his dissertation for publication in his spare time. In Washington, Simon Kuznets and Robert Nathan developed the national income accounts. At New York's Columbia University, the Statistical Research Group worked on the mathematics of probability, inventing, among other things, better ways of searching out the duds among bombs and artillery shells. Princeton's quest for a better adding machine led to the mainframe computer.

But it was the drama of the wartime mission that unfolded at the University of Chicago that captured the imagination of the economics profession. The Cowles Commission had pulled back to Chicago from remote Colorado Springs in 1939 and reorganized as a foundation. It shared office space with the Department of Economics. With the war's outbreak, the commission received a new assignment from the government: to build a working econometric model of the U.S. economy.

During the next ten years much of the future of economics took shape at Cowles. And it was here that the strands of economics began to differentiate themselves: Keynesian macro, econometrics, mathematical economics, and game theory. It was, in some sense, action "away from the ball," meaning that most eyes at the time were focused on what the Keynesian engineers in Cambridge, Mass., had to say about problems of war finance. The good news was that the science-minded group at Cowles produced a deeper than ever investigation of the logic of the Invisible Hand.

The bad news was that the Pin Factory was, once again, bracketed or ignored. The significance of increasing returns became even more obscure.

THE "DIRTY DOZEN" THAT assembled in Chicago was at least a little like the war movie of that name, except that Jacob Marschak's recruits specialized in statistics, economics, philosophy, mathematics, and strategy instead of mayhem, and they stayed put instead of traveling behind enemy lines. "Jascha" was another of the fathers of the Modern movement. A Menshevik refugee from the Russian revolution (and former economics reporter for the *Frankfurter Zeitung*), he had been with Von Neumann in Berlin before the war. He had been teaching at New York's New School for Social Research before he took the Cowles job. He had, in other words, a very broad view of developments, and he took advantage of the poor academic market to assemble a remarkable team.

There was the statistician Trygve Haavelmo, interned by the war, lent by the Nowegian embassy; Leo Hurwicz, a lawyer and mathematician from Poland; the budding measurement economist Lawrence Klein, Samuelson's brightest pupil, lured to Chicago despite his teacher's wish that he go to the Federal Reserve Bank of New York; Tjalling Koopmans, a Dutch physicist refitted as an economist. Herbert Simon, a psychologist, was a frequent visitor, as was the monetary theorist Don Patinkin. Von Neumann would drop in while changing trains, on his way to Los Alamos from Princeton to work on the atomic bomb. The economist Simon Kuznets came by to describe the social accounting framework he was building. Oscar

Lange, teaching mathematics at Chicago, would disappear from time to time in later years, only to turn up on the front pages, meeting with Stalin. In the evenings the team did skits. Down the street, physicists under Enrico Fermi were laboring in the squash courts beneath the football stadium to build an atomic pile. Various members of the two teams paid visits to each other's lunchrooms to compare notes.

The most distinctive innovation associated with the Cowles Commission in Chicago was probably the idea of the mathematical model itself—and its rapid recruitment to the cause of Keynesian macroeconomics. Simultaneous equations in those days were referred to as Cowles Commission methods. This was no longer the power of high school algebra to solve word problems. But neither were these chains of if-this-then-that reasoning yet mathematics from the farthest frontier. University-level calculus seemed to offer a way of clarifying assumptions until they were entirely noncontradictory, of replacing emotionally charged words with terms whose meaning was inescapably clear. Klein remembered, "We saw the world as the solution to an equation set and we were aiming to build a model that worked. We imagined that we held the well-being of the economy right in the palms of our hands." (And victory in the war as well.) And though the problem of separating cause and effect turned out to be more difficult that the Cowles economists had imagined, the term "model" before long replaced "hypothesis" in all but a few research outposts. If you didn't have a model, you were not entitled to enter the debate.

Then there was econometrics. Here the idea was to marry statistics to economics, the advent of statistical methods having been shown to be the most useful development in mathematics since the calculus. Much of life was chance, the Cowles economists recognized; that is, it was subject to random error. Any system of equations describing an equilibrium would be subject to random occurrences ("stochastic shocks") that contradicted the purely economic assumptions and might prevent the variable from taking the course implied by theory. How best to gauge cause and effect in such a complicated world? The subfield of regression analysis already had a long history in statistics as a means of sorting out cause and effect, of describing the correlation between one variable and another, in everything from celestial mechanics to human heredity. Economists adapted the tool to the study of their problems.

Mathematical economics was a third important development emanating from Cowles. Indeed, it led to the team's first concrete achievement—the discovery of a technique to solve the "shipping problem," namely, how to find the best route among many destinations, given the available ships, crews, cargos, dock facilities, and so on. (In peacetime this was known as the traveling salesman problem.) These were only scheduling problems, it was true, but deep down they were no different from other problems in economics; the idea was to allocate scarce resources so as to deliver the most matériel in the least time. It was the physicist turned economist Koopmans who in 1942 hit upon a practical mathematical system for making these decisions. Before long he found he was able to optimize a hundred variables or more. Years later the Americans learned that Leonid Kantorovich had made the same discovery in Leningrad in 1939, working on lumber manufacturing for the Soviet Union's plywood trust. And in 1947, while working for the U.S. Air Force, the mathematician George Dantzig came up with what turned out to be the best method of all for getting the most output from the fewest inputs and calculating the various trade-offs along the way. He called his technique the simplex method and described it as "climbing the beanpole." That homely figure of speech, familiar from any kitchen garden of that simpler time, was in essence what Dantzig's series of calculations looked like when envisioned in three dimensions. "The beanpole" was a geometric solid, a many-dimensioned polygon called a *polytope*. The problem solver went around its outside, checking each corner, turning this way and that, moving on each time from one vertex to the next, always in the direction of a better solution. Pivot, climb, pivot, climb some more, until you can go no higher—*climb the beanpole*.

Economists called the body of their new techniques linear programming. Why linear? Because its equations produced shapes with straight lines instead of the curves that Marshall's marginalism required—lines, planes, and hyperplanes (just as a line becomes a plane in two dimensions, planes become hyperplanes in three and more dimensions). Linear techniques were much better at describing the discrete this-or-that choices of real-world production and logistics problems than was calculus, which assumes that everything changed smoothly. Why programming? Because "scheduling" was too tame, and "planning" had undesirable overtones. Wasn't planning what communism was all about? What *they* were doing, economists slyly dubbed programming, since all military plans were already called programs, anyway.

In fact, the bland name for the new technique was even more subtly misleading. The new tools involved a dramatic departure from calculus. They were essentially geometrical, drawn from the branch of math known as topology. Ever since Descartes had shown how to graph equations, it had been known that there was a connection between algebra and geometry. For a time it was known simply as analytic geometry. Gradually the subject morphed into topology in the eighteenth century, when, after a visit to the Baltic city of Königsberg, the mathematician Euler had proved that it was impossible to travel its famous seven bridges without at some point walking the same route twice. From that problem Euler moved to mapping the various possible routes that a knight might follow in a game of chess. New techniques were then generalized to analyze three dimensions, to solids of all shapes and sizes, cones, polyhedrons, and the rest, and, soon enough, in mathematicians' customary fashion, to n dimensions. By the early twentieth century theorists had found their way to the abstraction known as Hilbert space—the infinitely many-dimensioned mathematical form, which Von Neumann adopted to characterize quantum mechanics.

Within a few years after the end of World War II, linear programming was described as being as significant as the discovery of double-entry bookkeeping in the Middle Ages. Eventually it provided the basis for applications ranging from managing the staggering complexity of a modern petroleum refinery to keeping track of all the operations of a fleet of commercial airplanes, from reservations to fueling requirements. For the economists it meant a shortcut to Marshall's global bird's-eye view of the economy, the everything-at-once treatment of which Walras had dreamed. Leontief, with his input-output table, had prepared a highly useful static snapshot of the economy. Now the idea was to turn it into a moving picture—a dynamic model of the economy as a whole with which economic changes could be followed, along long chains of mathematical reasoning to their most surprising and remote repercussions. So rapid was progress that economics had moved far beyond *Foundations* even before Samuelson's finished book appeared in 1947. And ten years later, Samuelson, Robert Solow, and Robert Dorfman had to write *Linear Programming and Economic Analysis* to introduce students to the new math.

The fourth and most far-reaching subject of all at Cowles originated not in Chicago but in Princeton, though news of it arrived regularly enough on the overnight train from Philadelphia. It was the publication in 1944 of *The Theory of Games and Economic Behavior*, a book devoted to the proposition that people were intelligent, that their actions anticipating and affecting another could be rigorously described. (Game theory might better have been dubbed strategic thought.) John von Neumann had arrived in Princeton in 1930, along with Einstein one of the first and most important intellectual refugees. The two men joined the Institute for Advanced Study when it was founded in 1933. Though Von Neumann had been interested in economics all along, he was not yet deeply involved.

An Austrian refugee named Oskar Morgenstern persuaded him to work up an earlier paper on the principles underlying parlor games into a full-scale book. Thus was strategic thinking introduced to economics. It was obvious that certain games had much in common with business situations, with strictly individual strategies as well as those that involved forming coalitions. And if that had been the end of it, *The Theory of Games* would have been a very short book.

Instead it was only the beginning. Most of the 600-odd pages of the book were taken up with math of the most abstruse sort. It turned out that Von Neumann had discovered linear programming for himself, at a famous seminar in Berlin in 1928, grabbing the chalk out of Jascha Marschak's hand and walking animatedly around the room, thinking out loud, until his friend reluctantly brought the meeting to a halt. Eventually economists saw that the math that Von Neumann had packed into his book was deeper and more general than the "activity analysis" being developed at Cowles, and absolutely central to the economic problem. But that was by no means obvious at the time. Within thirty years economists, too, were using "eigenvalues" and "eigenvectors," tools from Hilbert space that Von Neumann had introduced, to represent the variables of their systems. But to most economists in Chicago during the war, the hard mathematics of *The Theory of Games* might just as well have been another language.

All four strands of the Modern movement were present at the Cowles Commission in Chicago—not just the macroeconometric model building with which the group originally had been charged, and for which it eventually became famous, but Keynesian macro-economics, mathematical economics, and game theory as well. And since Cowles's heyday in Chicago lasted a dozen years, from 1942 until 1954, its work emphasized different skeins at different times. The only one of these fields where the Cowles Commission pioneered alone for any significant length of time was model building. Other centers contributed significantly in the remaining fields.

Remember, the economists at Cowles were still doing things with hand-cranked adding machines. The first electronic computers were just beginning to be invented, mainly at Princeton, under the fierce stimulus of the number-crunching necessary to build the atom bomb. Von Neumann was perhaps the only one among the economists who really *knew* what their capabilities might be. Yet even in those early days, it was possible to imagine the far-reaching possibilities of nearly costless, nearly instantaneous computation, if not yet how to get there.

Present in Chicago, however, was a fifth strand, comprising economists who shared office space with Cowles, but not convictions. These were the defenders of the Marshallian status quo. Not surprisingly, the hurly-burly of the Modern movement was galvanizing them, as well—to resist.

IN ALL GREAT ENTERPRISES it helps to have a foe. Cowles's "enemy," at least at first, was the National Bureau of Economic Research. The

NBER was one of those research institutes founded in the 1920s, loosely based upon a German model—the Brookings Institution in Washington was another—to provide a source of relatively disinterested advice to policy makers. In both cases the idea was to build an alternative to the cacophony of special interests and immoderate cranks. The NBER approach was thoroughly institutional and empirical. Simon Kuznets pioneered in the creation of the national income accounts. Wassily Leontief found his first refuge in the United States there. A number of diligent scholars signed on as researchers, Solomon Fabricant, Arthur Burns, and Geoffrey Moore among them. But in the mid-1930s, the NBER's biggest catch was an up-and-comer named Milton Friedman.

Friedman was an extraordinary individual—practical, inventive, skeptical, naturally combative. Born in 1912, he attended college at Rutgers, learned economics as a graduate student at Chicago (where he and the undergraduate Paul Samuelson first met). But economic circumstances forced Friedman to leave Chicago in 1935 without completing his dissertation, and a proper academic appointment had eluded him for a decade. He lectured part-time at Columbia University in New York while he worked in Washington for the National Resources Commission, a short-lived creation of the New Deal. In 1937 he took a job at the NBER in New York.

Even before the war, however, the NBER was in a strategic retreat, losing its top talent to university departments. In 1940 the newly married Friedman (he had met his wife, Rose Director, when they were in graduate school together) left New York for a teaching job at the University of Wisconsin. After an ugly display of the anti-Semitism that still afflicted most American universities, he left Madison a year later for a job in the Division of Tax Research of the Treasury Department. In 1943 he moved back to Columbia, doing applied statistical research for the War Department (and finally received his Ph.D. there in 1946, for the work he had done at the NBER in the thirties). In 1945, he joined George Stigler at the University of Minnesota. When Stigler's appointment at the University of Chicago stalled the next year over Stigler's too-enthusiastic opposition to rent control measures, the department turned to his friend instead. Thus it was that Friedman returned to Chicago in 1946. He was home.

In Chicago, Friedman discovered an important ally, a political exile from Iowa. Theodore W. Schultz was an original, son of a South Dakota farmer, who had written his thesis at the University of Wisconsin on increasing returns in agriculture, about the same time Allyn Young was giving his famous talk, in Scotland, about economic progress. As a professor at Iowa State, Schultz had become embroiled in a brouhaha. In a departmental working paper, a student had argued that, at least during wartime, restrictions on the manufacture of oleomargarine be relaxed, since it was less expensive to produce. The butter lobby, which was doing everything it could to keep the cheaper substitute out of the grocery stores, insisted that the pamphlet be withdrawn The administration capitulated. Schultz resigned. He arrived at the Social Science Research Building in Chicago in 1943.

Friedman became the leader of the Chicago school—the *second* Chicago school, in fact, for he soon would displace his teachers Frank Knight, Henry Simons, Lloyd Mints, and Paul Douglas with a series of younger men. For the Chicagoans, Alfred Marshall was still the bible. *The General Theory* was a dubious achievement. *The Theory of Games* was itself a mathematical game. And imperfect competition was a snare and a delusion. At least the latter was easily dismissed. In "An Essay on Methodology of Positive Economic," Friedman gave Chamberlin the back of his hand. He then set out, slowly and deliberately, to counter and roll back Keynesian dogma. The centerpiece of his effort, a meticulous empirical study called *A Monetary History of the United States*, challenged the standard interpretation of the cause of the Great Depression. It appeared only in 1962. The Chicagoans couldn't very well call themselves Classicals. Keynes had triumphed too completely over Marshall for that. They identified themselves as monetarists instead.

The only other rival school of thought that darkened Friedman's horizon in the early 1950s was, unfortunately, the one whose headquarters shared office space with his own department—that is, the Cowles Foundation. Friedman feared that his economics department was in danger of being hijacked by mathematicians whose legitimacy he doubted. "I was, and still am, a persistent critic of . . . the Cowles approach," he wrote as recently as 1998. Its methods he considered too highfalutin'—antidemocratic and, as Marshall had felt, prone to error.

For their part, members of the Cowles group felt somewhat persecuted by Friedman. He disrupted their workshops with lengthy monologues. He opposed their appointments. Kenneth Arrow was one of the young Moderns who spent a year in Chicago in the late 1940s. As he recalls it, Friedman and his colleagues thought it was all wild stuff. "We felt sort of bunched together. But we were kind of feared, too. It was a funny kind of being persecuted . . . but we were taken seriously, even when we were just this little group, five or six people together at Chicago." The newcomers were bubbling over with new ideas, shouting at each other in excitement with each new proof or counterexample, making aggressive claims for the importance of their work.

In truth there was an unattractive side to the new high mathematical style that was coming to dominate the Cowles approach. It derived from mathematics as it was being set out in the higher realms of universities after the war, at least in Europe. A good taste of it can be had from considering the personage of the mysterious N. Bourbaki, leader of the French axiomatization movement and author of a series of extremely rigorous papers. It turned out that N. Bourbaki was no person at all, but rather a group of French mathematicians who wrote elaborate graduate texts and ascribed their authorship to a mythical retired army general. Their enthusiasm inspired a craze for formalism among mathematicians that in the 1950s and 1960s spread even to American grade schools in the form of "the new math"—set theory for kindergartners. The air of Gallic campiness and condescension emanating from mathematics departments in European and American universities left a bad taste in many mouths, nowhere more so than in the American Midwest.

Moreover, many Chicagoans remained skeptical about the gains to be had from the new high-tech methods. A simple story illustrates why it was easy enough to believe in the efficacy of the old ways.

During the war the economist George Stigler had been given the task of calculating the least annual cost for an adequate diet. This is typical of the kind of practical problems on which economists worked in those days, particularly at the Statistical Research Group. Stigler devised a diet based on the substitution of certain foods by others, which gave more nutrition per dollar. He then examined a few of the 510 possible ways to combine the selected foods. These were possibilities he chose because they seemed to box the compass of the extremes. In the end, he didn't claim that he had found the single cheapest possibility. But he gave reasons for thinking that he had gotten close.

After the war, the diet problem was one of the first tests to which George Dantzig's new simplex method of linear programming was put. His approach involved nine equations in seventy-seven unknowns, he recalled in his book *Linear Programming and Extensions*. Using hand-operated desk calculators, some 120 man-days were required to obtain a solution. Stigler's solution (expressed in 1945 dollars) turned out to be only 24 cents higher than the true minimum per year of $39.69. Hadn't that been close enough? Stigler returned to Chicago in 1956.

Few could imagine the extent to which the advent of the computer and advances in mathematical technique would transform the utility of the new methods. Calculations that had been no more than a goal in the beginning came to be performed with a few quick keystrokes. Before long, men would be flying to the moon. In the early 1950s, however, all anyone knew in Chicago (at least in the Department of Economics) was that "programming" really meant planning. And as Robert Lucas later recalled, at free-market Chicago in the 1950s, antipathy toward any sort of planning was very great. Surely the old methods were good enough.

Tension between the Cowles Foundation and the economics department slowly mounted throughout the early 1950s, aggravated by the dark Chicago winters. The safety of the campus deteriorated as the surrounding neighborhoods filled up with displaced workers from the rural South. The University of Chicago briefly considered moving to the country altogether. Friction over appointments increased. (Friedman doesn't wear hair shirts; he gives them, said one participant in the discussions.) In 1953 the Cowles Foundation announced it would move to Yale.

Leaving Chicago in the next two years was the flower of a generation of mathematical economists—Tjalling Koopmans, Gerard Debreu, Jacob Marschak, Roy Radner, and Martin Beckmann among Cowles's own professors. Others who had left Chicago earlier included Herbert Simon, Lawrence Klein, Harry Markowitz, and Kenneth Arrow. Counting the visitors who no longer came, no fewer than six future winners of the Nobel Prize were driven from Hyde Park, nearly as many as those who stayed.

The Modern movement had lost its home. For a little while Purdue University became a major center. Gradually more important centers coalesced: in California (where Arrow and Marschak had gone), in Pittsburgh (Herb Simon), in Rochester (Lionel McKenzie), in Philadelphia (Lawrence Klein), New York (Harry Markowitz), and, of course, at Yale.

And MIT? In Cambridge there was a subtle but distinct resistance to the methods of the Modern movement. There were plenty of mathematical economists on the market in the 1950s, but Paul Samuelson chose men of a more practical bent, in keeping with the macroeconomics program of the Keynesian revolution. The task of "operationalizing" these soon produced a distinctive MIT style, a series of general equilibrium models of various phenomena—savings behavior, financial and currency markets, economic growth, government debt, unemployment, and inflation. These were "Volkswagen" models, in one student's evocative phrase, economical engines for thinking that were no-frills, simple, and easy to use—a few key variables suggestively connected by economic reasoning and chosen for their relevance to policy. They were relatively easy to explain to policy makers as well. The nuts-and-bolts conceptual arrangement of the economy of the United States was in large measure designed at MIT in Cambridge in the years after World War II. Harvard's economics department, at the other end of the little city, struggled to keep up.

For its influence on practical affairs, MIT paid a price, which wouldn't become apparent for many years. The brightest students still flocked to MIT's campus in grimy East Cambridge, where the fragrance of petrochemical refining and soapmaking mingled occasionally, when the wind was right, with the smell of chocolate (candy having been a high-tech industry in Boston since the eighteenth century). But at a certain point the brightest economist not already on the premises decided to go to the other end of town.

When, in the early 1960s, MIT and Harvard competed aggressively to lure Kenneth Arrow, Arrow chose Harvard and the die was cast. It may be that Arrow was simply attracted to the idea of being part of a great old university, where his colleagues would include historians, philosophers and classics scholars instead of scientists and engineers. Or it may have been that the "house view" at MIT of what constituted really interesting economics was simply too confining for him. (It might also have been "inefficient" to have both Samuelson and Arrow under the same roof, ventured their fellow theorist Lionel McKenzie many years later. "They were both stars, but they were very different, and they tended to dim each other's brilliance.") In any event, MIT remained oriented to teaching modern economic management, and, with Arrow, Harvard had found a new way back into the race.

And so by 1954, when the Cowles Commission left Chicago, the architecture of postwar economics was set. Before the war, the leading centers of learning had been the department of Cambridge University and the London School of Economics in England; and Harvard University, Columbia University, and the University of Chicago in the United States. Now there emerged two dominant new poles, both of them in the New World: MIT in Cambridge, Massachusetts, and Chicago.

Each department had a leader. Friedman and Samuelson were friendly rivals. They had known each other since the very beginning of their careers. They were temperamentally very different, but they shared the characteristics of two persons whose scientific stance had co-evolved. Both were committed to what we have been calling the clinical/engineering point of view. Within its bounds, their departments approached matters from the opposite ends of the spectrum.

The Keynesians at MIT, who believed macroeconomic glitches were real and dangerous, emphasized regulation and fiscal policy. The counter-Keynesians at Chicago condemned this as "fine-tuning" and taught the magic of the market and the likelihood that perverse effects would arise from attempts to interfere.

And in less-celebrated universities around the country, like so many guerrillas in the hills, worked the Moderns.

CHAPTER ELEVEN

The Residual and
Its Critics

WHEN WORLD WAR II ENDED suddenly, in 1945, many economists feared that peace would bring a return to the stagnation of the 1930s. After all, Europe and Japan were in ashes. And every American war since the Revolution had been followed by a general business collapse. The Federal Reserve Board predicted a slump. Paul Samuelson himself took to the pages of the *New Republic* in 1944 to warn "Depression Ahead." American soldiers in the Pacific joked, "Golden Gate in '48, unemployment line in '49."

Instead, the postwar years turned into a sustained boom unprecedented in the annals of world history. An undetected trove of liquid assets accumulated by households during wartime stringency fueled the boom. Keynesian policies got the credit. The "panics" of the preceding century became "recessions," events of limited duration, modest proportions, and mild consequences. "Automatic stabilizers"—withholding taxes and social security programs—dampened the swings. Trade boomed and incomes rose. A "neoclassical synthesis" was proclaimed, a body of knowledge on which 95 percent of all economists could agree. Cambridge and Chicago settled down to an extended period of problem solving, a shared commitment to the engineering perspective, and, otherwise, polite agreement to disagree.

Economists' stock rose steadily on the bourse of public opinion, especially after John F. Kennedy was elected president in 1960 and invited the leaders of the new economics to Washington—Samuelson, Solow, James Tobin, Arrow. To be sure, the Cold War was the central feature of the landscape. There had been *Sputnik*, followed by the race to the moon. The competition between the industrial democracies and centrally planned dictatorships of Russia and China was one more reason that the economists' services were so highly valued. *Time* magazine put John Maynard Keynes on its cover in 1965, nineteen years after his death, canonizing him as the architect of the post-war boom.

Yet one important puzzle remained in technical economics in the early 1950s—the explanation of the boom itself. Companies were bigger. Competition seemed less intense. And yet the economy was growing faster than it had ever grown before. Keynes might have solved the underconsumption problem, by getting the government involved. But how did diminished savings translate into economic growth? What had happened to the supposedly inevitable logic of diminishing returns?

Once again somebody would have to reconcile the contradictions between the Invisible Hand and the Pin Factory—the supposedly inescapable with the frankly unmistakable. This time a model, a Keynesian model, would be required. Another new concept would emerge. Before long it would come to be known as the Residual.

IN THE EARLY 1950s most of what the Keynesian tradition had to say about the wealth of nations was contained in a couple of swiftly improvised models. Neither one seemed to capture the essence of the problem. Before the war Keynes's fellow economist (and biographer) Roy Harrod had tried to put businessmen's "animal spirits" into the equation. (The phrase had been employed by Keynes to describe the psychology that led to booms.) Harrod's model suggested that the economy could grow forever; also, that doubling the savings rate would double the rate of growth. The world didn't seem to behave that way.

In 1946 another, more troubling possibility had been raised by an economist named Evsey Domar: the economy might become more and more unstable, forever tottering between explosive inflation or prolonged unemployment. The Domar model presented what was known as a knife edge—a small change in behavior, and the outcome would spiral rapidly in one direction or the other. (Something like this view undergirt George Orwell's popular novel *1984*.) The world didn't seem to be much like that, either.

Then a young former GI named Robert Solow stepped up to the task. It wasn't the first time that Solow volunteered for a tricky mission. Born in 1924 in Brooklyn, he graduated from high school in 1940 and entered Harvard College on scholarship that same fall. Though Keynes's ideas were in the air among the graduate students, he caught not a whiff as a freshman. The ideas were too new and Harvard economics was too sclerotic at the time. In 1942 Solow volunteered for the army. After three intense years as a combat intelligence noncom in the Italian campaign, he returned to Harvard in the fall of 1945. There he acquired a new teacher, Wassily Leontief, the man who ten years before had taught Paul Samuelson. Leontief persuaded Solow to take calculus. ("It was amazing that [mathematics] was such a big deal in those days. People got hot under the collar about it.")

He returned to New York, to Columbia, in order to learn some statistics, then went back to finish his Ph.D. at Harvard. Soon he was teaching a course in business cycles at MIT. Only later, he recalled, did he learn that its real name was Macro. He had become a full-fledged soldier of the revolution. Before long he was collaborating on a book introducing other economists to the mysteries of the economic applications of the linear programming techniques that had been developed during the war. That led, naturally enough, to the models by Frank Ramsey and John von Neumann designed to show how economies grew over time. It occurred to him, Solow later said, that neither man had been trained as an economist. The process didn't seem to be the kind of simple expansion that Ramsey or Von Neumann had envisaged, any more than it resembled the worlds of Harrod or Domar. So Solow set out to make a model of his own.

What does it take to build a good model? George Shackle, an especially acute expositor of the methods of modern economics, has described the experience of leaving the world itself in order to reduce it to its bare essentials. The world is "richly detailed, fluid, living and ultimately vague." The model must be stringent if it is to be of any use. Assumptions must be sufficiently simple and precise to allow for the play of logic and mathematics, yet not so restrictive as to eliminate the mechanism itself. The model maker works forward and backward, Shackle says, always wondering whether a slightly different set of assumptions would yield a completely different and perhaps more illuminating result. "The model is a work of art, freely composed within the constraints of a particular art form, namely the logical binding together of propositions. In this bounded freedom, it resembles any other art form: the sonnet, the symphony, the cabinet maker's or architect's conception. . . ."

Economist that Solow was, his basic innovation was to make his model of production depend on substitution. In the Domar model there had been no possibility of substituting labor for capital in production. The ratios were fixed, and steady growth occurred only under certain rigidly specified conditions. Solow replaced the fixed capital/output ratio of the Harrod and Domar models with the relatively new concept of a variable production function, whose advantages were twofold. The convention permitted producers to shift back and forth, using capital when labor was too expensive and vice versa. As a result, no longer did the model present a knife-edge problem. The new mechanism also accommodated a term determined outside the model—a parameter, a "given"—that described the rate of technical change.

No fancy mathematics was required—no fancier than calculus, anyway. In its language, a production function describes the relationship between inputs and outputs. Similar functions had been extensively developed in the early 1950s to describe the relationship between what consumers saved and what they spent (consumption functions). Solow adopted a form that had been developed in connection with the controversies over marginal productivity theory in the 1920s by the mathematician Charles Cobb and the economist Paul Douglas to describe data that showed that the share of income going to workers and to owners of capital had remained remarkably steady over time, at least in the American economy. (Wages accounted for 75 percent of output in the years between 1899 and 1922.) Much more general functions would serve better, he said, and went on, with others, to develop them. For the most part, the profession was content with the easy version.

For the purposes of his model, Solow maintained the assumption of perfect competition. Capital and labor would be paid their marginal products, and if either changed on its own, there would be diminishing returns. Whatever fraction of the growth of actual output couldn't be ascribed to either would be assigned to the "technical change" parameter in the model—to A of (t), as Solow designated it in the equation $Y = A(t)F(K, L)$. The equation itself meant nothing more forbidding than that the growth of output/income is a function of the accumulation of labor and capital multiplied by some arbitrary constant representing the rate of growth of knowledge. Increasing returns were a possibility, he noted in a footnote, but they were not necessary to the analysis.

Finally, to make the model work, Solow needed an explicit assumption about the rate at which technical progress happens, about A of (t) in the model. He found it in the calendar, in the shortcut assumption that knowledge would increase steadily with the passage of time, year after year. There was no discussion here of the Pin Factory. As a graduate student Solow had studied economic history and read A. P. Usher's *History of Mechanical Inventions* (Usher being Harvard's preeminent economic historian). He had read a certain amount of British economic history. Mostly he had read John Stuart Mill on the implications of diminishing returns for the stationary state. And in the end he saw very littler reason to differ with him. He would take the same approach. Assume knowledge is increasing exogenously. Assume that growth gradually will converge to a steady state—the point at which every little bit of additional capital that is put away just makes up for depreciation and population growth. At that point, adulthood, or bliss, or whatever you wanted to call it will have arrived and growth will cease.

Certainly those who were less concerned with the foundations of things were well aware that a "research revolution" was shaking up corporate America in the mid-1950s—sharp journalists such as Leonard Silk and nonmathematical economists, including Theodore Levitt and Sidney Schoeffler, had called attention to the trend in articles and books. Later Solow described technology in his model as being a public good, rather like ham radio. It was the result of something that the government was doing, there for anyone who wanted to take the trouble to tune it in. The mathematical economist—the counterpart of the careful cabinetmaker, the architect, the poet—found it easy enough in 1956 to ascribe this growth of knowledge to noneconomic background forces. And to assume that it was pretty much beyond the abilities of economic policy to affect, much less control. The real action would be with manipulation of traditional economic variables, such as capital accumulation, the savings rate, or labor supply.

The effect was to restate mathematically the position John Stuart Mill had taken a century before: "In so far as the economical condition of nations turns on the state of physical knowledge, it is a subject for the physical sciences and the arts founded on them. Political economy concerns itself only with the psychological and institutional causes of growth." Solow puts it somewhat differently: "Perfectly arbitrary changes over time in the production function can be contemplated in principle, but are hardly likely to lead to systematic conclusions." The significance, however, was the same. $A(t)$, meaning knowledge, was assumed to grow steadily, naturally, with the passage of time. There would be no room in this story for the history of the canals or the railroads!

"A CONTRIBUTION TO the Theory of Economic Growth" (in the *Quarterly Journal of Economics*) appeared just about the time that the first satellite sailed into orbit around Earth—the Soviet *Sputnik*. The Solow model proved to be invaluable for thinking about the market economies of the West. Its cardinal characteristic was that its equilibrium was *general*: its elements were connected in such a way that, when the growth rate of the labor force changed, so did the capital output ratio. Now the system could adjust to any given rate of factor growth and eventually approach a steady state of proportional expansion. Moreover, it was dynamic, not static; it gave an account of a system in motion, a stylized animation if not a complete moving picture that described a few key changing variables over time.

The really effective rendering of the new formulation came in the shape of a diagram designed to illustrate the path of balanced growth. Solow hit on it one day while taking a child to the pediatrician. He borrowed some paper (ripped from a prescription pad) and sketched his idea on it. Two intersecting curves depict the model's key equations, the production function and another describing the rate of capital accumulation. All the really interesting questions can be easily discussed in terms of capital per worker and output per worker. Suppose investment per person increases 1 percent. What would be the effect on ouput? On workers' savings? The model was a practical tool. "I really don't know how you could run an economy without it," says Solow.

The surprising implication of the Solow model was that the savings rate didn't really matter for the growth rate. The Harrod and Domar models suggested that all that poor countries had to do in order to speed up their rate of growth was to double savings, by the simple expedient of tax increases, perhaps, as in, say, the Soviet Union. The Solow model suggested that the effect of such "capital deepening" on the *rate* of growth would be transitory (though there would be a permanent effect on the *level* of output for all future time). How soon? Years? Decades? It didn't matter. Eventually such measures would run into diminishing returns, as workers' wages rose in relation to the cost of the new machines. A nation couldn't save itself into a higher rate of growth. Only population growth and the rate of technological change could accomplish that.

It was the 1957 follow-up article, "Technical Change and the Aggregate Production Function," that was the real eye-opener. When Solow applied his model data for U.S. gross national product in order to estimate the relative contributions of capital and technical change to growth from 1909 to 1949, out popped another surprising conclusion. Assuming each received its marginal product, increased inputs of capital and labor explained barely half of the increased output. Once adjustments were made for increased population, additions to capital explained barely an eighth: fully 85 percent of the increase was unexplained by what was in the model. This was the Residual, the portion of growth that the model did not explain.

LOOKING TO A RESIDUAL for evidence of unseen forces was an old and useful trick in science. In 1846 the planet Neptune was discovered thanks to a residual in the calculations of Uranus's orbit; the neutrino was only a measurement residual for many years until the existence of the subatomic particle was experimentally confirmed in the 1950s. Paul Samuelson says that Solow was like Enrico Fermi, meaning an imaginative theorist who could also get things to work. The assumption was that A of (t), the rate of technical change, must explain the rest, by enhancing general productivity.

Here was the answer to the question of why the economy kept climbing the mountain of diminishing returns. It had relatively little to do with labor or capital accumulation. "Technical progress," the growth of knowledge as measured by the Residual, was creating the new wealth. Readers of Smith, Mill, Marshall, and Schumpeter knew that technical change was real, important, and quite different in its fundamental character from the conventional inputs of labor and capital. Solow's model made the point in modern, mathematical language, and even if the source of the increasing returns lay outside the model, it was segregated there in such a way that the contribution of knowledge to productivity could be measured. The two papers together constituted a rhetorical triumph of the first magnitude.

It could be said—indeed, it was said—that Solow was merely translating Mill into calculus (calculus was a long step forward in America at the time). Or it could be said, with equal justice (though hardly anyone did at the time), that the Residual was strong evidence, adduced from a model, that Schumpeter had been right after all. Technology was far and away its most important source of growth. Labor unions could forget Ricardo's warnings against new machinery. They could stop worrying and learn to love the cornucopia of new innovations.

Keynesian economics in general and the Solow model in particular now became blueprints for the Cold War. Technology would be the dominant engine of growth. Responsibilities were apportioned between the public and the private sectors. Government steadied the business cycle and funded the universities. Capital and labor made peace and agreed to share the gains from growth.

Once growth had been fit into the Keynesian system, Solow appeared to lose interest in it. He returned to working on what seemed the most pressing problems in the late 1950s and early 1960s—competing successfully with the Soviet Union and smoothing the ups and downs of the business cycle. It wasn't long before he and Paul Samuelson turned their attention to what they designated the Phillips curve—an empirical regularity reported by a New Zealand economist, A. W. Phillips, that suggested a trade-off between unemployment and inflation. For the next fifteen years the center ring of macroeconomic thought concerned itself with question of whether this trade-off could be manipulated to achieve better economic performance. Might a little more inflation mean a little less unemployment? Economists in the1960s were deeply interested in the possibilities of such "fine-tuning."

In 1962 Solow wrote the portion of the report of the Council of Economic Advisers that dealt with optimal economic growth. It set the stage for the Kennedy tax cuts of 1964, which were said to be about removing impediments to growth. Behind the scenes he continued to play an important part as a friend to technical change, persuading the unions that it would be in their interest to embrace new techniques, even when job loss was the most immediate and most visible result.

THE REPUBLIC OF ECONOMICS is a big place. Consensus is elusive, and there were plenty of economists who figured that the riddle of growth hadn't been solved by the Solow model, with its not-my-table exogenous technology variable doing almost all the work. The Residual was "the measure of our ignorance," according to Stanford's Moses Abramovitz. "Naming is not explaining," declared Zvi Griliches, a Chicago econometrician. (Not long afterwards the Residual was rechristened Total Factor Productivity.)

The Keynesians in Cambridge, England, were especially

aggrieved. They disputed the entire idea of aggregate production function. ("A parable that can explain nothing but itself," snorted Joan Robinson.) The Schumpeterians were vexed as well. In his last days Schumpeter had made his headquarters the Center for Entrepreneurial Studies, at the Harvard Business School. The tradition continued there after his death, producing in due course the great historian of business Alfred Chandler, among others. In Chicago, Theodore Schultz beavered away on the concept of embodied skill and schooling that he called human capital. By 1965 the econometricians had made their answer. Griliches (who was Schultz's student) and Dale Jorgenson of the University of California at Berkeley announced a program to "endogenize" technical change—that is, to explain it in strictly economic terms and thus make the Residual disappear. And, of course, the mathematical economists produced a high-tech version of the Solow model with which to experiment.

But the most interesting attempt to go beyond the Solow model unfolded at the RAND Corporation. Set up after the war by the U.S. Air Force in Santa Monica, California, as a "university without students," the Research *and* Development Corporation was intended to keep some of the best and brightest scientists and engineers working on problems of defense. And for a time it attracted some of the deepest minds of the generation.

In the mid-1950s planning disciplines developed during World War II were all the rage at the Pentagon and in engineering schools—"systems analysis" and "systems dynamics." Among RAND economists (and not a few practitioners of R&D), the fear had grown that top-down administration would eliminate competition and choke off promising unorthodox approaches to scientific and engineering problems. The massive planning required for the Atlas intercontinental ballistic missile program forced the issue. It was at this point that RAND economists went public. "We simply don't have the required degree of foresight nor the ability to determine what we shall be able to learn and know," warned Richard Nelson and Burton Klein, a few months after the Soviets shocked the Americans by beating them into space with *Sputnik*. "We need *more* competition, duplication and 'confusion,' not less."

A frequent visitor to RAND in those days was Kenneth Arrow. Even then, in his early thirties, it was obvious he was one of the best economists of his generation. Born in 1921, nine years younger than Friedman, six years younger than Samuelson, three years older than Solow, he was perhaps the one who had been most severely affected by the Great Depression. His father, a previously successful Brooklyn businessman, had been ruined by the crash. So Arrow attended New York's free City College, graduating in 1940, flirting briefly with a career as an actuary, then going on with a scholarship to Columbia University, where he studied mathematical statistics with Harold Hotelling. "I realized I had found my niche," he recalled.

Indeed he had. Arrow's thesis, delayed by four years of wartime military service (and what he has described as a nagging fear that he might not live up to very high expectations), created almost out of thin air the field known today as social choice—the formal study of various paradoxes and possibilities that arise from the institutions of democratic voting. (He had started out investigating shareholder control of larger corporations.) Then at Cowles came various proofs of the existence of competitive equilibrium, solutions to a knotty problem that led to a very useful confirmation of the internal consistency of Walras's original everything-at-once intuition. By the early 1950s nobody understood the logic of the Invisible Hand better than Arrow, and he proceeded to invent a formal theory of uncertainty, which turned out to be of great significance. By the time he began regularly visiting RAND, he was working on a series of problems in which persons on opposite sides of a deal possessed very different degrees of information.

The early memos of the Air Force strategists at RAND got Arrow thinking about economic aspects of military research and development, for what was more uncertain than the process of discovery? (Hence the RAND investigators' enthusiasm for redundant, parallel investigations.) Risk certainly was central to the arms race. But then Arrow concluded that two *other* unusual attributes affected the production of knowledge as well. For one thing, new know-how often was hard to hang on to. It wasn't "appropriable," meaning that the person who created and paid for it couldn't necessarily expect to benefit exclusively from it. Other people would soon copy it. For another, you couldn't buy just a little bit of knowledge. New knowledge was *indivisible*, in that it entailed a certain fixed cost before its benefit could be enjoyed. Moreover, the need for it in a given situation was independent of its scale. You had to pay up whether you intended to use it a little or a lot.

By now a certain amount of confusion attended the use of the word "indivisible." In public finance, remember, a good was said to be indivisible if its benefits were freely available to all. National defense was indivisible. So was police protection, or the signal of a lighthouse or a radio broadcast. For Edward Chamberlin, however, and others working in the theory of production, the meaning was just slightly different. An indivisible good was one that was either altogether present or it was not. It was "lumpy." You couldn't buy just a little bit; you had to pay for it all before you could use it even once. You couldn't have a half a piece of new knowledge, any more than you could find a use for half a bridge. Then again, once you had it, there was no obvious limit on the number of times you could use it. And it was this quality of indivisibility, said Arrow, which meant that investment in knowledge "obeys the law of increasing returns."

There were plenty of practical ways around the appropriability problem in the real world—patents, secrecy, and the like (though patents tended to keep markets undesirably small). But the "indivisibility" of knowledge—the fixed cost entailed—was a harder problem, at least for the economic theorist. The implication was that whoever first got a bit of knowledge—about, say, the manufacture of pins—could use it to cut his prices, to make more pins, to accumulate more knowledge, to cut his prices further, and eventually, through the logic of increasing returns, to take over his market.

In hopes of finding something concrete to say about the accumulation of knowledge, Arrow built a model of knowledge accumulated through experience. Practice, experience, and research were all different, he knew; he chose experience because it was the easiest of the three to depict, because R&D required the expenditure of cash, and practice took time, whereas experience-knowledge was a side effect of production undertaken for its own sake. He called it learning-by-doing.

To deal with the aspect of indivisibility, Arrow had thus turned to the "externalities" device, just as Alfred Marshall had seventy-five years before. With learning-by-doing, the knowledge gained could be thought of as an accidental by-product of production, not fundamentally different from any other uncompensated spillover of production—the light from a lighthouse, say, or that radio broadcast. The world seemed to work this way. After all, companies building ships and airplanes found that annual output per worker increased steadily for fifteen years, with no additional investment. (This had been dubbed the Horndal effect, after a Swedish steel mill where it had been observed.)

To make the model work, Arrow borrowed a little-known modeling convention known as rational expectations. That is, he simply assumed that everybody *already* knew everything there was to know, as soon as it became known by others. The effect was to build the equivalent of Solow's radio broadcast into the model. It was a short-cut, but then taking shortcuts is what modelers did. Instead of spelling out various canny, forward-looking behaviors by which other steel-makers would take advantage of Horndal's spillovers, it simply asserted that they would be successful in finding out what their neighbors already knew. Perhaps manufacturers merely opened their window, and the new knowledge, the magical "something in the air," flowed in. And just as they had in Marshall's system, the external increasing returns in Arrow's model made everything come out right. Spillovers would increase with scale, as the industry grew. They ensured that no firm would use its own learning to build a monopoly.

Arrow's discussion of the peculiar economics of knowledge was presented at a meeting in Minneapolis in 1960. The learning-by-doing model followed in 1962. By then Arrow had gone off to work on Kennedy's Council of Economic Advisers. For a few years there was great excitement among some economists. Increasing returns had finally been rendered respectable by formalization. Others tried without much success to get at the details of the diffusion of knowledge—most notably Richard Nelson and Edmund Phelps.

Then it turned out that the mathematics was too much. Arrow's model didn't have the well-behaved qualities expected of a reliable guide to action. It was unstable. Little changes threw it off. So the learning-by-doing model failed to become an important part of economists' tool kit. Instead, it became part of the underground river of thinking about externalities and increasing returns. By the late 1960s enthusiasm for externalities had petered out.

That didn't prevent the next generation of business consultants from trying to turn "the learning curve" (as "experience" came to be called) into a business panacea. For a little while, in the heyday of the Boston Consulting Group, market share was all, because it was supposed to lead directly to increasing returns. But enhanced profitability was elusive, for those spillovers were real enough: it was hard to hang on to the gains.

One part of Arrow's paper, at least, became a standard feature of the landscape of textbook economics—the three reasons why a free-enterprise economy couldn't be counted on the produce enough fundamental new knowledge. Knowledge was nonappropriable. It was indivisible, meaning that it generated increasing returns. And its production was intrinsically uncertain. In the face of such routine market failures, the government would regularly have to take a hand. The National Science Foundation had, at least, a secure foundation in theory.

AGAINST THIS BACKGROUND the last and, in many ways, the most interesting attempt to go beyond the Solow model was the project undertaken by young economists who were his students at MIT. Not that there was anything wrong with the Solow model; it just wasn't intellectually satisfying to have everything that was really important, all the Schumpeter jazz, going on outside. This attempt, in the mid-1960s, sought to capture the role that the growth of knowledge and monopolistic competition played in the process.

In the early 1960s the brightest students from around the world flocked to MIT. It had become a self-conscious citadel of economic science, emphasizing personal disinterest and public spirit in equal measure. The economics faculty lunched together daily at a

Stammtisch, a large table customarily reserved for them in the faculty club. Samuelson declined to go to Washington in order to continue to preside over students' education; Solow took a low-visibility high-level job on the Council of Economic Advisers but hurried home each week to meet his classes. The brightest junior faculty turned up in Cambridge year after year to teach. At MIT they still marvel at those golden years, when an endless stream of bright young men and women marched through the doors to teach or to learn.

Among them in 1964 was the assistant professor Karl Shell. As a doctoral student at Stanford, he had been initiated into the mysteries of growth theory by Arrow. Indeed, Shell's dissertation, based on Arrow's learning-by-doing model, was one in which technological knowledge accumulated, financed by the government, creating increasing returns. He, too, came at the growth problem with an itch to write technology *into* the model instead of leaving it out.

There was the excitement of a new technique, originating in, of all places, the Soviet Union. A strong school of topological math had flourished in Moscow since the 1920s, supported by the government's lively interest in practical applications, everything from weapons research to the control of industrial processes. Being mathematicians, and therefore internationalists, such Russians also maintained contact with the West, to the extent that they were able. And in the early 1960s the talk was all of Pontryagin's "maximum principle," described in his *Mathematical Theory of Optimal Processes*, published in Russian in 1961 and translated into English the next year. The maximum principle offered a new and powerful way of connecting the old calculus-of-variations algebra to the new topology. Paul Samuelson kept track of developments in Russia through his friends in Boston's substantial refugee community and discreet visits with the occasional defector. (He had learned as early as 1945 of Leonid Kantorovich's work on linear programming, for example.) Yes, Samuelson told the luncheon *Stammtisch*, many of the academicians in the circle around the legendary blind mathematician (Pontryagin) apparently were becoming anti-Semites, but the technique described in the book was real and useful. It could be adapted to economics. Among its other attractions, it might in the right hands provide a way of addressing increasing returns and still making the math and economics come out right.

In 1964 Arrow's other prize pupil, Hirofumi Uzawa, moved from Stanford to Chicago. The seminar on growth that Uzawa had been leading moved with him. Now there were sovereigns in the air. Chicago was signaling a willingness to compete in model building by hiring Uzawa. His friend Shell was already at MIT. The joint effort might produce a successful model of technical change. The legend of Uzawa's lengthy meetings—and the exuberant beer-drinking sessions afterwards—was growing. Supported by the National Science Foundation, Uzawa and Shell invited a dozen of their best students to Chicago the next summer, including several from MIT.

It was a luminous time. The young people were rambunctious. The possibilities seemed endless. The Cambridge group—George Akerlof, Joseph Stiglitz, William Nordhaus, Eytan Sheshinski, Mrinal Datta-Chaudhuri, Giorgio La Malfa—stopped at Stiglitz's parents' house in Gary, Indiana, on the way out to Chicago. They repaired to Akerlof's family house on New Hampshire's Squam Lake when they were done. During the intervening month they talked growth theory day and night. "Friendships and rivalries strengthened in the Chicago heat," as Shell delicately put it many years later. The economists felt they were on the verge of creating a dynamic theory of historical change. Sheshinski recalled, "We felt we were in touch with the secrets of the universe." The same kind of excitement obtained among the young economists that, for others, arose from reading the remarkable book by Thomas Kuhn, *The Structure of Scientific Revolutions*, which had appeared three years earlier. The topic of the growth of knowledge was on many minds in the mid-1960s.

About what happened next there is much disagreement, even now. At the end of the session in Chicago, a few members of the Chicago group traveled to Stanford University, where a conference and a monthlong workshop on optimal growth were under way at the Center for Advanced Research in Behavioral Science. The conference had been organized by Kenneth Arrow and was attended by many of the senior figures in the field, among them Frank Hahn, Lionel McKenzie, Tjalling Koopmans, and Carl Christian von

Weizsäcker. The meeting turned out to be something of a climax to a series of conferences devoted to what up to then had been the hottest topic in mathematical economics: could economic growth be speeded up through policy? (Previously researchers had met in Cambridge, England, in July 1963, and a few months later at the Vatican; and in the summer of 1964, in Rochester, New York.) Exciting new theorems about the existence of "turnpikes" were being proved and disproved (routes by which economies might swiftly move to higher levels of industrial development through forced investment in heavy industry). "Golden rules" of capital accumulation were being proposed (how much to save and how much to consume?). Macroeconomic models of technical change were introduced.

What happened in the summer of 1965? The youngsters were discouraged by their elders from pursuing their ambitions. The requisite mathematics was too fancy. The concerns might be interesting, but the models were not easily managed or controlled or even understood. They wouldn't mathematically behave themselves; depending on the starting point, they were as likely to exhibit explosive growth or contract into a black hole–like depression, instead of the reliable stability that characterized the Solow model. What economics needed going forward, they were told, was more concern with the here and now. For several who were involved in the intellectual debates of that summer, it is still a painful subject, requiring much delicacy and tact.

So the papers that the MIT students had written that summer were collected and published as *Essays on the Theory of Optimal Economic Growth*, edited by Shell. The book appeared without fanfare in 1967. There was little to indicate that the technical questions with which the young economists had been wrestling were much the same as those addressed that year in a strictly literary fashion in John Kenneth Galbraith's *The New Industrial State*. Shell wrote up the model of his thesis for the *American Economic Review* in 1966 and for the conference volume. Sheshinski published a note in the *AER*. Nordhaus, who had written a model of monopolistic competition for his MIT thesis, at the last minute took it out. Other young growth theorists got the message. James Mirrlees took up optimal taxation. Edmund Phelps returned to macroeconomics. Uzawa became absorbed in radical politics in Japan and all but left economics for many years.

The effect was to redirect the efforts of the young toward small models and practical applications—and lead them to put aside their interest in growth theory or forget about it altogether, at a time when much growth in the global economy was taking place. The brilliant young MIT students who had spent the hot summer of 1965 in Chicago moved on to other topics with great success. But the mission that had taken them to the university's Hyde Park campus eventually was abandoned by all but Shell. Their effort had been, in effect, written off as a Lost Patrol. The main line of advance lay somewhere else.

A BENEDICTION on growth theory was pronounced by Solow himself in 1969. In a series of lectures at the University of Warwick, he went back carefully over what he thought had been gained. The Residual was a useful concept. But by now pretty much all the juice had been squeezed out of the orange. People would continue to write more elaborate versions of the model, with fancier mathematics; that was how economists got ahead. But he wasn't expecting usable insights into real economies.

Models like his didn't lead directly to prescriptions for policy, said Solow. "But neither are they a game. They are more like reconnaissance exercises. If you want to know what it's like out there, it's all right to send two or three fellows in sneakers to find out the lay of the land and whether it will support human life. If it turns out to be worth settling, then that requires an altogether bigger operation"— the tedious work of building a large-scale econometric model and assembling a mountain of data. Theory had no more to offer.

In such terms did MIT regularly reemphasize its commitment to the art of the practical, and its conviction that the features of the new map had already been pretty well established. When the veteran Italian economic journalist Arrigo Levi called on MIT's rising young star Lester Thurow in 1969, Thurow articulated what by then had become the official version. "There are no new discoveries," he told the Italian journalist. "All the great discoveries have been made."

CHAPTER TWELVE

The Infinite-Dimensional Spreadsheet

IT WAS IN 1969 that economics reached its high point in popular esteem. Europe, Japan, and the United States were enjoying the longest sustained business expansion ever recorded—the capstone to an astonishing quarter century of growth since the end of World War II. The business cycle seemed to have been tamed, if not eliminated altogether, after 150 years during which it regularly threatened economic collapse. The Americans had just landed on the moon.

So after much deliberation, Swedish authorities created a new Nobel Prize for economics, in addition to the original Nobel Prizes in physics, chemistry, medicine, literature, and peace. Specifically, the impulse was to commemorate the founding, three centuries earlier in Stockholm, of the world's first central bank. More generally, the new prize was designed either to recognize economics' coming-of-age or to hasten its real maturity, much as a famous British Admiralty prize had in the eighteenth century brought forth the marine chronometer and established the modern age of navigation. Who could tell which? It scarcely mattered. The world's most respected brand was extended, for the first and perhaps the only time.

After all, the reasoning went, central banking had turned out to be an invention of fundamental significance, widely imitated and ultimately indispensable. Economists had become increasingly clear about how central banking worked (and sometimes failed to work), expanding credit, preventing bank runs, skewing incentives to invest. The result had been generally faster and more dependable growth and enhanced stability. Economics seemed to be following the same pattern of scientific advance as physics (think of Maxwell), or medicine, perhaps, in prior centuries—from tinkering and observation to successful manipulation and the sound theoretical underpinnings of a successful science.

Never mind that certain differences of opinion remained. What the public saw were the Keynesians in Cambridge, Massachusetts, and in Chicago the defenders of the old Marshallian orthodoxy now known as monetarists. In Cambridge, England, were the critical outsiders who had been left behind, eventually to be labeled the crits. This was economics as it is remembered in the mind's eye, at least for those of a certain generation, and a cheerful and orderly world it was.

Yet within a few years pandemonium reigned, inside economics and out. Within the profession the argument started out between the Keynesian exponents of activist macroeconomic management and their skeptical critics—differences of opinion among liberals and conservatives. But these political differences of opinion quickly escalated into technical issues: what exactly was to be modeled, and how? Which theoretical orientation was best supported by the complicated historical data? Behind the scenes furious arguments raged about the significance in economics of uncertainty, information, and expectations.

By the mid-1970s theorists were embroiled in something of a civil war. At its center was the question of which models to prefer. It became difficult for the theorists to communicate across the divide. Older citizens of economics left the stage with bitter denunciations. Civilians freely opined about "the crisis in economics" (though it is unlikely that any no centrist economist ever used that term). *Newsweek*'s Robert Samuelson, a respected commentator on economics (and no relation to Paul) opined, "Probably the only people who think economics deserves a Nobel Prize are the economists themselves."

What the public missed, and what much of the profession failed to understand, was that the arguments were mainly about new mathematical tools, employed to address familiar economic problems. Young economists turned to rocket science for mathematical techniques with which to depict more realistically the processes by which individuals made their decisions over time. The advent of the cheap computer began to make itself felt.

In the end, however, none of the new tools turned out to be more valuable than the homegrown, axiomatically based theory of general equilibrium.

RECALL FOR A MOMENT the beginnings of this feud: the Cowles Commission in the early 1950s, on the eve of its divorce from the University of Chicago. No single incident better captures the tenor of the times than the oral examination in 1952 of the twenty-five-year-old Harry Markowitz for his Ph.D. Under Jacob Marschak, Markowitz had begun an investigation of the reasons for financial diversification. He set out to analyze the problems that investors faced in assembling a portfolio of stocks. Using linear programming techniques, he came up with a rigorous new way of assessing the trade-off between risk and rate of return—of selecting an "efficient" portfolio, we would say today. The problem was in many ways analogous to the diet problem that George Dantzig had solved with such satisfying precision, but more complicated.

On Markowitz's thesis committee was Milton Friedman. Shortly after the graduate student began his defense, Friedman said, "Harry, I don't see anything wrong with the math here but I have a problem. This isn't a dissertation in economics, and we can't give you a PhD in economics for a dissertation that's not economics. It's not math, it's not economics, it's not even business administration."* This is a common enough reaction to the advent of new knowledge, of course. Dogma is dogma, wherever it occurs. But that day in Hyde Park, Marschak prevailed over Friedman; Markowitz got his degree.

---

* The incident is described by Peter Bernstein in *Capital Ideas: The Improbable Origins of Modern Wall Street.*

Indeed, some 38 years later, he received the Nobel Prize in Economics for the skein of work his thesis began.

But in one respect Friedman was correct. Markowitz's field needed a new name. Today we call it finance. But application to investment problems was just one among myriad possibilities that the new planning tools presented. Finance was only part of a whole second wave of research excitement that was unfolding at Cowles, begun several years after the Keynesian revolution was encoded during the war. In the early 1950s the excitement around Cowles was again palpable.

Nobody had a better intuitive feeling for the new possibilities than the polymath Kenneth Arrow. The sources of Arrow's genius are, as genius always is, mysterious. A summer job working as an actuary gave him a practical acquaintance with oddsmaking. His father's bankruptcy in the Great Depression deepened his appreciation of uncertainty. And he had the advantage of having read Von Neumann's *Theory of Games* when he was twenty-three years old.

Excitement about new mathematics was sweeping up young theorists just entering the field. Arrow arrived at the Cowles Commission as an assistant professor at the University of Chicago for the year 1948–49. In a memoir he conveys a little of the atmosphere in which social science was coming to be done. He had gone to hear Franco Modigliani debate rent control. While he was listening, it occurred to him that, if different kinds of housing were considered to be different commodities, then most consumers buy zero of most kinds. What did it mean, then, to prove that the allocation of housing was optimal? Arrow puzzled over what seemed a real conundrum until, at a seminar given by Paul Samuelson, he was about to ask the presenter's opinion when he "realized from his diagram that the separating hyperplane theorem supplied the answer."

Those separating hyperplanes, a central concept from the theory of convex sets, would solve a great many theoretical problems for the Cowles group, once Arrow succeeded in giving them an economic interpretation. We are, to put it mildly, deep in the realm of hearsay evidence. What exactly was a hyperplane? A plane that existed in three or more dimensions. What did hyperplanes separate? An indif-

ference curve from a transformation curve. The juncture would produce a line; the line's slope could be understood as a relative price.

Economists were finding that they could exploit a property of the
geometry known as duality, meaning that every problem stated in
terms of a linear program was intimately related to a second problem called its dual. This was what Paul Samuelson had foreseen. Any
economic problem could be worked from either end—solve the
pricing problem, and you get the answer to the allocation problem,
too. Hyperplanes also played a computational role in Dantzig's simplex method for linear programming, separating feasible solutions
from ones that could not be achieved. A typical program would have
inequalities stating that resources used up in the program can't
exceed what is available. Any resource with slack must have zero
shadow price. If the positive shadow prices are known, their inequalities must be equations, and can be solved by conventional methods.
Clear enough? If not, sign up at a local college for an introductory
course in mathematical economics. Economics had gone high-tech.
Marshall's "book of curves" had become an atlas of *shapes*.

Von Neumann had been right, Arrow decided. Calculus wasn't
nearly as versatile as set theory/topology. There were things one
couldn't do with calculus, or do only much more laboriously than
with topological methods. Big gains in generality and simplicity
were to be had by embracing a higher degree of mathematical
abstraction. Shortly after Arrow left Chicago, a jaunty young Frenchman named Gerard Debreu arrived. Debreu independently reached
many of the same conclusions.

In 1951 both Arrow and Debreu published separate studies (and,
independently, Lionel McKenzie as well) showing how set theory
and convex analysis could be used to determine when the equations
describing an economy had a solution, thereby solving one of the
deepest riddles of the new economics. Henceforth there would be
inequalities instead of equations, spaces instead of points on lines,
production possibility frontiers instead of geometric diagrams of
supply and demand. "Climbing the beanpole"—and the practical
wartime exigencies of scheduling ships and equipping armies—had
led to a mathematical wonderland above the clouds.

Was all this new equipment really necessary? Naturally there were plenty of skeptics, and not just the relatively few important literary economists who remained. Mathematical economists were divided, too. Koopmans pointed out that the same objections to new methods had been raised in physics twenty years before, when quantum theorists had first turned to set theory to describe the "state" of an atom. He and the other mathematical economists were not daunted in their effort. Negative numbers had also seemed at best an empty formalism when they were discovered by mathematicians and logicians in the first centuries A.D. For hundreds of years they were a topic of ridicule and doubt among mathematicians. Then, in the thirteenth century, in a problem concerning money, Leonardo Fibonacci interpreted them as the possibility of a loss. Indian logicians reached the same conclusions. Negative numbers have been with us ever since.

IN 1953 ARROW SHOWED how the new math might be useful, by giving set theory a solid economic application. Traders and economists for centuries had understood how to write an option contract—that is, how to add to a physical commodity a description of the date and location and precise circumstances under which its delivery would take place (for instance, if there was a freeze). Already in the 1930s, John Hicks had dated all the commodities in his analysis, such that wheat delivered in May might have a different price from wheat delivered in August. (Writing futures contracts was a common enough practice among farmers, after all.) Now Arrow took the analysis a long step forward.

In a seven-page paper for a conference organized in Paris, he generalized the idea of an options market to include everything in the economy, and in every conceivable situation, too. That is, using the new tools of set theory and topology, he wrote a model in which the same physical commodity existed for anything and everything as if in a futures market, by adding to the physical definition of each commodity an accompanying definition of the "state of the world" in which it would be available. This was a description so precise that it would define completely not only the initial holdings of goods but all the technological possibilities as well. Uncertainty then became a statistical conception, a matter of knowing the likelihood that one possibility would have eventuated at the stated place and time.

The new conceptual apparatus became known as the "state-contingent" formulation. It enabled economists to imagine a world in which there would be a market for every conceivable sort of commodity or asset under every conceivable condition. "The complete market," Arrow called it. Even externalities could be nicely covered by the new formulation, it turned out. No longer did they have to be described as simply "something in the air." Instead, they could be described as "commodities which pass from one individual to another but for which no suitable market exists"—meaning, as Ronald Coase later pointed out, that property rights to them (or to freedom from them) had been incompletely spelled out.

Implicit in this "contingent claim" formulation was the idea of a kind of universal insurance against any conceivable risk. The value of a life insurance policy in the event of a death as opposed to a year of perfect health. A bushel of wheat if there was plenty of rain in August, the same bushel if there wasn't. A share of common stock if the company met its earnings target, the same share if it did better, or worse. Arrow's insight had transformed general equilibrium theory into a theory of uncertainty—of a world in which anything that *could* happen would be assigned a probability and treated as if it might. Actual contingent contracts could be written for such goods, if a market was established, and buyers and sellers with their different estimates of the probabilities could trade them. Indeed, practical traders had been doing as much in grain pits and insurance markets for centuries. For such abstractions, powerful mathematical constructs would be required up to and including Hilbert space. Here were the beginnings of a deep theoretical understanding of a familiar practice.

The 1950s were years of rapid progress in mathematical economics. The toolbox continued to grow. Before the war it consisted almost entirely of differential calculus and matrix algebra. Now, according to Gerard Debreu, it added convex analysis, set theory, general topology and algebraic topology, measure theory, infinite-dimensional vector space theory, global analysis, and nonstandard analysis—and that, he said, was by no means the whole list. In 1959 Debreu published *Theory of Value: An Axiomatic Analysis of Economic Equilibrium*. It rapidly emerged as the standard version of the new topological economics, the neatest and most compact model of an economy since Quesnay's *tableau économique*, and vastly more general.

Coded and installed on computers, the state-contingent Arrow-Debreu model became, in effect, a spreadsheet, years before recalculating elementary computer spreadsheets had been invented. After all, a spreadsheet is just a bunch of equations coded into a computer to describe relationships between numbers arrayed in rows and columns. Arrow and Debreu's concept was no ordinary spreadsheet, however; thanks to set theory and the mathematics of convexity, it was an infinite-dimensional spreadsheet, with vectors instead of columns and rows, capable of describing, at least in theory, all the possibilities for all the markets for all the commodities in the world.

The framework was waiting to be put to work to serve any purpose that imaginative economists might dream up. Before long Herbert Scarf, a mathematician who had begun working with Arrow at RAND, learned enough economics to show how the steps of the proofs themselves could be combined with the national income accounts to calculate magnitudes of interdependence in the real world. Under the tutelage of Scarf, by now a professor of economics at Yale, a generation of young economists refined the methods of computable general equilibrium to gauge how any particular policy change would affect the economic system as a whole.

All this took place far, far away from the front pages of newspapers or, for that matter, from the seminars of leading Keynesian economists. Years later, when economists would argue among themselves about who had been the greatest economist of the twentieth century—Keynes? Schumpeter? Von Neumann? Samuelson? Friedman?—the answer that won out among the top economists, more often than not, was Kenneth Arrow.

CHAPTER THIRTEEN

Economists Turn to Rocket Science, and "Model" Becomes a Verb

THE TOOL-MAKING investments of the Modern movement began to pay off in the 1970s. Equipped with the abstractions of game theory and the infinite-dimensional spreadsheet, would-be scientists among the economists began to challenge the engineers—Keynesians and monetarists alike. The Moderns sought to provide more realistic treatments of familiar issues—inflation and monopolistic competition chief among them—than the old techniques would permit. And, in due course, the Moderns won the day. By the end of the decade, the familiar Keynesian/monetarist dichotomy had all but disappeared, a least among those at the forefront of the field. It was supplanted by a new distinction, between Freshwater and Saltwater macroeconomics. Many of the arguments were familiar. Now, however, they were conducted in a different language.

The starting point of the debate was inflation. By the end of the 1960s, economics had no bigger problem. In their paper about the Phillips curve, Samuelson and Solow had suggested an engineering solution—a little unemployment might serve to reduce inflation. A little inflation might reduce unemployment. For a few years the Phillips curve dominated macroeconomics. The trouble was, the trade-off didn't seem to work. Unemployment rose, but inflation wasn't any lower than before. The key factor, economists agreed, was that people now *expected* inflation. They had gotten wise to what the government was doing.

Economists had always known that forecasts routinely affect economic outcomes. If people expect a price increase, they buy supplies in anticipation and hold off selling until it occurs, thereby creating a self-fulfilling rise in prices that eventually collapses when too many people do the same thing. Investors and producers engage in still more complicated behavior. In some sense such departures from equilibrium were what Keynes was all about. So, since the 1930s, economists worked on incorporating expectations, however mechanically, into their formal accounts.

The standard textbook demonstrations of how the mere passage of the time necessary to bring a product to market created fluctuations in market prices mattered was called the cobweb theorem, after the look of graphical treatments of the lags involved in the interaction. The standard example came to be the cycle of interdependent corn and hog prices. Then, in 1935, the young Ronald Coase (and R. F. Fowler) showed that the pig-breeding cycle in England lasted four years, instead of the two years that the cobweb theorem predicted. Why was that? Perhaps because farmers would seek to take account of whatever additional information was available—bacon imports and shifts in demand—knowing that more accurate forecasts would mean higher profits. The argument foreshadowed the psychological assumption that came to be known as *rational* expectations.

By the late 1950s the cobweb had evolved into a more sophisticated version called *adaptive* expectations. Human beings were still backward looking. Now, however, they were expected to factor in the mistakes they had made, but only after they made them. They learned from experience, but otherwise had no imagination. Most Keynesian models relied on the adaptive expectations assumption, not because Keynesians necessarily believed in the psychological caricature of *homo economicus* as a creature of habit, easily fooled (though certainly some did), but because it was convenient. The pioneering economists of the 1940s and 1950s constructed their models with cumbersome mathematical tools that had been invented to

control chemical plants, to make plywood, and to build radio transmitters and receivers. No wonder that they depicted people who
could be expected to yield passively to policies designed to control
them.

Chicagoans, on the other hand, with few mathematical aspirations to encumber them, still assumed "a little Scotsman in every
man." Men and women were seen to be shrewd, forward-looking
actors, capable of gathering information and taking into account the
opinions of others (including those whose aim was to manipulate
them). For models populated by myriad Scots to be tractable, however, more sophisticated modeling techniques would be required.

The man who solved the problem was Robert Lucas. As a Chicago
undergraduate in the 1950s, Lucas had studied history. At a certain
point he decided he wanted to do economics. Making up for lost
time on the eve of graduate school, Lucas read Paul Samuelson's
Foundations over the summer. By carefully working it through, he
discovered that, by the first day of class, he had become "as good an
economic technician as anyone on the Chicago faculty."

Thereafter Milton Friedman's discussions of price theory in the
classroom became doubly exhilarating. First there was the sheer
quality of the talk: it was "unique in my experience," Lucas later
wrote. Then, after each class, Lucas hurried home to translate what
Friedman had said into the math he had learned from Samuelson. "I
knew I would never be able to think as fast as Friedman, but I also
knew that if I developed a reliable, systematic way for approaching
economic problems, I would end up in the right place."

"I loved the *Foundations*," Lucas recalled many years later. "Like so
many others in my cohort, I internalized its view that if I couldn't
formulate a problem in economic theory mathematically, I didn't
know what I was doing. I came to the position that mathematical
analysis is not one of many ways of doing economic theory. It is the
only way. Economic theory *is* mathematical analysis. Everything else
is just pictures and talk."

THE DEVICE TO WHICH Lucas turned to solve his problem was the
assumption of rational expectations—the compressed future-perfect

view of the world that Kenneth Arrow had used to make spillovers work in his model of learning-by-doing. Like Arrow, Lucas didn't want to bother with the details of how it happened; he simply assumed that word would get around. The rational expectations assumption is simply a shortcut, he explained. "[It] describes the outcome of a much more complicated process. But it doesn't describe the actual thought process that people use in trying to figure out the future. Our behavior is adaptive. We try some mode of behavior. If it is successful, we do it again. If not, we try something else. Rational expectations describe the situation when you've got it right." It was the future-perfect state that would be arrived at eventually.

Next Lucas went looking for mathematical tools that would allow him to model a series of changes in expectations: that is, a sequence of individuals' decisions, each one of which would depend on those that had gone before, and which would include the effects of occasional unexpected events ("stochastic shocks," in the language of statistics). He sought out a 1957 book by Richard Bellman, *Dynamic Programming*.* Bellman was a mathematician working at the RAND Corporation, quite literally a rocket scientist. He had invented a set of techniques designed to optimize decisions in which long chains of choices had to be made amid changing circumstances—if, for example, you wanted to fire a missile into the upper atmosphere and hit a target halfway around the globe, or even travel to the moon. The same kinds of decision processes were at the heart of much less exotic activities, Bellman noted: the bidding systems in contract bridge, for instance, or the raise, counterraise, and call of poker, with its particularly interesting opportunities for bluffing. Lucas hoped the same methods could be applied equally to calculate a point at which to spend or save, to decide when to draw down inventory, or to switch from stocks to bonds. Anything that required a formal statement of the links between present and future was a candidate to be improved by rocket science.

---

* Bellman's 1984 *Eye of the Hurricane: An Autobiography* offers a fascinating glimpse of the life of a gifted mathematician (who was also a sharp observer) working at the intersection of high science and engineering during World War II.

The new methods were dubbed *dynamic* programming, since "dynamic" connoted history and change. Alternatively, they were labeled as *recursive* methods, because the same general structure of the problem recurred again and again. The underlying mathematics were considerable more complicated than simply climbing the bean-pole. (Although as Bellman described it, the basic rule was deceptively simple: "do the best you can from where you are.") What was the difference between optimal control and dynamic programming? It was largely a matter of time. Because dynamic programming allowed constant revision to get the best possible result, you didn't have to plan the whole journey step by step before you began, as with Ramsey's calculus of variations, or even linear programming. You could improvise, do things on the fly, making allowances for the things you didn't know, for the unexpected twists and turns that inevitably occurred along the way.

How to give the problem an economic setting? It was when he was trying to describe investment behavior that Lucas realized that the infinite-dimensional spreadsheet was the ideal framework if it could be put to work to describe the various possible outcomes. Lucas and his friend Edward C. Prescott worked day and night to master the new math, and contingent-claim apparatus of the Arrow-Debreu model. Once fully understood, the result was electrifying to other macroeconomists. The new techniques could make *everybody* an optimizer in the model, not just the system planner. Instead of firms acting as if they thought that current prices would hold forever, companies would constantly calculate and recalculate the value of their investments, on the basis of rational expectations about future prices. That is, they would behave as if they were run by real people. Lucas and Prescott had created a model of a decentralized and highly uncertain world. They called their paper "Investment under Uncertainty."

This was "new classical macroeconomics"—"classical" because it assumed a Scotsman in every man; "macro" because it entailed a theory of the business cycle; and "new," because it was very different from the *neo*classical dogma that had been embraced by Keynesians and monetarists alike. This remarkable transformation swept through the upper atmosphere of economics in the 1970s. Olivier Blanchard, who lived through it as a young man, later explained it this way: "If people and firms had rational expectations, it was wrong to think of policy as the control of a complicated but passive system. Rather, the right way was to think of policy as a game between policy makers and the economy. The right tool was thus not optimal control, but game theory."

The 1970s saw a cascade of breakthroughs: concepts that had long been familiar to central bankers (at least the *best* central bankers) now received a mathematical exposition. Credibility became a key consideration; reputation, transparency, and independence all came to be seen as crucial elements of economic policy. Thanks to the mathematical richness of the infinite-dimensional spreadsheet, the old literary distinction between the short run and the long period gave way to a distinction between expected outcomes and unexpected ones. Equilibrium had come to be understood as whatever happened next.

NEARLY SIMULTANEOUSLY other economists were learning to incorporate into their models not expectations but different degrees of information. Here the key figure was a young mathematical economist named George Akerlof. Born in 1940, Akerlof showed up at MIT in the autumn of 1962, fresh from Yale College and full of enthusiasm for mathematics. He spent most of his extra energy during his first year in a course on algebraic topology. Everybody at MIT learned growth theory in those days, so he became Solow's student. Among his fellow students were Joseph Stiglitz, William Nordhaus, and Eytan Sheshinski—the boys who went to Chicago.

But the issues in growth theory left Akerlof cold. The work he had done in Chicago demonstrated conclusively the stability of something called a "putty-clay" model, which he "had been told was one of the burning topics in economic growth." Distinguishing between fixed and variable capital-labor ratios of investment goods (clay and putty) did not seem very important at all to him. He wanted to know how real markets actually worked. He graduated from MIT in 1966 and took a job at the University of California at Berkeley.

Before long he decided to study the big annual variations in the sale of new cars. Maybe the sources of volatility in automobile sales, whatever they were, would shed some light on the sources of volatility in setting wages and prices on the mechanics of the business cycle. A major reason people bought so many new cars, Akerlof found, was that they mistrusted the motives of used-car salesmen. "If he wants to sell it, it's probably because it's a lemon, and I don't want to buy it." Economists had begun calling this a problem of "asymmetric information," in that one party ordinarily knew something the other didn't. Such considerations turned out to be old hat to horse traders, but Akerlof didn't know it at the time.

Today the mechanism that Akerlof had identified is called adverse selection. Fears might be such that the market for used cars might diminish, perhaps even collapse. Akerlof soon realized that it wasn't confined to cars. Adverse selection might set in with *any* market in which quality was difficult to assess, the markets for loans or insurance, for instance. He demonstrated the result to his satisfaction (along the way discarding the abstruse topological proofs he preferred in favor of more standard approaches), sent the paper in, and went off to India for a year, hoping to gain a firsthand appreciation of why the country was so poor. Meanwhile, the paper on new-car sales was rejected several times, as being too trivial to merit publication or, in case of the referee for the University of Chicago's *Journal of Political Economy*, because it was obviously wrong. *Obviously?* Certainly, replied the referee; if the paper were correct, economics would be different from what it was. "The Market for 'Lemons'" finally appeared in 1970, in the *Quarterly Journal of Economics*. It was an instant success, and, before long, economics was different than what it had been.

The study of used cars turned out to be the beginning of the road back to monopolistic competition. Barely a year later a young Harvard graduate student named Michael Spence showed one way how sellers could work their way out of the predicament that Akerlof had described. If they were students entering the labor market, they could invest in an advanced degree. Taking some expensive step to demonstrate quality Spence called signaling behavior. His model was as tight as "Lemons," and still more broadly applicable. "Market Signaling" was later said to have launched a thousand other dissertations, for it proved to be useful wherever there were gaps in the information available to buyers: in job markets, financial markets, markets for consumer durables, pharmaceuticals, and the like. Here was a way of formally describing the intricate process that Edward Chamberlin thirty years earlier had labeled product differentiation—everything from advertising to design.

A third young economist joined in the chase. Whereas Spence had explained signaling, Joseph Stiglitz now identified *screening* mechanisms in which valuable information was elicited in various ways: for example, the trick by which insurance companies divided customers into risk classes by offering policies with different deductibles. Soon Stiglitz extended his analysis to finance in order to explain credit rationing, to job markets to explain high (efficiency) wages designed to deter workers who might otherwise shirk.

The irrepressible Stiglitz's research style was almost the precise opposite of Spence's. He had turned up at MIT fresh from a tumultuous student council presidency at Amherst College (he campaigned to abolish its fraternities, marched on Washington with Martin Luther King) but a full year ahead of his scheduled graduation. Famously bright, he was determined to make an impression. By the end of his first year, he was editing the first volume of Paul Samuelson's *Collected Papers*. Stiglitz wrote a lengthy monograph that had to be cut into little papers before any could see the light of day. He gave a legendary eight-hour lecture to an audience in Japan. Controversy drew him like a bear to honey. Stiglitz's work seemed to touch on anything and everything that was exciting: growth, general equilibrium, public finance, corporate finance, the theory of the firm under uncertainty, missing markets, comparative economics, and, most successfully of all, the economics of information.

THE NEW TECHNIQUES provoked great battles—Lucas's applications of the infinite-dimensional spreadsheet in particular. But gradually the Moderns were victorious. Whichever the angle of approach— rational expectations or asymmetric information, macro or micro—

the gains in understanding of economics' traditional problems with the new methods were simply too great to ignore.

That did not mean, however, that Modern methods produced complete agreement, far from it. Just as those who in the 1930s embraced the new interpretation of economics as engineering had divided themselves as Keynesians and monetarists, so the Moderns split into two camps—New Classicals and New Keynesians, they called themselves for a time. The new divisions mapped smoothly to the old.

The New Classicals had a head start. They had pioneered the methods, after all. They emphasized the convenience of the assumption of perfect competition, the likelihood of various forms of government failure, the possibility that the problem of involuntary unemployment had been exaggerated. For a little while it looked as if those political positions were somehow implicit in the tools.

Then the Keynesians went to work. They embraced the new methods. They built general equilibrium models, assumed rational expectations, and learned to use the infinite-dimensional spreadsheet, with its explicit links between present and future. Soon they were stressing the same variety of imperfections, frictions, and asymmetries that had been identified by their predecessors; naturally, their preferred solutions usually involved some form of regulation. The Phillips curve made a comeback, suitably modified to account for expectations and surprise shocks. These were *New* Keynesians.

So at some point, a wag distinguished between Freshwater and Saltwater macroeconomics. Freshwater macro dominated at Chicago, Minnesota, Rochester, Carnegie Mellon, inland universities situated on rivers and lakes; Saltwater macro was the ruling fashion among coastal universities, at MIT, Harvard, Yale, Princeton, Stanford, Berkeley, and many places in between. The profession immediately embraced the terms as a way of signifying how greatly the methods of the Modern movement had changed the old way of doing things. Old-style Keynesian and monetarist doctrines ceased to command a following among the young.

Many years later Akerlof traced the origins of the new methods back to the early days of growth theory. The early growth theorists, led by Robert Solow, had built the first models that departed slightly from the norms of perfect competition. Before the early 1960s, he recalled, theorists rarely constructed models whose purpose was to capture unique institutions or the characteristics of particular markets. Chamberlin was the notable exception. But while monopolistic competition was taught to graduate students and even a few undergraduates, it constituted an excursion into the countryside, for those with a day or two to spare.

Those "special" models attempted to depict features of the world that were just too difficult to capture, or even to understand very clearly: vintage capital, human capital, learning-by-doing, his own model of "putty" and "clay" goods. But these early models of economic growth had sowed the seeds for a revolution. Almost inevitably, Akerlof wrote, asymmetric information was among the first payoffs in the hands of veterans of the Lost Patrol. He could just as easily have cited the developments in finance, or Freshwater macro. Taken altogether, however, the result was undeniable. Thanks to the new methods—game theory, set theory, rocket science, and all the rest—economic theory was learning to say much more about the real world.

It was in the summer of 1969, he recalled, that he first heard the word "model" used not just as a noun but also as a verb.

ALL THE WHILE the Swedes awarded their new Nobel Prizes, guiding the public and the press toward the future through what amounted to the judicious use of a rearview mirror. The Nobel committee had begun writing a popular version of the recent history of thought. Gradually the new prize won wide acceptance.

The first award, in 1969, went to Ragnar Frisch and Jan Tinbergen, the planners who in the 1930 had been such forces in the founding of the Econometric Society—economists who, in the United States, were completely unknown to the general public. The next prize went to the forty-five-year-old Paul Samuelson, the third to Simon Kuznets for national income accounts, the fourth to Sir John Hicks and Kenneth Arrow, and the fifth to Wassily Leontief for his input-output table. After that the Swedes relaxed long enough to give the prize to one of their own, Gunnar Myrdal, along with the great

Austrian economist Friederich von Hayek, representing opposing poles of a single tradition. The next year it went to the linear programming toolmakers in economics, Tjalling Koopmans and Leonid Kantorovich.

Only then, in 1976, did the Swedes turn to Milton Friedman, the man who a quarter century before had run Koopmans out of town. In another fifteen years they would give the prize to Koopmans's student Harry Markowitz as well. Inexplicably, even mysteriously, they waited until 1987 to recognize Solow's contribution, thus obfuscating a major axis of advance. Not until 1994 did the Swedes finally confer an award on John Nash (and John Harsanyi and Reinhard Selten), the first award (but not the last) to recognize the centrality to economics of a skein of developments in game theory that had begun nearly fifty years before.* Nevertheless, by the end of the 1970s, the Moderns had completely won the day in the top graduate schools. By the 1990s they had won in Stockholm as well.

As usual, the new techniques also meant that a certain amount of hollowing out took place, as economists solved the easy problem first. This time, ironically, it was growth theory that was brushed aside. That it should be eclipsed in the 1970s and 1980s was doubly odd, because so much of the turmoil in the world economy had to do with growth: the productivity slowdown, high inflation, the rise of Asian "tigers," the return to prominence of Europe, and so on. But business cycles and policy effectiveness were on economists' minds; besides, the main issues in growth theory were considered to have been largely settled.

Like the map of Africa, the Solow model of the sources of growth consisted of bold outlines, with little interior detail and most of the interesting action deliberately left out. But if large areas of the modern economy were still marked "here there be tigers," young economists could be expected to venture soon into the unknown areas, on mapping expeditions of their own.

* Even then the committee had to fend off the efforts of a dissenter seeking to sabotage the award in a meeting of the Royal Swedish Academy of Sciences on the day of the vote, an episode described in Sylvia Nasar's *A Beautiful Mind: A Biography of John Forbes Nash, Jr., Winner of the Nobel Prize in Economics, 1994.*

PART
II

CHAPTER FOURTEEN

New Departures

A WATERSHED IS rarely obvious. A small rise, an otherwise unremarkable summit, and streams that would have drained in one direction now flow in another, not just one stream but many, apparently unrelated, which nevertheless combine and combine again until they become mighty rivers. In the history of economic policy, the 1970s were as much a watershed as were the 1930s—maybe more so. But it was not obvious at the time.

The decade's global economic turmoil presented a crisis of a very different sort from the Great Depression—double-digit inflation rather than stagnation; relative decline; vertigo, not despair. In the industrial democracies, the sense was widespread that things were spinning out of control. The command economies appeared to some observers to be on the march; to others, to be falling farther behind. The north-south disparity seemed to widen. Most of the nations of the Third World despaired of ever catching up. Only a handful of nations—Japan and the Asian "tigers" of Taiwan, Korea, Hong Kong, and Singapore seemed to have mastered the secrets of growth.

The hundreds of students who in the mid-1970s enrolled in graduate programs of economics in search of riddles to answer and problems to solve were, in a way, as much children of a crisis as the students who had taken up the discipline in the 1930s. There were so many things to worry about in the seventies—inflation, unemployment, resource scarcity, the productivity slowdown. The spirit of the times was captured somehow by the title of a Led Zeppelin song (and later a concert film and finally a movie comedy about those years), "Dazed and Confused." Meanwhile, memories of the Great Depression were fading. The recessions since World War II had been mild events. Preventing slumps no longer seemed a daunting task.

Indeed, the most pressing problem was again what it had been at the very birth of modern economics, three hundred years before. Why were some nations growing so much faster than others? Why had others slowed down? The young didn't arrive in classrooms to find that question written on blackboards, of course. Only later did it become clear, gradually, how the topic of growth was supplanting economic stabilization as the most interesting problem of the day. In the 1970s the fastest-growing nation in the world was Japan. The Japanese onslaught against American automotive manufacturing was becoming apparent. How could so great an industrial advantage be so quickly undermined? How did the little island nation achieve such phenomenal rates of growth? What was the secret of its success?

So IT WAS that a twenty-four-year-old MIT graduate student named Paul Krugman one day found himself listening to a California businessman describing his fears about how Japan was using its enormous protected home market as a practice field in which to prepare to conquer global markets. The year was 1978. First it had been cameras and motorcycles. Now the Japanese manufacturers were mastering automobiles. The American television, videotape recorder, and other consumer electronics industries were under siege. Sophisticated Californians now understood that semiconductors, an American invention of barely twenty years before, would be the next big target. The mechanism in each case was the same. There would be heavy investment in the latest manufacturing processes. Long production runs for domestic markets would cover fixed costs. As manufacturing techniques improved, export markets would be targeted, with goods priced incrementally lower in overseas markets.

As he listened to the California businessman that day, Krugman mentally rehearsed the view of international trade he had been taught. It was the standard one, enshrined in textbooks since the time of Ricardo, that there exists a natural pattern of specialization among nations, based on national differences in natural resource endowments. The automatic forces of perfect competition and constant returns to scale could be depended upon to achieve the correct arrangement among them. Portugal would export wine, England wool, the United States timber, and so on. Trade among nations would compensate for the unequal distribution of productive resources—land and people alike—and development would spread evenly over the world.

There would be occasional departures from the norm, Krugman understood, but they would be handled in the usual way, as afterthoughts. Trade theory had been codified by theorists in the 1930s, formalized in the 1940s by Paul Samuelson as the Samuelson-Stolper theorem. Few apostles of trade had been more clever at adapting and extending this standard model than Samuelson's pupil and Krugman's teacher, Jagdish Bhagwati. No wonder that by the time Krugman arrived at Bhagwati's door, the impression was widespread that virtually all the interesting work had been done.

The businessman didn't seem to understand the principle of comparative advantage, Krugman thought. Nor did he share economists' "homeostatic" view of the world—the conviction that automatic market forces inevitably would restore a "natural" pattern of trade and specialization. The executive had no coherent model of his own, just a powerful conviction that the facts of the world in which he operated were very different from the economic doctrines that Krugman and others were being taught in the schools.

By any standard, Krugman was an interesting young man. He had grown up on Long Island, and thrilled as a boy to the *Foundation Trilogy* by Isaac Asimov, with its crafty, heroic psychohistorians—mathematical social scientists who could manage the destinies of galactic empires with a few well-chosen equations. He went to Yale for college, where he worked for his professor William Nordhaus on the world market for energy. (In a summer econometrics project, he found that people would cut back on oil consumption if the price went up!) After graduating from Yale, he moved in the fall of 1975 to MIT, where Nordhaus had gone to school.

MIT was still the single best place in the world to learn economics by a wide margin, thanks to the quality and commitment to teaching of its faculty. (It may still be so, but not by so wide a margin.) And so a disproportionate share of the most promising new students entering the field chose to accept its offer of admission. Naturally all were eager to distinguish themselves. At one point Krugman wrote a paper on the economics of interstellar trade, as a joke, in which he sought to adjust interest rates to take account of general relativity.

The making of small mathematical models came easily to Krugman. He had, it seemed, a knack for making the kinds of simplifying assumptions that rendered his models tractable but not trivial. He learned the newest mathematical techniques. There was great excitement in those days about the tools. He wrote a paper on speculative attacks on currencies that turned out to herald a new view of the determination of exchange rates. He didn't bother even to include it in his thesis, which reflected the dominating fashions of the day—extending standard Keynesian views in new directions with rational expectations models of international trade. Yet Krugman left graduate school (in June 1977) without direction and went back to Yale to teach. "I was not even sure if I really liked research," he has recalled.

Yet, what if the businessman was right? Over the years many politicians and some economists—all the way back to Alexander Hamilton and before—had espoused the protection of infant industries on the grounds that market share alone conferred great advantages through the magic of increasing returns. In 1961 an MIT student named Staffan Burenstam Linder had hypothesized about a "home-market effect," whereby nations might take advantage of trade embargoes or themselves ban imports in order to enter markets for which domestic demand remained high. Linder was thinking of Volvo, which had entered the automotive business during World War II, when the importation of most cars to Sweden was forbidden. Having learned carmaking during the few years when it was protected from foreign competition, Volvo came to dominate the Scandinavian market and in the 1960s was beginning to learn to sell its automobiles overseas, even in the United States.

The Swedish entry into the American market was an anomaly, Linder recognized. It wasn't supposed to happen in the Ricardian scheme of things. Standard theory predicted that ever-increasing specialization would take its course among nations: cars would be made in England, trains in Germany, planes in the United States, and any such home-market effects as Volvo should be weak and rapidly washed out. Yet, Linder noted, industrial countries tended to increase exports in all categories at the same time, and they exported mainly to one another. The United States sent Ford cars and Boeing airplanes to Germany, Germany sent Fokker airplanes and Volkswagens to the United States. Subsequently this became known as "the puzzle of intra-industry trade."

Suppose the Japanese were doing exactly what the Swedes had done, Krugman wondered, but on a grander scale? Suppose they were relying on protectionist policies to shelter not just automobiles but an ever-changing mix of products—chain saws one year, lawn mowers and outboard motors the next, until they had achieved the advantages of scale in the home market and thereafter could sell at lower costs abroad? A nation of clever manipulators—call them strategic traders—could use the government to their advantage, passing laws and coordinating firms' efforts to achieve effects that otherwise might occur only by happenstance, if at all. First they would target motorcycles. Then cars. Then airplanes. Then computers. Other nations could be driven out of particular businesses altogether. Once forced out, they might find it impossible to come back.

But then, what seemed reasonable to a businessman was preposterous to a properly trained economist—or, rather, a possibility all but impossible to entertain. Without a model of the process the businessman described, it was impossible systematically to conceive of such an effect, much less seriously gauge its magnitude.

As IT HAPPENED, questions of this sort were very much on the minds of economists in Cambridge, Massachusetts, in the mid-1970s, but they were working in a different part of the forest. In the early 1970s, the subdiscipline known as industrial organization (IO) had suddenly come alive, thanks to the new signaling and screening models developed by Akerlof, Spence, Stiglitz, and others. The action in IO was fast and furious. The U.S. government's antitrust suits against IBM and AT&T were going forward. The Bell and RAND journals of economics had opened for business, emphasizing applied economics. New tools had been created by a new generation of young game theorists (David Kreps, Paul Milgrom, John Roberts, and Robert Wilson in particular), building on a series of lofty abstractions developed by theorists in the 1950s and 1960s (by John Nash, John Harsanyi, Reinhard Selten, Robert Aumann, and others).

Questions about how single firms might come to dominate their markets were being asked in formal language, with increasing success. Why did they undertake some activities and not others? How were they governed and financed? When did they prefer hierarchy and when not? And at the center of it all were problems of increasing returns. The new models showed how firms could earn increasing returns by expanding the variety of their products, burnishing their brand name or using a wide variety of other means to block their competition. Young economists were still taught that monopolistic competition was a dead end, at least as far as an overall theory was concerned, but it might have a few concrete applications after all. The problem of the Pin Factory suddenly came to life.

It was in one such model of monopolistic competition that Krugman found the key to his problem. Avinash Dixit and Joseph Stiglitz had devised it a year or so before, for a very different purpose—as a means of investigating whether "product proliferation" was harmful to the economy. A popular theory at the time held that the proliferation of "brands" was partly to blame for inflation. They wondered, could excessive variety be used as a strategy? Had giant food-processing oligopolies put too many varieties on supermarket shelves, in hopes of crowding competitors out of the market? That meant finding a way to say something about optimal variety.

The problem of variety had been framed fifty years before by

Columbia's Harold Hotelling in terms of spatial location—three gasoline stations grouped around a single intersection, say, each selling the same things. Now Dixit and Stiglitz changed the problem slightly. The competition was several monopoly products, each a little different from the others—breakfast cereals and shelf space instead of gas stations. They postulated a consumer with a taste for variety, characterizing his utility function with a mathematical technique known as "additive separability" in such a way as to make him fit neatly into the world according to Arrow-Debreu (those separating hyperplanes again!). Dixit later recalled, "Joe and I knew that we were doing something new in building a tractable general equilibrium model with imperfect competition, but we didn't recognize that it would have so many uses—obviously, otherwise we would have written all those subsequent papers ourselves!"

This was the "beautiful little model" of differentiated products that Krugman thought might be adapted to his problem. (He had learned about it in a course on monopolistic competition taught by Robert Solow.) It turned out, as often happens, that many other persons had devised similar models about the same time.* Yet for many applications, including the one Krugman had in mind, Dixit-Stiglitz's was the most useful formulation—another of those economical and easy-to-use "Volkswagen" models that were the hallmark of MIT.†

In these circumstances in January 1978 Krugman went to see his MIT faculty adviser, Rudiger Dornbusch, a leading authority in international economics. Almost as an afterthought he described his conversation with the businessman, and wondered whether it might pay to try to make a monopolistically competitive trade model. Dornbusch was immediately enthusiastic. Krugman went home to work.

---

* Kelvin Lancaster in 1975, Michael Spence in 1976, Dixit and Stiglitz in 1977, Steve Salop in 1979.
† A lucid discussion of the advantages of the Dixit-Stiglitz model can be found in *The Spatial Economy: Cities, Regions, and International Trade*, by Masahisa Fujita, Paul Krugman, and Anthony J. Venables.

KRUGMAN WAS ABOUT to join the long list of those who had argued over two centuries that increasing returns or falling costs implied a role for government in trade policy—John Rae, Friederich List, John Stuart Mill, Frank Graham, Staffan Linder. It is odd now to think that economists were still using mathematized versions of the corn model as recently as the mid-1970s—a single composite good no different from all other goods. But the tools to do otherwise did not exist, so that was how economics was done.

Unlike those who had gone before, however, Krugman had access to an extensive array of new conceptual tools. As he began to think seriously about the problem, the difficulties started to resolve. Some goods in the model would be proprietary products, like airplanes, with no immediate substitutes. Their manufacturers could set their prices monopolistically (within reason). Other goods would be like corn: many sellers, many buyers, perfect substitutes. Their level would be determined by plain old supply and demand. Suddenly the road ahead seemed completely clear. He stayed up all night in excitement. "I knew within a few hours that I had the key to my whole career in hand," he wrote later in an autobiographical essay, "Incidents from My Career."

And in short order, using proper economic logic, he had demonstrated how it might be possible not just for a firm but for an entire nation to lock in certain advantages, to lock out competitors. "I suddenly realized the remarkable extent to which the methodology of economics creates blind spots. We just don't see what we can't model."

A dramatic new vista had opened. With the new models, Krugman could show how increasing returns and general equilibrium might coexist. If one country got a head start in mass production of some sophisticated good for which there were no near-substitutes—cars, say, or airplanes or silicon chips—it might keep it. Specialization would lower unit costs. Others could find it impossible to break in.

The implication was that markets couldn't necessarily be counted upon to "get things right." Disturbances might grow over time, rather than returning to "normal." In the language of theory, there might be multiple equilibria: this was a highly subversive result, because it undercut the welfare theorems and implied a role for government. Apparently there really *were* circumstances in which the ministry of trade could lend a helping hand. In the context of the late 1970s, his model told a potentially explosive story. The principle of geographical differences, of comparative advantage, was no longer the only possible explanation of patterns of international specialization. Sometimes history itself—whatever country got a good start— might be the cause.

Alas, the model had too many loose ends to be persuasive by the standards of the day. For instance, economists typically wanted just one outcome rather than many. If many were possible, they wanted to know more or less exactly what they were. So Krugman's next year was deeply frustrating. Journals rejected his paper. Senior colleagues ignored him or disparaged his work. In contrast to the latest theorizing in the high-flying literature of rational expectations, his model was almost embarrassingly low-tech. Yale turned him down for a research fellowship. The difficulties continued. His little model was incomplete.

Then, in the spring of 1979, while sitting at Logan Airport in Boston on the way to Minneapolis to give a talk, he discerned a way to integrate the warring principles of monopolistic competition and comparative advantage—an analytical trick rendered clear by an ingenious graphical device. Later he described the events of that first evening as being typical of a particular process. "A foggy idea played with occasionally, sometimes for years at a time until at last an event causes the fog to lift, revealing an almost fully developed model." In this case the vision was increasing returns to scale in several different industries engaged in international competition. The business executive's fear about Japan—first lawn mowers, then automobiles, then semiconductors—had been expressed as part of a consistent story. "Obviously nations are not firms—they cannot be driven altogether out of business. But perhaps a nation can be driven out of *some* businesses, so that in fact temporary shocks *can* have permanent effects on trade."

In July, Krugman took his model to the first ever Summer Institute of the National Bureau of Economic Research. (Only the year before the NBER had moved to Cambridge from New York.) The Summer Institute in Cambridge has since become a venerable institution. Then it was a more modest affair, but well attended by young economists eager to make their marks.

"I still think, with all the things that I have done since, that the hour and a half in which I presented that paper was the best 90 minutes of my life," Krugman wrote many years later. "There's a corny scene in the movie 'Coal Miner's Daughter,' in which the young Loretta Lynn performs for the first time in a noisy bar, and little by little everyone gets quiet and starts to listen to her singing. Well, that's what it felt like. I had, all at once, made it." He was twenty-six years old.

KRUGMAN'S SUCCESS in the summer of 1979 earned him immediate entry into the invisible college of persons working on international trade at the uppermost levels of the field. (Ordinarily it takes two such contributions, but then he had that currency paper lying around unpublished.) There exists a nearly constant stream of meetings in cities around the world; the airplane trips between them provide participants a chance to write for the next. There is no telling when something truly interesting will erupt. Krugman recalled one such international trade conference from those years, held in a Milan classroom: "The room was shabby, with seats so uncomfortable that several older participants ended up with back problems. The hotel was decent but austere. Yet I can assure you that there was more real insight in the discussion than you will find in a dozen G-7 summits. I hope that I never forget that it is young economists in blue jeans, not famous officials in pinstripes, who really have interesting things to say."

In the summer of 1980 the big meeting in international trade and finance was a three-week summer workshop at the University of Warwick in England. Warwick, not far from Oxford, was a second-tier school with a reputation for serious economics. The idea was to bring the top people in the field to mix and mingle with a few hand-picked youngsters each summer, to discuss the most recent controversies and learn the latest techniques. At Warwick that summer was a rich mix, twenty-eight visitors in all: distinguished elders still working in the field, energetic midcareer scholars vying to move to the next level, and a sprinkling of talented young postdocs just starting out, one of whom was Krugman.

Exchange rates received top billing at Warwick that year. The mathematics of uncertainty was another hot topic: Avinash Dixit and Robert Pindyck had begun introducing trade economists to the infinite-dimensional spreadsheet of Arrow-Debreu. Imperfect competition was not the only topic on the agenda, or even the most important one. Krugman brought a paper (joint with James Brander) on "reciprocal dumping." The size of the market seemed important here; circumstances would favor the low-cast producer in the larger country.

This time Krugman's presentation didn't go so well. The usual objections were raised. The elders of the council were skeptical, critical. One dubbed Krugman and Brander "the imperfect competitors." The venerable Charles P. Kindleberger teed off on "those who need formal models to understand the intuitively obvious." The idea of increasing returns in international trade had been thoroughly ventilated long before—in his 1953 textbook, in Tinbergen's text the next year, in the 1929 article by John Williams on which their discussion had been based. "I recall the joy in Cambridge, Mass. when Kenneth Arrow made increasing returns respectable by formalizing it. [But] . . . I confess some irritation over Krugman's defense of his international trade theory as new because it offers a well-worn truth in equation form."

The young, however, those interested in formalization, were very much intrigued. One attendee was particularly impressed by the logic and the novelty of Krugman's layered approach to trade. Elhanan Helpman in 1980 was thirty-four. He was a leader of the rising generation, a student of Kenneth Arrow at Harvard who had a reputation among his peers for being as scrupulous as he was imaginative. He had been born in Dzalabad, in the former Soviet Union. He grew up in Poland until the family emigrated to Israel in 1957. He was planning to become an engineer after his military service, but a chance encounter with the fat Hebrew version of Samuelson's textbook on a fellow soldier's desk led to a change of plans. ("I started to read it and I simply could not stop.") Helpman entered Tel Aviv University in 1966, graduated, and then moved to Harvard University.

In 1982 Helpman invited Krugman to share some tasks for a new handbook of the theory of international trade. A research partnership developed, and before long they decided to write a book together. A deeper, wider truth was embodied in the otherwise disconnected papers about patterns of international trade that were suddenly appearing in all corners of the realm. They set out to provide a systematic exposition of the theory of monopolistic competition applied to trade. The strategy paid off when their monograph, *Market Structure and Foreign Trade: Increasing Returns, Imperfect Competition, and the International Economy*, appeared in 1985 to wide acclaim. Reviewing the book, Robert Lucas wrote, "The useful development of an economic idea depends critically on one's ability to formalize it accurately and tractably. . . . The book is a brilliant success." Strong praise from the citadel of perfect competition that for thirty years had been the University of Chicago! Such is the persuasive power of an equation that encapsulates a well-worn truth.

Monopolistic competition swept through trade theory, quickly and completely. The "new" economics of international trade was well suited to the world of the early 1980s. Instead of a homogeneous global trade in corn, or wine and wool, economists now viewed international commerce as consisting of two broad tiers: an underlying trade in commodities and services characterized by perfect competition and driven by comparative advantage; and an upper level of monopolistic competition in which great multinational corporations abetted by friendly government subsidies periodically mounted assaults on each other's markets, and specialization was determined by market size.

Both types of trade would produce mutual gains. But if the former advantages arose from the distribution of natural resources, then logic of the upper level was nothing more than the result of history—whoever had gotten to lawn mowers or airplanes or computers first. Perhaps that explained Japan's success. Maybe, for that matter, it explained the success of Boeing or IBM. The new findings could hardly have been more relevant. Governments were continually prodded to adopt "industrial policies" and to engage in "strategic trade." Apparently the only question was whether the new policies were hard or easy to apply.

IN THE SUMMER of 1980, when monopolistic competition was being "discovered" by the trade economists meeting in Warwick, the public mind in America was focused on the excitement of a political campaign. Ronald Reagan was running for president against Jimmy Carter. Carter was the incumbent, but Reagan possessed a peculiar advantage. He was said to be in the van of a revolution. Perhaps he was—certainly we have since come to speak of the Reagan revolution, meaning a whole range of attitudes toward interdependence and personal responsibility—but that was not the revolution with which he was identified at the time. In the summer of 1980, the "supply-side revolution" was building toward a boil—no real revolution at all but rather an insurrection staged mainly in the media.

As we have seen, it is not unusual for outsiders to muscle onto the stage in times of crisis. Sometimes it even pays off. During the 1930s John Maynard Keynes injected himself into the center of the debate over the causes of the depression, and though he probably confused the issue in some respects while drawing attention to himself, he offered a story about "getting stuck," about multiple equilibria, that could be widely shared by technical economists. As grandstanders go, Keynes was the height of respectability. The little band of outsiders who sought to hijack the debate in the 1970s suffered greatly by comparison. Supply-side economics is the aspect of the late 1970s and early 1980s that has proved to be most confusing to those who follow developments in economics, all the more so because of the shadowy presence behind the scenes of an influential economist, Robert Mundell.

Far more visible among the supply-siders was Jude Wanniski, who had begun his working life as a newspaperman in Las Vegas. He went on to become (like the fabulist journalist Hunter S. Thompson) a feature writer for Dow Jones's ill-fated weekly newspaper *National Observer* and, eventually, an editorial writer for the *Wall Street Journal*. In the early-1970s Wanniski caught a whiff of the excitement that was spreading from Chicago in economics in those days. He did not burden himself with overreporting. First in a 1975 article for the quarterly journal *Public Interest*, then in a 1978 book called *The Way the World Works: How Economics Fail—and Succeed*, Wanniski asserted that something he called "the Mundell-Laffer hypothesis" was revolutionizing the field.

What exactly was the Mundell-Laffer hypothesis? To the extent it existed at all outside Wanniski's imagination, it would be fair to describe this hypothesis as a broad general equilibrium view of the world, in which everything was connected to everything else, especially the choices of work and leisure. Much more narrowly, it had found expression in something called "the monetary approach to the balance of payments," which was discussed extensively in the Workshop in International Economics at the University of Chicago in the early 1970s when Mundell was a professor there. Arthur Laffer was an associate professor of business economics, recently arrived from graduate school at Stanford, serving intermittently in Washington, and Mundell's friend throughout.

For a few exciting years Mundell and his fellow professor Harry Johnson had regularly battled Milton Friedman over exchange rate policy. Currencies should float freely, argued Friedman. That way the central bank could keep control of the money supply. Doomed to fail, argued Mundell and Johnson, because capital had become mobile. In an open economy, fiscal and monetary policy worked very differently depending on the exchange rate regime. Friedman won the policy battle. The system that Keynes had designed at Bretton Woods was coming apart. Floating rates soon would be the rule. But Mundell won the methodological war (and, just as quickly, was overturned himself in the particulars). The issue was Friedman's penchant for partial equilibrium analysis and its ultimate futility. In the real world, *ceteris* never remained *paribus* for long. Now Mundell had a model—a general equilibrium model that showed how everything-at-once would work. One young international economist

(Michael Darby) compared the excitement over the monetary approach to the balance of payments to the hullabaloo that had attended Robert Solow's growth model fifteen years before.

In fact, Mundell had spelled out his much broader vision of an interdependent world in plain English in 1968 in a fascinating little manifesto, *Man and Economics*. Among the insights: "Competition can take two forms: Competition is personal when the competitors can be readily identified and singled out; it is impersonal when they cannot." Hertz and Avis on the one hand, the wheat market on the other. Vintage Chamberlin, and pretty nearly exactly what Krugman had written down so successfully with mathematical logic in 1979. But instead of setting out models, *Man and Economics* lapsed frequently into free verse. (Sample stanza: *Outputs, inputs / Goods and factors. / Inventions, patents, / Plays by actors. / Goodness!*) At one point, joked Mundell's student Rudiger Dornbusch, "I was a little late for one of his lectures. Perhaps I missed the model?"

Confusion about the new ideas was the rule; confusion between the realms was routine. As far as can be told, Wanniski never so much as mentioned *Man and Economics* in print. Certainly the economics profession paid it no need. Nor did Mundell and Laffer ever produce a single journal article together. Nor did either man ever address the Meetings in those years. Laffer left Chicago for a job in government. Mundell grew more eccentric and discontent. In 1971 he stalked out of the University of Chicago and took a job teaching at the University of Waterloo in his native Canada instead ("At last Waterloo has met its Napoleon" quipped Richard Caves). What was most concrete in Mundell's vision—the monetary approach to the balance of payments—was taken over and developed by other professors, notably Jacob Frenkel and Dornbusch. Laffer, to his credit, at least produced a textbook in international economics (with Marc Miles) in 1982 before disappearing into the shadowlands of consulting, just as the excitement over increasing returns rendered the text completely obsolete.

Even after Columbia University hired him in 1974, Mundell remained out of the mainstream. He stayed on the sidelines of economics for more than a decade, dabbling in policy but publishing little and teaching less. Gradually Mundell returned to serious economics. Eventually, Dornbusch persuaded the Swedes to honor his old teacher with the Nobel Prize. But the citation dwelt on the contribution he made in the 1950s; it didn't mention the supply-side years. And Mundell's Nobel lecture, a disjointed defense of the gold standard, persuaded few.

For a little while, though, the supply-siders dominated the policy debate, and for many years thereafter retained a forceful voice, thanks mainly to Robert Bartley, editorial-page editor of the *Wall Street Journal*. ("He taught me the power of the outrageous," said Bartley of Wanniski.) Often there was enough truth in what they said to render it plausible; never enough to allow it to be pinned down. The supply-siders asserted that cutting taxes would make the economy grow faster, thus flatly contradicting the Solow model. They may even have been right.

But they made no attempt to map their conclusions to the carefully modeled consensus. They ignored most of what had been said before. They eschewed conventional language: supply-siders' real preoccupation was with economic *growth*, though they didn't say so. They rattled on about supply, supply, supply. While the increasing-returns revolution gathered steam in the profession in the meeting at the University of Warwick, the supply-siders conducted their business in the newspapers.

CHAPTER FIFTEEN

"That's Stupid!"

ELSEWHERE THAT SUMMER of 1980 a young student named Paul Romer prepared to return to graduate school. He had taken a year-long break from formal schooling, accompanying his Toronto-born physician wife to Kingston, Ontario, while she completed her training as a medical resident at the university hospital there. Over the course of the year, he had decided on a thesis topic. He would build a new model of economic growth. It would start with falling costs, which had characterized the past two hundred years. They could be explained, he thought, by the growth of knowledge, so his model would treat technological change as internal to its system instead of exogenous. It would also describe a world where growth was actually speeding up, instead of slowing down.

Situated on the north shore of Lake Ontario, at the point where the easternmost of the Great Lakes flows into the St. Lawrence River, Kingston is nothing if not out of the way. Once it had been important militarily. As late as 1848 the last fortified tower had been built to defend against an American invasion. Now the city was home to one of Canada's best universities. Queen's University was a collecting point for the brightest kids in a large population. Romer had no difficulty keeping busy.

By day he attended classes to build his skills at math and economics. By night he worked on the topic he expected would become his dissertation. In June he packed up his wife in the family Volkswagen and a rental truck and together drove the length of the Great Lakes. He would resume his graduate education at the University of Chicago, where three years earlier he had been an undergraduate.

Romer possessed a special qualification for his task. The preceding summer he had completed the course work and passed the field examinations for his Ph.D. in economics at MIT. He would be taking what he had learned in Cambridge to the department that was its fiercest rival on the planet. There is nothing like putting yourself on both sides of a civil war to acquaint yourself with the inner workings of a controversy.

ROMER HAD BEEN among the twenty or so economics students who arrived at MIT in the fall of 1977. Up to that point there was nothing obvious to set him apart—except, perhaps, his very high grades as an undergraduate math major at Chicago.

Born in Colorado in 1955, he was the second of seven children. His father was for many years a farmer, John Deere equipment dealer, aviation academy proprietor, home builder, ski area developer, and, eventually, a politician. He also was a lawyer who had studied for a time at Yale Divinity School. In 1966, when Paul was eleven, Roy Romer ran for the U.S. Senate and lost. He reentered politics in 1974, when Richard Lamm won the governorship and named Romer chief of staff. In 1982 he was elected state treasurer and finally, in 1986, governor of the state himself. Beatrice Romer was a housewife, attentive to her children. After Paul came home deeply excited about his role in a grade school class play—having been cast as a tree—she switched him, midyear, to a private school. She wanted him to be more extensively challenged.

Thereafter, school learning became his characteristic mode of self-expression. He attended Phillips Exeter Academy, in New Hampshire, for his last two years of high school, but as a rebellious junior he did so poorly that he spent his senior year on an exchange program in France, giving up high school wrestling and skipping the usual round of interviews and college visits. Among the colleges to which he applied, only the University of Chicago sent an acceptance. So, like the molecular biologist James D. Watson, Paul Samuelson, and Robert Lucas before him, Romer enrolled in the famously intense university on Chicago's South Side. He entered as a freshman in the Watergate summer of 1973.

With its free-wheeling intellectual excitement, Chicago quickly undid whatever harm Exeter had inflicted on his independence of mind: no line of inquiry was forbidden. For most of his undergraduate career, Romer planned to become a cosmologist. But by the mid-1970s the great postwar boom in basic science clearly was running out of steam, and the prospects of a life meditating on the origins of the universe seemed less attractive going forward. Then, for a time, he thought of becoming a corporate lawyer. But a late course in price theory steered him toward economics itself, at least as an intermediate step to a legal career; technical economics in those days was making substantial inroads into law. MIT admitted him to its graduate program. After graduating with a degree in mathematics in 1977, he thus returned to the East.

Romer arrived at MIT with almost no previous formal training in economics, perhaps the first such walk-on since Robert C. Merton had arrived from Caltech eight years earlier. Unlike Merton, he didn't shine. He had learned a fair amount of economics over beer from his undergraduate roommate at Chicago, David Gordon (who is today a professor of economics at Clemson University), but MIT in those days was full of polished Europeans, many of whom already possessed master's degrees in economics. It was easy to get lost in the crowd. Samuelson and Solow were teaching less than before. The lines now formed outside the offices of Stanley Fischer and Rudi Dornbusch, who had brought to Cambridge the new learning from Chicago. Fischer's *Lectures on Macroeconomics*, written with his colleague Olivier Blanchard, was the fashionable graduate macro text. In a brilliant final burst of energy devoted to Keynesian economics, everybody was trying to build rational expectations into macroeconomic models—including, for a time, Romer and Paul Krugman, who had graduated the year before. Romer hung out with the other two Freshwater types—Bruce Smith, who had learned his economics at Minnesota, and David Levine from UCLA. There was plenty of talk.

One night a burglar crept through a window into the bedroom of Romer's apartment in Cambridge. As the startled graduate student slipped out the front door, he met the young Canadian woman who lived across the hall, going to work in the predawn darkness. He borrowed her phone to call police. Virginia Langmuir was doing a year of residency at the Massachusetts General Hospital. They fell in love and married. He wrote a required econometrics paper on the economics of breaking and entering. Romer took his field exams at MIT, passed them easily, then prepared to return with Langmuir to Canada for a year.

After two years of MIT he was no longer thinking of becoming a lawyer. But neither would he return to Cambridge. The topics that interested him increasingly had little resonance at MIT. During his second year Solow had told an audience (elsewhere), "Anyone working inside economic theory these days knows in his or her bones that growth theory is not a promising pond for an enterprising theorist to fish in. . . . I think growth theory is at least temporarily played out." Romer and his wife decided that he would follow her to Queen's, but that when he returned to school to write his dissertation in economics, it would be to the University of Chicago.

There was no invitation, no assurance it would work. Indeed, for taking communion at one high church of economics and then switching to the other, there was no precedent.

SO OFF THEY WENT to Canada. Queen's University had more than its share of good departments, economics and computer science among them, with tight (if largely invisible) links to the corridors of power. Most prominent of its forty-odd economists was Robert Lipsey, a theorist sometimes mentioned as a candidate for a Nobel Prize. But the teacher there who for Romer turned out to be most important was named Russell Davidson, one of those utterly self-reliant characters who pop up with some regularity in academia.

The son of a Scottish sea captain, Davidson had done physics at Edinburgh University and, in 1966, wound up working as a research assistant to the noted chemist Ilya Prigogine, first in Belgium, then at the University of Texas. With a glut in the market for physicists developing in the 1970s, Davidson retooled as an econometrician during a single year at the University of British Columbia, such was the overlap of the math, and earned a second Ph.D. At Queen's he taught the course on growth from a reader of the important recent contributions (compiled by Amartya Sen), learning the papers himself in order to teach them, one at a time. "This was immediately after people had been doing work in the style of Pontryagin. I wanted to see what to make of Richard Bellman, to see what was in the black box bag of tricks, wanted to exercise my economic intuition as much as anything else."

One day Davidson was presenting the Von Neumann model of growth to his class. This was the classic 1937 paper in which, among other things, Von Neumann employed topology to prove for the first time the existence of equilibrium in an economic model. The ten-page paper, whose beginnings went back to the 1928 seminar in Berlin in which Von Neumann had leapt to his feet to interrupt Marschak, solved a number of deep problems in early general equilibrium theory, long before they were commonly recognized as problems at all. Not until Arrow and Debreu began to build on their foundations around 1950 would their significance come clear. According to the intellectual historian Jürg Niehans, "Never has one fundamental idea had so many fruitful ramifications."

The mathematical profundity, however, had been purchased at the price of realism. In the Von Neumann model (as in the earlier model of Gustav Cassel, on which it was based), all inputs and outputs grow at a constant rate: a fixed set of goods "breeds" an ever larger collection of such goods, as if by magic. Steel produces more steel, corn produces more corn. Nothing changes; the economy just grows. At one point in the exposition, Romer blurted out, "But that's stupid!" Mildly, Davidson replied, "Stupid? Yes, well, perhaps, but we're going to cover it anyway."

Romer had been caught, momentarily, in a kind of time warp. As a graduate student at MIT, he had been taught the Solow model of economic growth, with its exogenously increasing knowledge as a kind of public good. The Von Neumann model was precisely the convention that the Solow model and its Keynesian predecessors had been designed to supplant. In the older model, technology was assumed to be unchanging for simplicity's sake—growth was the product of capital multiplied by a technological constant (hence the designation AK, by which Von Neumann–style models are known today, the letter A being the commonly agreed-upon designation for technology, with K the usual symbol for capital). The Solow model was far more appealing than that. The rate of technical change was set exogenously, but at least technological knowledge was assumed to grow, and its magnitude could be gauged through the clever use of a residual.

The older model had a different rhetorical style, however, and a much more general ambition. It was Romer's first glimpse of the power of the Modern program. For all its usefulness, there was something quick and dirty about the Solow model, Romer thought. After they learn it, a lot of people pull up and say, "Forget it, it's not possible to think about the big problems." In the Von Neumann model, Romer suddenly glimpsed how it was possible to grapple with the deepest questions of how the world changes over time. "I never had seen that before, though I saw lots more when I got to Chicago."

Romer recalled the incident in a talk he gave much later. He acknowledged that he had failed to appreciate the subtlety of Von Neumann's contribution. "It is also clear that I was not very tactful." But his subsequent work had persuaded him that his harsh initial judgment of the paper's description of *growth* itself was correct. "In place of a discussion of new products, new processes, universities, private research labs, patent law, scientific inquiry—all the things that seemed to me then and still seem to me now to be at the heart of economic growth—the model blithely offers up an attractive mathematical assumption that cannot be given any meaningful interpretation."

So with the self-assurance of a twenty-four-year-old, Romer decided to build a better model of economic growth, whose mainspring would be based on this intuition. It would be better than Von

Neumann's, in that it would include knowledge. It would be better than Solow's, too, in that the new knowledge would arise from purposeful decisions within the system. No one ever invested in R&D for private gain in the Solow model; everyone simply benefited from spillovers from government research. Above all, it would be contemporary, taking advantage of the mathematical generality of the tools that economists had developed since the 1940s, the infinite-dimensional spreadsheet in particular.

Years later Romer spoke of the year in Kingston as a halcyon period, during which he slowly came to grips with the problem, one clean sheet of paper after another.

> The first interaction I can remember is playing with some control theory model and coming to the first recognition that there was a way to get at growth if I built in some increasing returns. The next thing I remember is one of these episodes, pencil and yellow pad. When you do that, there are all these ups and down in the process, sometimes you think you've really got it, other times you think you're at a dead end. I remember trying to go to bed one night at a point where I had some success, because it's hard to relax when you think it's all falling apart. There's this pacing you try to do, you try to quit before it can fall apart again. . . . The moment (that) you look for is when you reach a kind of completion. You don't want to interrupt when things are progressing, when you've tied off a piece. I remembered somebody's description of the life of a poet: you are only a poet at the moment you finish the last line in the poem. Before then, you are a failed poet; after that, you are an ex-poet. At those moments of completion, I felt like an economist.

He applied to Chicago as a graduate student and was admitted. Langmuir obtained a research fellowship at the University of Chicago hospital.

IN RETROSPECT the remarkable thing about Romer's project is how completely at odds it was with the spirit of the times in which it was conceived. While the general pessimism of the 1970s never rose to the level of the apprehension during the Great Depression, much less the desperation of the Napoleonic Wars, there was in many quarters a certain longing attachment to doom. Pop models dominated public consciousness: there were the Club of Rome Report, the Population Bomb, the End of Capitalism, and other gloomy scenarios. Pessimism extended deep into the economics profession itself.

As always there were other voices, operating in the tradition of Godwin and Condorcet, ebullient popularizers of old-fashioned views derived from Adam Smith—the economist Julian Simon and the supply-side journalist George Gilder, to name two of the more appealing. But inside the profession, in the graduate schools, among the established figures of authority, there was very little interest in growth theory at the end of the 1970s.

It was precisely then that Romer took the other side of the argument. Human living conditions had been improving dramatically for at least a couple of centuries, he reasoned. Why not expect that the trend would continue? In his model, growth would continue indefinitely, for decades, even centuries into the future.

"I wasn't thinking about picking a fight with the doomsters or about what government should do," Romer said much later, when the work was done. "I just wanted to understand. The economics I had learned in graduate school were mostly right and depended really centrally on diminishing returns. Yet here was this one phenomenon that seemed to go in just exactly the opposite direction. The question was, how to reconcile the contradiction?"

CHAPTER SIXTEEN

In Hyde Park

ROMER HAD NO DIFFICULTY translating the economics he had learned at MIT into Chicagoese when he arrived at the Social Sciences Building on the Hyde Park campus in June of 1980. Ordinarily students take the department's core exams only after completing Chicago's two-year sequence of courses. Robert Lucas had taken his during January of his first year. Romer arranged to take them as soon as he arrived. He passed immediately. It was as good a way as any of advertising his presence among the rest of the graduate students. He was, he felt, back home.

In fact, Chicago was the perfect place for Romer's project. A passionate dedication to scholarship and pure research was in its genes. Lawrence Kimpton, its sixth president, had described the university as a place "where one is always in principle allowed to pose the hardest question possible—of a student, a teacher, a colleague—and feel entitled to expect gratitude rather than resentment for one's effort." Taking ideas seriously, Chicagoans liked to say, was what the university was about.

Romer didn't just walk in and start talking, of course. He enrolled in several advanced courses as he prepared to write his thesis. He took the course that Lucas was teaching, a course on how to write a paper: "He'd come in and show us from class to class where he had gotten to," Romer remembers. He connected, too, with Chicago's other reigning guru of mathematical economics, José Scheinkman, who taught a course on the mathematics of intertemporal optimization—the logic of choice over time. Scheinkman agreed to supervise Romer's dissertation. Lucas soon joined his committee.

THE CHICAGO ECONOMICS DEPARTMENT of 1980 was deeply divided. It was twenty-five years since the Cowles Commission had left. And for all that time the literary, price-theoretic approach, the second Chicago school, had dominated the department. But pressure, both internal and from the other centers of the discipline, was becoming very great. In the early 1980s the Chicago department's members were once again in the throes of having to speak two languages. This time the mathematical approach rapidly gained the upper hand.

The old literary school was breaking up: Milton Friedman had enjoyed remarkable success in his battle with Keynes, regularly going over the heads of his fellow economists to appeal directly to the general public. *Capitalism and Freedom*, a remarkable little book, had sold tens of thousands of copies since it was published in 1962. It persuaded countless young persons, including the youthful Romer, that conservative didn't have to mean dumb. In other quarters he was famous for his dueling columns with Paul Samuelson in *Newsweek*. And in 1980 Friedman and his wife starred in a ten-part television series shown around the world. The accompanying book, *Free to Choose*, became a best seller. Later that year his friend Ronald Reagan was elected president. But Friedman had bypass surgery in 1972, and in 1977 he kept a long-standing promise to his wife, Rose, to retire to California. George Stigler was still teaching in the business school. By 1982, however, he was preoccupied with the events surrounding his Nobel Prize, and preparing to write his autobiography. In the economics department, the other heavyweights of the old school—D. Gale Johnson, Arnold Harberger, and Theodore Schultz—were consulting to industrializing nations.

Meanwhile the mathematical tilt increased. Chicago had hired its first cutting-edge mathematical economist in 1971, a Berkeley Ph.D. named William "Buz" Brock. Brock in turn had scouted out Lucas and, in the same year, José Scheinkman. Of those who made present-day Chicago economics what it is, Scheinkman, a French-Brazilian of infectious high spirits, is perhaps the least known. (After a quarter century in Hyde Park, he moved to Princeton University in 1999.) Arriving later were Thomas Sargent, who today teaches at New York University, and Lars Hansen, still in Chicago. Lucas's and Sargent's disagreements with the Keynesians were by then well enough understood to have been recognized as a school, as Freshwater macro. In Chicago—and Minnesota, Rochester, and Pittsburgh (Carnegie Mellon)—these were the New Classicals, great believers in the Invisible Hand, very high-tech, and appealing to the young.

The new mathematical style didn't persuade everyone among the rising generation at Chicago, naturally. Almost immediately a new group among the faculty emerged, labor economists, both theorists and econometricians who were more interested in what they could learn about the workings of particular markets than in generalizing about the behavior of the economy as a whole. Led by Gary Becker, Sherwin Rosen, Sam Peltzman, and James Heckman, these were economists operating more nearly in the old Marshallian tradition that Friedman had championed and that (with its Keynesian add-ons) Paul Samuelson had designated neoclassical. They updated their methods constantly, as Friedman had updated his. But however esoteric their work became, expressed now in models and heavily buttressed with econometrics, they still considered themselves to be applied price theorists—not literary economists by any means, but neither high-tech acolytes of the Modern movement. For a time the joke was that Brock was the mole who had destroyed Chicago. In the early 1980s the department was just barely holding together. Worn down by the tension between the factions, this most affable of men—an accomplished tap dancer, no less!—left Hyde Park for the University of Wisconsin in 1981. The divisions deepened.

Departmental politics were less important for graduate students. Technique was their primary concern. It was an outgrowth of his thesis topic that Romer spent more time with the mathematician Ivar Ekeland, an expert on convex analysis who was visiting the math department, than with the economics department's spiritual leader (and future Nobel laureate) Gary Becker. The traditional Chicagoan who took the greatest interest in Romer's work was Sherwin Rosen, a price theorist and student of specialization recently recruited from the University of Rochester to be, for all practical purposes, George Stigler's heir. (Remember, it was Stigler who in 1951 had identified the paradox of the Pin Factory.) When he learned that Romer was working on increasing returns, Rosen told the young mathematical economist about the paper that Allyn Young had written in 1928. Romer says he remembers thinking at the time how woolly seemed Young's emphasis on cumulative causation.

Had he been in the habit of expressing his economics in literary terms, Romer might have said that he planned to characterize knowledge and show how it could accumulate in the same way as any other form of capital. Remember the basic intuition: new products, new processes, entrepreneurs, universities, private research labs, patent law, scientific inquiry—all were to be at the heart of economic growth.

But, like any good scientist, Romer had learned to be professionally modest and oblique. "I don't think I wanted to over-claim that 'I'm going to bring knowledge in,'" he later said. "This is the kind of thing you get beat up for. . . . Lots of people had thought about increasing returns and growth before me. I was just following a problem where it led."

WHERE IT LED was to the kinds of powerful general equilibrium models that had emerged in the 1950s to describe the behavior of people, corporations, and governments over time—specifically, to a version published more or less simultaneously in 1965 by David Cass and Tjalling Koopmans. The Cass-Koopmans model did the same things that the Solow model did, but with the intertemporal optimization bells and whistles that Lucas had pioneered. Frank Ramsey's lone planner had become a competitive industry, or an economy composed entirely of canny Scots looking out for themselves. Cass-Koopmans was, in other words, a much more general version, and for this reason, Romer scarcely looked at Solow's version as he began his work; by the standards of the 1980s, it seemed not so much a Volkswagen as a Model T. Still less did he think to consult the many literary economists who previously had tackled the problem of increasing returns. "In a way," he later recalled, "it shows how far we had come. Things that had been pretty hard to sort out became much easier to say in math." (Here, as usual, we stress the hearsay rule.)

Romer wanted a model in which growth could continue indefinitely. There would be no looming steady state. In the Solow model the economy inevitably reached a kind of adulthood in fifty or a hundred years and stopped growing altogether. Growth itself was but a stage. In the classics department down the hall, professors taught cyclical and stage theories of all kinds, the philosophical histories of Polybius, Saint Augustine, Vico, Kant, Condorecet, Hegel, and Teilhard de Chardin. Economists were not thought to dabble in such matters, but in fact a tacit view of the long-term future of the human race was hidden in the Solow model: the assumption that nations soon would converge to a steady state.

Remember, the strictly empirical problem Romer was addressing was the reality that growth seemed to have been speeding up for more than a century instead of slowing down, as had been expected. He reasoned that it must have to do with the internal dynamic of science: the more you learn, the faster you learn new things. If knowledge was the source of increasing returns, then accumulating more of it should mean faster growth—which was, in fact, the record of the preceding two hundred years.

But there was no readily available metaphor for the world that he imagined and was trying to capture, one in which it was to be expected that humankind would still be discovering new mysteries a thousand years into the future. For his own purposes, then, to remind himself what he was driving at, Romer occasionally turned to the view of growth embodied in the popular television series *Star Trek*, about the distant future, in which nations rose and fell but the species went on innovating and expanding outward, if not forever, at least for a good long time. The argument was not couched in these colorful terms, of course. Instead, it was increasing returns to knowledge versus diminishing returns to land, labor, and capital. He couldn't have been any more obscure if he had proposed to do it in code.

With the math, Romer quickly ran into the problem of the Pin Factory. "I'd been working on a social planner model like Ramsey, where the planner maximizes in the context of increasing returns to knowledge. I could get growth that was speeding up that way, which is what I wanted, but I thought that it couldn't be decentralized into a competitive equilibrium. Having pretty much captured the world in the way that interested me [speeding up growth], it didn't seem consistent with the market."

The problem was that a single firm would take advantage of increasing returns to knowledge to monopolize its markets and destroy the assumption of perfect competition. It would have happened every time. There was nothing to prevent it. There was no fun in making a model of *that*, since it clearly was not what happened ordinarily, if ever. "I remember having a conversation with Lucas where he said, 'Well, why don't you use external increasing returns?' So that's where it first came up, as a mathematical strategy for dealing with this awkward fact that there would be just one big firm."

The role of knowledge spillovers in Romer's first model was the same as it had been in Marshall's book—to assure that new technology could not be appropriated even though it was privately financed. Marshall's "trade knowledge that cannot be kept secret"—his beneficial externalities—would cancel out increasing internal returns. Romer hadn't yet read Marshall. He didn't know even about the use of spillovers that Arrow had made in learning-by-doing twenty years before. Instead, he went straight to the mathematical frontier and prepared to build a model from scratch.

THERE WERE MYRIAD DETAILS to be attended to, mostly mathematical. There was, for example, the question of *which* rocket science planning technique to adopt. Pontryagin's or Bellman's? Both had to do with describing the passage of time. Romer had shown up at Chicago doing the Pontryagin-style continuous time techniques that he had learned from Russell Davidson. The method was ill suited for use with the infinite-dimensional spreadsheet of Arrow-Debreu, whose use in macroeconomics Robert Lucas was popularizing at the time. But expected and unexpected outcomes didn't seem very important to the analysis of growth. So Romer stuck with the more familiar technique, Pontryagin-style math. It let him track the evolution of his variables in time without having to show time explicitly.

Then there was the problem of multiple equilibria, meaning that, as always with positive feedback, things could come out in more than just one way. Perturbations might prove irreversible, rather than return to "normal." (This was, of course, the same problem that Krugman had solved for trade the year before, but Romer didn't know about that, either.) Then such multiple equilibria had to be laboriously calculated. Graphical representation of them was known as a phase diagram. The personal computer had barely been invented; the necessary mathematical software was years away. Romer drew his phase diagrams by hand.

The biggest technical issue had to do with demonstrating the stability of the model. This was the "knife-edge" problem that had defeated Shell and Stiglitz and Arrow fifteen years earlier. Such were the assumptions that individual utility might become unbounded—might become infinite—if one parameter were just slightly changed, in which case, the model would be useless, the property in question being known as the transversality condition. The techniques he used to solve the problem were based on ones developed by Lucas and Prescott in their 1971 paper "Investment under Uncertainty." The mathematician Ekeland helped him out. He solved it to his own and to his teachers' satisfaction, publishing separately in *Econometrica* a short paper on the infinite-dimensional optimization problems that arose. In the end he produced a model that was well behaved.

Once he built spillovers into his model, Romer had a world that looked much like Marshall's system, though he wouldn't have described it that way at the time. Perfect competition was preserved. Product exhaustion, the condition imposed by marginal productivity theory, Euler's theorem and all that, was maintained. There would be nothing left over to pay technology. And yet the economy would exhibit aggregate increasing returns. Solow had solved the problem by bringing in new knowledge from outside the model, as had Mill. Romer went in the opposite direction, as had Marshall: his accumulating knowledge came from new investments; it was then communicated to all the rest by means of spillovers. Spillovers meant that growth would occur endogenously in his system, from forces internal to his account. And these external economies constituted a strong defense, at least intuitively, against the possibility that a single firm would take over the world, just as they had for Marshall.

Romer was so absorbed in the math that he didn't think very hard about what that meant. It came as a shock, he recalls, while otherwise beavering away in Regenstein Library, to read an editorial arguing that the space race had been good for economic growth, and realize that the abstractions in which he was investing so heavily might one day have practical applications.

LATE IN 1981 Romer completed his thesis, completed it enough, anyway, to begin looking for a job. "Dynamic Competitive Equilibria with Externalities, Increasing Returns and Unbounded Growth" had taken more than a year to write. By the time it was formally submitted, it had been compressed to 143 pages, most of them containing forbiddingly difficult math.

There was a curt nod in the direction of the historical literature. ("Although the mathematical details have not previously been worked out, the underlying ideas for this kind of model are quite old. . . . [I]n a less precise form, the notion that growth is driven by some kind of increasing return is as old as the attack on the ideas of Malthus.") There was also a determined attempt to show the relevance of the model to the real world. A table of the best available data (that of Simon Kuznets) showed that since 1841 the rate of growth in the four leading industrial nations had been speeding up, not slowing down.

What kind of change might be considered truly exogenous in his model? Romer offered a concrete example. During a climatological warming trend in the Middle Ages, presumably caused by perturbations in the orbit of Earth, he noted that the northern limit of grain cultivation in Europe crept a hundred miles to the north—a fact recognized by contemporaries. Farms were correspondingly more productive as a result. That was exogenous change, he wrote. No human action could possibly have produced the result. But when yields of domestic wheat rose steadily during those same years while wild grain yields remained the same, the change should be understood as having occurred *within* the system—that is, endogenously. Farmers purposely planted the better strains and threw the worse away.

The centerpiece of the thesis was the model itself, thirty compact pages of formal notation that set forth the world whose workings Romer had wanted to describe. There were increasing returns to scale in aggregate production, thanks to "the intangible capital good, knowledge," which in turn was embodied in capital-related spillovers. A suitable yardstick was proposed, measured in units defined by hypothetical costs of production. Romer mapped out and carefully defined certain places where the market failed because inventors had insufficient reason to invest their efforts; any gains they made would quickly vanish through the spillover mechanism. It thus turned out there would be systematic underinvestment in new knowledge. The proofs occupied nearly half the manuscript—hard going for all but the most mathematically adroit. It is safe to say that few besides his committee ever read Romer's thesis.

There was, however, no palaver, no comparison with the Solow model, no calling attention to the significance that the model had no steady state, that the rate of growth actually accelerated somewhat over time. About tools he had developed, Romer was downright assertive. The very first paragraph of his thesis noted that the mathematics he had devised for calculating nonefficient equilibria might have application throughout economics, any time a significant market failure might occur—in the theory of the firm, in asset pricing, in macroeconomic fluctuations, and so on, everyplace where spillovers might bring about suboptimal results. It was one of those tricks that made everything come out right that had found great favor in Chicago.

About the policy implications of his model for growth, on the other hand, Romer was reticent—not surprisingly, perhaps, because the implications did not seem very Chicagoan at all. It appeared that government subsidies could sometimes improve economic performance. But it might matter quite a lot exactly what the subsidy encouraged, he noted. It didn't seem right to him that productivity could be increased by subsidizing output with, say, trade quotas. More likely, productivity would improve if government policy subsidized the construction of new plants with new technology instead.

Another eighteen months of polishing were required before Romer formally submitted his dissertation, three more years before its model was published in a journal. Yet for those on the frontier of economics, when they first worked through the argument, at whatever stage of its refinement, they knew that the world had changed. "People say that it was formally the same as the model Ken Arrow wrote down fifteen years before," George Akerlof said many years later. "But that is an invalid complaint. When Paul wrote that paper, somehow everybody understood that the ballgame had changed. It was like the moment in [Henry James's novel] *The Golden Bowl*, when a look passes between the husband and the wife, and suddenly everybody knows that she had had an affair. Suddenly, somehow everyone just *knew* there was a great deal of new economics to be explored."

As HE PREPARED to leave Chicago, Romer made the inevitable trip to the hiring hall. The Meetings in December 1981 were in Washington, D.C. (for many years they took place between Christmas and New Year's). Reaganomics dominated the trendier sessions that year; in the exhibit hall the conservative American Enterprise Institute boasted, "The *New York Times* calls us the hottest show around." The ideological celebration was no more than distant thunder in the suites and cavernous room where job interviews took place. There the idea is to impress sufficiently in a short conversation to be invited to campus to give a talk about one's dissertation.

Romer was asked to talk at several places, Harvard among them, but not at MIT. Cambridge, Massachusetts, is a small place, however, and the MIT assistant professors Tim Kehoe and Lawrence Summers attended the Harvard talk. They were sufficiently impressed that they enlisted Stanley Fischer in a swift and successful campaign to offer Romer a teaching job at MIT, sight otherwise unseen by the faculty. Other offers came from Wisconsin, Carnegie-Mellon, and the University of Rochester. Rochester offered the best situation for his wife. So in June the Romers packed up again and retraced their steps along the Great Lakes. By now they had an infant son.

CHAPTER SEVENTEEN

The U-Turn

THE UNIVERSITY OF ROCHESTER was one of the places to which MIT professors sent their intellectual daughters when, in the 1930s, 1940s, 1950s, and 1960s, they couldn't be admitted to Harvard, Yale, or Princeton. It possessed a tough-minded, egalitarian temperament that in those days could be found in almost no other research university in the East. It was not surprising that this was so. In the early nineteenth century Rochester had become a focal point for the fierce energy, religious and secular, that had swept across upstate New York with the opening of the Erie Canal. The Mormon Church started in upstate New York. So did the women's suffrage movement. So did John D. Rockefeller, whose contributions would be very influential in shaping the University of Chicago. So did Eastman Kodak and, in due course, much of the rest of the U.S. optical/imaging industry, which remained a thriving presence in the city. In short, Rochester was a good place for a young theorist interested in economic growth.

Romer arrived there in the spring of 1982. As an assistant professor at the beginning of his career, he was expected to pursue several parallel projects at once. He had to satisfy his Chicago dissertation supervisor José Scheinkman on the math in his not-quite-finished thesis. He was expected to carve out a portion of it to be published as a paper in a journal. He was to begin to teach for the first time, devising a course on money and banking. He was starting a family with a physician partner who was as dedicated to her work as he was to his own. Another child, a daughter, would be born in 1984. Yet such was the culture of the Rochester economics department that he also had plenty of time to think. There was, at least, no pressure to show off.

The longer Romer thought, the more convinced he became that the approach to the problem to which he had devoted his last two years at Chicago would ultimately lead to a dead end. Knowledge spillovers were important, he decided, but they were not enough. They captured one aspect of the situation well enough, but they obscured another.

So within a year of leaving Chicago, the twenty-seven-year-old theorist discarded the model of perfect competition he had pursued so laboriously in his thesis. He began experimenting instead with aggregate models of monopolistic competition—the approach that had been developed fifty years before in Cambridge, Massachusetts, and which traditionally Chicago despised. An 180-degree turn is a rare event for any scholar, all the more rare for one just starting out. This wasn't merely taking a different tack. The newly minted Ph.D. was changing sides in economics' civil war—again.

THE PROBLEM WITH the perfect-competition story, with the side-effects approach of uncompensated external economies, was that it failed to capture the reality of, among other places, downtown Rochester. "Something in the air" made sense up to a point, however hard it might be to say exactly what the "something" was. There were indeed things that were obvious in Rochester, in any city, to anyone who walked down the street. In Rochester, for instance, one of the obvious facts was that its companies kept investing substantial sums in R&D.

It was clear that those costly decisions signified that firms expected to make a return on their investment. They maintained labs, hired chemists, employed lawyers. Secrets, patents, copyrights, trademarks, and, often enough, the determination to remain on the technology's cutting edge were the keys to the city's prosperity. There was a controversy in the local newspapers at about this time concerning the university's reluctance to admit a Fuji executive to its business school, for fear that he would gain too much insight into Kodak business secrets. In Rochester, apparently, there were some very important things that didn't spill over. Or at least possessors of these proprietary advantages sought mightily to prevent it from happening.

In the purely spillover world of Romer's thesis, there was no place for any of this kind of purposeful activity. If Kodak produced a new high-speed film, Fuji would know all about it the next day. There could be no incentive to accumulate private knowledge under these circumstances, since it would never help you more than your competitor. If, on the other hand, Romer had allowed in his dissertation's model for the possibility that Kodak could keep even a little bit of the information secret, the model would have had a serious flaw, because Kodak would have increasing returns and eventually would take over the whole industry. He would have been back in the world of the Pin Factory, in which monopoly was the ordinary outcome.

In his dissertation Romer had finessed the issue. There, if Kodak got some proprietary knowledge, Fuji got some of the benefit, but not as much—enough to keep Kodak from taking over the entire market. Hidden in a production function was an assumption that Kodak could not grow past a certain point, because it would face increasing costs in connection with its knowledge—that there was a limit to how big it could grow. It was a shortcut. The assumption was crucial to getting incentives for innovation into the model, while still making things come out all right.

Romer hadn't bothered doing with his rising-cost assumption what he had done in his thesis with the concept of exogeneity. He hadn't illustrated it with a real-world example. "I didn't actually go out into the world and try to look for a piece of knowledge, to test it, to see if you ran into increasing costs when you tried to use it. The thing was that I had taken a shortcut through a rough spot in the reasoning. The math highlighted it, and each time I returned the math tripped me up. It wouldn't let me alone. I had to go back and deal with it."

WHEN ROMER BEGAN THINKING about what exactly might constitute a new and valuable piece of knowledge worth spending money on, he soon decided it must indeed be something like a new good, a successfully differentiated product. A faster type of film, say, one of greater sensitivity to light than the others.

After all, he reasoned, most new knowledge in the private sector comes about because of a process of trial and error, of experimentation, of explicit research and development. People who commission it know what they are doing, and they invest because they hope they'll make a profit. True, the new knowledge often proves to be of some benefit to others, but that's not what investors in its accumulation are after. They're looking not for spillovers but for new products that they can sell. They're seeking to "differentiate their product," to *specialize* in its production and sale.

But specialists can hope to make a profit only if they can keep their discoveries or procedures secret for a time, or protect their new knowledge with a patent or copyright, or realize some other inimitable cost advantage in manufacturing, distribution, or sales. They have to cover their fixed costs—the costs of going into business in the first place, before a single item can be sold. That means they have to be price *makers*. They have to act, or try to act, at least for a time, like monopolists.

It was the same logic that had led Edward Chamberlin to monopolistic competition sixty years before. But Romer wasn't reading Chamberlin. He was writing math in such a way as to describe the world he saw, and in this case plausibly to describe why private parties would want to invest in the production of knowledge. One of the fruits of the Modern movement was that researchers no longer had to form their thoughts in natural language. They could cut straight to far more precise mathematical formulations.

The mathematics of fixed costs had to do with "nonconvexities." The tools of convex analysis that Romer had grown accustomed to using in graduate school in Chicago were insufficient here, because fixed costs introduced a certain lumpiness into the world; that is, they were *indivisibilities*—just as you couldn't make money from half a bridge, you couldn't sell your new film until you had invented and developed it. Indeed, nonconvexity was a fancy way of saying indivisibility, and the presence of indivisibilities, of course, signaled the possibility of increasing returns. Convexity described the familiar case of increasing costs and decreasing returns; nonconvexity meant decreasing costs and increasing returns.

Beyond its ordinary meaning—curving outward like the surface of a sphere—the term "convexity" had a special significance for economics. All the analysis of perfect competition had come to be built upon the logic of convex sets, just as during the preceding century it had been built on calculus—set theory had trumped calculus by dispensing with some of its unrealistic assumptions about the "smoothness" of the world. In return, economics got inequalities instead of equations—statements that carved out whole sets of points instead of simply describing a line. George Dantzig's beanpole, as a rough-shaped cone, was a convex set. So were all the other higher abstractions, borrowed from rocket science, which economists had found so useful. The infinite-dimensional spreadsheet was anchored in convexity. The separating hyperplane theorem was a standard tool of convex analysis. It could be used to establish something as grand as competitive equilibrium, or to illustrate the supposition that any difference between market prices and natural prices will soon be erased by adjustments in price and quantity. To define "convex" was easy enough: a set is convex if it contains a line drawn between any two of its points. Peter Newman, an editor of *The New Palgrave: A Dictionary of Economics*, memorably put it this way: pyramids are convex sets and Frisbees are not. Golf balls are almost-convex sets, whose near-spherical surface is covered with the little nonconvexities that we call dimples.

Nonconvexities spelled big trouble for mathematical economists, just as monopolies pose big problems for students of the Invisible Hand. For mathematical economists, though, it was easier to be clear about what nonconvexities entailed for a general equilibrium model than to talk about monopolistic competition. Long afterwards, explaining the controversies to a lay audience, Romer reduced the matter to just two dimensions. He distinguished between circles, which were convex sets, and *crushed* or dented circles, which were nonconvexities. (A cross section of a Frisbee would look like a circle that had been crushed so thoroughly as to resemble a C.)

The crushed-circle shape had obsessed him for ten or fifteen years,

Romer said. It had come to represent something very important in economics. But if his listeners didn't already understand the connection between things and knowledge, and the way in which the circle had come to represent the former and the crushed circle the latter, then he couldn't take them through it mathematically—not in that hall, anyway. "I can't show how the process of [mathematical] distillation, of sculpting away, strips the complexity of the world down to two geometrical shapes." If only he could, he said, he would be able to give his audience a Ph.D. in economics at the end of the talk.

Gradually Romer became aware of the existence of an extensive literature of fixed costs. Many people had wrestled with the problem over the years, beginning with a series of nineteenth century French engineers who, he learned, had more or less invented microeconomics fifty years before Alfred Marshall, working through successively the economics of the construction of roads, canals, and railways. He read Jules Dupuit, the chief engineer of Paris, who in the mid-nineteenth century had become an expert on the provision of all kinds of public goods—not just bridges and highways but also canals, railroads, municipal water systems, sewage services, and flood control projects—only to be ignored by Alfred Marshall. What is the difference between the decision to build a bridge and the decision to build a Pin Factory? Very little. A little farther down this road lay intellectual property. "Once you start looking for fixed costs," wrote Romer, "you start to see them everywhere."

The point is that "the literature" of economics played a relatively small part in Romer's thought. He was reading not Chamberlin and Schumpeter but Rockafellar—not John D. Rockefeller but R. T. Rockafellar the mathematician, whose book *Convex Analysis* undergirt the present-day field. Even in those days any number of people wanted to talk about knowledge workers and intellectual property. But none had much stomach for working through the transversality conditions in infinite-dimensional spaces. Yet it was the mathematics that in the end would expose the contradiction in the phrase.

About this time Romer remembered Sherwin Rosen's suggestion. He went back and read Allyn Young's lecture, "Increasing Returns and Economic Progress." This time Young's argument seemed to make more sense.

What Allyn Young had so boldly told his listeners in 1928 was that Adam Smith had missed the point. By concentrating single-mindedly on what went on *inside* the walls of the Pin Factory, he had overlooked the essential matter of the pin industry's relationship with its neighbors. The subdivision and repetition of complex tasks was only part of the story of the division of labor—the less important part at that. The invention of *new* tools and machinery and *new* materials and designs involved the division of labor as well. Often this transformation was described simply as "progress."

In fact, if you examined only a single firm or even a single industry, you would have difficulty seeing the unfolding essence of this evolutionary process, Young said. He illustrated what he had in mind with his thumbnail history of the printing industry. When the printing press was newly conceived, its inventors had to design and manufacture presses for themselves. They had to formulate special ink and train workers. They had to search out customers for their books.

As the printing trade grew, however, firms arose that did nothing *except* manufacture presses. Those presses would be sold to would-be competitors. The successors of the early printers, Young wrote, were not just the specialized printshops of the present day but the press makers, wood pulp suppliers, papermakers, ink manufacturers, type manufacturers (and designers), lithographers, press builders, and so on, not to mention the suppliers of steel, chemicals, electricity, machine tools, and countless other intermediate goods on whom these manufacturers depended.

True, sometimes the process worked the other way around: a book publisher might buy a paper company to assure a steady source of supply. But such *integration* seemed to be a function of maturity. A young and growing industry specializes and *dis-integrates*; that is, artisans leave established firms and go into business for themselves, supplying several competing firms with components. There are spin-offs, breakaways, start-ups.

The driving force behind these new companies ordinarily was an entrepreneurial search for *new* markets. But the entrepreneur had to have a new product. For that a certain scale of operations was necessary, a sufficiently large market for the business to flourish. It wouldn't make sense to make a hammer to drive a single nail, or to fill a factory with specially constructed jigs, gauges, lathes, drills, presses, and conveyors to build a hundred cars.

But if the hammer came into common usage, if enough cars could be sold, then unit costs would fall and specialization would begin to pay off. This is what it means to say that the division of labor—the degree of specialization—is limited by the size of the market. Adam Smith himself had said as much when he observed that a porter required a city to make a living and that a baker required at least a small town. Isolated farmers baked their own bread.

Smith had been so clear about so much else. Why not this? Why hadn't he taken his observation a step further, to note that increasing returns/falling costs seemed to be associated mainly with machines—two-wheeled luggage carts, for example, or convection ovens? And why wasn't his omission quickly spotted? The hollowing out that took place when Ricardo introduced formal methods with his corn model is easy enough to understand. But why were the next generations of economists, John Stuart Mill in particular (and excepting, of course, Karl Marx), so *incurious* about the determinants of a flood of new inventions?

The answer, Allyn Young had surmised, may have been that by the mid-nineteenth century economic progress had been so steady for so long that it simply seemed to grow out of the nature of things. In any event, this steady growth of knowledge was taken for granted by Mill and his fellow economists. "If they had looked back," Young wrote, "they would have seen that there were centuries during which there were few significant changes in either agricultural or industrial methods. But they were living in an age when men had turned their faces in a new direction. . . . Improvements, then, were not something to be explained. They were natural phenomena, like the precession of the equinoxes."

The economics of "improvements" was precisely what Romer was endeavoring trying to explain.

WHEN HE TURNED to Marshall, Romer found that the inventor of external increasing returns himself had described them in the classic passage as arising from two different sources. There was the "trade-knowledge that couldn't be kept secret." There were also the "subsidiary trades," whose emergence depended on the emergence of "machinery of the most highly specialized character." Marshall, too, was really writing then about specialization. But so quickly did he skate over the central point that it was scarcely noticed.

Somebody had to help the baker and the porter to get started. Specialization inevitably entailed a fixed cost, the expense necessary to get an activity up and running. The baker had first to rent a shop and buy an oven; the porter needed a luggage cart. Marshall had much to say about the relationship between fixed costs and variable costs, meaning expenses that would increase or not, depending on how heavily a facility might be used. But he had relatively little to say about the introduction of new goods.

Instead, there were externalities—that "something in the air." "I remember trying to formalize Marshall," Romer later recalled.

> People were bugging me that I didn't know the literature. . . . The truth is, I'm pretty sure that Marshall introduced spillovers the same way I did, to deal with the technical problem, to make sure the math came out right. But the way he deals with it in the book is to say, "Oh, here's this natural problem, there is something important about knowledge, it is very hard to contain, I'm just observing the world, it seems like an important feature, so let me build it in." You could talk about spillovers in that form without explaining they were solving this mathematical problem. He wanted increasing returns, because he wanted things to be getting better over time. But he also wanted to preserve competition among many firms.

Returning to the world periodically in search of relevant examples of the phenomena he was describing was not "dumbing down," Romer said. It was a crucial part of the process. "Once you've erected the mathematical machinery and understood how it works, you've got to cut back to the world to see whether you've cut to the essence of it. I often draw a picture for my students of different levels. The highest degree of abstraction is at the top, the closest contact to the world of our senses at the bottom. The theorist follows a trajectory within these bounds. You zoom up, spend some time, and zoom back down again."

To clarify matters, then, he would make a model of specialization with *no* spillovers.

The next problem Romer faced had to do with describing an increasing *variety* of goods. It was in some ways the same problem that had confronted Paul Krugman when he set out to model competition among different kinds of high-tech goods in international trade. And it led directly to the same tool—the Dixit-Stiglitz model of monopolistic competition (and to the rest of the family of related models that had been taught in graduate school). There was, however, a key difference.

Whereas Krugman had taken the array of different goods as fixed, Romer's problem was to describe the new goods' origin, for he wanted a dynamic model of growth. So he reinterpreted the consumption function of the Dixit-Stiglitz model as a production function, to describe a world in which production of final goods depended on a large number of intermediate goods. After all, when you wrote it down, the model of the market for new kinds of film was little different from the market for breakfast cereals already on the supermarket shelves. It simply required a different motivation. (Later he discovered that Wilfred Ethier of the University of Pennsylvania had already done the same thing for a model of trade.)

With a relative handful of equations, Romer wrote a general description of a *cornucopia* turning out a steady succession of new goods. None of the goods would be a perfect substitute for any other. There would be pins. There would be room for all the other kinds of fasteners that could be designed and produced—staples, brads, paper clips, buttons, rivets, bobby pins.

Every firm wanting to enter the marketplace would incur an initial fixed cost to design a new type of fastener—a set of blueprints that could be sent to a machine shop for fabrication. Every firm would then act as a small monopolist, setting the prices of its fasteners well above cost, hoping that there would be a stream of profits sufficient to pay for the design and enter the business in the first place. Many firms would fail, of course, but the resulting equilibrium among those who succeeded would be one in which each of these firms made the zero profit that was the hallmark of a fully competitive industry. If there was something more to do, they would do it.

All this was couched in terms of convexity *and* nonconvexity. True, nonconvex analysis was not attractive pedagogically. "It meant you couldn't just turn the [mathematical] crank" and have unassailable results stream out. It had the advantage, however, of describing a world in which a semiconductor manufacturer might have to invest hundred of millions of dollars in design before it could manufacture a new single chip.

Before long, Romer possessed a model capable of describing in a general way the ongoing process of specialization—of the increasing division of labor. It would be a kind of cornucopia machine, forever spilling out new goods. Whether the setup was literary or mathematical, though, the initial formulation of the problem sounded more like a description of the Yellow Pages of a telephone directory than an economics text. But then, in a certain way the Yellow Pages *were* the point—both of Young's capsule history of the printing industry and of Romer's model of it. There were phone books and newspapers and pulp fiction and church programs, all the other broad array of possible printing tasks, and all the array of machinery and raw materials required to accomplish them. Young's phrase "an increasingly intricate nexus of specialised undertakings" now had a mathematical representation.

This is the model that later would be called neo-Schumpeterian, one that depended on the introduction of new goods to make it work. The new model was far from perfect. There was plenty of creation in it, but no destruction. The old goods never disappeared. The measure of a country was the size of its population, meaning that a big nation like China should grow much faster than a small closed economy. But the basic point was clear: specialization, meaning new goods, and the increasing returns that came with them, was the key to rising output. It was a very big step beyond his dissertation.

Once again, Romer didn't come to the subject of specialization by reading Schumpeter on, say, the differences between a stagecoach and a railway carriage, or a system of canals and a modern automotive highway system, even though Schumpeter had written suggestively about just this. Indeed, only in the late stages of its development had it occurred to Romer that he was himself recapitulating, mathematically, the progression from Alfred Marshall to Edward Chamberlin and Joan Robinson that, earlier in the century, had taken years to unfold in words. Those differences of opinion could be resolved much more rapidly and completely in the concise language of math. His thinking flowed from the mathematical logic of the problem, he said, from the Cass-Koopmans model and "a clean sheet of paper."

THE DECISION TO ADOPT the monopolistic competition approach was no small matter in the extended world of Chicago of the early 1980s. (In this sense Rochester was very much a satellite.) The old guard of the Chicago school still fiercely disapproved of the doctrine. And for a time, Romer recalled, the question of how to proceed was genuinely open in his mind—perfect competition or market power? Chicago or Cambridge? Then he decided that the math he had been working with in Chicago just wouldn't accommodate the facts. "I realized I'd have to give up convexity to talk about the things that interested me." He bade farewell to the conventions of perfect competition and to most of Freshwater economics.

Later he recalled that he might never have managed to reverse himself if not for the guiding presence in Rochester of Lionel McKenzie, the man who had created the university's economics department and who exemplified its style. McKenzie was a courtly exponent of mathematical economics of sufficient stature that, when Stanford needed a theorist to replace the great Kenneth Arrow in the early 1960s, it turned to McKenzie. He declined, preferring to run what was, in effect, a finishing school for topflight research economists. He supervised or taught a succession of students who in due course would become leaders of the profession themselves: José Scheinkman (later of Chicago and Princeton), Jerry Green (of Har-

vard), Hugo Sonnenschein (later president of the University of
Chicago). McKenzie remembers Romer as a man who, like the others, had largely taught himself. His own role, he said, was to provide
the necessary cover for the younger man to complete the investigations culminating in his U-turn. Stop badgering Romer on the
antecedents of his work, the older man told his colleagues: "We don't
want to turn him into a contributor of notes."

JUST SETTING OUT on his career, Romer had more pressing concerns
than debugging a new model. There was, for example, the task of
structuring a paper or two out of his thesis. The technical discussion
of the knife-edge matter—"when apparently reasonable problems
can fail to have a solution"—became the *Econometrica* paper: "Cake-
eating, Chattering and Jumps: Existence Results for Variational
Problems." That was easy enough. Then he boiled down the spillover
approach and submitted a paper called "Increasing Returns and
Long-Run Growth" to the *Journal of Political Economy*. There he ran
into problems.

One referee's report recommended in favor of publication, the
other against. Much the same thing had happened to Paul Krugman
a few years before with his paper on increasing returns and international trade. "It was not malicious," recalls José Scheinkman, who as
editor of the journal recused himself in favor of Jim Heckman. "It
was someone who just didn't understand. Mathematical economics
was somewhere else in those days." The situation was delicate; the
Chicago department, which edited and owned the *JPE* (as Harvard
owned the *Quarterly Journal of Economics*, or *QJE*), bent over back-
wards to avoid the appearance of favoritism, and, normally, mixed
referee reports would give reason to reject. Instead, Heckman sided
with the positive review. "I thought the article should be published,"
he says. And so, in the *JPE* of October 1986 it was. In due course the
spillover paper became known as Romer '86.

The irony was that Romer no longer believed his result. That is, he
no longer considered externalities to offer a promising approach to
capturing the economics of knowledge. So into the published version he slipped a semaphore to signal, as least to careful readers, that

his thinking had changed. "It is now clear that these changes in organization cannot be rigorously treated as technological externalities," he wrote. "Formally, increased specialization opens new markets and introduces new goods. All producers in the industry may benefit from the introduction of these [new] goods, but they are *goods*, not technological externalities" (emphasis added).

And with that sentence, he undermined everything that had gone before.

CHAPTER EIGHTEEN

The Keyboard, the City, and the World

THERE EXISTS AN intellectual snapshot of the state of thought in serious economics on the eve of its transformation. It was taken, naturally enough, at the Meetings, the ones held in Dallas in December 1984. It consists of a slim book that was produced from a session called "Economic History and the Modern Economist." It is a group self-portrait showing where the best men of economics' "greatest generation" stood near the ends of their careers when they gathered in a ballroom of the Dallas Hilton to discuss the relationship of economic theory to history.

Plenty of history is being made in the world in the winter of 1984. No longer are pin factories and Wedgwood china or railroads the interesting news. Apple has marketed a "personal computer," and IBM has made it a household word. Now the computer giant is preparing to introduce its new "Topview" system—a clever idea that would permit users to work on more than one program at once by dividing the screen into separate "windows." One of its vendors, a tiny company named Microsoft, is racing to develop an alternative. The Defense Department has opened its ARPANET computer network to overseas traffic; the new network has been dubbed the Internet. At the insistence of the Justice Department, the Bell telephone monopoly is being broken up. Most of its assets spun off to shareholders, though some of its property (its UNIX computer operating system, for example) is pretty much given away. And in the infant field of biotechnology, news of the discovery of a new chemical tool known as polymerase chain reaction is slowly spreading. It is a technique that permits endless amplification of the slightest bit of DNA. No one yet knows the uses to which it will be put.

A political revolution, too, is under way. China is busily "growing out of the plan"; Guangdong Province, following the example of nearby Hong Kong, is joining the global economy. Ronald Reagan has been reelected president of the United States. The Cold War is entering its climactic phase. There are war fears at the highest levels of governments. In London, KGB agents have been directed to track the spot price offered by blood banks by officials worried that a sharp rise would be a signal that the West was preparing to mount a surprise attack. The American central bank is in the fifth year of an epic battle against world inflation. The power over oil prices of the Organization of Petroleum Exporting Countries (OPEC) is nearly broken. The Third World debt crisis is growing worse.

The distinguished men who have gathered for the session in Dallas are not uninterested in current events, but neither have they come to talk about them—they are concerned chiefly with economics' authority as a science. Many of the foremost students of growth and development of two generations are here. The makers of the Modern program in growth economics are present; so are some of those who feel they have been steamrollered by them. In the session chair is the Nobel laureate W. Arthur Lewis of Princeton University, author of a highly influential model of economic development; among the panelists, representing theory, are his fellow Nobelist Kenneth Arrow and Robert Solow, not yet a laureate. Speaking for history are Paul David and Peter Temin. Donald McCloskey (later Deirdre) and Gavin Wright are the discussants; in the audience are the historical economists W. W. Rostow and Charles Kindleberger. It's a growth economics Who's Who.

Yale's William Parker, who has organized the session, opens with a denunciation of the mathematical turn that economics has taken. As dean of American economic historians, he laments the decline of the sort of historical economics that had flourished in England and Germany and the concomitant rise to world dominion of formal theory and econometrics mainly from the United States. The values that were formerly inculcated—the knowledge of institutions, the social concepts, the moral zeal—have been lost, he says. Before long, economists themselves will have been left behind, "paddling a canoe around cool, mathematical backwaters." Real life—"with its excitement, its turbulence, its freshness, its power"—will have passed them by.

Kenneth Arrow weighs in for the theorists. Economic history is like the history of the natural world as interpreted by geology, he says. The most basic mechanisms of geology are understood by standard chemistry and physics. Virtually all its work now takes place in a lab, where experiments quickly yield understanding. Yet geology is a flourishing subject, Arrow says, because people are interested in particulars. For the same reason economic history is a fount of interesting questions that only economic theory properly applied can answer. For instance, why is health care organized the way it is?

Somewhere in between is Robert Solow. Is something missing from economics? The answer is yes, he says, beginning with a little humility in the form of Damon Runyon's law, to the effect that "nothing between humans goes off at odds of more than three to one." (Runyon is famous as, among other things, the source of the musical play *Guys and Dolls*.) The hard sciences excel at dealing with complex systems, says Solow, because they can isolate, they can experiment, and they can make repeated observations under controlled conditions wherein the forces being studied are not swamped by the noise. The hard sciences are good for topics like the hydrogen atom or the optic nerve. But most topics in economics are far more complex than these. The interplay between social institutions and behavior is crucial. Axiom-based economic science may be doomed to fail because of this complexity, says Solow. He is not prepared to abandon it, but doesn't expect a lot.

When Paul David rises to speak, audience members lean slightly forward in their chairs. David is an economic historian, perhaps the brightest light of the rising generation. No historian has worked harder to master the new wave of formalization, yet David remains an ingenious critic. He understands its limitations, and the subversive nature of the story he is about to tell.

His topic is the lowly typewriter; specifically, what happened as it emerged over several years in the 1870s from a series of machine shops in Milwaukee. The typewriter that David presents is not just a piece of hardware, a bundle of moving parts of varying designs. It is a "complex of production" combining the hardware of differing machines with the "software" of the typists' skills in using them.

When the "Type Writer" was first introduced, an army of clerks and copyists were practicing penmanship. Now stenographers and secretaries would become "typists." But typists would have to learn how to use the new machines before typewriters could be adopted for widespread use.

For a time there were many different typewriter companies, David says, and even many competing keyboard designs. The skills of the operators quickly became a key factor in determining which ones would thrive. A spirited competition developed among rival manufacturers to offer the most popular features. Business colleges and handbook publishers vied to teach typists the latest and most productive touch-typing techniques. Speed-typing contests and other marketing ploys emphasized various selling points. Gradually one keyboard design began to outdistance all others: the now familiar configuration of four rows of keys operating long levers that strike upward.

The curiosity here is the QWERTY arrangement. Why should those letters be placed on the keyboard as they are? Other manufacturers offered other arrangements of the letters on the keyboard that they claimed were better—more logically arranged with respect to the frequency with which the letters were used. But even though it was often claimed (and sometimes demonstrated) that such alternative arrangements facilitated quicker movement of the fingers over the keys, typists entering the workforce preferred to learn the QWERTY system because there were many more such machines in use. Their laboriously acquired touch-typing skills had to be portable, after all. So gradually the QWERTY keyboard became known as "the universal." Its adoption by various manufacturers had created a virtuous circle. The other designs slowly disappeared from use.

This is, of course, a slightly more complicated version of the story of the Pin Factory—of monopolistic competition and increasing returns. The QWERTY design is what we have come to call an "open" standard, as opposed to a proprietary one such as the Windows operating system for personal computers. Nobody owns the rights to it. Anyone is free to adopt it for personal use. But the effect of its increasing adoption is the same, to reinforce the tendency to standardization.

Yet David describes all this to his listeners as if for the first time, and in a certain sense it is. Only a decade earlier Jeff Rohlfs at Bell Labs identified "network externalities" as a key attribute of communications networks. Rohlfs described as "bandwagon effects" the cumulative benefits that consumers enjoyed as a result of others' using the same product or service—or failed to enjoy, since he was writing about AT&T's disastrous "Picturephone" project.

Now, in 1984, Paul David speaks of the "lock-in" of a de facto standard as a result of "system scale economies" (such as the decreasing costs of having a secretary type a letter) and "technical interrelatedness" (later dubbed strategic complementarity) between the "software" of touch-typing techniques to which all those secretaries have become habituated and the hardware of the keyboard itself. Such outcomes were "path-dependent," he says, meaning they could not be easily reversed. QWERTY would flourish, and all other keyboard systems would fail, even if they turned out to be better.

And indeed, just such a better system was shown to exist, said David. An "ideal" keyboard, designed once certain mechanical problems had been solved, placed the letters DHIATENSOR in the home row. This "more sensible" arrangement of the keys permitted typists to spell 70 percent of the words in the English language with the letters in just one row. It seemed to promise faster typing speeds. But by the time it was introduced, in 1893, the QWERTY keyboard was already known as the universal. And when a university professor named August Dvorak tried in the 1940s to market a slightly improved version with the claim that the increased efficiency of the new keyboard would pay for retraining of typists within two weeks, his efforts went nowhere. The QWERTY standard, David asserts, was a case of "market failure"—in this case, failure to halt a takeover by a second-rate system.

It's not that David is unaware of other instances of where the market "doesn't work" or works too well. The Stanford professor is one of the handful of scholars who have kept alive the memory of Allyn Young and his paper "Increasing Returns and Economic Progress." He knows all about the underground history of positive feedback, and understands that his fellow panelists are high priests of the Modern program and won't be impressed by one more story of multiple equilibria, meaning the existence of more than one possible outcome, a "suboptimal" outcome at that, which is the inevitable concomitant of the presence of increasing returns. In fact, David surely understands that the whole apparatus of monopolistic competition was devised fifty years earlier to deal with situations exactly like these. He probably even remembers a key passage in Marshall's *Principles* on multiple equilibria—a footnote to an appendix, no less. Hints were given, Marshall wrote, about the difficulty of applying the equilibrium concept in situations of increasing returns. What about a commodity that, in the beginning, would appeal mainly to the rich? It might occur to someone that ordinary folk would like such an item, if only it could be brought within their price range. New methods would be devised. Other manufacturers would follow suit. And before long, "instead of a few hundreds being sold weekly at so many shillings, tens of thousand are sold for an equal number of pence." The price might jump from one stable equilibrium to another, wrote the eminent economist, at least in theory. Say hello to the Model T Ford!

But David is in a race with a Stanford colleague, Brian Arthur, a race to say what is distinctive about the changes taking place outside the hotel walls. It will be ten more years before people begin to speak of a "new" economy, but already great excitement is in the air. No wonder, therefore, that as he relates his tale, David affects the air of a magician pulling rabbits out of a hat. "I believe there are many more

QWERTY worlds lying out there in the past, on the very edges of the modern economic analyst's tidy universe; worlds we do not yet fully perceive or understand, but whose influence, like that of dark stars, extends nonetheless to shape the visible orbits of our contemporary economic affairs." The implication of increasing returns is much the same for Paul David that it was fifty years before for Alfred Marshall's successor, Pigou—or for the international trade economist Paul Krugman, for that matter. Increasing returns were an open invitation to government intervention. In this case, if the ostensibly sovereign consumer could be locked into an inferior keyboard design by the exertions of a powerful first mover, then the Invisible Hand couldn't be depended on automatically to produce the single best outcome in keyboards or, perhaps, for other things as well. David is clearly thinking of computer software. The door is open to government intervention to somehow improve the result. That was the moral of what Krugman will soon be calling QWERTY-nomics.

Brian Arthur is not Paul David's only rival in this explanation derby. A young graduate student named Ward Hanson has begun lecturing around the Stanford campus on what he describes as technological "orphans" and "bandwagons"—victims and beneficiaries, respectively, of increasing returns. Two sets of young microeconomists on opposite coasts are about to publish formal models of what quickly become known as network externalities—the gains arising from other people's use of similar or compatible products. With the new models of monopolistic competition, Michael Katz and Carl Shapiro (at Princeton) and Joseph Farrell and Garth Saloner (at Berkeley and Stanford) show how the kind of positive feedback effects that David is stressing may dominate outcomes in many markets besides that of typewriters. "Network industries" will eventually include (for instance) telecommunications, computers, banking, broadcasting, airlines, and markets for information. Here is all the more reason for David to press his claim. Though he mentions the term only once in Dallas, "increasing returns" is a phrase on the tip of the modern tongue.

Viewed in retrospect, the controversies of the Dallas meeting have an old-timey flavor, as of something already in the archives. The language is awkward. There is no mention of knowledge or the problem that new goods pose to conventional analysis. The discussion is stilted. The meeting has the character of a last hurrah. Conspicuously missing from the discussion that day in Dallas is any mention of the up-and-coming generation of economists—the kids, now in their late twenties or early thirties, who are making a revolution far away from the Meetings. This is not particularly surprising, for Paul Krugman, Elhanan Helpman, Paul Romer, and the rest are excited and hard at work among themselves. At the Ecole Nationale des Ponts et Chausseés, in France, Jean Tirole has begun writing *The Theory of Industrial Organization*, the book that will put monopolistic competition at the center of microeconomics once and for all. No controversy disturbs the discussion of theory and history in Dallas that day. The panelists are, without exception, members of the older generation, talking among themselves.

Now THE SCENE SHIFTS to England. It is nearly a year later, December 1985. A distinguished lecturer has been called upon to give the Marshall Lectures at Cambridge University. Invited lectures are inevitably somewhat fancy; a thought leader has been called upon to instruct the field. The Marshall lectures, established in 1932, are among the fanciest of all such talks. There is added drama insofar as the economics faculty at Cambridge is sharply divided on the invitation. It is barely twelve months since Paul David gave his talk in Dallas. The claims of the new growth theory are about to be asserted for the first time. But no one in Cambridge knows that yet.

At the age of forty-eight, Robert Lucas has become the most influential economics theorist in the world. He has been a professor at the University of Chicago for a dozen years. His views about the importance of modeling alert and forward-looking human behavior have conquered first the rest of the Chicago department and then most of the rising generation of macroeconomists. Yet the controversy has lingered on, in the form of a sterile and sometimes bitter antagonism between Freshwater and Saltwater economists, as the New Classicals and New Keynesians have come to be known. Lucas has dueled repeatedly with MIT economists, with Robert Solow in particular, over alternative strategies of model building. He is not a high priest of the axiomatic approach, but he is a big user of its tools—of dynamic programming and the Arrow-Debreu infinite-dimensional spreadsheet in particular. He is precisely the sort of theorist whose relevance was doubted in Dallas. In Cambridge, England, his model-building style is actively disparaged.

So in Cambridge, Lucas is entering a charged situation. By most reckonings economics at the thousand-year-old university on the river Cam has been in decline since 1937, when Hicks left for Manchester on the eve of World War II. It still has its stars, including a few world-class mathematical economists. But Cambridge economics is dominated by proud defenders of the old literary tradition. Its saints are Joan Robinson and Nicholas Kaldor, who fought a long rearguard campaign against the North American mathematical tradition. By 1985 its reputation in economics is as something of a backwater, a little like Oxford in the days when Adam Smith was an undergraduate there.

The surprising thing is that Lucas doesn't plan to talk about the studies of money and the business cycles for which he is famous. He has written to his host, the mathematical economist Frank Hahn, offering to reappear for a third hour, in order to discuss this controversial work. But, in a way that reminds friends of when the serious young student sat for his core exam after only a few months in the classroom, Lucas has decided that his Marshall Lectures will be on a topic—economic growth—about which he has not previously published a word.

"We knew we were going to hear something about development, but we didn't have a clue," says Tim Kehoe, who was visiting Cambridge as a young postdoc. The day gets off to a rocky start with an eleven o'clock sherry. David Canning, another young economist who was there, remembers, "I think I was one of the first people to talk to him. I said something as small talk and he thought he was being attacked. And he went ballistic. Tim had to say, 'David is trying to be nice.' He was a bit prickly at that stage."

After an hour or so of social conversation, the audience streams into the auditorium of Lady Mitchell Hall, the incredibly ugly building next to the economics faculty building. Lucas is introduced. He begins to talk, quite nervously at first. Soon it is clear, to at least some of those in the hall, that something fundamental is in the works.

LUCAS WASTES NO TIME setting the stage for his inquiry. The title he has chosen is "On the Mechanics of Economic Development," unusual in that it combines the theorist's quest for mechanism with a concern for a field, economic development, in which theory ordinarily is anathema. Though he does not employ the phrase itself, he immediately makes it clear that his topic is the wealth of nations.

With a few matter-of-fact strokes, Lucas sketches some indicative disparities as they existed in 1980. Among industrial market economies, Switzerland to Ireland, per capita income averages $10,000. Meanwhile, India's is $240, Haiti's $270, and so on. The difference is fortyfold. Since $240 is not enough to sustain life for a year in England, no matter how carefully it is husbanded, the comparison needs to be taken with a grain of salt, Lucas says. Nevertheless, the gap is enormous—and persistent.

Lucas doesn't mention the industrial revolution, either, but that sequence of events clearly is on his mind—whatever constituted that "sequence of events." Some countries have industrial revolutions, or rather participate fully in them, while others don't. "A few centuries ago, some of us moved into a phase of sustained economic growth while others did not, and out of this ill-understood process emerged the unequal world we know today."

Yet why should this inequality be permanent? All the experience of recent years shows that it was possible to close the gap, at least under some circumstances. The "miracles" of Japan and the four Asian "tigers" of South Korea, Taiwan, Hong Kong, and Singapore offer the best demonstration that growth rates can differ. Indeed, growth rates varied greatly from place to place and from time to time. The world's industrial economies grew at an annual average of 3.6 percent for twenty years. Meanwhile, Japan averaged 7.1 percent growth a year, Egypt 3.4 percent, the United States at 2.3 percent, and India 1.4 percent. With rates like these, Lucas observes, Japanese incomes would double every ten years; India would require fifty years to do the same. "I do not see how one can look at figures like these without seeing them as representing *possibilities*," says Lucas. "Is there some action a government of India could take that would lead the Indian economy to grow like Indonesia's or Egypt's? If so, *what* exactly? If not, what is it about 'the nature of India' that makes it so? The consequences for human welfare involved in questions like these are simply staggering: Once one starts to think about them, it is hard to think about anything else."

NEXT COMES A DISCUSSION of economists' chief tool for thinking about such differentials, the reigning model of economic growth—the neoclassical Solow model. This is familiar territory to his Cambridge audience. Many of them resent the Solow model for the way it undercuts the traditional reading of Marx, because the engine of the Solow model is not the capital accumulation that preoccupies most modern-day Marxists but rather the steady advent of new technology. (Marxism has drifted a long way from the "critical history of technology" that the master had in mind!) Admittedly, Solow takes this relentless growth of knowledge as a given. It is not analyzed or explained. His Residual, the portion of growth that cannot be accounted for by the addition of more capital or more labor, is a powerful rhetorical device nonetheless. It has stopped in its tracks a good deal of talk about class warfare. On the other hand, the audience knows that Lucas and Solow have been bitter antagonists for twenty years. Something must be up.

About the *form* of the Solow model, Lucas is nothing but admiring. It exhibits the characteristics that all good models should have, he says. It is compact, consistent with the rest of what we know about economics; it squares with the broad outlines of the history of the United States and the other industrial economies. It has paid off handsomely with certain kinds of understanding, revealing things that other models could not. For example, the idea that tax cuts designed to stimulate savings could have large, sustained effects on growth rates, was highly influential in American politics in the 1980s—the supply-siders and all that. "It is so reasonable, and it may even be true," says Lucas. "But the clear implication of the Solow model is that it is not." This is precisely the kind of experimentation with alternative assumptions that's needed to bolster confidence that the theorist is on the right track, he says.

But it is not taxes that are on Lucas's mind. He wants to talk about the gap between rich and poor. This is the "convergence debate," or the expectation that countries around the world will grow at different rates, with the poor ordinarily growing faster than the rich, until they all enjoy pretty much the same level of income. The convergence hypothesis was introduced to modern economics by the great historian Alexander Gerschenkron in a famous 1952 paper called "Economic Backwardness in Historical Perspective." Talk about convergence, or the lack of it, has been simmering in technical circles at least since Richard Easterlin of the University of Southern California put the question "Why Isn't the Whole World Developed?" in a celebrated presidential address to the Economic History Association in 1981.

Now Lucas asks whether the Solow model is an adequate model of economic development. It is not, he says. In fact, it is a failure, because its chief prediction is precisely that poor countries will grow faster than rich ones in per capita income until wealth is spread smoothly and evenly over the surface of the earth. Yet as the quick comparisons that he cited at the beginning of his talk clearly demonstrate, it hasn't happened, says Lucas. The Solow model seems to apply only to developed countries. Maybe these wealthy nations will converge among themselves. A few Asian nations seem to have made the jump. But most of the rest of the world seems stuck. "I suppose this is why we think of 'growth' and 'development' as distinct fields," says Lucas, "with growth theory defined as those aspects of economic growth we have some understanding of, and development defined as those we don't."

Moreover, he says, if you take the Solow model apart, you can see *why* convergence doesn't occur. It is because of another theoretical anomaly—the one-way traffic in human beings. Across national borders, labor migrates to capital, and not, with rare exceptions, the other way around. In Lucas's hands this is somehow a startling observation. Within nations there is often considerable factor mobility. In the United States, for example, labor moved from the South to the North in the twentieth century for jobs with auto manufacturers; textiles plants moved from New England to the South in the nineteenth century in search of cheaper labor.

But not even during the long era of global colonialism, when the European nations governed global dominions through military power, and when there was relatively little political risk to consider in making such decisions about where to locate, was had there much movement of capital to the low-income countries. Rich countries simply went on growing richer and more highly specialized. Poor people migrate to rich areas, hardly ever the other way around.

BY NOW THE AUDIENCE is thoroughly confused. Lucas is making a familiar point—familiar, at least, to those in Lady Mitchell Hall—that sometimes markets do not work. In fact, it is the same point that Paul David made in 1984 in his lecture about the QWERTY keyboard. The Chicago theorist lecturing in Cambridge has identified a "suboptimal" outcome that is hard to explain on the logic of competition. The failure of convergence to occur, of the gap to narrow, is as much an affront to standard theory as is the possibility that a less efficient keyboard design might triumph. The market does not seem to "work" to produce the expected outcome. Some kind of lock-in is occurring. A certain preoccupation with market failure is to be expected from David, who is, after all, a representative of the tradition of Cambridge, Massachusetts. Coming from Lucas, however, it is a total surprise.

In all other respects, the two differ widely in their methods. Whereas the historian works in English with suggestive parables, the theorist presents models. Whereas David's emphasis is on particular markets, Lucas's approach is definitely macro. Moreover, Lucas began his career as an econometrician. Now he wants data so that his models that can be put on a computer and *run*, so their weak links can be identified. On this one point, though, they seem to be in agreement. Whether the phenomenon in question is the QWERTY keyboard or the global distribution of income, the pattern of lock-in—that the rich should get richer and the poor stay poor—is just the opposite of what the standard model predicts. Each real-world system seems to exhibit increasing returns. As a result, there are multiple equilibria, when there should be just one.

However much Lucas admires Solow as a model builder, it is clear he is disparaging the ability of Solow's model to explain the facts. The Solow model relies on technology to explain growth over time. And among developed nations, at least, it seems to work pretty well to explain differentials, though it fails completely with poorer nations. To bridge the gap, Lucas says he will offer "an alternative engine of economic growth, or at least a complementary one," such as might account for the failure to catch up. He has in mind an old Chicago standby, human capital. But not just human capital as commonly understood, general skill levels, but human capital spillovers. And this, too, takes his audience aback, for it was in Cambridge a hundred years earlier that externalities were identified by Marshall and assigned a central economic role. It is a cheeky Chicagoan indeed who travels to Cambridge in order to lecture his listeners on their significance.

About these spillovers Lucas is somewhat apologetic. It was true that their nature might be hard to grasp, intellectually and empirically. Then again, he says, human capital itself, meaning general skill level, seemed an ethereal concept when first introduced—"at least it did to me." Yet once the idea of human capital had been elucidated and refined by many minds and hands over many years, the idea of the valuable skills possessed by individuals turned out to be a highly useful concept, illuminating (among other things) the choices people make between work and leisure; the level of earnings they attain in the workplace, and the division of responsibilities within families. "After two decades of research applications of human capital theory," says Lucas, "We have learned to 'see' it in a wide variety of phenomena, just as meteorology has taught us to 'see' the advent of a warm front in a bank of clouds or 'feel' it in the mugginess of the air."

Okay, then. Suppose that human capital externalities really do constitute "a powerful unseen force is at work in economic life." (Even the phrasing of Lucas lecture is reminiscent of Paul David's explanation of why things sometimes get stuck—those "dark stars" that shape the visible orbits of contemporary economic affairs.) Suppose that spillovers from people working in close quarters are in fact an "alternative engine of economic growth." How exactly do they work?

AT THIS POINT Lucas begins to build a model. "We want a formalism that will let us think about people's decisions to acquire knowledge," he says.

> Suppose there are N workers in total, with skill levels h ranging from 0 to infinity. Let there be $N(h)$ workers with skill level h, so that $N = N(h)dh$. Suppose a worker with skill h devotes a fraction $u(h)$ of his non-leisure time to current production, and the remaining $1-u(h)$ to human capital accumulation. Then the effective workforce in production—the analogue to $N(t)$ in equation (2)—is the sum $N^e = \int_0^\infty u(h)N(h)hdh$ of the skill-weighted manhours devoted to current production. Thus if output is a function of total capital K and effective labor N^e is $F(K, N^e)$, the hourly wage of a worker at skill h is $F_N(K, N^e)h$ and his total earnings are $F_N(K, N^e)hu(h)$.

This is a standard opening gambit in an execise in model building. But what does all that *mean*? Most of those in his Cambridge audience are as baffled as if he had been speaking Greek. For those not well versed in formal language, and that includes most of his audience this day, $Hu(h)$ indeed! Lucas is preparing to define and isolate the aggregate effect of whatever spillovers may exist as a function of the average level of skill. "We know from ordinary experience," he says, that group interactions sometimes are central to individual productivity. These involve groups larger than the immediate family and smaller than the human race as a whole; human capital accumulation is a *social activity* involving groups of people "in a way that has no counterpart in the accumulation of physical capital." Human capital is at least partly about rubbing elbows. So what are the mechanics? What's the difference between internal and external effects?

It is in fact Romer's model of the increasing returns arising from spillovers that Lucas is using. He gives his student full credit. He locates the young man's work in the illustrious tradition extending back to Kenneth Arrow and Hirofumi Uzawa in the mid-1960s. That makes Romer's sudden appearance in the middle of the "convergence" debate all the more remarkable. Remember, this is December 1985. Romer is three years out of school, almost completely unknown to the profession. The appearance of his first article, in the 1986 *JPE*, is still some months in the future.

Lucas has greatly simplified the mathematics of the dissertation, trimming away the knife-edge problem, adopting a simpler, more robust formulation, almost in the accessible style of Solow. Instead of differential equations and phase planes, there is algebra.

But Lucas has made one important change. Romer's concept of accumulating "knowledge" has been relabeled "human capital externalities." Yet in just three paragraphs of mathematical exposition, Lucas has replaced Solow's concept of exogenous technology, increasing automatically and inexorably, year after year as $A(t)$, with a very different concept: H^Y, designating human capital spillovers, or the uncompensated influences that people have on the productivity of others. He even assigns a value to the effect of these spillovers on U.S. production, guesstimating that it might be 0.4, meaning that output is nearly half as much again as it would be without spillovers. That 40 percent is meant to represent how much more productive individuals have become than they would be otherwise, thanks to their membership in companies, unions, universities—teams of all sorts.

About eliminating knowledge from his calculations, at least as a commodity apart of its human instantiation, Lucas makes scant apology. There cannot be just one correct answer as to the extent of the spillovers, he says. Some knowledge remains relatively closely held for decades. Other discoveries become common property almost immediately—the development of a new mathematical result, for example. So his model features an infinitely lived family as a typical agent, passing down its secrets from one generation to the next, as well as technology modeled in Solow fashion, as an exogenous force.

This is not quite the Pin Factory, but it is getting closer. Lucas has backed up to the subject of increasing returns. This is, after all, why externalities were invented. For the next forty minutes he conducts a clinic. He introduces a second model to consider how increasing returns implied by human capital externalities might affect international trade. This one has two goods instead of just one: he calls them computers and potatoes. His idea is to open up the original model to capture its possibilities for international trade. Remember, Lucas is interested in the effects of human capital spillovers on the differences in the wealth of nations. Isn't trade the likeliest mechanism by which industrial revolutions can spread from place to place?

In Lucas's second model a nation that learns to produce computers more and more cheaply can substitute in its favor, consuming more calculations and fewer potatoes. This is the familiar learning curve, in which positive feedback takes over and undermines the principle of comparative advantage. But instead of providing a mechanism for catch-up, as Lucas hoped, his learning-curve model implies the reverse. Rich countries capture the advantages of their spillovers. The poor countries export their brightest people to the developed countries and otherwise remain poor. "Under these dynamics, then, an economy beginning with low levels of human and physical capital will remain permanently below a better endowed economy." The first model suggests a subsidy to schooling. The second points toward infant industry protection. Lucas is apologetic. Picking winners for the government to subsidize is easy in the model. Says Lucas, "If only it were so in reality!"

Now Lucas has taken his listeners all the way back to Pigou, just as Paul David did in Dallas the year before. An interest in aggressive trade policy is in the air in the mid-1980s, as it was in the 1920s. It was downright salacious to bring up the Cambridge professor whose elaboration of the Marshallian "laws of return" put industrial policy on policy makers' agenda in the 1920s. But, even so, Lucas's highly technical talk about how competition might fail to produce the expected convergence among nations, because of the unobserved force that he ascribed to human capital spillovers, might have been pretty completely ignored—except for the way that he ended his talk.

Without some way to *measure* the supposed external effects, it hardly matters what they are called, says Lucas. The force they represent will remain mysterious. "If these features of behavior were all of the observable consequences of the idea of human capital, then I think it would make little difference if we simply renamed this force, say, the Protestant ethic or the Spirit of History or just 'factor X.'" Spillovers will remain what they were for Marshall, an ineffable "something in the air." Then again, Lucas continues, a little in the manner of Detective Columbo, perhaps there is a way to "see" those spillovers, after all.

What about big-city rents?

THE MODERN CITY is a puzzle for economists, says Lucas. According to the standard economic model, it should not exist. It "is like the nucleus of an atom: If we postulate only the usual list of economic forces, cities should fly apart. . . . A city is simply a collection of factors of production—capital, people and land—and land is always far cheaper outside cities than inside." Yet people don't spread themselves out evenly over the landscape. They throng to central cities, with their tall buildings and narrow streets. Yes, people like to live near shopping, and shops need to be located near their customers, "but circular considerations of this kind explain only shopping centers, not cities." So what holds a city together? Why do people want to live cheek by jowl?

For his expert, Lucas turns not to another economist but to a shrewd describer of cities in the real world—to the author-activist Jane Jacobs. Her *Death and Life of Great American Cities* in 1961 was immensely successful as a tract against planning and large-scale "urban renewal." But it was not taken seriously by economists. So in 1969 in the *Economy of Cities*, she set out to explain how they worked. The book, Lucas says, "seems to me mainly and convincingly concerned (though she does not use this term) with the external effects of human capital."

The very definition of a city, says Jacobs, is a settlement that generates its own growth. People in cities proceed by adding new work to old. In a chapter on how new work begins, there is a charming story of the development of the bra. The dressmaker Ida Rosenthal was dissatisfied with the way her dresses hung on her customers, over their various corsets, chemises, and ferris waists. She experimented with improvements and at one point invented the first brassiere. For a time she gave away a free brassiere with each new dress. Fairly quickly, though, she abandoned dressmaking altogether in favor of going into business to manufacture and distribute brassieres themselves. The secret of a city's success in creating new work, is the extensive cross-fertilization that takes place in its various neighborhoods, according to Jacob. The garment district of New York City, where Ida Rosenthal invented the bra, is a warren of designers and manufacturers, peering over each other's shoulders, anticipating each other's designs, solving problems, and creating new work. So is its financial district, its diamond district, its advertising district, its publishing district, and so on. Lucas observes that the neighborhoods that Jacobs describes with such affection are as much intellectual centers in their own ways as are the city's universities: Columbia, say, or NYU. The ideas in each place are different, but the process is highly similar. "To an outsider, it even *looks* the same," says Lucas: "A collection of people doing pretty much the same thing, each emphasizing his own originality and uniqueness." In other words, Jacobs is saying, smart people throng to a city because that's where the talent is.

What Lucas adds to Jacobs's account is the disarmingly simple observation that cities are more expensive than other places. People pay money, lots of it, for the privilege of living in Manhattan. Price is only a fleeting and oblique consideration for Jacobs. For Lucas it is absolutely central. If people pay higher prices, it must be because they think they will derive some advantage for being in the center in the city.

This consideration may prove to be the yardstick that enables economists to "see" human capital externalities. If spillovers are indeed the invisible force that binds cities together, as if they were the nucleus of an atom, then land rents should provide an indirect measure of this force, he says, in much the same way that differential earnings have come to be seen as a measure of the productive effects of internalized social capital. Perhaps someday we will "see" spillovers in a rent gradient as reliably as an approaching warm front can be inferred from a bank of clouds. "What can people be paying Manhattan or downtown Chicago rents *for*, if not for being near other people?" asks Lucas.

And with that, more or less, he is done.

FROM THE AUDIENCE there is stony silence. The leftists are scandalized by the mathematical sortie into the development economics that they think of as definitely being *their* turf. The Keynesians are infuriated by what they consider to be an attack on Solow. Lucas's approach seems completely at odds with the discourse to which nearly everyone in the hall has been accustomed. The faculty, polite in the lecture room, turn vicious among themselves in the coffee room. Lucas goes off for a bunch of beers. Tim Kehoe and David Canning, the young postdocs, are among the few who like what they have heard—but even they aren't entirely sure. "When I heard Romer, I knew it at once," recalled Canning many years later. "I'm not going to say with Lucas I recognized it. Still, the guy was doing what I'd like to do. He was saying, 'This is important,' taking fairly standard things, twisting them around in a new way, getting a new take to see what direction it might be interesting to go."

It would take nearly three years for "On the Mechanics of Economic Development" to find a home in print. The paper was too long for most economic journals. Explication is not a common form. Yet Lucas's Marshall Lectures now become the provocation by which a great deal of economics is gradually transformed. It emphasizes different facts, poses different questions. Before long it has changed the fundamental focus of economics, taking the emphasis off business cycles and putting it on growth. The peroration of its introductory section ("The consequences for human welfare involved in questions like these are simply staggering: Once one starts to think about them, it is hard to think of anything else") will become the most frequently quoted passage since Keynes wrote that "the ideas of economists and political philosophers . . . are more powerful than is commonly understood." Moreover, "Mechanics" seems to be offering the torch to the next generation, to Krugman and Romer and the others; if not exactly passing it, then at least holding it out, challenging the youngsters to wrestle for its possession. So among macroeconomists, at least among the young ones, the preprint of Lucas's lectures passed rapidly from hand to hand.

Read twenty years later, the address is startlingly ambiguous. Lucas has given an account of lock-in quite different from Paul David's. Yet exactly what it is that is giving rise to the differences between rich and poor nations, between city and country, is not yet clear—nor is it yet obvious what, if anything, these mechanics have in common with the story of the QWERTY keyboard. Was it positive feedback? Were there barriers of some kind? For whatever reason, there is lock-in; things become *stuck*. The aggregate case is awfully complicated. But the example of the city, with its high-rent sky-scraper district, takes what otherwise would be an abstruse quarrel among professional economists and transplants it to the realm of universal experience and common sense.

When Paul David broached the question of lock-in stemming from increasing returns in terms of typewriter keyboards, it was no more than distant thunder. But with his modern mathematics Lucas has forcefully injected the riddle of positive feedback into the central problem of the day—the rapid growth of some nations and relative stagnation of others.

Those who read "On the Mechanics of Economic Development" carefully knew that *something* had changed that day in Lady Mitchell Hall—that economics itself had somehow swung upon its hinge. The transformation seemed to have to do with increasing returns. But at the end of 1985 it was clear only that Lucas had picked a fight with Solow, an indisputably great scholar who inexplicably hadn't yet received his Nobel Prize. Could Solow's recognition somehow now be imperiled by what Lucas had to say? That possibility, ridiculous though it was, merely served to inflame the passions. At that point perhaps only Paul Romer thoroughly understood that his old teacher had picked a fight not just with Solow but with Romer too.

CHAPTER NINETEEN

Recombinations

LUCAS'S "MECHANICS" LECTURES caught the profession by surprise. His argument enraged some economists and startled or puzzled others. It was his first word on the subject of growth. It seemed to have come completely out of the blue. And even though his interest in the possibility of market failure seemed curiously in tune with fifty years of the Keynesian tradition, it was unfamiliar enough when expressed in the vernacular of Freshwater economics that the lectures at first caused more consternation than anything else, and in most quarters they were studiously ignored. A few young researchers, however, were galvanized into immediate action.

The notion that trade and migration must be strongly linked to economic growth was hardly new. Nor was the insight that cities must be central to economic progress. Perhaps the real news from Lucas's lectures was his identification of lock-in as a potentially serious puzzle. It was one thing when Paul David described positive feedback in terms of a typewriter keyboard. Now Chicago's leading economist invoked spillovers to call into doubt the surefire dependability of the Invisible Hand. ("It was like the conversion of Paul for the Christians," said David Canning.) Was there a trick up his sleeve? Meanwhile, the relatively easy-to-use mathematical restatement of Romer's model offered the least conservative among his readers a chance to investigate a whole range of topics involving positive feed-back that had gone mostly unexamined for a century.

So in the first few months of 1986, a series of recombinations occurred, as a handful of researchers committed themselves to new lines of work, pursuing new insights across old boundaries. It was as if mapping parties were landing at scattered locations on a large and unfamiliar continent—the continent of increasing returns. Researchers in very different fields took their bearings and set out to explore.

AFTER CAMBRIDGE, Lucas continued his trip, flying to Tel Aviv, to present his new ideas about human capital spillovers in a series of seminars. Remarkably, for someone who was in the process of reori-enting economics to the differences among the nations of the world, it was the first time he had ever traveled abroad. A friend, Asaf Razin, told him about a paper by Paul Krugman on increasing returns and trade that had been making the rounds. One look was sufficient to persuade Lucas that Krugman was investigating more or less the same problem, albeit from a slightly different perspective, and had anticipated him. So Lucas gave credit for the two-sector model he had developed to Krugman instead, adding a prominent citation to "Mechanics."

On the surface the two papers could hardly have been more differ-ent. Krugman's sounded like more of a policy brief than a contribu-tion to mainstream economic research. With a customary flourish, he called it "The Narrow Moving Band, the Dutch Disease and the Com-petitive Consequences of Mrs. Thatcher: Notes on Trade in the Pres-ence of Dynamic Scale Economies." He illustrated its applicability to situations of Japan, the Netherlands, and the United Kingdom.

At its heart was a model in which entire countries got ahead on the basis of manufacturing specialties usually incorporated only at the level of the firm—"the learning curve," he called it, following Arrow. The spillovers here arose simply from the history of a partic-ular neighborhood, rather that from increasing returns of monopo-listic competition of the sort that had characterized Krugman's work in trade. They were the result of Marshallian spillovers, in other words. The broad result was thus the same as in Lucas's potatoes-and-computers model. Some countries got ahead and stayed there. Others fell behind. Convergence failed. Krugman's paper was published in the *Journal of Development Economics* in 1987.

There could have been few greater surprises than to find Lucas making common cause with an apostle of the new monopolistic competition, even though the particular "Moving Band" paper he was citing depended instead on spillovers from otherwise perfect competition for its increasing returns. Within a couple of years Lucas would go further. Praising the codification of the new work on monopolistic competition on which Helpman and Krugman had collaborated, *Market Structure and Foreign Trade*, he explained his reasons.

David Ricardo's formalization of the principle of comparative advantage had worked well through successive elaborations for 150 years, according to Lucas. And the resource-based model still accounted for much of world trade. "Wine is still moving from Portugal to England and not the other way around. But why are Volkswagens moving from Germany to Italy and Fiats from Italy to Germany?"

The answer, Lucas said, seemed to lead back to Adam Smith's ideas on specialization, increasing returns and market size. But until the first models appeared in which it was possible actually to calculate equilibria in the presence of increasing returns—to square the Pin Factory with the Invisible Hand—Smith's ideas, like Chamberlin's monopolistic competition doctrine, remained the source of various "rules of thumb," rather than a viable analytical framework for dealing with trade.

Now, thanks especially to the appearance of the Dixit-Stigliz model, with its variety-loving representative consumer, it was possible to capture the benefits of specialization and thus to pursue a rigorous theory of monopolistically competitive industry. That was what the "new international economics" was all about. Most of the signs still suggested that free trade was beneficial to consumers. But there were some surprising implications, too. And "once one moves away from competitive assumptions welfare questions involve complicated, second-best balancing of different kinds of distortions."

How to go about such balancing? Helpman and Krugman had shown *how* and *why* it all depends, and what could be done to make it simpler. Such tractability was all.

If the youthful Krugman was pleased by the recognition in early 1986 of the novelty of his results by the leading figures of the Chicago school, there is no record of it. He was busy tidying up an address on new trade theory for an address to the Fifth World Conference of the Econometric Society in 1987. The new trade theory "might never be tied up in as neat a package" as the old, he said. But increasing returns were here to stay.

Meanwhile, Lucas himself was unsatisfied with his model—for precisely the reason that convergence failed to occur. Years later, he said, "I think, everyone thinks that trade is the key way to joining the industrial revolution, that the failures are the countries that cut themselves off, like the communists, the Latin Americans, the countries that follow a strategy of import substitution, like India." Rapid innovation was taking place elsewhere, and they missed out. The Asian nations that traded with the more advanced countries did well. Shouldn't it be possible to do some trade models that illuminate how that works? "Well, I didn't pull that off for that section [of my lectures]. In my model trade has the opposite effect. It just widens the gap. If you're trying to figure out why trade helps less-developed countries catch up, that model doesn't contribute anything."

The link between trade and growth went unexplored. Krugman didn't take up the growth chase. Neither did anybody else on the faculty at MIT—at least not immediately. Not until the autumn of 1987, nearly two years after Lucas's Cambridge lectures, did Assistant Professors Philippe Aghion and Peter Howitt begin an investigation of growth itself, not trade—just about the time Robert Solow's Nobel award was announced. In the interim, however, an MIT graduate student had signed on to the new work. A young Russian émigré named Andrei Shleifer had used a Romer-style spillover model in his 1986 thesis, showing how firms might time the introduction of new products to coincide with the business cycle, in order to boost share prices. For a time it was Shleifer who provided a crucial link between Cambridge and Chicago—a striking example of the interesting phenomenon in science in which the young, ostensibly those lowest on the totem pole, often play a critical role.

In Chicago faculty and students excitedly debated the appearance of Romer's paper in the *JPE*. In the autumn of 1986 Gary Becker described the department—indeed, all of economics—as unexpectedly being engaged in a "reexamination of specialization and the gains from trade along the entire spectrum" of economic activities, from the most intimate familial matters to the most complex postindustrial economies. Among the most excited were three bright young economists so inseparable in their published work that they were known as the trio. The trio consisted of Shleifer, Kevin Murphy, and Robert Vishny.

Shleifer was the most exotic figure of the three. He was born in 1961 in the Soviet Union. Both parents were engineers; they left the USSR in1976 on one of the first Jackson-Vanik visas with help from the Hebrew Immigrant Aid Society and, after five months in Italy, entered the United States and settled in Rochester, New York. (Shleifer was, he says, typical of the Jewish scientific elite, very good at blackboard science and math, "the kinds of things you can carry around in your head.") A Harvard College recruiter picked him out of an inner-city high school. He was off to Cambridge on scholarship with, he says, little more than the English he had learned from *Charlie's Angels*.

At one point in his sophomore year, Shleifer came to Larry Summers, then an assistant professor at MIT, to apprise him of a series of problems with his mathematics. It was love at first sight. "While characteristically unimpressed by the argument that his work contained flaws, Larry was sufficiently impressed to hire Andrei as his research assistant," according to Olivier Blanchard. Summers and Shleifer have been fast friends ever since. After college Shleifer moved on to graduate school at MIT. At one point, he visited Chicago for a few months; there he learned enough of the new mathematics of increasing returns to build "implementation cycles" into a model of the business cycle for a thesis. After a year teaching at Princeton, he was hired by Chicago in 1987.

Hardly less interesting was Kevin M. Murphy. He enrolled at Chicago as a graduate student in economics in 1982, not long after Shleifer left. Having been briefly a manager in a grocery store after college, Murphy took up economics at UCLA after deciding it would be more interesting than the supermarket life. A familiar story has him taking the graduate price theory course there, a feature of which was ritual humiliation of students by Socratic method at the hands of Armen Alchian, UCLA's near-substitute for Milton Friedman. Called upon, Murphy effortlessly kept pace with the professor. Unable to leave him behind, Alchian asserted that the student must have taken the class before. Murphy denied it. Alchian: Did too! Murphy: Did not!! Murphy got his Ph.D. in 1986 and immediately began teaching in Chicago's business school.

The third member of the trio was Robert Vishny. He was more conventional in all respects but one. He was an unusually canny investor, and the money management firm of which he was a cofounder (with Shleifer and Josef Lakonishok of the University of Illinois) has grown steadily over the years. Vishny arrived in Hyde Park in 1985 after graduating from MIT a year ahead of Shleifer. When Shleifer returned to Chicago from Princeton in 1987, he, Vishny, and Murphy became enthusiastic collaborators. Their famous first paper provided a striking illustration of the power of the new models of increasing returns to illuminate matters previously controversial.

In "Industrialization and the Big Push," the three young economists set out to show how government probably could rely on spillovers to foment economic growth. The "Big Push" idea had a long history in practice. Lenin's New Economic Policy of the 1920s, for example, was based on the conviction that the massive investment in basic industries such as electricity and steel would by itself permit Soviet Russia to break with its agricultural past.

In 1943 the Hungarian economist Paul Rosenstein-Rodin, working in wartime London, gave the strategy its name. (He was motivated partly by his reading of Allyn Young.) A successful big push might work in any underdeveloped country. It would have to get some people off the farm and into the cities, and then into the schools. It would have to beef up urban infrastructure as well. This sort of transition was expensive. Employers couldn't be expected to finance education, because they wouldn't be able to capture the return on their investment (the old problem of appropriability). They couldn't be counted on to improve infrastructure, because of all the free riders that indivisible benefits would create. Only government could be expected to have deep enough pockets to bear the large fixed costs, and enough power to force others to comply. Positive feedback would do the rest.

But, in the mainstream of the profession, the Hungarian's paper was ignored. Remember, economics in 1943 was embarking on a big push of its own—into formalization. Like Allyn Young's "Increasing Returns and Economic Progress" fifteen years before, Rosenstein-Rodin's "Big Push" paper attracted a great deal of attention. Indeed, it helped create a clear division between neoclassical economists, working on industrial economies, and other economists who worked on the problems of less-developed states. Among the latter the big-push model occasioned all kinds of arguments about various kinds of coordinated investment strategies designed to get things moving. But neoclassical economists, schooled in the mathematics of perfect competition and constant returns, failed to see that there could be any such thing as a multiple-equilibrium "underdevelopment trap." Mainstream economists concentrated instead on "investment gaps" or identified pools of surplus labor but otherwise ignored education and infrastructure. They built models with the tools they already had.

But now, in 1987, the mechanism underlying the sort of positive feedback that Lenin had envisaged had been rendered tractable by the newly stripped-down Romer model. Suddenly increasing returns were respectable again. It may have helped that Shleifer was a Soviet emigrant himself. In any event, the three young professors at the University of Chicago put together a series of models designed to show how a program such as Lenin's big push could work, at least in theory—how a nation might switch from a system of cottage production to an industrial system in the space of a relatively short time. Government could justify its intervention because spillovers would pay back the investment many times over. Such places might be not only permissible but even required. (Of course, nothing said that *only* the government could create a big push. Such an analysis might explain the mechanism at the heart of Henry Ford's celebrated offer in 1914 to pay his workers $5 a day, or something like $1,200 a year. Pay the automotive workers enough to buy the goods of other workers—shoemakers, bakers, candlestick makers—and soon enough these others, too, might earn $5 a day. And before long everybody would earn enough to be able to buy a car, because many more cars could be sold to the broader market, at prices eventually falling to barely more than $300 apiece—a textbook example of a virtuous circle that previously had been impossible to pin down analytically.)

This was exciting stuff. Increasing returns had long been the preserve of literary economists. Now young formalists were thronging to the topic, thanks to the appearance of the new mathematical tool. The "Big Push" paper, published in the *Journal of Political Economy* in 1989, was its first big hit (though by now Romer himself had moved well beyond the 1986 paper on which it was based). It was all the more striking to find conservative Chicago economists making the same kind of case for government intervention that Krugman and the new trade theorists had been making at MIT. (As Romer had discovered for himself, logic and evidence possess powers that sometimes trump the wishes of those who use them.) The point was not lost. More and more bright young people began to take an interest in the new economics of increasing returns.*

FOR ROMER a new problem had arisen. He had to differentiate his own views from those of his celebrated teacher. For a time before the Marshall Lectures, Romer had worried that he might be brushed aside altogether. The Lucas paper was circulating in draft through-

---

* It was the contrast between the trio's success in light of Rosenstein-Rodin's frustration that provided Krugman with the illustration for his parable about the temporary hollowing-out of the map of Africa.

out 1985, and Romer's increasing-returns paper hadn't yet been accepted by the *JPE*. He needn't have worried. Lucas was generous in his formal citations and informal comments. ("Paul was a student, and the one thing you never do is take credit for something a student has done.") Heckman had insisted that the paper be published.

Yet the fact remained that Lucas had taken Romer's "knowledge" variable and relabeled it human capital, thus considerably obscuring the case that Romer was trying to make. Moreover, Romer had changed his mind about the best method by which to make it, discarding the assumption of perfect competition for the new models of monopolistic competition. So even though Romer '86 was in mailboxes, the disclaimer he had inserted ("they are goods, not technological externalities") was clearly not enough. Romer was being identified with the Chicago Freshwater tradition at the very moment that in fact he resorted to Saltwater methods. How to spell out to others the reasons for his change of heart, starting with Lucas himself?

Though teaching in Rochester, Romer was a frequent visitor to Chicago in those days. Excitement boiled about the topic of increasing returns. At a certain point the argument became a conversation about what went on not in a city but in a single academic department. The framework had been introduced by Lucas himself in his lectures when he said, "Most of what we know we learn from other people. We pay tuition to a few of these teachers, either directly or indirectly by accepting lower pay so that we can hang around them, but most of it we get for free, and often in ways that are mutual— without a distinction between student and teacher."

To which Romer now replied in effect, you only *think* you're getting it free. Informal trading in the form of "relationships" more nearly described the most important interactions that took place in a department—lunch dates, office conversations, collaborations, recommendations, and the like. Certainly it was true that workshop and classroom discussions and the frequent conversations at the common lunch table generated plenty of authentic spillovers. And if you watched the corridors, you could see who was lunching with whom—at least that much was free. But how much more would you gain from being part of the private conversations at lunch?

What really was at work in the department (and nearly every-where else in the world), argued Romer, was a system of selectively doing business with one another—a system that could be described better as monopolistic competition than as an anonymous, friction-less exchange. Each teacher, each student sought to "differentiate his product" in the labor markets, to establish a claim to "a special some-thing extra," in order to trade with others on more favorable terms (to collect a rent). To be a little smarter, a little more widely read, a little more relentless, a little more cooperative—something, any-thing, to give the possessor an identity and an edge. Sometimes nothing more complicated than good will often was the currency here. More often it was the expectation of indefinite future gain. In his novel *The Bonfire of the Vanities*, Tom Wolfe describes the "favor bank"—an informal trading and accounting system operating over many years, sometimes on as tight a basis as favorable book reviews and wedding presents, at other times as diffuse as simple good will ("I knew your father"). "A deposit in the favor bank is not a *quid pro quo*," Wolfe wrote. "It's saving up for a rainy day."

This may have seemed to Lucas too mercenary a view of what goes on between human beings. He once said, "In my house we don't use words like 'marginal' every day. I don't find the language of econom-ics to be useful to think about individual decision problems. I also don't use economic principles at home. I try to use family loyalty or an exchange system; you help me, I'll help you." As in the family, so in the department: "[T]he benefits of colleagues from whom we hope to learn are tangible enough to lead us to spend a considerable fraction of our time fighting over who they shall be, and another fraction traveling to talk with those we wish we could have as col-leagues but cannot," Lucas had written. This kind of effect—he insisted it was external to the transaction—was common to all the arts and sciences, the "creative professions" in particular, Lucas said. Knowledge was something that could be accumulated essentially for free, just from being around dense clouds of educated persons.

Even though the ubiquity of less intense versions of the Lucas family favor bank was exactly the point he was striving to make, Romer's homily didn't resolve the argument, and when Lucas gave a lecture in another important series, this one at Northwestern University, in the spring of 1987, there were signs he was digging in to defend his position. Human capital spillovers would be enough to explain what went on.

ALL THAT SUMMER of 1986 Romer worked on a model of specialization and differentiation in the sense that Allyn Young had described it in 1928—"one kind of work leading to another," as Jane Jacobs put it forty years later. Was it spillovers that drew people to the cities? Or the opportunity to specialize? Or both? Romer solved the problem of separating himself from Lucas by devising a model in which economic growth depended *only* on the appearance of new goods to generate growth. That way, eventually, he could force the issue, or so he hoped.

He took time to search for lines of work parallel to his own. He cited Wilfred Ethier for the production function at which he had independently arrived. He cited Kenneth Judd for his work on patents at Chicago. There were serious distractions. After four years as state treasurer, Romer's father was running for governor of Colorado. He fought off the itch to work in the campaign.

In December 1986 Romer circulated two versions of his new model. The first, which went out as a working paper of the Rochester economics department, noted the links to Allyn Young and elaborated on the history of the treatment of increasing returns. Its contents were incorporated in bits and pieces in subsequent papers.

The second, a telegraphic version of the model itself, Romer presented at the Meetings in New Orleans in late December, on a program with Robert Lucas and Edward Prescott. The session concerned the effect of organizational arrangements on growth. The advantage was that the papers would be published in the *Proceedings*—Romer could officially join the monopolistic competition camp quickly, without a lot of complicated refereeing.

When "Growth Based on Increasing Return Due to Specialization" appeared five months later, in the May 1987 *AER*, it was scarcely noticed. It was too short. There was very little exposition of the math, because of the requirement that all such papers from the sessions be abbreviated. There was little attempt to relate the paper to what had gone before. "I don't think that paper influenced people very much," Romer remembers. Elsewhere that winter, though, there was plenty of excitement.

ABOUT THE SAME TIME as those meeting in New Orleans, a young Princeton professor name Gene Grossman went to Tel Aviv to see Elhanan Helpman. Grossman had tried to visit in 1982, but Helpman had been called up by the army during the crisis in Lebanon. Now he arrived in December 1986. The time was more auspicious.

Like other trade economists of his generation, Grossman had operated to some extent in the shadow of the more flamboyant Paul Krugman. He arrived at Yale the year Krugman was a senior at MIT the year Krugman left; and he had followed him into international economics, writing a well-received paper on strategic trade. He had attended the hotly competitive Bronx High School of Science: he possessed self-confidence bordering on the serene. Princeton gave Grossman tenure at the tender age of twenty-nine, only five years out of school. He married a fellow MIT economist, Jean Baldwin, whose father and brother were economists as well.

By now Helpman's partnership with Krugman was ending. Their second book, *Trade Policy and Market Structure*, would not be the ringing success that the first monograph had been. For whatever reason, Krugman was drifting off. When Grossman told Helpman that he was thinking of trying to put technology into the Ricardo model, the older man grinned and pulled out a drawerful of notes. And when Grossman returned to Princeton in early 1987, he was full of excitement. Avinash Dixit recalls, "I knew he had found the problem that would make his name."

CHAPTER TWENTY

Crazy Explanations

HAD IT APPEARED on its own, Romer's 1986 paper on growth through spillovers might have been ignored by all but the most mathematical few. The little paper in which he reversed himself in 1987, rejecting spillovers for specialization, was even more obscure. Who cared that a young rocket scientist in Rochester had changed his mind about a modeling convention? The effect of the Lucas lectures, however, was to call Romer to the attention of a much wider circle of economists. This newfound fame brought him an invitation to present a paper to the macroeconomics conference of the National Bureau of Economic Research, at a two-day meeting in Cambridge, Massachusetts, in March 1987.

The NBER was the center ring of policy-oriented economics in the industrial democracies, drawing the brightest young researchers from universities throughout the United States and around the world. The meeting was designed to showcase annually the most promising new work. In Colorado, Romer's father had been elected governor. The temptation to be relevant was very great.

There were big questions in the newspapers in those days. Mainly these had to do with the practical aftermath of the Reagan revolution: unemployment, exchange-rate fluctuations, the economic significance of budget deficits, north-south relations. But in 1987 the overarching riddle remained the productivity slowdown in the United States. So why not try to say something about it? After all, Romer's underlying point was that technical change was very much an economic phenomenon. What better way to demonstrate why this mattered than to show how his model, too, could be put to work in the growth-accounting tradition that had grown out of the Solow model?

To make to make his topic interesting to the Bureau audience, Romer therefore left the world of straightforward theorizing, as symbolized by the Invisible Hand and the Pin Factory. Instead, he applied his framework econometrically to some new data in such a way as to emphasize his differences with Solow. He called his paper "Crazy Explanations for the Productivity Slowdown." And with it Romer plunged headlong into the convergence debate about differing rates of economic growth among nations. The result, unfortunately, was to help send off a generation of young economists on what amounted to a wild-goose chase.

ROMER'S TITLE was meant to convey the novelty of his approach (and perhaps a little sangfroid as well; remember, he had nearly become a physicist). All the conventionally sensible ideas about the slowdown had already been tried and found wanting, Romer said. How about thinking outside the usual box? In a famous lecture, Wolfgang Pauli had attempted to solve all the outstanding problems in particle physics with a single equation. After Pauli had finished his talk, the great Danish physicist Niels Bohr had gently deflated his proposal, saying, "Herr Professor, we are all agreed that your theory is crazy. However, we are not convinced that it is crazy enough to be right. . . ."

What might constitute a theory crazy enough to be right for economics in 1987? Romer wanted to show that the very framework for growth accounting that arose from the Solow model ruled out the most interesting possibilities. Lagging productivity might stem from the sheer numbers of the postwar baby boom, Romer argued. Perhaps a glut of people had slowed capital investment and therefore the pace of technical change. And maybe situations in which relatively *fewer* people were available for work might force businesses to invent new machinery and thus stimulate more productive investments.

The possibility of a connection between population and the rate of new invention was hardly new. As Romer wrote, a dearth of labor had been the standard explanation for differences in British and American productivity in the nineteenth century. Plentiful land in the United States was thought to have raised wages in the United States relative to those in Britain. Higher wages increased the demand for labor-saving inventions. Ester Boserup, a Danish economist working for the United Nations, wrote books in 1965 and 1981 turning Malthus on his head, arguing that population pressure was the driving force behind technological progress. Romer wanted to show that all kinds of choices made in the public and private sectors—everything from education policy and trade regimes to systems of intellectual property rights—were likely to have a significant effect on national growth rates, too.

But within the framework of an exogenous growth model, the effect of a surplus of labor on technological change could not be addressed. No matter what was happening to the growth of the population, or to the rate of accumulation of capital (these, of course, could be investigated far into the night), the rate of increase of new knowledge would not be affected, since it was exogenous, determined by forces outside the model. It would continue to emanate, like radio broadcasts, from the nation's universities year after year. And since productivity depended on new knowledge more than on anything else, output wouldn't increase much no matter how quickly capital was accumulated.

As usual, Romer chose an example to illustrate his point—in this case, a story about horseshoes. Here, at least, the data on new ideas in a well-established market were fairly accessible. He noted that, in his study of patents, the economist Jacob Schmookler had shown that improvements in that ancient device had peaked in 1900 and continued until 1920, when automobiles took over the roads. What had given rise to the twentieth-century spike in patents? Presumably it was the size of the market, the sheer numbers of inventors at work on making ever more minute refinements for the enormous number of horses. There seemed to be nothing accidental or exogenous about the sudden surge of ingenuity. After all, horseshoes had been invented by the Romans in the second century A.D. "If strong demand can induce improvements in a 1700-year-old technology as simple as this," wrote Romer, "I find it incredible that we have now exhausted the opportunities for technological improvement in areas like steam-electric generation or chemical processing."

But the story of horseshoes was unlikely to be persuasive to the NBER audience. Romer needed models, and these he had—two of his own (the 1986 version, based on spillovers; and the new 1987 version, in which specialization did the work) and one identified with Solow (in which technology was exogenous). But if he wanted to subscribe to contemporary norms, and follow the example that Robert Lucas set in "Mechanics," he also needed *data*. And aside from Schmookler, Fritz Machlup (a Princeton University economist who had undertaken a mammoth historical study for the Ford Foundation), and a few other outsiders whose theories pointed to the potential usefulness of such metrics, no one actually collected data on the production of knowledge.

So Romer resorted to a time-honored trick. In hopes of showing that new knowledge was driving the system in some places faster than in others, he equated the growth of knowledge with the rate of capital investment. After all, most new machines represented significant advances over old ones. Maybe technical progress was "built-in" to new capital investment, and could be discerned if capital could be assigned a "vintage." This was the "embodiment" hypothesis and had been ventilated at some length after Solow himself introduced it in a paper called "Investment and Technical Progress," which appeared in 1959. The result was that the focus had remained on capital. More than a quarter century later, Romer observed, "No international agency publishes data series on the local production of knowledge and inward flows of knowledge. If you want to run regressions, investment in physical capital is a variable you can use, so I did." And because he was thirty-two years old and full of the excitement of the chase, he turned to a new and previously little-known data set to test his new and previously little-known theories.

IN THOSE DAYS the Penn World Table was very nearly new. Its significance as an international comparison of prices was little understood. That Simon Kuznets had begun in the 1930s to develop the international bookkeeping system known as the national accounts while teaching at the University of Pennsylvania was widely recognized. He had received the Nobel Prize in 1971 for that and other work. And Richard Stone, who had overseen the preparation of the first accounts, was himself honored with a Nobel in 1984. The trouble was that, as good as the data were for purposes of comparing the economic performance of individual countries over time, the accounts did not permit the comparison of one country to another, because no measures were taken to correct for the price levels that differed from country to country. It would have been too ambitious an effort systematically to collect prices all over the world in the early days.

The usual way of comparing wealth and productivity among nations was to rely on exchange rates. Economists would take the dollar value of everything the United States produced, the yen value of everything Japan produced, divide by the population of each country, adjust according to the current exchange, and compare. The trouble is that exchange rates are volatile, at least as volatile as stock markets, and this quick-and-dirty calculation doesn't necessarily reflect any underlying reality of relative prices.

The better alternative was to compare the purchasing power of different currencies over similar baskets of goods in different countries year after year. But to establish purchasing power parity (PPP) this way takes time and money to pay price collectors. The *Economist* magazine regularly reduces this comparison to sampling the prices of a Big Mac hamburger to make the point that the cost of living varies greatly from place to place. But clearly for proper comparisons a more elaborate basket of goods would be required.

The first systematic attempts to compare international prices were made by the United Nations in the 1960s, supported by the Ford Foundation and organized by Irving Kravis of the University of Pennsylvania, in the hope that the World Bank would eventually make the job its own. This the bank had declined to do. So a couple

of professors from the University of Pennsylvania, Alan Heston and
Robert Summers, had continued collecting prices themselves on a
shoestring budget. They, too, hoped that after a demonstration of
the data's usefulness, the bank would take the project over. The fact
that Summers was Paul Samuelson's brother and Larry Summers's
father lent a certain aura to the undertaking; by that time the son
was teaching at Harvard. And in 1986 the first Penn World Table
appeared, macro variables from the national income accounts of 115
countries converted to international prices. A floppy disk was tucked
into the inside cover of the *Quarterly Journal of Economics*, a first for
data sharing that marked an important departure in the history of
the new age of empirical economics. These were the data that Romer
employed for his comparison of long-term growth rates—a vast
improvement over the previously best available series.

Next Romer laid out three different growth models, two versions
of his increasing-returns story—spillovers and specialists—and
Solow's diminishing returns story. He compared them in the arcane
language of production functions with the data. In contrast to what
the Solow model predicted, low-income, low-capital countries
remained stuck behind, just as Lucas had argued fifteen months
before. By now the failure of convergence to have occurred was being
seen as considerably less damaging to the Solow model. The discussion quickly bogged down in the details of growth accounting. Com-
menting on Romer's paper at the NBER, Martin Neil Baily of the
Brookings Institution remarked, "I am not sure how compelling an
objection this is to orthodox theory. If you had told Bob Solow back
in 1956 that his theory would work for the United States, Europe and
Japan, but miss for Swaziland, he would have been pretty happy."

The fact remained: in every version of the Solow model, there was
little or no room for policy to affect growth rates, or for the conventional inputs of capital and labor in the model to explain them.
Technological progress was the engine of economic growth, but it
drove matters from outside the model.

The sudden appearance of two new versions of growth where formerly there had been only one canonical model was confusing, especially since Solow that very autumn finally would be anointed with a

Nobel Prize. More bewildering still were the implications that Romer drew from his exercise. If higher wages increased the incentive to innovate and invent, and this in turn led to spillovers in knowledge, then maybe Europe had the right idea: reduce hours worked, pump up wages, tolerate high unemployment rates, and expect investment and innovation to follow. Maybe the United States was right to borrow abroad, as long as the proceeds went to investments that would produce knowledge spillovers and not consumption. "We should be running as deep a trade deficit as possible for as long as we can get away with it," Romer wrote.

Unfortunately, Romer's ploy left nearly everybody behind. Wasn't he the one who had been going on for several years about the importance of knowledge? Now suddenly he was treating investment as a proxy for new ideas. The key assumption—that new knowledge was the important thing, not investment for investment's sake—was easy to miss. Faster capital accumulation leads to faster growth? There was nothing new about advocating tax-breaks for investment. Corporate lobbyists had been doing that for years.

All this was a little more wide-ranging than the community expected a thirty-two-year-old to be. It is fair to say that most of his listeners were mystified as Romer, in effect, thought out loud. Buzz can be amazingly inefficient in its early stages. Although they were researchers at the nation's top universities, most in the audience probably hadn't even heard of the Lucas lectures, much less read them (they didn't appear in print for another year). Still less were his listeners aware of Romer's turnaround, the fact that he was the proprietor of not one but two models of growth, spillovers and specialization, new and newer still, the latter contained in a talk at the December Meetings, not yet in print. Least of all were they prepared for Romer's sudden turn away from the style of theorizing with which he was just beginning to be identified and toward the sort of down-and-dirty econometrics with which he had little experience.

The result was that Romer's message—that the incentives to technical change were the important thing—was lost in translation. "Crazy Explanations" made it look to outsiders (and even many insiders) that he was giving up on everything for which he had worked during the preceding six years. It was as though he were dropping out of the derby. And since he seemed to agree that the really interesting subject was convergence, attention swiftly shifted to the paper's other novelty—the data.

ONE MAN, more than any other, saw the possibilities inherent in the appearance of the Penn World Table. At forty-three, Robert Barro was one of the brainiest of the rising generation in economics. He was also one of the prickliest. As an undergraduate, Barro had been an aspiring Caltech physicist. And for a time after gaining his economics Ph.D. from Harvard in 1969, he was an old-fashioned, if very high-tech, Keynesian.

But as a young assistant professor at Brown University, Barro made the transition to the new Freshwater style of macroeconomics with less effort than most—to the new math and the rational expectations assumption—if only because of his physics background. He moved to Chicago and there argued in an influential 1974 paper ("Are Government Bonds Net Wealth?") that deficits didn't have much economic effect, since persons with foresight would immediately reduce their current consumption in anticipation of future tax burdens—the "Ricardian equivalence" of borrowing and taxing, it was called, since David Ricardo was the first to note that a strictly logical person would behave in this fashion. This assume-a-Scotsman approach was especially infuriating to Keynesian economists, for whom a certain amount of cognitive fog on the part of consumers was a key assumption. By 1982 it was enough to win Barro a job at the University of Chicago as a full professor. He was viewed by many as being a suitable successor to Milton Friedman as an exponent of free-market economics.

Then, wholly unexpectedly, after the department two years later backed its longtime econometrician Jim Heckman for the Clark Medal, the award given biennially to the most accomplished economist under forty, Barro renounced his Chicago appointment and returned to Rochester, where he had been teaching before being called to Chicago. He had met Romer briefly before leaving; the two resumed a conversation upon his return, and continued it for a couple of years, until Barro visited Harvard in 1986 and joined its faculty in 1987.

Barro and Romer got along well, despite the difference of more than a decade in their ages. Almost no one was quicker than Barro to spot the significance of the new work on growth. After "Crazy Explanations" appeared, Barro and his research assistant Xavier Sala-i-Martin devised an alternative hypothesis about convergence— "conditional convergence," they called it, designed to explain why some countries caught up and others didn't. If a poor country maintained property rights, permitted markets to function, and accumulated a certain amount of human capital, it tended to converge with the industrial leaders. (The newly industrializing Asian countries provided a good example.) Countries that failed to establish certain basic institutions, on the other hand, tended to lag far behind. Just a few variables seemed to explain the differences in growth rates among the 115 countries of the Penn World Table.

The trouble was that the same kind of elaborate statistical analysis that identified the policies that made for conditional convergence— those famous "cross-country regressions"—could be brought to bear in support of other government interventions that could be undertaken in the name of enhancing growth. Infant industry protection, strong labor unions, housing subsidies, large transfer payments designed to promote equality—these were some of the policies whose supposedly positive effect on the growth rate was modeled and tested against the Heston-Summers data in the next few years.

"The 'Crazy Explanations' approach became a module that you could plug in to a bunch of other models," recalled Romer years later. "And then you could ask in a pretty simple way, 'Okay, so what if the government screwed up on income inequality?' You could set up a simple system and say, 'Okay, that's what its implications are for the growth rate.' Mathematically, you could never do that before with the Solow model, because nothing ever changed the growth rate.... Once you gave people this module that they could plug in, then they had lots of things that they could test."

Barro and Romer agreed to start a workshop in growth for the NBER. They invited contributions for an exploratory session to be presented at a ski meeting at Vail in the fall of 1987—an expensive venue that later nearly everyone quickly agreed ought not to be repeated. Spirits were high; feelings ran deep. Barro sought to take charge of the topic. By the time of the meeting, Romer had been dissuaded from the growth-accounting approach of "Crazy Explanations," mostly, he recalled, by a series of discussions with the economist Larry Christiano of Northwestern University about the difficulty of econometrically establishing the direction of causation. He was back on the track of trying to describe the economic role of knowledge. Years later, he wrote, "I wish I had stuck to my guns about the importance of the [simpler] kind of evidence. . . ."

IT WAS INEVITABLE that someone should come forward to defend the Solow model, to say that what was new in Romer wasn't important and that what was important had been said before. Nor was the direction surprising from which the defense was mounted. It was natural that Saltwater economics should offer a growth theory of its own. Perhaps with a little fixing up, the Solow model could be made to serve.

N. Gregory Mankiw was typical of many—of most, perhaps—of the students who went into economics at MIT in the 1960s, 1970s, and 1980s. These students tended to be passionate about economic policy. These were Saltwater types. Not for them the laissez-faire skepticism that was characteristic of their Freshwater counterparts, nor, for that matter, the deep-seated curiosity about the wellsprings of economic order that also was characteristic of Chicago. They were in Cambridge to master the tools that would permit them to improve an imperfect world. They called themselves New Keynesians.

This New Keynesian theory was, in many ways, a liberal doctrine. It had evolved in order to meet the challenge of the New Classical economics from Chicago and the other Freshwater ports. It taught that the traditional emphasis on the efficiency of the Invisible Hand was exaggerated, that imperfections were common in markets, that economic management of these market failures was virtually always needed in some degree, sometimes urgently. A long line of MIT economists had declared themselves New Keynesians: Stanley

Fischer, Olivier Blanchard, Alan Blinder, George Akerlof, Joseph Stiglitz, Janet Yellen, Michael Woodford, Larry Summers, and Ben Bernanke, to name some of the best-known. "Perhaps the invisible hand guides the economy in normal times," Mankiw wrote in an introduction to a survey of New Keynesian economics that he edited (with David Romer, who was no relation), "but the invisible hand is susceptible to paralysis."

But Saltwater macro also had its conservative side. In the early 1980s the influence of the Harvard economist Martin Feldstein was very great. He had become Harvard's best-known economist. He had trained Larry Summers, Jeffrey Sachs, and a substantial number of the best and the brightest of the coming generation. He was breathing new life into the National Bureau of Economic Research, newly relocated to Cambridge, midway between Harvard and MIT. But Feldstein himself never identified as a New Keynesian. Indeed, he had announced a "retreat from Keynes." He had become the mainstream conservative against whom the young honed their ideas. In 1982 Feldstein had agreed to become Ronald Reagan's chief economic adviser, helping to manage a tactical retreat from the more extravagant claims of the supply-side revolution. Among those he recruited for the council staff were Summers, Krugman, and Greg Mankiw.

Mankiw arrived at MIT in 1980, in the same autumn that Ronald Reagan was elected president. He came, with a National Science Foundation fellowship, straight from Princeton, where, as an undergraduate, he had been a championship sailor. Mankiw was no child of privilege, however, even though he had attended New Jersey's exclusive Pingry School (his mother worked to pay the tuition). His grandparents had emigrated from Ukraine on the eve of World War II. When an uncle was killed on Normandy Beach, the family blamed Franklin D. Roosevelt for insufficient preparation for the invasion and became staunch Republicans. His earliest political memory was of attending with his father a rally for the reelection of Richard Nixon in 1972.

How was it that conservatives like Feldstein and Mankiw were more drawn to Keynes than to the more severe traditions of Fresh-

water Chicago? Why not make common cause with Milton Friedman? There are at least two answers to this question. For one thing,
there was by now plenty of room in the Keynesian tradition for reasonable persons to disagree about the appropriate role of government in the economy. Public finance had become a hot field. The
advent of fast computers and the new tools of general equilibrium
theory made it possible to ask questions that hadn't been asked
before—about the perverse effects of taxation, about the interest-
group politics that underlay many government spending programs,
about the interaction of inflation and tax rules and savings and
investment decisions. Even fine-tuning turned out to have a counterpart view—fine-tuning via tax cuts instead of through government
borrowing. For another, economists' gains in prestige during the
preceding thirty years had been hard-won. There was a definite tendency to hang on to the influence that had been achieved.

By 1987 Mankiw had become the first MIT Ph.D. economist ever
to be hired by Harvard, a full professor at age twenty-nine. He was a
prolific writer on a broad range of topics. There was an occasional
mishap—in 1989 he very publicly forecast (with his friend David
Weil) a long-term crash in housing prices that never occurred—but
otherwise he was a master explicator and synthesizer. In 1992 he
vaulted into the forefront of his generation with his authorship of an
intermediate macroeconomics textbook, that being the traditional
point of entry for those preparing to write introductory texts.
Mankiw's surprising innovation: he reversed the usual order of topics, putting Keynesian stabilization toward the back of the book and
devoting the first part to a discussion of the determinants of the
wealth of nations. The centerpiece of the new text was a Saltwater/
New Keynesian model of economic growth.

Many years in preparation, the Saltwater rejoinder to the Romer
model of growth appeared in the *Quarterly Journal of Economics* in
May 1992. "This paper takes Robert Solow seriously," began the collaboration among Mankiw, Berkeley's David Romer, and Brown
University's David Weil. The echo of Chicago's take-no-prisoners
rhetoric in its first sentence was deliberate, though it is hard to say
exactly what "seriously" signified, aside from a flat-out challenge to

the criticisms that Robert Lucas had made in his Marshall Lectures. "This paper argues that the predictions of the Solow model are, to a first approximation, consistent with the evidence," the authors wrote. Moreover, if human capital were added in, then the Solow model could explain *all* the observed differences between the rates of growth of nations, at least if its cross-country regressions were evaluated on the standard grounds of "fit." Reports of its failure had been greatly exaggerated, the authors implied.

The key assumption was that all countries had access to the same pool of knowledge. Nothing was private for very long. Even the poorest countries had libraries, after all. Couldn't they simply buy whatever they wanted to manufacture and reverse engineer it? They would differ only in how they invested in physical and human capital to take advantage of the stock of knowledge.

The Mankiw-Romer-Weil model quickly became known as the augmented Solow model. Maybe neoclassical growth theory, suitably modified to reflect real differences in skill levels and education accumulation of human as well as physical capital, would serve well enough after all—in which case it would be preferred. The whole Keynesian system would remain intact. The chief difference between the new model and the old had to do with the speed of at which convergence could be expected to take place—thirty-five years instead of seventeen to get halfway to the steady state.

Romer and the rest of the endogenous growth camp greeted Mankiw-Romer-Weil with astonishment. Within a year of its publication, Gene Grossman and Elhanan Helpman had described its assumption of a common rate of technological progress in all ninety-eight countries over twenty-five years as "simply indefensible." Hadn't Japan considerably outstripped, say, the Central African Republic, in the acquisition of new technologies—both those new to the global economy and those simply new to Japan? At another point, Paul Romer wrote, "The answer implied by the model is so unsatisfying that it is hard to believe we are meant to take it seriously." For reasons that are unexplained, some countries save more and invest more in schooling, and these variations are said to explain *all* differences in growth rates. In other words, government policy and industrial organization have nothing to do with it. There was nothing here about head starts, development traps, knowledge transfer, patent law, foreign direct investment, infant industry protection—just the time-honored assertion that no policy could change the growth rate very much for very long. "The issue at hand is not whether the neoclassical model is exactly true," Mankiw told a meeting in 1995. "The issue is whether the model can even come close to making sense of international experience."

To be sure, there was considerable irony in Cambridge's defending the assumption of perfect competition and constant returns against a Chicagoan interested in increasing returns and monopolistic competition. A further irony was that Mankiw and Solow had attacked real business cycles theorists for making precisely the same kinds of global assumptions in a controversy only a couple of years before (see "Real Business Cycles: A New Keynesian Perspective"). But the fact remained that the Solow model was easy to teach. It fit well into the rest of the neoclassical synthesis. Students could easily work it through. Therefore it was the first model that they should see. Never mind that it required the assumption of perfect competition. The New Keynesians/Saltwater economists were determined to stand their ground, even at the cost of some derision. The Mankiw-Romer-Weil model fit the data in the Penn World Table. So what if it didn't fit a host of easily observed other facts?

Economists had begun to apply the standard lawyers' principle of stare decisis to their doctrines: change as little as possible. This conservatism was by no means confined to economics. The celebrated investor Charles Munger (Warren Buffett's partner) tells of a physician whose eye clinic at UCLA continued performing a cataract operation long after it was considered obsolete. When he asked why, the reply was, "Charlie, it's such a wonderful operation to teach." The doctor stopped using it only when his patients had voted with their feet.

So INSTEAD OF CLARIFYING the debate, Romer's "Crazy Explanations" paper at the NBER in the winter of 1987 wound up confusing it. Its use of the Heston-Summers data initiated a fad that would come to dominate the debate for the next decade—a vogue for rote statistical comparisons of the experiences of many countries in an attempt to pull explanatory rabbits out of hats. Convergence, or the lack thereof, was too big a question to be answered with any certainty. The why-are-we-so-rich-and-they-so-poor approach had become a cynical game. In time, simply pronouncing the words "cross-country growth regression" would elicit (as one practitioner put it) equal measures of scorn or disgust. For a time, however, it gave the impression of great excitement.

For Romer the first few months of 1987 were a period of great unhappiness. He had reasons to feel dissatisfied. He was stuck in Rochester, five years out of graduate school, with only two published papers on his résumé. The soon-to-be third item, the telegraphic little model of growth through specialization, had yet to appear in the proceedings issue of the *American Economic Review*, and there was something about it that just wasn't getting across. The soon-to-be fourth paper, "Crazy Explanations," had already given his critics an easy point of attack.

His major project of the moment was writing a note on the pricing of rides on ski lifts, in collaboration with Barro, an almost laughably narrow technical exercise, and now Barro had been called away from Rochester to Harvard. In Colorado, Romer's father was settling into the governor's office. Indeed, the young assistant professor, barely thirty years old, was seriously thinking about quitting economics and starting political consulting, going to work for his dad.

CHAPTER TWENTY-ONE

At the Ski Lift

WE WOULD LIKE to think that the light bulb goes on, all at once, in colorful locations—shouting Eureka! in the bathtub, the apple falling from the tree upon the head beneath. In fact, the discovery of the piece of the puzzle of economic growth that clarified the rest had its beginnings in a lunchroom conversation between Romer and Barro and others in the economics department at the University of Rochester.

Moreover, the key distinction did not emerge all at once. Only after a seemingly unrelated problem was analyzed, written up, published, challenged, and defended did a distinction emerge that, while useful in one respect, turned out to be crucial in another. It is true, however, that they were talking that day about the lines at Disneyland, and that the distinction that finally clarified the economics of knowledge emerged from a careful examination of the economics of ski lifts.

THE BARRO FAMILY had been to California on vacation. The economic problem that the father brought home with him was this: why were there long lines for rides inside the park? To an economist, especially one like Barro, long lines were prima facie evidence of market failure. Suppliers would do better if they raised prices. Yet

Disney charged a single fee to enter the park, after which all the rides were "free." Those ubiquitous lines were the result. Ski resorts did the same with lift tickets and rides. Why didn't operators use prices to eliminate the lines? Couldn't they make more money if they did?

This was just the kind of puzzle in price theory that young economists, at least Chicago school economists, liked to solve in order to display their comparative advantage in the profession. It was the autumn of 1986. Barro was forty-two. He had returned to Rochester after having stalked out of Chicago. He was cooling his heels, trying to decide where he belonged if not in Hyde Park. Romer, ten years his junior, was working on "Crazy Explanations." After some exploratory talk in the lunchroom, the two decided to write a joint paper about such bundled pricing schemes. Both were avid skiers, so they decided to concentrate on the specific case of ski lifts. The exercise might even yield a useful insight.

For a time they thought that the ski lift riddle must have to do with congestion, "the tragedy of the commons," the free use of a scarce resource. They revisited a famous economic parable about a well-maintained narrow road (too many travelers) parallel to a poorly kept broad highway (too few), in which the solution was a tollbooth on the narrow road. Perhaps the ski lift problem was another case of where property rights were the answer, a problem easily solved if only lift operators would charge for seats and raise their prices whenever demand peaked. Only gradually did it occur to Barro and Romer that the ski resort owners *did* raise their prices whenever demand was high. That was the point of the lengthening queues.

After a little reflection the coauthors concluded they had been looking at the wrong price. The relevant price was not the price of the daily lift ticket but, instead, the price per ride. This in turn depended on how many other people showed up on a given day. If a lift ticket cost ten dollars and long lines limited skiers to five runs, the price would be two dollars per ride. If no one showed up because it was cold or wet and skiers were able make twenty runs each, the price would be fifty cents per ride.

In fact, resort owners probably *were* charging as much as the market would bear. And they were doing it without appearing to be too greedy. Ride ticket pricing would be expensive to set up and monitor. On the other hand, the cost to skiers of waiting in line would seem small compared with the fixed cost of getting on the mountain in the first place. The effect of the queues was to make riders bear the uncertainty of how many other skiers would show up. The same idea explained why lift passes cost the same throughout the season; owners didn't raise the price but the lines are longer. Lengthening queues were an alternative to flexible money prices; they automatically adjusted the *real* prices that skiers paid. The moral of the story was that ski operators perhaps know something economists didn't—they were the ones who had prospered, after all.

"Ski-Lift Pricing, with Applications to Labor and Other Markets" appeared in the *American Economic Review* in December 1987. The whole analysis was nailed down neatly in general equilibrium math, and suggestively applied to phenomena ranging from the two-tier pricing system in the Paris Metro to various profit-sharing schemes among investment banking firms (the size of the year-end bonus, like the number of lift rides, depends on the number of persons enrolled). The paper was sufficiently clever to merit a write-up in the *Economist*, despite its equations ("Readers are advised to beware skiers sporting scientific calculators. They could be underground economists testing the Barro-Romer thesis"). By now Barro had been hired by Harvard University, making good on his gamble to quit Chicago. Romer, on the other hand, still in Rochester, was bogged down by the controversy surrounding "Crazy Explanations."

Then the ski lift paper turned out to have struck a completely unexpected nerve.

THE FIRST LETTER arrived at the offices of the *American Economic Review* in April 1988, another in May, and a third in September. The analysis of price flexibility and "package deals" in labor markets was all very well, wrote Tyler Cowen and Amihai Glazer. Doubtless the ski lift–pricing paper constituted a contribution to economic theory. But, wrote the young economists, colleagues at the University of California at Irvine—and it was a big "but"—"nowhere in the article or references is it indicated that the basic model is a rediscovery of the theory of clubs." Other writers were less polite. All leveled the same basic charge: Barro and Romer had reinvented the wheel in their paper and failed to cite the original wheel makers.

For nonspecialists to enter an unfamiliar area and fail to discover the relevant prior work would be a significant embarrassment. Appropriate citation of prior work was the fundamental currency of the recognition bank by which science operated. If their primary results really were already well known in the public economics literature, Barro and Romer would be forced to amend or even to retract their paper. As his commitment grew to cross-country comparisons of growth rates, Barro had lost interest in the exchange. For Romer, though, the task of translating the insights of "Ski-Lift Pricing" into the language of club theory was a welcome relief from the distractions of "Crazy Explanations."

Now Romer went back and read "An Economic Theory of Clubs," the 1965 *Economica* paper by James Buchanan that gave the field its name. When they wrote their paper, the pair knew only that the standard result in club theory contradicted their result, insisting that a usage fee for lift seats would be required to support an efficient allocation. This much background knowledge, at least, was in the air. But so broad and deep had the literature of economics grown in the years since World War II that only specialists in public finance could be reasonably expected to have read the classics of the field.

As it happened, James Buchanan was, briefly, a celebrity in 1987. The year before the "Ski-Lift Pricing" paper appeared, he had been awarded the Nobel Prize for economics for his lifetime of work on political decision making. In fact, his career makes an interesting story. As a graduate student at the University of Chicago in the winter of 1948, when the excitement of Cowles was at its zenith, Buchanan was among those who left Hyde Park altogether. He had concluded that economics was shifting away from its classical foundations and that "technique was replacing substance."

Besides, Buchanan had begun to read the great Swedish economist Knut Wicksell. He became preoccupied with the boundary between economics and politics. "Economists should cease proffering policy advice as if they were employed by a benevolent despot," he argued, "and instead turn their attention to the way in which political decisions were made." He challenged his fellow economists "to postulate some model of the state, of politics, before proceeding to analyze the effects of alternative policy measures." A series of essays in this vein put "political failure" on a par with "market failure" as a matter of legitimate interest to economists. Indeed, along with his coauthor Gordon Tullock and his fellow Chicago graduate student G. Warren Nutter, Buchanan built up a school of political economy—the "Virginia school"—whose views were similar to, though subtly different from, Chicago's own. But Buchanan never lost a taste for mathematical precision. And "An Economic Theory of Clubs" had launched a wide and deep literature.

From Buchanan, Romer learned that it was Paul Samuelson who had set the stage. Public finance was a very old field, enshrined in textbooks, laden with gradations and hazy distinctions. In 1954, piqued by a dare to show what the new formal language could do, Samuelson translated an important but little-known paper by his friend Richard Musgrave ("The Voluntary Exchange Theory of Public Economy") into the mathematical exposition of "The Pure Theory of Public Expenditure." Samuelson set out an extreme polar case between public and private. There were conventional goods like bread, whose total can be parceled out to individuals, with one man having a loaf fewer if another has a loaf more. There also were public consumption goods, such as a display of fireworks or a national defense. These were provided for each person to enjoy or not, according to his taste, "but with no subtraction from any other's consumption." There followed three pages that, for those able to follow the math, transformed the field. Forty years later Jim Heckman remembered, "I read Musgrave as a student and to be honest nothing was clear. The 3-pager by Samuleson made everything very clear to me and I can still recite its proofs." Samuelson later noted ruefully that his formalization may have cost his friend an eventual Nobel Prize.

It was to this literature that Buchanan in 1965 had added the concept of "club goods," a catchall term for a broad spectrum of goods that were neither purely public nor purely private—a class of things that, somewhat misleadingly, had previously been called "impure" public goods.* Clubs were groups that shared something valuable exclusively among their members—swimming pools, golf courses, ski mountains, toll roads, trades associations, and so on. Club goods depended critically on *excludability* to make them work. The exclusion mechanism could be a guard, a gate, a fence, a ticket office, a checklist maintained by a greeter at a door—anything that served to let member in and keep nonmembers out. Club theory was a way of identifying impure public goods and disentangling the relationship between their costs and the groups that consumed them.

Club theory was mainly about congestion. Swimming pools were a good example. They were impure public goods in Buchanan's scheme of things, at least up to a point. Many people could belong to a swimming club. Swimmers could take turns with the diving board. Several people could even swim laps in a single lane, as long as they were evenly spaced and swam at about the same speed. But sooner or later there would be a problem with overcrowding. At that point someone presumably would build another swimming pool.

Among club theorists inclined to math, some of the proudest achievements were those that showed that so long as the size of the market is big compared with the number of clubs, the market will produce enough swimming pools, and the price of a membership will be set competitively. For the purposes of high-end general equilibrium models, the gist of the analysis was that memberships in swimming clubs are intermediate goods that end up behaving like purely rival goods, and that perfect competition obtains in the end. In other words, club theory required no significant nonconvexities in the math. Club theory quickly became standard treatment for any number of problems: schools, highways, information networks,

---

* Others had hit on similar ideas at about the same time. Charles Tiebout had anticipated some applications in a famous 1956 paper about the factors that led consumers to prefer one suburb to another—public schools, for example. Mancur Olson zeroed in on the general behavior of political interest groups a few years later in *The Logic of Collective Action*.

communication systems, national parks, waterways, and the electro-magnetic spectrum.

Before long, however, it became clear to public finance theorists that a better term than "public" would be required to describe the underlying characteristics of goods that clubs provided to their membership. It was one thing to describe public goods like national defense or streetlights as "pure." But "impure" or "mixed goods" didn't capture the characteristic these goods had in common with the warning provided by a lighthouse or a subway ride or the opportunity to play a round of golf at a country club. "Club" goods filled only part of what Buchanan called the "awesome Samuelson gap" on the spectrum between purely private consumption and those public goods that everyone enjoyed no matter what. "Collective" goods wasn't a much better. A few years later, Richard Musgrave of Harvard University, by then the doyen of public finance economists, added a chapter to his famous textbook, *Public Finance in Theory and Practice*, on what he identified as "social goods."

The distinguishing thing about the club goods is that they "weren't used up" in consumption, Buchanan noted, at least not by any one individual. Many people could enjoy their benefit at the same time. But eventually, of course, their benefits *were* exhausted; the swimming pool became crowded. So now Musgrave changed the terminology, adding a distinction between rival goods and nonrival goods. Nonrival goods were those that were available to all and without mutual interference. Rival goods were those whose benefits were enjoyed by their purchasers. Food, clothing, housing, automobiles, and so on. The key here was the mechanism of exclusion. "A hamburger eaten by A cannot be eaten by B." But what about a bridge for which tolls might or might not be charged, or a broadcast that might be susceptible to jamming? Thus Musgrave produced a little table that looked like this.

	Exclusion	
	Feasible	Not Feasible
Rival	1	2
Nonrival	3	4

Market provision worked well enough only in case 1, Musgrave wrote. In each of the other three cases, the market failed. Especially interesting was case 2—the case of the bridge, a broadcast, cross-town traffic in Manhattan on a busy afternoon. In principle, you'd like to be able to auction off or otherwise sell the right to travel along Forty-second Street, wrote Musgrave, just as you might charge a toll for a bridge, but it wasn't feasible (though someday, he noted, it might be). Better to call all these cases of market failure "social goods."

(In 1955 Buchanan had noted that, strictly speaking, not even a pair of shoes was truly rival. Shoes could be lent or, as at a bowling alley, rented. Too bad he didn't extend the "cooperative membership" properties in which he was interested in the other direction, toward goods whose consumption could be more widely shared than shoes. Many years later Elhanan Helpman sighed, "He came so close!")

Romer encountered the rival/nonrival distinction in a textbook (*The Theory Externalities, Public Goods, and Club Goods*, by Richard Cornes and Todd Sandler) and immediately found it useful. As he thought about the chairlift problem, however, it struck him that his club theorist readers were missing the point. Rides on ski lifts were not like swimming pools. You either had a seat on a chairlift or you didn't. They were purely *rival* goods—once you were in a particular seat, it was yours. Nobody else could share it. There was an element of crowding, but it was not an important thing, at least not from the point of view of the operator or, for that matter, of the skier. If the ride was taken to be the basic good instead of the lift ticket, then the pricing behavior of the operators made perfect sense. Their arrangement was designed to raise the most revenue and let queuing do the rest. Romer sat down to write a rejoinder to the letter writers for publication in the *American Economic Review*.

Before he could finish his reply, however, Romer's attention suddenly snapped back to economic growth. For what was the knowledge whose accumulation he had set out to describe if not a wildly various collection of nonrival goods?

HERE IN THE ATTIC of the economics of public finance was a concept that, just possibly, could make sense of the most basic economics of growth. Certainly it could be put to use. For the very meaning of a nonrival good was that it was an item which is not "used up" when consumed, or employed as an input in a production process. The design for a fast new photographic film, for example.

When Romer looked at the public finance textbooks to see how the term was being employed, he found that the distinction between rival and nonrival goods was being narrowly applied to goods previously defined as clubs. For instance, Tyler Cowen, the theorist whose letter had initiated the exercise, was writing a primer on public goods and externalities at about the same time. (He had moved to George Mason University.) To illustrate the concept, he chose a cinema:

> A movie theater provides an example of nonrivalrous consumption. Up to the point of crowding, it is possible to allow additional individuals to enter a theater and watch the movie without infringing on the consumption of those already in the audience. Because one individual's consumption of a movie (unlike, say, a banana or a pair of eyeglasses) does not prevent another individual from consuming the same good, it is not rivalrous.

The really interesting nonrival good in this example, however, is not a seat in the theater, however many seats there might be. It is the movie itself. The theater would fill up, there might be a line around the block, but the film could be shown in theaters all across the country—across the world. It could be shown on airplanes, on television, sold to consumers on disks. Sequels to it could be made. The film was the property of its owners; but others—the stars, the composer of its music—had rights as well. Most of these many sorts of exhibition rights were highly excludable, thanks to various contracts that lawyers had drawn up. The lawyers were specialists in *intellectual property*. But none of this had anything to do with club theory.

More curious still, Romer discovered that club theorists were using the concept interchangeably with indivisibility; "nonrivalry of benefits, see indivisibility," was the index entry in the Cornes and Sandler text. Remember, a good was said to be indivisible if there was a minimum size beneath which it was unavailable. You could have half a box of cereal, but not half a bridge over a river. An indivisibility, as we have seen, or its mathematical representation, a nonconvexity, arose anytime there was a fixed cost. The fixed cost of making a movie, for example?

Now Romer reread Arrow's two papers on the economics of knowledge from the early 1960s. It was here, he realized, that matters had gone off track. Arrow had identified three special characteristics of knowledge that made it different from other things. Its successful production was inherently *uncertain*. Once produced, new knowledge often was *inappropriable*—the person who brought it into the world might have no way to capitalize on it, since it can be possessed at best only imperfectly. And, finally, it was *indivisible*—its use led to decreasing average costs (or, to put it another way, to increasing returns), since, like the warning provided by a lighthouse, the requirement for knowledge in a given activity was independent of its scale.

What Arrow had called appropriability mapped neatly onto the concept of excludability in club theory. This much was simply a mirror image. It didn't matter whether a patent made your discovery appropriable to you or excludable to others.

But the unique thing about knowledge was not so much its indivisibility but rather its nonrivalry. There was indeed something indivisible about a lighthouse or a recording or a software program. It didn't exist until it was built or made or turned on, and doing that inevitably entailed a fixed cost. Once created, however, a nonrival good could be copied endlessly at almost no cost and used over and over again, without being "used up." Many people could possess it precisely because it was nonrival. It was indivisible, too. But its indivisibility was not the important thing.

A nonrivalrous good could be almost anything whose content lent itself to copying. A symphony, or the performance of it by a particular orchestra; a painting, or a reproduction of it on a coffee mug; a chemical formula, or its instantiation in a pharmaceutical pill. Indeed, it was when excludability entered the picture that things got really interesting. Nonrival goods were excludable in varying degrees, depending on the circumstances. The seat at a concert, for example. But suppose the concertgoer held a tape recorder in his lap? In the composer's heyday, the operas of Puccini were rehearsed without their arias, lest newspaper reporters memorize the melodies, write them down in musical notation, and tip them to the eager public. Secrecy was one device to preserve commercially valuable nonrival goods. Patents, trademarks, secret ingredients, access codes, proprietary standards, continual innovation were some others.

Gradually, a chart took shape in Romer's mind. It looked something like this:

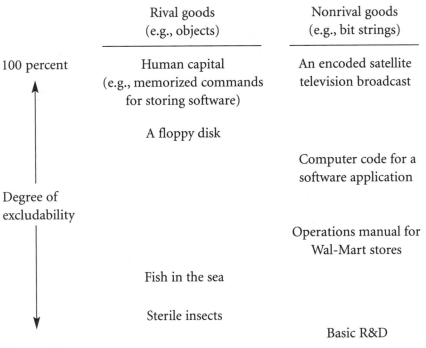

	Rival goods (e.g., objects)	Nonrival goods (e.g., bit strings)
100 percent	Human capital (e.g., memorized commands for storing software)	An encoded satellite television broadcast
	A floppy disk	
		Computer code for a software application
Degree of excludability		Operations manual for Wal-Mart stores
	Fish in the sea	
	Sterile insects	
		Basic R&D
0 percent		

The new typology solved a lot of problems. Under the press of events, public finance economists such as Tyler Cowen and Hal Varian had begun speaking of "private markets for public goods." But surely such terminology obscured the issues. What was *public* about Microsoft's Windows operating system for personal computers, even though the software quickly became an industry standard? What was *private* about the English language, even though each person possessed it individually? How much easier was it to speak of markets for nonrival goods?

Here was a means of unraveling the extensive collection of related concepts that had accumulated over the years—public goods, externalities, indivisibilities, nonconvexities, missing markets, poorly defined property rights—concepts whose common denominator was that they were associated with the malfunctioning of the market.* For a nonrival good—a lighthouse, for example—was very different from a spillover. There might very well be uncompensated side effects in principle, but in practice the cost of building and maintaining a needed lighthouse was more likely to be shared than to be undertaken by public authorities or remain unmet. It was for lack of this more precise terminology that Paul Samuelson's textbook had gone through fifteen editions describing lighthouses as public goods and asserting that they could only be provided only by the state—despite a drop-dead article in 1974 by Ronald Coase demonstrating that lighthouses had often, even *ordinarily*, been privately provided. Lighthouses were nonrival, partially excludable goods. So were articles in scientific journals, the private reports of industrial research laboratories, the design and techniques of manufacture of consumer goods such as Wedgwood china. The externalities were real enough, but the deeper and more interesting phenomenon was their nonrivalry. The economics of nonrival goods were very different from those of people and things.

In the spring of 1987, however, as Barro and Romer put the finishing touches on "Ski-Lift Pricing," all this lay in the future. The very beginnings of the controversy with the club theorists was still more than a year away. Not until 1992 did the chart appear. In a matter of weeks, however, the ski lift paper opened the first door to the future.

The observation that prices might be flexible even when they appeared to be sticky—the take-home message of "Ski-lift Pricing"—was the sort of insight that Chicago economists prized. Romer was

---

* The phrase is that of Andreas Papandreou in *Externality and Institutions*.

invited to talk about the analysis at a workshop at the University of Chicago. It was a few weeks after the disappointments of "Crazy Explanations." With its combination of taut price theory and high math, the paper appealed to both camps in the Chicago department, the applied price theorists as well as the Modernist faction in the department.

Indeed, the Chicago outing paid off beyond all reasonable expectations. A few weeks after the seminar, José Scheinkman called his former pupil, six years out of graduate school, with an offer: to return as a full professor. It wasn't an altogether easy decision. Romer's wife had a better offer to do medical research in California. But his was the career that needed a boost.

Romer accepted, effective January 1988. His regrets over the "Crazy Explanations" misadventure at the NBER were forgotten. He was ready to go back to work on the model of growth by specialization that he had hurriedly published in his 1987 note, to unpack it and figure out where spillovers fit into the story. Instead of quitting economics, he would be returning to his alma mater. And he was at last within sight of his goal.

CHAPTER TWENTY-TWO

"Endogenous Technological Change"

IT WAS A FINE SITE for a tournament—the banks of a river flowing north from Lake Erie to Niagara Falls, except that instead of a sun-dappled meadow, the lists were located in the fluorescent recesses of a Hilton Hotel situated between ribbons of highways that lay along the water's edge. Buffalo in those days looked as though it had seen a war. With the strong dollar of the early 1980s, many of its jobs had gone overseas.

It was here that various conflicting theories of economic growth were arrayed against one another at a conference held on Memorial Day weekend, 1988. The idea was to assess the potential of the varieties of "new" growth theory that had arisen in the years since Romer submitted his thesis on increasing returns five years before. The economists had been looking for an excuse to gather, to lay out the competing views that had dominated conversation for several years. It amounted to a jousting contest among the various parties to the debate. Romer, newly appointed at the University of Chicago, brought a paper. So did MIT's Paul Krugman, Harvard's Robert Barro, Chicago's Gary Becker (with a coauthor, the youthful Kevin Murphy), and the econometrician Dale Jorgenson of Harvard. Among the discussants were many of the rising stars of the next generation—Larry Summers, Gene Grossman, Andrei Shleifer, and Robert Vishny. Many senior figures turned out as well—Lucas from

Chicago, Stanley Fischer from MIT, Robert Hall from Stanford, Edward Prescott from the University of Minnesota, Finis Welch from Texas A&M. Lending gravity to the occasion was the foreknowledge that the best papers would be published in the University of Chicago's flagship journal, the *Journal of Political Economy*. They would enter the literature under the sponsorship of the University of Chicago.

The timing of the meeting seemed to be vaguely connected to the presidential election of 1988; it was billed the First International Conference of the Institute for the Study of Free Enterprise Systems. Funds had been obtained by Buffalo's congressman, Jack Kemp. The supply-sider (and onetime quarterback for the Buffalo Bills) had been hoping to deny George Bush the Republican nomination that summer. His closest adviser was Jude Wanniski. A handful of news reporters and other observers had been invited by the Smith Richardson Foundation, another of the meeting's sponsors. The sponsorship may have been political, but the economists who gathered in Buffalo were detached and serene. The participants didn't care who was paying the bills.

Among the papers presented in Buffalo that day was Romer's "Micro Foundations for Aggregate Technological Change." The other papers swiftly faded into the background—Becker and Murphy's perfectly competitive model of the demographic transition, Krugman's attempt to link trade and growth, Jorgenson's study of the effects of tax policy on growth, another AK model in the spirit of Von Neumann. But "Micro Foundations" was the article that in due course would be retitled "Endogenous Technological Change"—that is, it would become Romer '90. For it was in this unlikely setting that the concept of intellectual property was, if not exactly "discovered," then formally characterized for the first time in the context of growth theory, embedded in an aggregate-level model of the economy, describing knowledge as both an input and an output of production, in a way that permitted economists to take account of its significance. There were sovereigns in the air.

THE NEW PAPER BEGAN by asserting the claim that it was knowledge, not physical factors, whose accumulation was the really important thing. The basic raw materials that were combined to yield utility were pretty much the same as they had always been, Romer wrote, but the means by which they were combined had become vastly more sophisticated, especially in recent years:

> A hundred years ago, all we could do to get visual stimulation from iron oxide was to make it into pigment and spread it on fibers that are woven into canvas. (Canvas itself was a big improvement over cave walls.) Now we know how to spread iron oxide on long reels of plastic tape, and use it with copper, silicon, petroleum, iron, and other assorted raw materials that have been mixed together to make television sets and video tape recorders:

In Buffalo, Romer wasn't yet using the term "nonrival" knowledge. Instead, he employed the distinction between "embodied knowledge" (meaning human capital that didn't outlive the individual) and "disembodied" knowledge (that did), which dated back to the days of the Lost Patrol. The clarifying controversy with the club theorists that would lead to nonrival, partially excludable terminology had barely begun. The first letter arrived only a week before the conference. The new language would jell only slowly. In the next few years, Romer would experiment with language, occasionally using "recipes" and "blueprints" and "ideas" as synonyms for "instructions." He would shy away consistently from the curiously misleading expression "intellectual capital," and from the slangy distinction among hardware, software, and "wetware," meaning brains or human capital.

Gradually the terminology evolved, as the concepts' interpreters experimented with their use. Rival and nonrival properties came to be identified with concrete objects and incorporeal ideas, and then shortened by synecdoche to atoms and bits. The distinction didn't replace the public/private dichotomy of political discourse. It augmented and reinforced it instead. In thinking about rival goods, Romer had gained a sharper appreciation of the properties of nonrival goods he was working with in growth theory. He understood better what made knowledge unique. And, for the first time, he saw how it was that Kenneth Arrow had sent the profession off on a wrong track in 1962 with his discussion of the indivisibility of new ideas, their irreducible "lumpiness." New ideas were indeed lumpy, because they involved a fixed cost. You couldn't buy just half of one. Like one of Dupuit's bridges, they would serve no useful purpose until they had been achieved, often at considerable expense. But lots of things in this world were lumpy. What made a new idea similar to, but ultimately different from, a bridge was that, unlike a bridge, a new idea could be used by any number of people at the same time, often without any diminution of its usefulness, and usually without much (or even any) compensation.

From the beginning the great charm of nonrivalry had been its capacity to explain the mechanism underlying Adam Smith's dictum that "the division of labor is limited by the extent of the market." Allyn Young had sought only to describe the "increasingly intricate nexus of specialized undertakings [that] has inserted itself between the producer of the raw material and the consumer of the final product." Now Romer had untangled the mechanism that related specialization to market size. It was the fixed cost of finding a set of new instructions. You wouldn't make a hammer to drive a single nail, or a newfangled trap to catch a single mouse, but the bigger the market, the more copies of a new design could be sold. The cost was unrelated to the number of times the design was used; hence the origins of the declining average costs that created increasing returns: sell a hundred hammers, and break even; sell a million, and get rich. And a truly large market was capable of supporting incalculably many specialists whose inputs contributed to the final product.

> Cave painting was a do-it-yourself proposition, and even 100 years ago, the chain of individuals and firms that intervened between the collection of pigment and fibers for canvas and the sale of a painting was relatively short and simple. Today, a consumer of home videos takes advantage of the work of tens of thousands, perhaps hundreds of thousands, of specialized workers and firms spread around the globe.

The division of labor—the market for specialists and their inventions—was limited mainly by the market's size.

Romer's telegraphic model of growth by specialization in 1987 had made it seem that population might be the key—that whoever had the biggest internal market should grow the fastest. If that were so, China should long ago have outstripped Great Britain. This time Romer was more careful about the links between the stock of specially trained human capital and the growth of knowledge that he built into the Buffalo model. After all, it wasn't raw labor that performed R&D; it was engineers and scientists and other highly skilled workers. The Buffalo model was clear about why population was not the right measure of size. More important, it showed how, by opening markets to new knowledge, trade policy could affect not just welfare (as had long been argued) but the rate of growth itself. The economics of creating ideas were very different from those of making things, because ideas, from intellectual property to the most basic research, could be copied practically without cost and used by any number of persons at the same time.

Thus innovations—the various new "sets of instructions" that arose and the entrepreneurs who put them to use—were the key to growth. It was true that assembling old materials in new ways always required additional human capital (in the form of increased training) and more physical capital, but the costs of finding new sets of instructions were the really interesting thing. People cooked up the new instructions in the hope of making money, then either kept secret some aspects of them, patented them, or used the advantage of their newfound knowledge to keep going forward to create still more new knowledge.

THE SECOND NOVEL CLAIM of the paper flowed from the first. It had to do with the ubiquity of monopolistic competition. To Romer it was obvious that the existence of the rights associated with intellectual property—and, more important, with trade secrets and general know-how—meant the presence of monopolistic competition throughout the economy, of price making, and not just textbooks, but cornflakes, stamping mills, oysters, everything that could be branded or otherwise successfully differentiated. And here the concept of a fixed cost was the vital link.

The other growth models in Buffalo that day preserved price-taking behavior—that is, perfect competition. Robert Lucas didn't bring a model, but in the preceding year he had swiftly glossed over the distinction that Romer was putting at the center of his analysis. To Lucas both batting skills and textbook knowledge were forms of "human capital." Both entailed a fixed cost: George Brett had to practice baseball; the authors had to write their book. Each worked in anticipation of a stream of earnings. So why bother to make a distinction? Each could be captured by a standard model of perfect competition, with its elegant mathematics of convexity. But then, wrote Romer, the convexity assumption "is precisely what must be abandoned in a mode that allows for knowledge that is disembodied and that evolves endogenously."

True, he acknowledged, whatever monopoly rights might be established to new knowledge, laboriously acquired, tended to evanesce, sooner or later. This is where spillovers came in—Marshall's trade knowledge that couldn't be kept secret. Romer wrote, "As is quite clear from the experience of video tape recording (a technology developed by a firm in the United States, refined by firms in Japan, and copied by firms in Korea), a technological innovation can be copied and used without the consent of the developer." Patents and secrets might limit the extent of the unauthorized use, but this didn't change the fact that knowledge, especially the variety known as intellectual property, was very different from human capital—it was easy to copy.

The new model thus differed from both the Chicago and the Solow models in two crucial respects. It contained a research and development sector, which used valuable resources to produce more new instructions, carefully embedded in the decentralized general equilibrium framework we have been calling the infinite-dimensional spreadsheet. This is what it meant to say technical change was "endogenous."

Second, the Romer model took monopolistic competition for granted. The Pin Factory had become an engine of growth, perhaps, as Schumpeter had argued, *the* engine of growth. No longer were the advantages of technical superiority to be understood as a case of "market failure." They were part of the rules of the game, were assumed to be the result of manufacturing or marketing advantages that could be kept secret for a time, or protected by a patent or a trademark, such that the manufacturer would be able to keep sales prices far above marginal costs, at least for a time—and so earn back its investment in new know-how. Increasing returns would be the norm, in many if not most situations.

Moreover, the special "copying" property of knowledge—that it could be used by the same person over and over again, or by any number of persons at the same time—was not an inconvenient fact that could be assumed away simply by assigning property rights. Property rights were the standard solution to most problems, according to most Chicago economists. And indeed, intellectual property was as ubiquitous and various as the customs and laws that had grown up, over the centuries, to deal with it.

But who could say with any certainty what should be regarded as appropriable and what should not? Who would advocate giving Newton or Leibniz a patent on the calculus? Or Einstein a copyright on the formula $E = mc^2$? Or David Ho a royalty on his AIDS combination drug therapy? Or William Kellogg a trademark that entitled him alone to manufacture breakfast cereal from corn? How broad should these protections be? How long should such state-sanctioned monopolies last? What alternative institutions might be set in motion, educating the workforce, producing new knowledge, and diffusing it? These were among the most important policy questions of the new economics of knowledge. But there were no pat answers to them. They required that social choices be made. They required a policy, just as central banking required a monetary policy, or stabilization required a fiscal policy.

The knowledge that accumulated in Romer's model was quite different from the concept of *information*, as it had been introduced to technical economics fifteen years earlier by the great papers on asymmetric information, "lemons" and signaling and screening. Information consists of facts, not necessarily dependable, that may or may not be gleaned. There's something intrinsically loose about information, even in its plural form, which is data, until it is attached to a particular rival good involved in a transaction. Much of the new theory of mechanism design has to do with getting buyers and sellers to disclose relevant information that they alone possess.

Knowledge, on the other hand, connotes understanding, both of a set of facts and of the ideas that have been inferred from them. The essence of knowledge is structure. Here again, the distinctions between rivalry and nonrivalry and the degree of excludability are useful. Part of the process in the creation of useful knowledge is to take bits of information that are specific to a person or thing and generalize them so that they apply broadly, thereby turning private information into knowledge that many can use.

Here is a simple example. When Vasco da Gama sailed out of Lisbon in 1497 around the Cape of Good Hope on his way to India, scurvy was an utterly mysterious disease, often fatal, and thought to be infectious. Da Gama eventually lost 100 out of 160 men to it. When he put in near present-day Mozambique for a time, some of his sailors ate oranges and recovered. At this point, he had some information, though it was of no value to him, much less to the wider world: "God was gracious, the air was good and the men got better." In 1617 John Woodall made the leap from specific information about particular people to knowledge that would be useful for everyone. Perhaps sailors got better because they ate fruit and perhaps this same approach would work for everyone. He described the illness in *The Surgeon's Mate* and recommended lemon juice as a preventative. The East India Company began issuing lemon juice to its sailors on the strength of his advice. Eighty years later, authorities had become more matter-of-fact: a 1699 tract on medicine asserted that the worst case of scurvy would disappear after two weeks of eating oranges and lemons in Cadiz. "This is not a relation of one or two persons only, but what is generally agreed upon, and allowed by all to be the truth."

But only when the British naval surgeon James Lind invented the first modern clinical trial in 1747 was the point finally hammered home. Twelve sick sailors on a lengthy voyage were divided into six groups, fed the same diet and administered different daily supplements—apple juice, elixir vitriol (dilute sulfuric acid), vinegar, a mixture of herbs and spices, a pint of seawater, a couple of oranges, and a lemon. When the last group alone recovered quickly and completely, Lind ended the trial and gave oranges to everyone. At that point the antiscorbutic properties of citrus had become inarguable knowledge. Even then it took another fifty years to persuade the Royal Navy to make citrus juice part of the standard ration (and thereby turn Brit sailors into limeys). And not until the twentieth century was the role of vitamins in nutrition firmly established, vitamin C identified and synthesized, and vitamin pills invented and marketed. All the usual varieties of rival and nonrival partially excludable goods are to be found in this history, among knowledge and information goods alike, but it is ultimately a story about the growth of knowledge, not about the exchange of information.

None of this was in the paper, but all of it was implicit in the analysis of knowledge as both input and output in "Endogenous Technological Change." Knowledge is information after it has become proven valuable and, at least potentially, nonrival. It may or may not be excludible. The history of writing about the role of knowledge in economics recapitulates this story, of course. Marshall had said as much. Hayek in 1945 had written on "the use of knowledge in society." Some of the choicest observations were made in the 1960s by the economist Simon Kuznets. Consultants wrote plenty of books about knowledge and knowledge management in the 1980s and 1990s, starting with Peter Drucker. Savants contributed some memorable shorthand, including the distinction between atoms and bits, and Stewart Brand's observation "Information wants to be free, and information also wants to be very expensive" lacks only the observation that information is also expensive to produce. But it is the last word in these matters that we care about, not the first. The most widely shared ideas—"judgments concerning which universal agreement can be obtained," in the philosopher Norman Campbell's phrase—are the ones that become science or, in this case, economics.

In effect, Romer had challenged his fellow Chicagoans to a contest. Either explain the existence of specialization and intellectual property in some other way, or print the article and accept the consequences. If he won, the tools of monopolistic competition would finally be recognized by Chicago's flagship *Journal of Political Economy*. A forty-year, fingers-in-the-ears standoff between Chicago and Cambridge would be over.* The process of coming to terms would have begun.

The question Romer had framed as a graduate student had an answer now. All that remained was that it should be understood. How could economics be right about so much and fundamentally wrong about growth? The answer was that a basic economic principle was missing—the principle of the nonrivalry of knowledge as the fundamental source of increasing returns. Scarcity was indeed a cardinal principle of economics, but it was not the only cardinal principle. The economics of knowledge was about abundance. And for the previous several centuries, at least, abundance had routinely trumped scarcity.

It was in Buffalo that propertized knowledge—intellectual property, capable of commanding a monopoly rent—made its appearance for the first time in the kind of aggregate analysis that constituted mainstream economics. But you had to lean close and pay attention to know it. "Intellectual property" was on no one's lips on leaving the meeting in the Hilton.

Outside the profession the meeting in Buffalo produced few waves. From a distance of years, we can see that many careers shifted onto different paths not long thereafter. Barro made a specialty of cross-country regressions. Krugman turned his attention to geography. Stan Fischer prepared to become chief economist for the World Bank, on his way to the International Monetary Fund. Larry Summers returned to work on the Dukakis campaign. The defense of the Solow model passed to the next generation. The collaboration

---

* In an autobiography published nearly simultaneously with the appearance of Romer's paper, George Stigler crowed that Chicago's victory over monopolistic competition had been complete. "Scarcely a trace" of the Chamberlinian tradition remained in the work of economists, he wrote in *Memoirs of an Unregulated Economist* in 1988. In fact, Chamberlin's ideas had never gone away, as illustrated in Jean Tirole's *The Theory of Industrial Organization*, published that same year. Now Krugman in international trade, and Romer in growth, had taken monopolistic competition to a new level, demonstrating that it was indispensable to understanding not just the details of a single industry but the economy in general. No wonder Stigler and Milton Friedman stayed away from Buffalo!

between Gregory Mankiw, David Romer, and David Weil that eventually led to the "augmented" Solow model known as Mankiw-Romer-Weil, with its assumption that everyone in the world has access to the same great pool of common knowledge, was then only beginning to take shape. Its appearance in print was still four years away.

In what sense, then, was the meeting in Buffalo a tournament? Compared with, say, the single most famous dinner party in the history of modern economics, not much at all. That was the night Ronald Coase came to dinner at Aaron Director's home to defend his views of transaction costs against a skeptical Chicago department. Coase had submitted a paper arguing that simply assigning property rights and then letting market processes take their course was usually a better solution than costly government regulation. The referees were certain that something was wrong with his argument. Hence the occasion of the dinner. George Stigler later recalled, "In the course of two hours of argument the vote went from twenty against and one for Coase to twenty-one for Coase." Midway, Milton Friedman opened fire, and the bullets hit everyone but Coase. "What an exhilarating event!" wrote Stigler. The guests said good night knowing that intellectual history had been made.

In Buffalo there was no such moment of climax, no scales falling from all eyes, no common perception that participants had witnessed the entry into the macroeconomics literature of the first successful account of the aggregate economics of knowledge. (Never mind the ghost of Joseph Schumpeter, a spirit generally summoned by economists when they lack a concrete result.) The excitement was unmistakable, but it was ill defined. Only gradually did it become a conviction shared by many that the world had changed once and for all that day.

EVEN BEFORE BUFFALO a race had developed to connect the growth literature with issues of market structure. With its wave after wave of new goods, Romer's model of the processes of aggregate growth had plenty of job creation in it, but no job ever disappeared. Soon three different teams of researchers were already at work on the problem of "creative destruction" that Schumpeter had described so evocatively in 1942.

Economic progress, in a capitalist society, means turmoil. And in this turmoil competition works in a manner completely different from the way it would work in a stationary process, however perfectly competitive. Possibilities of gains to be reaped by producing new things or by producing old things more cheaply are constantly materializing and calling for new investments.

This was the literature of "quality ladders" or "creative destruction," depending on who did the modeling—Gene Grossman and Elhanen Helpman, or Phillipe Aghion. (Paul Segerstrom, T. C. A. Anant, and Elias Dinopoulos also had an early horse in the race.) The idea was to decompose the process of technological advance, to describe what went on in industrial organization within and between those waves of development. At times competition among the economists working on models to convey various Schumpeterian mechanisms was intense. In the end there was plenty of credit to go around. And in 1996 Princeton's Gene Grossman was chosen to produce a two-volume reader, *Economic Growth: Theory and Evidence*, designed to showcase what had been learned.

Economists had lost interest in economic growth after 1970, Grossman wrote. That was the year that Robert Solow published his benediction in the Radcliffe Lectures. However many interesting questions might still have remained then, Grossman continued, it was clear that the neoclassical model "could not deliver all of the answers." Empirical work, lacking guidance from theory, became clouded. Growth accounting became increasingly sterile.

"But all of that changed in the mid-1980s," wrote Grossman, when two events kindled a sharp revival of interest. "First, Paul Romer completed a dissertation at the University of Chicago. . . . Second, Robert Summers and Alan Heston assembled internationally comparable data on gross domestic product and its components for over 100 countries and made their data readily available. . . ." Thereafter Grossman carefully laid out what he considered the thirty-seven most important papers in the new literature, arranged by categories: convergence, cross-country correlates, AK models, externality-based models, innovation-based models, and so on. It had been quite an effusion of work.

THE SHOCKWAVES FROM BUFFALO were still spreading in the spring of 1989 when Robert Solow's former students gathered at the brand-new hotel in Kendall Square to honor their teacher with a Festschrift, a collection of essays in his honor, on the occasion of his sixty-fifth birthday. MIT had transformed East Cambridge in the forty years since Solow had joined the faculty. The Marriott had risen where once burlesque halls and soap factories had stood.

Just eighteen months earlier Solow had been honored by the Nobel Foundation. Yet there was something about his long wait that seemed to leave a bad taste. Was it that the Swedes had given the prize first to the professional skeptic James Buchanan? It didn't matter this bright evening. Solow's students and friends turned out in force, including a galaxy of star contributors: Avinash Dixit, Frank Hahn, Eytan Sheshinski, Joseph Stiglitz, Robert Hall, Larry Summers, Martin Baily, Bill Nordhaus, Olivier Blanchard, Peter Diamond, George Akerlof, Robert Gordon, and, of course, Paul Samuelson. It was a proud day for MIT.

From the perspective of Cambridge, Massachusetts, the endogenous growth literature appeared in the late 1980s to be almost entirely a Freshwater phenomenon, another trick like real business cycles, another affront from the New Classicals at the University of Chicago to East Coast good sense. The very fact that its signal developments had occurred along the shores of the Great Lakes in Hamilton, Ontario, Chicago, Rochester, and Buffalo put it under suspicion. That it had borrowed the Dixit-Stiglitz model was particularly resented by some.

Never mind that the Chicagoans had finally adopted the approach pioneered by Samuelson and Solow, the use of small models, focusing on particular issues. The prevailing attitude was one of irritation, Joe Stiglitz's in particular. Stiglitz told the audience that all that stuff had been tried before, especially by members of the group that traveled to Chicago in the summer of 1965. "We knew how to construct models that 'worked,' but we felt uneasy making these special assumptions" that were required, he said; it took "a certain amount of chutzpah" to proceed where they had failed. He complained that the work of his colleagues and his own had been "curiously ignored."

(It was in the early 1990s that I first employed the phrase "the lost patrol" to describe the group that included Stiglitz, Sheshinski, Akerlof, and Nordhaus working around Kenneth Arrow's students Uzawa and Shell in Chicago in the summer of 1965. I meant that the importance they attached to capturing the growth of knowledge in formal models was discounted by the leaders of the profession. The act of reporting then on participants' differing views of the episode caused a certain amount of tension among friends. This is regrettable, but is not surprising. Almost inevitably, there is something intolerant about a great school. Not for nothing do scientists borrow the term "dogma" to describe whatever happens to be the prevailing view of the problems whose answers are within reach at any particular moment. The important thing is that no one was really lost in Chicago, and the men who were involved were successful in economics and remained friends. In 2004, at a farmhouse in Umbria near the old Roman spa town of Chiusi, Joe Stiglitz hosted a reunion for several of those who some forty years before had sought, with high excitement but little effect, to establish the economics of knowledge as a domain unto itself—including Karl Shell, George Akerlof, and Ned Phelps.)

It fell to Akerlof to remind the audience in Cambridge of just how perspicacious Solow had been in regard to the issues raised by the new growth theorists. He did so by quoting what Solow had said in his 1980 presidential address.

> There's a large element of Rorschach in the way each of us responds to this tension [regarding the importance of market failure.] . . . A hopeless eclectic without any strength of character, like me, has a terrible time of it. If I may invoke the names of two of my most awesome predecessors as president of this association, I need only listen to Milton Friedman talk for a minute and my mind floods with thoughts of increasing returns to scale, oligopolistic interdependence, consumer ignorance, environmental pollution and on and on. There is almost no cure of it, except to listen for a minute to John Kenneth Galbraith, in which case all I can think of are the discipline of competition, the large number of substitutes for any commodity, the stupidities of regulation, the Pareto optimality of Walrasian equilibrium, the impor-

tance of decentralizing decision-making to where the knowledge is, and on and on. Sometimes I think it is only my weakness of character that keeps me from making obvious errors.

That was the essence of self-deprecating Solovian wit—sly and razor sharp—that had made Solow beloved by generations of students at MIT. The eclecticism, on the other hand, was precisely the tendency that infuriated Solow's Chicago critics. Weren't the brightest students in the profession working furiously to narrow the issue of monopolistic competition even as Akerlof invoked his teacher's view that all of it was just an ambiguous Rorschach test? But in a room of five hundred admirers, it was the essence of Solow's character that was on display that night, like a shining suit of armor—loyal, graceful, kind, temperate, resolute. Economics probably did not have a more influential teacher in those years—a softhearted, tough-minded mathematical Mr. Chips.

THE POLISHED VERSION of Romer's Buffalo paper finally appeared in mailboxes in October 1990. This time there had been no problem with the referees at the *Journal of Political Economy*. He had changed the terminology, had changed the mathematics, too: giving up the grand choice-theoretic optimization framework he had developed in his thesis in favor of more commonly used shorthand techniques at the urging of Helpman and Grossman. Much later, looking back, Romer would say,

> Remember my thesis, and how it was articulated, I had these general equilibrium ambitions, I was hoping people would pay attention to that, but they didn't. On the other hand it was a little too abstract for the Solow types, the MIT types, who said, just give me the equation, don't worry about the logic and assumptions. I don't think either of those paths ultimately would have led to the clarification of what do we mean by an externality, as opposed to what do we mean why a nonrival good. That's where the rigor and logic of GE math really paid off.

But in 1990 the paper was upstaged by world events. The Berlin Wall had fallen the year before. The Soviet Union was dissolving. The slow-motion collapse of communism seemed to be the ultimate victory for the forces of the Invisible Hand. The gap between current events and developments at economics' frontier was very great.

The situation in economics became even more confusing when, in the spring of 1989, to general astonishment, Romer suddenly resigned his professorship at the University of Chicago after barely a year on the job and moved to California without a university appointment. His wife's fellowship had turned into an unpleasant difference of opinion with a lab chief over research strategy. She didn't like the long Chicago winter. The Romer children were reaching school age. It was time to make a choice. The matter came to a head just about the time of the first NBER meeting and the Solow Festschrift.

Sherwin Rosen, then chairman of the Chicago department, argued passionately that by leaving Chicago without a job, Romer would be ruining his academic career, hardly less than had Mundell, who twenty years before had walked away from Chicago to the University of Waterloo. Romer reckoned that some other San Francisco Bay area university would pick him up, either Berkeley or Stanford. If not, there was always politics, or software development—he often had thought of starting a company of some sort. His decision to leave the University of Chicago without a firm offer from a California school was only a little more unusual than his decision, a decade earlier, to submit his dissertation at Chicago rather than at MIT.

In the fall of 1989 Romer obtained a one-year fellowship at the Center for Advanced Study in Behavioral Science, which was perched on a hill overlooking the Stanford campus. The NBER office in a nearby grove of trees gave him an office, too. So did the Hoover Institution. He moved his family to the Stanford suburbs. And the next spring the economics department of the University of California at Berkeley offered him a tenured professorship. In September 1990 Romer began commuting the thirty miles to Berkeley several times each week to teach.

Behind him in Chicago there was confusion and resentment.

CHAPTER TWENTY-THREE

Conjectures and Refutations

IN *THE STRUCTURE OF SCIENTIFIC REVOLUTIONS*, Thomas Kuhn put the question succinctly. Suppose some well-trained young persons working in a discipline have a big idea in the nighttime; they propose a new interpretation of a problem that heretofore has defied resolution. "How are they able, what must they do, to convert the entire profession . . . to their way of seeing science and the world?"

By 1989 the increasing-returns revolution was in the hands of a hard core of leaders committed to following the logic of positive feedback in general equilibrium models wherever it might lead—Krugman, Romer, Helpman, and Grossman chief among them. (An alternative approach to specialization and increasing returns was emerging meanwhile at Monash University in Australia, under the leadership of Xiaokai Yang, a Chinese expatriate who had spent a decade in prison during the Cultural Revolution before eventually obtaining a Princeton Ph.D.) Sensing opportunity, both scientific and personal, others now joined the chase. A few were established researchers. Most were graduate students just entering the profession in the late 1980s and early 1990s.

It was twenty years since economics had been so embroiled in controversy, the last time having been the beginnings of the rational expectations revolution. There were discoveries to be made, reputations to be earned. The new ideas were a tonic to the young.

The new models of the growth of knowledge were employed in a campaign that resembled island-hopping in a great campaign. Plant a flag of applicability here, demonstrate relevance there, create a staging area, close in on a persuasive demonstration. The reasons given for preferring the new work were the usual ones. It addressed problems that the old growth couldn't handle and solved them. It anticipated problems that old growth hadn't recognized. It rendered clear what once had been hazy. Soon all the smartest kids in macro were at work, investigating the relationship between scale and specialization.

ONE OF THE FIRST extensions of new theory was to the growth of cities. What made them work? What kept them going? Why did they arise in the first place? Obvious as these questions were, the answers were anything but obvious. As Robert Lucas noted in his Marshall Lectures, "If we postulate only the usual list of economic forces, cities should fly apart."

At the University of Chicago a young graduate student named Edward Glaeser came to José Scheinkman with a proposal. Glaeser was fresh out of college at Princeton. There he had learned about the economics of increasing returns from Andrei Shleifer. Why not devise a test of Lucas's proposition about cities and increasing returns? If knowledge spillovers were as important as he and Romer and Lucas thought they were, there ought to be some way of demonstrating it by comparing metropolitan growth rates. With the aid of his teachers Scheinkman and Shleifer, Glaeser identified three competing theories about growth that were then making the rounds.

The first was a story about *concentration*. Companies like Eastman Kodak stayed in one place, grew big, prospered as they spent more and more money on learning how to do old things better and new things first. The implication was that monopolies were good for growth, because big companies had money for corporate R&D, power to restrict the flow of ideas, and marketing capabilities sufficient to capture more of the fruit of their investments in R&D. This view went back to Schumpeter.

The second story emphasized *competition* within industries. Glaeser called this the Michael Porter story, after the prominent business strategist. Porter had argued in *The Competitive Advantage of*

Nations that it was not monopoly that fostered growth but rather vigorous local competition based on shared technologies among companies in the *same* industries—"clusters," he called them. Company towns such as Detroit or Pittsburgh could be expected to stagnate, while localities such as Silicon Valley, where spying, imitation, and job switching were common, and hundreds of rival firms competed with one another, were more likely to foster sustained advantage.

The third story took industrial *diversity* to be the key, rather than specialization, because the most important knowledge transfers often seemed to come from outside the core industry. No economist had championed the diversity story (though something of the argument can be found in the writings of Alfred Marshall, cheek by jowl with the concentration story), so this view was ascribed to Jane Jacobs, the well-known critic and urban activist.

In a few memorable pages in *The Economy of Cities* in 1969, Jacobs had laid out the parallel histories of the English cities of Birmingham and Manchester in order to make her point. In the mid-nineteenth century, she noted, highly concentrated Manchester was the envy of the world. Observers as various as Benjamin Disraeli and Karl Marx described it as the city of the future. Its huge textile mills were organized rank on rank, as far as the eye could see. The city fathers ran their enterprises from their lunch clubs—more like Detroit than the highly fragmented and competitive Silicon Valley.

Birmingham, on the other hand, resembled neither place. It was a city of small organizations, doing bits and pieces of work for one another, with workers forever walking out of existing firms to go into business for themselves, dealing in steel, glass, leather, hardware, guns, jewelry, trinkets, pen points, toys. It was, she wrote, "a little hard to say just what Birmingham was living on because it had no obvious specialty of the kind that made Manchester's economy so easy to understand and so impressive."

Yet, by the late twentieth century, only two cities in England remained vibrant: Birmingham and the even more diverse London. As a company town, Manchester had turned out to be vulnerable to obsolescence; Birmingham, on the other hand, had remained a center of development throughout. "Cities are places where adding new work to older work proceeds vigorously," wrote Jacobs, because it was the rapid interactions among persons from quite different walks of life that was the secret of their vitality. Chance favored the environment that was more complicated and diverse. Unexpected juxtaposition was the important thing.

So which attribute was more likely to produce growth? Concentration? Or competition? Or diversity? For data Glaeser turned to the Standard Industrial Classification (SIC) system, a hierarchical nomenclature a little like the Linnaen system (by which living organisms are sorted according to kingdom, phylum, class, order, family, genus, and species). The SIC had been created by the U.S. Census Bureau to keep track of the changing American economy—a data set that ordinarily enjoyed little standing in technical economics. Glaeser looked at sixty-eight American cities between 1956 and 1987.

He found that, instead of growing faster, cities where big companies were overrepresented grew at a somewhat slower pace than the rest. The evidence was mixed on Porter-style strong local competition in particular industries, and consistent with Jacobs's view of the importance of a high degree of variety. This was not particularly surprising. Folk wisdom had long held that a diversified city like New York or Chicago could be expected to do better over time than a highly specialized manufacturing center such as Detroit or Pittsburgh. Marshall himself had said as much.

The paper by itself settled nothing. It didn't appear in print until 1992, by which time Romer himself had moved far beyond the pure spillover approach of 1986, to a monopolistic competition model much like Jacobs's argument, but more precise. Yet Glaeser's thesis raised eyebrows among economists, because it disclosed a new line of investigation into a range of phenomena previously taken for granted. It employed a new source of data as well, one whose introduction eventually proved a good deal more exciting than the Penn World Table numbers—the SIC system. Knowledge and specialization were on the table, however imperfectly understood. Glaeser went on to write many illuminating papers about cities, regions, neighborhoods, and nations.

ANOTHER PROVOCATIVE application of the new growth model had to do with population. The innovator was an unusual fellow named

Michael Kremer. After graduating from Harvard College in 1985, Kremer spent a year teaching high school in Kenya, followed by three more years as executive director of the program that sent him there. There is nothing like living in Africa to get you thinking about economic development. Kremer returned to Harvard as a graduate student in 1989, just as the excitement about increasing returns was at its height. Before long he decided to study the relationship between population and technological change.

The proposition that a growing population would mean faster technological change had long been part of the underground river of arguments about increasing returns. After all, a preoccupation with diminishing returns and "carrying capacity" was a recent development—really dating back only to Malthus and Ricardo. Before that, for most of human history, a growing human population had been deemed a good thing, not least because it meant there would be more innovation aimed at the betterment of humankind.* A more common interpretation in recent years was that it was population pressure that drove technological change. Kremer's bright idea about the relationship between population and technology was to examine the evidence over a sufficiently long period that cause and effect just might stand out—from the very beginnings of the human race.

First, Kremer built a model. In this highly stylized version of the literature of endogenous technological change, each individual would earn a subsistence living, and each individual's chance of discovering something worthwhile would be exactly the same, independent of population. The fraction of resources devoted to research always remained the same as well. Thus technological knowledge would increase with population, and population with technology, thanks to the nonrivalry of knowledge, because "the cost of inventing a new technology is independent of the number of people who use it."

---

* No less than the founder of political economy, Sir William Petty, wrote, "[I]t is more likely that one ingenious curious man may be found among 4 million persons than among 400 persons." Adam Smith understood the possibilities in much the same way: the more people, the great the extent of the market, the more specialization could take place, including the advent of specialists known as inventors.

Next, Kremer assembled a long-term history of the human population. The various estimates of anthropologists and archaeologists tell an interesting, if not especially surprising, story. A million years ago the human population of the earth totaled something like 125,000 persons. For many millennia, the growth rate of the human population was very low. At the dawn of the technology of writing, around 12,000 years ago, it had risen to perhaps 4 million persons and, by the time of Christ, to around 170 million. Perhaps a billion persons were alive when steam power made its appearance; the number had doubled by the 1920s, at which point hybrid corn was introduced. Fifty years later, some 4 billion persons trod the earth and, by 2006, world population was nearly 6.5 billion persons.

In "Population Growth and Technological Change: One Million B.C. to 1990," Kremer discussed his findings. What had actually happened to the human race was more or less exactly what the Romer model predicted. The technologies in question included discoveries of the most fundamental kind—the uses of fire, of hunting and fishing, of agriculture, of the wheel, of cities, of mechanized industry, of germ theory and public health. Since these technologies could be expected to diffuse fairly rapidly around the world once they were invented, the relevant number was the *global* human population, at least from the standpoint of a million years. Technological progress, in other words, had led to increases in population rather than to higher living standards, as human beings spread over the global landscape. On all available evidence, the great mass of humans weren't living much better in 1800 than they had been 12,000 years before—just a little above subsistence.

Then, at a certain point, what is known as the demographic transition began to occur. The steady growth of population began to level off. More people made a broader market, a broader market enabled more specialization, more specialization created greater wealth, greater wealth supported more people, until greater wealth eventually staunched the growth of population, at least in the nations that experienced the industrial revolution. The mechanism seemed to be the same (though not quite so pointedly hopeful, Kremer noted) as that proposed by Ted Baxter, the windy anchorman of

The Mary Tyler Moore Show, who planned to have six children in hopes that one would solve the population problem.

Starting about 1950, with population at around 2.5 billion, the increase in the rate of global population growth leveled off, while the population itself continued to grow at around 2 percent a year. For almost all of human history, then, Malthus had been right: technological progress led to increased population, not to higher living standards. But now, something had definitely happened. When Kremer ran his models, they were consistent with a spike. Electrical engineers had written down an equation where population growth increased with population, showed that it fit the data, and slapped a ruler on it. It indicated that world population would become infinite on November 13 in 2028—a Friday, naturally. But the research production functions of Kremer's model suggested that population growth rates would eventually decline—not because of mass starvation and environmental collapse but rather because increasing income would lead to lower fertility around the world—as, indeed, they had in the past 150 years, starting with the richest countries.

Kremer had produced rough but powerful evidence that Smith's dictum worked both ways. The division of labor was limited by the extent of the market—in this case, the human population. But the growth of knowledge, of specialization, had ultimately removed the traditional limits on the size of the human community. The same point could be made in reverse, because the melting of the polar ice-caps 10,000 years ago created a natural experiment, in the form of technologically separate areas—the Old World and the New World. At that point the land bridges between Eurasia and North America, between Australia and Tasmania and Flinders Island, disappeared. Before the melt, Kremer wrote, humans made their way slowly from continent to continent. Presumably the inhabitants of all these areas had access to the same technology—fire, stone and metal tools, hunting and fighting techniques. The Solow model, in which technology increased steadily irrespective of population density or land area, might expect that all regions would be on a par when Columbus's voyages began the process of reestablishing technological contact among the regions.

But, of course, it was the Old World, with the greatest landmass, that had the greatest population density and the highest technological level, followed by the Americas, with their cities, extensive agriculture, and intricate calendars. Australia was a distant third, with a population of hunters and gatherers. Tasmania lacked even the basic technologies that the Australians enjoyed, such as fire making, spear throwing, and tool building. And on Flinders Island, cut off from Tasmania about 8,700 years ago, was evidence of the possibility of technological regress. The last inhabitants of that tiny island died out about 4,000 years after they were cut off from the larger community, having lost the ability to make bone tools. Small numbers meant no specialization.

The mystery was the demographic transition. What caused birthrates to drop in countries when they reached a certain level of income?

Kremer's article appeared in the *Quarterly Journal of Economics* in 1993, along with several seminal papers in the new growth literature. It was quickly recognized as a classic, for having driven home so clearly the far-reaching economic implications of the nonrivalry of knowledge. Kremer, too, went on to produce a long stream of interesting articles, including an eye-opening proposal on how a purchase commitment for vaccines—in effect, a prize like the one famously given for a reliable marine chronometer—might both spur innovation and help the poor. If some nonrival goods were so important for human welfare, Kremer asked, wasn't it possible to imagine new institutions to produce them? He returned to Harvard. He became a consultant to the Gates Foundation. And, in 2002, he founded the Bureau for Research and Economic Analysis of Development Projects, or BREAD, to study the microeconomics of development.

THERE WERE many others. In 1991 Paul David again attracted a good deal of attention with a paper called "The Computer and the Dynamo." His idea was to compare the history of productivity gains arising from the rollout of electricity in the years between 1880 and 1930 with those associated with the advent of the computer. He demonstrated that the age of electricity had arrived not all at once but rather in two distinct bursts of technological imagination. The first, a gross mode in which "electric dynamos" replaced steam engines for the task of providing brute power, occurred during the last quarter of the nineteenth century. The second phase consisted of a more far-reaching set of applications that occurred mostly during the second quarter of the twentieth century, when engineers found ways to miniaturize electrical motors and work them into myriad uses not previously practicable, from refrigerators to radios. The same thing might be expected of computers, wrote David, as designers succeeded in working smart chips into everything from automobiles to credit cards. Perhaps the productivity problem so much in the news in the 1980s was a matter of what he called "technological presbyopia," meaning "sharp vision of the distant technological future, coupled with an inability to see clearly the nearer portion of the transition path."

Before long, Timothy Bresnahan and Manuel Trajtenberg generalized such comparisons, by advancing the concept of "general purpose technologies." GPTs were seminal innovations whose adoption displayed similar trajectories of useful applications—not just computers and electric motors but also watermills, steam engines, internal combustion engines, railways, canals, and the like. Bresnahan had done pioneering work on computerization by banks and other financial institutions; Traitenberg had written an influential study of the benefits of CAT scanners. The model they devised seemed to describe the arc of these sorts of less visible innovations, too—the typewriter, the banking computer, the camera, computer assisted imaging techniques. An example is in the post-1845 history of the application of the turret lathe, which had turned out (in Stanford economic historian Nathan Rosenberg's classic story of technological interdependence) to be the key to manufacturing all kinds of interchangeable parts work. GPTs quickly became a familiar part of the jargon of growth. Meanwhile, UCLA's Kenneth Sokoloff, an economic historian who as early as 1988 had used the new models to demonstrate that inventive activity originates around transportation centers and follows the system as it expands (the division of labor is limited by the extent of the market), found that low fees and simple procedures in the United States opened the patent system in the nineteenth century to a far wider range of creative individuals than did class-conscious European systems did. Economics was becoming more like the "critical history of technology" that had been the dream of Karl Marx.

Elsewhere, the new work on networks was beginning to pay off in microeconomics. Industrial networks themselves were not new, of course. Railroads, gas and electric grids, telegraph, telephone, and typewriter systems had existed for a century or more. That success often depended on "bandwagon" effects had been recognized in a general way at least as far back as Thorstein Veblen's book *Imperial Germany and the Industrial Revolution.* (England had taken the lead in railroading, only to lose out to Germany when its carriages were too narrow to ride on the improved wider rails that were subsequently adopted on the Continent.) But these industries had been labeled natural monopolies because of their tendency to produce increasing returns. They were classified as market failures, separated from "normal" competitive economics, their underlying similarities (high fixed costs, low marginal costs) not parsed in any detail. When *The New Palgrave* dictionary was announced in Dallas in 1984, the same year that Paul David gave his QWERTY paper, neither "networks" nor "standards" rated an entry.

Now a new generation of young economists who had cut their teeth on the Dixit-Stiglitz model of monopolistic competition went to work. They sunk their teeth into the concept of "network externalities." A series of new terms entered the vocabulary: The *interoperability* of competing standards became a key issue, meaning their compatability. So did the overall *complementarity* of various components in a system that had to operate smoothly together if they were to operate at all. *Switching costs* were to be considered, for learning a new operating system was a time-consuming business. *Lock-in* was a possibility. However new and exciting to economists these considerations might be, they had been familiar to the builders of entrepreneurial businesses for decades, even for centuries. The details were hammered out in a series of remarkable antitrust cases. What gradually emerged in microeconomics was what Katz and Shapiro described as the "hardware/software/wetware paradigm"—precisely what Paul David had illustrated so provocatively a decade earlier with his parable of typewriters, keyboards, and typists and a striking corroboration of Romer's findings.

A vast new continent opened up. Young economists suddenly were free to explore various connections between political institutions and growth that had been off-limits to them with the Solow model. The early 1990s saw many other pathbreaking papers. "Schumpeter Might Be Right" was the title of Robert King and Ross Levine's study of the significance of finance to growth. In "How High Are the Giant's Shoulders?" Ricardo Caballero and Adam Jaffe commenced the measurement of knowledge spillovers. Torsten Persson and Guido Tabellini asked suggestively, "Is Inequality harmful for Growth?" Soon enough Alberto Alesina and Dani Rodrik affirmed their conclusion: maldistribution slows growth through confiscatory tax rates on human capital. Then Daron Acemoglu and James Robinson began a lengthy investigation of the legacy of colonial institutions, culminating in a lnadmark book, *Economic Origins of Dictatorship and Democracy*. In time the excitement spread to more speculative fields in which networks seemed to be involved. To banks. To money itself. Language. Religion. The norms and skills reflexively labeled social capital. Many various sorts of "favor banks" came to be seen as networks in which the existence of externalities played a major role. Before long, macroeconomists and microeconomists were reading the same books, books about historical and institutional change, which they had not read before.*

Macroeconomics was moving beyond stabilization, trade policy,

---

* Titles suddenly popular among economists included Douglass North, *Institutions, Institutional Change and Economic Performance*; Richard Nelson and Sidney Winter, *An Evolutionary Theory of Economic Change*; Nathan Rosenberg and L. E. Birdzell Jr., *How the West Grew Rich: The Economic Transformation of the Industrial World*; Joel Mokyr, *The Lever of Riches: Technological Creativity and Economic Progress*; David Landes, *The Wealth and Poverty of Nations: Why Some Are So Rich and Some So Poor*; Eric Jones, *The European Miracle*; Paul Bairoch, *Cities and Economic Development: From the Dawn of History to the Present*; Jared Diamond, *Guns, Germs, and Steel: The Fates of Human Societies*; and Alexander Gerschenkron, *Economic Backwardness in Historical Perspective: A Book of Essays*.

and the marginal tax rate. Microeconomics was moving beyond industrial organization. Development economics in particular was transformed. For fifty years old growth theory had emphasized foreign aid to fill the gap between savings and investment, or education, or population control. But as William Easterly wrote in *The Elusive Quest for Growth: Economists' Adventures and Misadventures in the Tropics*, "None of these elixirs has worked as promised, because not all the participants in the creation of economic growth had the right incentives." New growth theory focused attention on issues that had previously been far from the spotlight: the significance of institutions, of law in particular; the role of multinational firms as transmitters of knowledge; the usefulness of export enclaves as a means of attracting foreign direct investment to developing nations (and the significance of corruption as a means of repulsing it); the possibilities inherent in microlending; the importance of geography, climate, and disease as fundamental determinants to be addressed; and so on. Soon literally dozens of economists were working on all kinds of angles.

IN ALL THE VAST SWIRL of 1989, no player in this drama was left out more completely than the man who shared an office suite with Paul Samuelson and Bob Solow, the putative star of the next generation at MIT, namely Paul Krugman. Romer had beaten him to growth. Grossman had stepped into his partnership with Helpman. His Buffalo paper, which was to have vaulted him to near the head of the parade, had been withdrawn.

For a time Krugman cast about. He wrote a paper (with Elise Brezis and Daniel Tsiddon) on "leap-frogging" in international competition. The paper made a stab at explaining the empirical regularity known as Caldwell's law—the fact, according to the historian of technology Donald Caldwell, that for several hundred years no nation had retained economic and technological leadership for very long. But "A Theory of Cycles in National Technology Leadership" wasn't published until 1993. By then its observation that the Japanese might be overtaking the Americans seemed out of date.

Before long, Krugman had found another starring role. If he

couldn't apply the logic of increasing returns to the growth of entire economies over time, perhaps he could deal with changes in the landscape. He took up economic geography.

Geography in 1985 was a sleepy backwater, not because its leading economists were dumb, but because they lacked the general equilibrium modeling tools that had created new trade and new growth economics. The field had grown up with a distinctive style of its own, thanks to its having been something of a cul-de-sac. Other disciplines concerned with cities had grown up around economic geography, to deal with the positive feedback processes that economics left out: regional science, development economics, systems dynamics, urban planning. Writers such as Lewis Mumford and Jane Jacobs had developed comfortable niches of their own.

It was about this time that William Cronon's influential book about the natural history of Chicago appeared. *Nature's Metropolis: Chicago and the Great West* made clear the role of chance and history in determining the distribution of settlements over the landscape. In Chicago's case, the self-reinforcing logic of centralization arose initially from the fact that the city formed at precisely the point at which the passage from the Great Lakes watershed to the Mississippi watershed was shortest, no more that the portage of a canoe over a dune, from Lake Michigan to the Chicago River. This arrangement Cronon called first nature. It was followed by second nature, which conferred even stronger advantages. Because it was a hub of water transportation, Chicago became a railroad hub and, later, an air travel hub. The rest—lumber, wheat, meatpacking, farm machinery, oil, steel, manufacturing, insurance, financial markets—followed in due course.

This was a story about increasing returns. Alfred Marshall had written, "When a city has thus chosen a location for itself, it is likely to stay there long," invoking the mysteries that were no mysteries but rather in the air—meaning know-how—to explain increasing returns. Now Krugman brought the same formal apparatus that he had created for trade. The reigning model since 1974 had been one of systems of cities, administered largely by real estate developers— revealing enough, but lacking a satisfying generality. Starting in

1991, with "Increasing Returns and Economic Geography" in the *Journal of Political Economy*, Krugman was able to restate in a series of formal models what Marshall had been driving at. These models, in turn, touched off a flurry of work by others on the countervailing forces of centralization and dispersal. Old debates in economics were rejuvenated by the high-tech apparatus. But Krugman reported that when he excitedly described some of the work in economic geography to a noneconomist friend, the latter replied, "Isn't that all kind of obvious?" A series of lectures explaining the new economic geography led him, however, to develop the mapping Africa parable. "A properly modeled idea is, in modern economics, the moral equivalent of a properly surveyed region for eighteenth-century mapmakers," he said.

In a series of articles and books, Krugman made escalating claims for the significance and success of the new economic geography, which he hoped would soon become a field as important as international trade. It was, he said, "a story of breathtaking scope." At one talk graduate students handed out T-shirts with the slogan "Space, the final frontier." His colleagues smiled at the circus atmosphere. As he sometimes did, Krugman occasionally went too far. But in working through the microfoundations of the urban landscape, he was answering questions that few had thought to even ask. Once again Krugman had accomplished quite a lot.

A BACKLASH AGAINST the new models of knowledge accumulation developed in the early 1990s, among growth researchers who had been raised on the Solow model. This was not surprising, for the new knowledge-based framework with its generalized increasing returns threatened the eventual destruction of a good deal of intellectual property—some of it mathematical, some philosophical. Many mid-career economists disparaged the significance of the new developments. Others claimed that they had known it all along.

A rich tradition of growth accounting had grown up around the Solow model. The Mankiw-Romer-Weil model appeared formally in 1992. Almost immediately it was christened the augmented Solow model. The implication was that simply adding human capital might be enough to account for all the observed differences in the wealth of nations. Maybe differences in the rate at which new knowledge was produced had relatively little to do with it, since essentially the same knowledge was available to all. Maybe convergence to the steady state was the important thing after all. A youthful economist named Alwyn Young dubbed this response "the Neoclassical Revival." By mid-1994 it was in full swing.

Young was an especially influential figure in this matter. (He was, despite the similarities of their names, no relation to Allyn Young.) His "Tale of Two Cities" appeared in 1992, a case study of the postwar growth experiences of Hong Kong and Singapore—small city-states and former British colonies similar enough institutionally to be comparable, yet quite different in critical respects.

The similarities between the island nations were plain enough, Young noted. Neither one had much in the way of natural resources beyond the location of its superb natural harbor. Both were populated mainly by immigrants from southern China. The same industries flourished and declined in both: from textiles to clothing, plastics, and electronics and, in the 1980s, from manufacturing generally to banking and other financial services. In 1960 the GDP of each was about the same.

Then there were the differences. Hong Kong's population was thought to be more educated than Singapore's, having among it a large portion of middle-class entrepreneurs who fled Shanghai after the Communist revolution. Its government had maintained a policy of laissez-faire with respect to nearly everything but land (it kept large portions of premium land off the market until demand for it reached a certain point). The government of Singapore, on the other hand, had been aggressively *dirigiste*, "picking winners" among up-and-coming industries, pursuing an aggressive policy of forced saving, and soliciting foreign direct investment from abroad. Thus Hong Kong's invest rate had remained at around 20 percent of GDP since 1960, while Singapore's had climbed from 13 percent to an astonishing 40 percent of GDP annually since the 1970s. It was these differences that made his tale especially useful to proprietors of competing theories, Young wrote.

The main result: although Singapore had invested nearly twice as much as Hong Kong for nearly twenty-five years, it had grown no faster. The implication was that its leaders had been too eager to chase each new fad: microelectronics, computers, financial services, biotech. For all the frenetic upgrading, Singapore's citizens were worse off than their counterparts in highly diversified Hong Kong. (The story of Manchester and Birmingham once again!) Young was a master of the underlying data; he thought carefully about the numbers and what they meant. He was reluctant to draw a firm conclusion. This much was clear, he wrote: the new growth models, though far from definitive, had "liberated the profession from the intellectual straightjacket of the neoclassical growth model," which for the most part had "relegated technical change and long-run growth to the realm of the unexplainable."

Then, two years later, in "The Tryanny of Numbers," the scrupulous Young skinned back a little. "This is a fairly boring and technical paper, and is intentionally so," he began. He would provide no new interpretations of the East Asian growth expecience, derive no surprising theoretical implications, draw no new implications from the subtleties of East Asian government interventions to excite the policy activist. He just wanted to get the numbers right. But when he did, in a careful study of the experiences of Hong Kong, Singapore, Taiwan, and South Korea, the result looked surprisingly like what the Solow model would predict: rapid catch-up followed by convergence to some sort of steady state. The East Asian "growth miracle" of increasing living standards was primarily the result of one-shot increases in well-understood factors, according to Young—higher participation rates, increased shares of investment, the shift of farm labor to manufacturing, more education. If the same technology was equally available around the world, apparently there was no royal road to faster growth. His conclusion: "Neo-classical growth theory, with its emphasis on level changes in income, and its well-articulated quantitative framework, can explain most, if not all, of the differences between the performances of the newly industrializing countries and other post-war economies."

Young's retreat was very influential. Paul Krugman made a similar point about Japan. He compared its experience since World War II to that of Russia—a burst of growth followed by extended stagnation. Soon Dale Jorgenson was predicting that U.S. growth would drop to near zero in the next century. New exercises in international growth accounting were proposed (by Robert Hall and Charles Jones, by Peter Klenow and Andrés Rodriguez-Clare), in order to clarify the roles of education and knowledge flows in fostering growth. The effect of all the careful econometric work was to shift a large portion of the debate away from the nature of growth itself to the much more complicated problem of international convergence. The neoclassical revival was highly popular in the mid-1990s. Perhaps the Solow model of factor accumulation with exogenous technical change was good enough after all.

ONE CHALLENGE to Romer '90 stood out more than any other. With his expectation that rates of growth would accelerate, Romer had made an assumption directly contrary to that of the Solow model—that tomorrow's opportunities would be more or less the same as those of yesterday and today. But suppose most of the important discoveries had already been made? What if investment in the growth of knowledge, too, was subject to diminishing returns?

The challenger was Charles I. Jones, "Chad" to his friends, a researcher who had the good fortune to be born at exactly the right time. He graduated from Harvard College in 1989, then spent four years at MIT. In a couple of papers in 1995, he pointed out that for most of a century spending on R&D had increased, education had become broader and deeper, openness to trade had increased at home and abroad—yet instead of speeding up, average growth rates in the United States had been relatively constant for a century. All these developments were supposed to increase the rate of growth. So what was really going on?

Jones set about unpacking the "technology production function" of the Romer model, examining the abstract equations that described how researchers produced new ideas one at a time, to see exactly what they implied. He found that they depended in part on a series of assumptions about knowledge itself. In Romer '90 the production function for ideas made a generous assumption: that spillovers from new knowledge eventually became universal, that therefore the more that became known, the more new ideas would be discovered. Everybody gained from the advent of new tools. And indeed, the discovery of calculus, the invention of the laser, and the development of integrated circuits had clearly increased the productivity of later researchers. This had been labeled the "standing on the shoulders of giants" effect.

On the other hand, perhaps increasing numbers of researchers simply got in each other's way, a little like drivers thronging a highway to a popular destination. Given the nonrivalry of ideas, it would be wasteful if six people routinely simultaneously invented the same idea (a familiar phenomenon to students of "patent-races"). Such research congestion Jones described as "stepping on toes." Would its effect be greater or less than "standing on shoulders"?

And what about the nature of the mysteries of the world themselves? Suppose the discoveries humankind had already made were the most important ones, and that it would become progressively more difficult to find the next really important advance? Perhaps a "fishing out" process was at work. In that case the rapid progress of the previous several centuries might slow down as competition among ever larger teams of cooperating scientists found fewer new ideas.

Jones's role was to give the new ideas an ever more rigorous exposition. He noted, as we saw, that U.S. growth rates had remained relatively constant for the last century, despite the growing resources devoted to R&D. What were the implications of that? What was the contribution of a steadily growing population? How could we know whether there was too much or too little R&D? At the AEA Meetings in Chicago in 2000, Romer put together three sessions dedicated to ventilating issues like these, eleven papers treating one aspect or another of the question "Is Technological Progress Speeding Up or Slowing Down?" There were no satisfying answers, but plenty of interesting questions.

Meanwhile, Jones moved to Berkeley from Stanford and broadened out his work. With Robert Hall he created a new growth-accounting framework; with Peter Klenow of Stanford he took over the NBER program on growth and fluctuations. He wrote an introductory text, kept up a steady stream of research ("Was the Industrial Revolution Inevitable?"), contributed a survey article on the economics of knowledge ("Growth and Ideas") to a new handbook of growth theory, and, along with Klenow and David Weil of Brown University, exemplified the next generation of growth theorists.

THROUGH IT ALL Romer kept working. He was able to do so because thanks to his new association with the Canadian Institute for Advanced Research (CIAR). The brainchild of a restless epidemiologist with the unlikely name of J. Fraser Mustard, the CIAR had been put together in the early 1980s, out of thin air (and with a good deal of corporate funding), as a means of enabling Canadian researchers to tap into the latest developments taking place in several fields— almost all of them somewhere else.

The idea was to fund the work of a few dozen talented individuals working abroad in fields such as cosmology, evolutionary biology, neural and quantum computation, and new economic growth theory, in exchange for occasional working visits to Canada. One result was that a great line of talent in many disciplines periodically trooped to Canadian cities for many years. Another was that Romer was able to put a good deal of energy into cleaning up his project. He wrote several more papers tying up loose ends, then put the topic aside. After a dozen years, he figured it was complete. He began thinking about other skeins of work. And in 1996 he accepted an offer from the Stanford Business School and, with some regret, stopped commuting to Berkeley. After six years he was home.

Before closing up, he made a reply of sorts to critics. "New Goods, Old Theory, and the Welfare Costs of Trade Restrictions" is not one of his finest papers. It tries to do too many things. But it is among his most provocative. In it he addressed a particularly perplexing question. The tacit assumption of a typical infinite-dimensional spreadsheet model was that the set of goods in an economy never changes, he noted. Yet, of course, the set of goods was *constantly* changing. The significance of the fact that it does had been recognized for at least 150 years, ever since the French engineer Jules Dupuit had spelled out the uncertainties involved in deciding whether or not to build a new bridge. The mathematical difficulty of modeling new goods presumably was only party of the story. How could economics have gone so long without developing a vocabulary for speaking clearly about the new? Whence the deep philosophical aversion to imagining the new?

For an answer, Romer turned to *The Great Chain of Being: A Study of the History of an Idea*, by Arthur O. Lovejoy. In that celebrated book, published in 1936, Lovejoy identified a certain habit of thought in the intellectual history of the West, sometimes explicit, sometimes not—the conviction that everything that *could* be created *had been* created. He traced the history of this "strange and pregnant theorem of the 'fullness' of the realization of conceptual possibility in actuality" from its origins in Plato through the various forms it took, in religion, philosophy, art, literature, politics, and science, connecting episodes in different disciplines not seemingly connected at all on the surface. Seeing those connections is, of course, a big part of the thrill of the book.

Originally, Lovejoy wrote, plenitude was an answer to a question it was natural to ask—why was the world what it was? Because the Creator, or the Idea of the Good, or God, had made it so. And it was in the nature of such a Creator that no genuine possibility of being could remain unfulfilled, because, as Plato wrote, "nothing incomplete is beautiful." Such a God could no more surpass himself than he could do a sloppy job. Thus the contents of the world were a *plenum formarum*, a full and general assembly of the range of possible things.

Lovejoy conducted readers on an extraordinary tour of the implications of this view. There was the Great Chain of Being itself, as described by Thomas Aquinas, in which "the lowest member of the higher genus is always found to border upon . . . the highest member of the lower genus." There was the new cosmography of Tycho Brahe and Copernicus, in which the discovery of a comet—literally something *new* under the sun—led to the replacement of the fenced-about world of the ancients with the assumption of a decentralized, infinite, *and* infinitely populous universe. Leibniz, co-inventor of the calculus, stated the "law of continuity" thusly: "All the different classes of beings which taken together make up the universe are, in the ideas of God who knows distinctly their essential gradations, only so many ordinates of a single curve so closely united that it would be impossible to place others between any two of them, since that would imply disorder and imperfection."

Little more than a century later, disquieting discoveries of extinctions and of fossils led to a frantic search for "missing links" and to the temporalizing of the chain of being, meaning its conversion from a static inventory of creatures to a *program*, in which the world was gradually evolving from a lower to a higher degree of fullness and perfection. Finally, though, came the great shattering blow to the assumption of plenitude—when Charles Darwin titled his book *On the Origin of Species*, rather than the *Origin of the Species*, thereby giving us an image of a world of trial-and-error and happenstance, a world of coming from, not going toward.

Romer picked up the story not long after Marshall, with the doctrine of *natura non facit saltum*, that there could be no gaps or missing links, that everything was perfectly divisible. Economists recognized that the set of traded goods in an economy is always changing, he wrote, but according to the economic version of plenitude, such turbulence was an epiphenomenon of no fundamental interest. The insistence of economists like Schumpeter and Young that the creation of new goods was of fundamental importance had been disregarded. "[I]n our post-WWII enthusiasm for distilling 'the miracle of the market' down to its mathematical essence, economists have generally been willing to push these issues aside. Decentralized markets could be shown to get everything right but only by assuming that half of our basic economic problem . . . had already been solved." With the infinite-dimensional spreadsheet of Arrow-Debreu, he said, all the relevant dated and state-contingent goods already have been selected; all that remains is to allocate them among a set of existing uses. To an economist the plenitude assumption means "we can therefore assume that we are always in the interior of the goods space." The set is convex. The distortions caused by the monopoly rights necessary to call new goods into existence in the first place are simply assumed away.

Romer traced the hold on our imagination of the plenitude assumption to a deeply rooted human desire to understand the world. "If we admit that new things can happen—that there are many things that could exist that do not yet exist—we undermine our most common explanation of why the world is the way it is: It has to be this way for it could not have turned out otherwise." And yet in the context of biological evolution, plenitude turned out to be not just wrong, he wrote, but wildly misleading. If the world had not been hit by the asteroid that destroyed the dinosaurs, life on Earth today would be different in ways we could scarcely begin to imagine. So, too, in economics there has been a reluctance to believe new things can happen, and *could* have happened at any point in the past. When dissenting economists insist on the importance of what they call disequilibrium behavior, he said, part of what they mean is that only a sparse set of goods can exist in any real economy, so genuinely new goods can always be added. "Only a failure of imagination, the same one that leads the man on the street to suppose that everything has already been invented, leads us to believe that all of the relevant institutions have been designed and that all of the policy levers have been found."

Romer's excursion into the history of ideas was quickly over. "New Goods, Old Theory, and the Welfare Costs of Trade Restrictions" moved quickly into a discussion of public economics, fixed costs, Harold Hotelling, and Jules Dupuit. The penalty imposed by isolation from the flow of new ideas was probably far greater than usually thought. But his point was made. He opened the door to philosophical excavation of foundations that will take many years to complete. By now he was accustomed to being told that new growth theory was not new. It might not *be* new. But it was *about* newness.

CHAPTER TWENTY-FOUR

A Short History
of the Cost of Lighting

VERY FEW ARGUMENTS in economics are ever settled. The question of which model to prefer is not easily resolved. In physics whatever doubts existed about the significance of $E = mc^2$ were settled once and for all among scientists and laymen alike by the detonation of a nuclear fission bomb. But there are few such explosive confirmations in economics. That is not to say that there are none.

The controversy over the economics of knowledge was interrupted in December 1993 by news of a study that, by itself, would all but resolve the question of which model of economic growth to prefer, fundamentally. Regression analysis is all very well. But a good experiment is can make the case for a new idea with overwhelming rhetorical force.

The conventional wisdom is that economics can't have experiments. Here, however, was a case drawn from human history, not even a "thought experiment" but a real one, with the ultimate in hard data. No purchasing-power parity adjustment was necessary. No cross-country comparisons were required.

Clearly technological change has been the major source of economic growth. On that much both the Solow and the Romer models could agree. But was the growth of knowledge a fundamentally economic process? Or were its wellsprings still so mysterious or intractable that they should remain out of bounds to economists? Exogenous? Or endogenous? Black box? Or not? The nub of the question concerned the implications for policy. Was growth a matter for economic policy for sovereign nations? Or was there nothing much to be done about it?

The shape of the data was as singular as a mushroom cloud.

THE EXPERIMENTER was William Nordhaus, the same Nordhaus who as an MIT graduate student in 1967 had tried to build R&D into the Solow growth model, using monopolistic competition. That section was dropped from his dissertation, and from the book that it became, *Invention, Growth, and Welfare: A Theoretical Treatment of Technological Change.* It was eventually published as a short paper in the 1969 proceedings of the *AER.* Whatever disappointment he felt as a young man, he had never showed it. He returned to Yale University to teach (he had been captain of the ski team as an undergraduate there), and applied himself to a variety of topics connected with the environment, mineral depletion, and, of course, the energy crisis.

Over the next thirty-five years Nordhaus blossomed into an unusual combination of inventive thinker and useful citizen. Work that he began in the early 1970s on extending the national income accounts to include the environment steadily bore fruit. He became a leading expert on global warming and on nonmarket accounting in general. From 1977 to 1979 he was a member of President Jimmy Carter's Council of Economic Advisers, then provost of Yale University and, for a time, vice president for finance and administration. In 1985 he joined Paul Samuelson as coauthor of his famous text, whose eighteenth edition was published in the fall of 2004.

The conventional wisdom is that the best experiments are connected in the mind of the experimenter with the proof of some bold hypothesis. William Harvey's vivid experiment on circulation of the blood, for example, was designed to demonstrate that the body works in a certain fashion. Was any such intent on Nordhaus's mind when he conceived the experiment? No, he says—at least not consciously. When he started, in the 1970s, he was only trying to get a handle on the price of oil.

The year was 1974. Nordhaus was a newly tenured professor at Yale, affiliated with the Cowles Foundation. Like nearly every other economist in that year in which oil prices quadrupled, thanks to OPEC, he was thinking about the energy problem. Because of his dissertation, he well understood that technical change was one of the predictable responses to the higher price of oil.

True, purchasers would cut back on the oil they purchased and seek substitute sources, such as natural gas. True, too, prospectors would seek and find new reserves. Supply and demand would seek an equilibrium. But inventors, meanwhile, would go to work to find more efficient ways to make the most out of whatever oil was available—inventors of all sorts, to be found inside corporations and outside of them, not only at lab benches but in purchasing departments as well. Of the factors that would influence the future price and availability of oil, Nordhaus guessed, technical change probably was the most potent. How to illuminate the question?

What Nordhaus wanted was a measure of the cost not of crude petroleum but of the uses to which the products refined from it were put to create things wanted for their own sake—heat, light, travel, work—and not only substances refined from oil, but the various fuels that had been put to those same uses before oil was discovered, and the substitutes for oil that had emerged subsequently as well: electricity and gas and solar and nuclear power. He wanted to measure the *output* of whatever fuel was employed, in terms of the work it performed, rather than the various *inputs*, meaning the price of the fuel and whatever additional equipment was required to convert it to work—the furnace, the lamp, the car. Theorists call this a *true* cost-of-living index, one that measures the cost of goods and services that are wanted for their own sakes instead of relying on a rule of thumb (a production function) to calculate the yield from the prices and quantities of the ingredients.

But then, output was notoriously hard to measure, especially where changing technology is involved. For example, how to compare the transportation furnished by a car with that of a train or a horse? How to compare the reach of a copyist employed to communicate your views with that of a printing press or a copy machine? Or a monotonous diet of beer and bread with one that included sushi and Moon Pies? The energy represented by a barrel of oil was especially difficult to pin down. It could be put to so many different uses in the modern age. For this reason economists had hit on the idea of service characteristics, meaning the underlying utility that the customer seeks from the good that he purchases.

To simplify matters, therefore, Nordhaus zeroed in on a consumer good whose nature hadn't changed very much in hundreds of thousands of years—the cost of lighting a room at night. Nighttime illumination is one of humankind's oldest consumer goods. It was an uncommon luxury for thousand of years, gradually giving way to an entitlement, but never changing in its most essential characteristics, regardless of whether it is thrown up by a fire in a dark cave, an oil lamp in a Pompeiian villa, a candle in an eighteenth-century drawing room, or a warm pink bulb in a late twentieth-century kitchen. The great virtue of the cost of lighting was that it would be easy to measure. The inputs to produce it would vary greatly, of course. So would the efficiency with which they were converted into illumination. But the nature of output would remain the same. Light was light.

So Nordhaus became a student of the history of lighting. He perused old histories of lighting and nineteenth-century laboratory notebooks. He combed through the work of anthropologists, all the way back to the discoverers of the Beijing cave that contained the earliest-known ashes of a hearth fire. He described the history of lighting technology in the following table.

MILESTONES IN THE HISTORY OF LIGHTING

1,420,000 B.C.	Fire used by Australopithicus
500,000 B.C.	Fire used by Beijing man
38,000–9000 B.C.	Stone fat-burning lamps with wicks used in southern Europe
3000 B.C.	Candlesticks recovered from Egypt and Crete
2000 B.C.	Babylonian market for lighting fuel (sesame oil)

1292	Paris tax rolls list 72 chandlers (candle makers)
Middle Ages	Tallow candles in wide use in western Europe
1784	Discovery of Argand oil lamp
1792	William Murdock uses coal gas illumination in his Cornwall home
1794	William Murdock uses coal gas illumination in his Birmingham offices
1800s	Candle technology improved by the use of stearic acid, spermaceti and paraffin wax
1820	Gas street lighting installed in Pall Mall, London
1855	Benjamin Sillman Jr. experiments with "rock oil"
1860	Demonstration of electric-discharge lamp by Royal Society of London
1860s	Development of kerosene lamps
1876	William Wallace's 500-candlepower arc lights, displayed at the Centennial Exposition in Philadephia
1879	Swan and Edison invent carbon-filament incandescent lamp
1880s	Welsbach gas mantle
1882	Pearl Street station (New York) opens with first electrical service
1920s	High-pressure Mercury-vapor-discharge and Sodium-discharge lamps
1930s	Development of Mercury-vapor-filled fluorescent tub
1931	Development of Sodium-vapor lamp
1980s	Marketing of compact fluorescent bulb

SOURCE: Timothy F. Bresnahan and Robert J. Gordon, *The Economics of New Goods* (Chicago: University of Chicago Press, 1997)

With his rough history of the technology of illumination complete, the next step would be to estimate the efficiency of each light-producing apparatus. Now Nordhaus had to become more precise. What exactly did he mean by illumination? For his purposes, it was the simple flow of light that mattered—its flux, measured in lumen-hours per thousand Btus. He noted the many aspects of lighting that are important to us today because they can easily be controlled—color, dependability, convenience, and safety. These he simply left out of his calculations altogether, for the variation was simply too great to measure. True, improvements in all of these factors were part of what we meant when we spoke of a higher standard of living. But such considerations detracted from the point that he was most interested in investigating, which was the extent of the improvement in the sheer efficiency of its provision over the years, both of finding fuel and turning it into light.

The experiment became a hobby. Sometimes he found data on the differing efficiency with which various technologies produced illumination that had been collected carefully by others in the course of work. One researcher in 1855 had examined the illuminating possibilities of "rock oil," just about the time it was discovered in large quantities in Pennsylvania. Another in 1938 carefully compared data on candles, town gas, kerosene, and electricity (observing, in the process, that "the discovery of petroleum in Pennsylvania gave kerosene to the world, and life to the few remaining whales").

At other times Nordhaus had to make the measurements himself. One day he burned twenty-one pounds of wood in his home fireplace and calculated that it produced an average of 2.1 footcandles of illumination for about three and a half hours, or about 17 lumens per pound. Another time he bought a little terra-cotta lamp dating from Roman times. He rigged it with a wick from a modern candle and fired it up with sesame oil brought from the little Himalayan principality of Hunza. A quarter cup burned for seventeen hours and produced 28 lumens, a major improvement over logs. He combined his own results with nineteenth-century engineering data, as carefully as he could. The result was an index of the price of lighting expressed in cents per lumen-hour.

Even then, however, Nordhaus was not finished. The nominal price alone could give a distorted picture of improvements in living standards. A case in point: a modern hundred-watt bulb, burning three hours a night, would produce 1.5 lumen-hours of illumination per year. At the beginning of the nineteenth century, a similar amount of light would have required burning 17,000 candles. To buy them an average worker would have had to work a thousand hours, or nearly half a year. Naturally, nobody thought that much light was needed. It would be necessary, therefore, to calculate a labor price of light. Good data on average wages was available since 1800. But for three critical junctures before that, Nordhaus made his own estimates—the length of time it might have taken an artisan to make a soapstone lamp and earn the money for some sesame oil, to catch a duck for its fat, to gather wood for a fire.

Half a million years ago, Beijing man would have worked sixteen hours a week to gather wood to illuminate his cave, he estimated. A Neolithic man, burning animal fat, would have spent only a little less time chasing down and rendering the duck. A Babylonian man, on the other hand, would have worked just ten hours a week for an equivalent amount of lamp oil, and both the quality of light and the ease with which it could be controlled were much improved. Some four thousand years later, at the beginning of the nineteenth century, candle technology had improved matters further still—but only by a factor of ten. In the end Nordhaus had a history of the true price of a lumen-hour of the cost of lighting, expressed in terms of a carpenter's wage, dating back to the dawn of human use of tools.

Then, some fifteen years after the oil crisis in which he first conceived it, Nordhaus realized that his project might have some bearing on a larger issue. The oil crisis had abated in the 1980s. But the controversies among economists over the sources of growth had heated up. It hadn't escaped him that his cost-of-lighting index bore directly on the Solow-Lucas-Romer debate.

So Nordhaus neatened up his data, cut it back to the mere 4,000 years for which he had money wages and prices—the 2,000 years before the Christian era began and 2,000 years after. He took it first to the NBER in December 1993, then to a meeting of the Conference on Research in Income and Wealth in Williamsburg, Virginia, the next April. Somewhat disarmingly, he titled it "Do Real Income and Real Wage Measures Capture Reality? The History of Lighting Suggests Not."

THERE ARE FEW more remarkable pictures in all of economics than Nordhaus's chart "Labor Price of Light: 1750 B.C. to present." It shows the rough cost of illuminating a room at night over a period of four thousand years. For almost forty centuries there is barely perceptible movement. Then, suddenly, starting around 1800, the cost of light falls off a cliff and begins declining at a rate approximating a right angle. You don't see many right angles in economics.

LABOR PRICE OF LIGHT: 1750 B.C. TO PRESENT

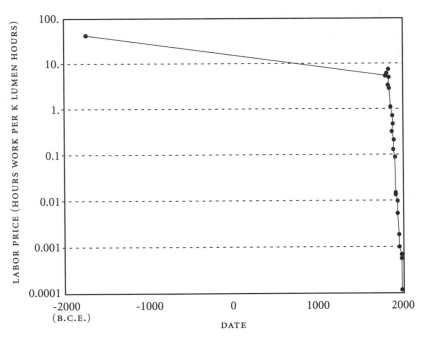

SOURCE: Bresnahan and Gordon, *The Economics of New Goods*

In this chart the history of the human race falls neatly into two parts. For most of its history humankind worked fairly hard for what little light it was able to obtain. People simply tended to go to bed when it got dark. For something like half a million years—from the time of the first fires in caves until candles illuminated the whole of the palace at Versailles—there is no evidence of any very great change in the labor price of light. It declined, to be sure, but the gradual improvement in lighting technology over the millennia was too slow for most generations to be aware of it.

By the beginning of the eighteenth century, the taste for lighting had been broadly enough acquired that the authorities had begun to tax windows (a good proxy for wealth) and candles. Between 1711 and 1750 the real price of candles in England rose by something like a third, causing cutbacks all around—a somewhat different kind of "dark age," according to Roger Fouquet and Peter J. G. Pearson, who studied the history of English lighting. Adam Smith, among others, inveighed against the tax on candles as being unfair to the poor; John Stuart Mill observed a "deformity of buildings" caused by the windows tax.

Then abruptly, about 1800, the cost of illuminating a room at night began to drop, year after year. Shortages of fuel came and went, but none could deflect the trend. Gaslight cost a tenth as much as candlelight; kerosene a tenth as much as gas. Electricity, starting in the 1880s, was the real wonder. Within a decade or so it ceased to pose a danger to its users. And by the twentieth century, nearly constant improvements were taken for granted.

To put it another way, ordinary people became rich. The real wage exploded, at least the real wage measured in terms of the cost of light. Illumination went from being a major heading in the consumer basket to being so small a fraction of consumption that, by the 1940s, it was expected that soon it might be free.

That was the essence of the experience of economic growth. The concept itself emerged only slowly in economic discourse from the nineteenth-century notion of "the national dividend." For a long time it was more or less synonymous with "the standard of living." Only after Robert Solow's growth model appeared did economists become much more careful about its definition. And now Nordhaus was warning that the official estimates of growth, conceptually at least, were way off, because of the manner in which new goods were linked into the index. Estimates of real income were only as good as the price indices were accurate. And it seemed that prices indices, by their very nature, simply ignored the most important technological revolutions.

When Nordhaus compared the light component of the consumer price index since 1800 with his own index, he found that the stories diverged radically. Money prices had risen three- to fivefold in 200 years, or only half as fast as the overall CPI. But in his own, "true" price index, money prices had steadily *fallen* year after year, until they were merely a tenth of 1 percent in 2000 what they had been when Thomas Jefferson was in the White House. And when he compared the changes in the purchasing power of a laborer's wage over

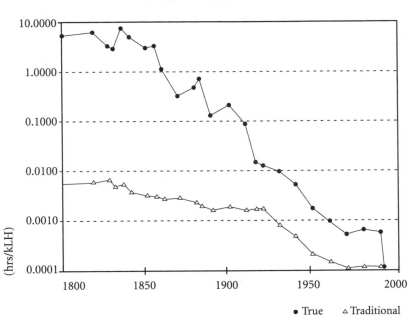

THE TRUE AND THE TRADITIONAL STORIES
OF THE LABOR PRICE OF LIGHT

• True   △ Traditional

SOURCE: Bresnahan and Gordon, *The Economics of New Goods* (University of
Chicago Press.) © 1997 by the National Bureau of Economic Research

those two centuries, he produced the picture above. On this one particular heading, the traditional story was off by *three orders of magnitude,* or a factor of a thousandfold!

It was not just light whose provision had greatly changed. Automobiles had replaced horses, television had replaced cinema, air
travel had replaced trains, and pharmaceuticals had replaced snake
oil. The only product that, superficially, had remained the same was
food. When he toted up the effect of all the "tectonic shifts" (a distinction very much in the Schumpeterian tradition) that had
occurred—in household appliances, medical care, utilities, telecom-
munication, transportation, and electronics—as opposed to the
run-of-the-mill improvements, which price indices were designed to
capture, and changes in "seismically active" sectors (tenements give
way to tract homes and high-rise apartments), Nordhaus concluded
that conventional measures of real output and real wages dramati-

cally understate the extent to which standards of living have improved. "The lowly toilet is classified as furniture but delivers a service that would delight a medieval prince," he wrote.

(A battle of such anecdotes, he warned, was likely to turn out to be a war of attrition, "because the number of products involved far outnumbers the number of interested and competent economists and statisticians." His suggestion: take a stratified sample of commodities from the CPI and put a dozen teams of economists to work on it for half a dozen years, estimating the "true" price of services delivered by those items, in the spirit of his experiment with the cost of light. There had been careful studies of televisions, pharmaceuticals, and computers, he said, but none for bananas, haircuts, or church sermons. He found it hard to think of a more exciting and worthwhile topic in applied economics.)

The real power of the Nordhaus experiment is to subvert the normal telling of the story. Was a 10,000-fold increase in the standard of living (as measured by the cost of light) sufficient to avert a proletarian revolution? *Why* did the improvements in the technology of illumination begin exactly when they did? What kept them going once they had begun? How much longer could they continue? (Not long after Nordhaus published his paper, the Department of Energy announced that scientists working in one of its labs had hit on a technique that promised a another tenfold improvement in the efficiency of fluorescent lighting.) What was it that happened around 1800 that made the years thereafter so very different from the years before? "I don't see how you can look at that chart," said Nordhaus, "without thinking of the industrial revolution."

"INDUSTRIAL REVOLUTION" is a term so common today that it is hard to imagine a time when it wasn't part of our everyday language. The term was employed by the French as early as the 1820s, and then Marx introduced it in his hazy way to economics. But not until Arnold Toynbee gave a famous lecture in 1888 did the term enter common parlance. Remember, barely fifty years before, Ricardo and Malthus had adamantly dismissed the possibility of an industrial revolution.

By the 1890s it was clear they had been wrong. "The bitter argument between the economists and human beings has ended in the conversion of the economists," wrote Toynbee. He was a trifle premature. Instead, two broad traditions had developed during the nineteenth century. Non-economists—"human beings," as Toynbee described them, saw the change as not just technological but also social, intellectual, religious, cultural, and political. These students now produced whole departments of knowledge, histories of all sorts, theories of all kinds.

The more general theoretical approach was dominated by Karl Marx. But Alexis de Tocqueville and Edmund Burke established a parallax view of politics. Max Weber turned Marx's idea on its head, forcefully suggesting that it was religious conviction in the form of a Protestant ethic that had produced capitalism, not the other way around, and so helped establish sociology as a subject in its own right. Emile Durkheim took up the division of labor from a different angle, and built bridges to the loosely structured discipline of anthropology. Less durable attempts to parse the great changes of the last few hundred years ran in every conceivable direction.

The main line of descent however, from Adam Smith through Max Weber, down to Alfred Chandler and Thomas Kuhn, with their histories of business and science in the present day, can be described as a preoccupation with the causes and the consequences of specialization—that is, with the underlying significance of the Pin Factory.

The economists, on the other hand, have given us growth theory. What do growth theorists have to say about the history of the true cost of light?

AMONG THOSE LEAST SURPRISED by his student Nordhaus's remarkable exercise was Robert Solow. After all, he had come up with the same answer, at first cut. Accumulation of capital is not the dominant force. Could modern abundance have been achieved by adding millions more candles? It was unlikely. More coal miners and farmers? Probably not. Remember Solow's initial calculation of the Residual of seven-eighths of increased output that could not be explained by the additions to the stocks of capital and labor. If the same methodology were applied to Nordhaus's data for the cost of light, the Residual might very well be 99 percent. Almost all of the action was in technological change.

On the other hand, Solow observed, there was nothing in the light experiment to tell you what fraction of national income you should commit to R&D. Nor was there anything to tell you what national income would have been without it. For Solow the new models were suggestive, but they were not yet fully formed.

For Lucas, who had been so keen on identifying policies that might improve the lot of the poor, the demographic transition was the key. Insofar as the industrial revolution was defined as a matter of sustained income growth, it was not exclusively, or even primarily, a technological event. "A small group of leisured aristocrats can produce Greek philosophy or Portuguese navigation," he wrote, "but this is not the way that the industrial revolution came about." Instead, a large fraction of the population changed the horizons of the lives they imagined for themselves—defying their parents, leaving their villages, taking work in impersonal cities, losing touch with their children themselves, in order to enjoy a standard of living that had suddenly begun to rise for large numbers of people. Economic development required "a million mutinies" against the traditions of the past, Lucas wrote, adopting a phrase from the novelist V. S. Naipaul, whose classic *A House for Mr. Biswas* described the passage of one family in three generations from the sugarcane fields of rural Trinidad to Oxford University.

Without wishing to dispute the place of knowledge in the growth equation, Lucas wrote, he wanted to make a complementary point. "Growth in the stock of useful knowledge does not generate sustained improvement in living standards unless it raises the return to investing in human capital in most families." The important thing was to get a fertility term into the model, Lucas wrote. Blueprints by themselves were not enough.

And Romer? If technical change matters so much, he asked, can we afford to continue to leave its secret rhythms unexplained? No wonder that the Lost Patrol thought it had tumbled on "secrets of the universe" when in 1965 it began examining the systems of incentives to knowledge creation and diffusion. To treat all this story as being outside the capacity of economics to influence or explain—as exogenous to economic models—is indeed, as Schumpeter had once described it, like playing *Hamlet* without the prince.

On the other hand, Romer's model underscored the importance of incentives to invention that were created by institutions. Consider the other developments that began to take hold in the late eighteenth century—the Declaration of Independence of Britain's North American colonies; in France, the Declaration of the Rights of Man. Changes in the law of property and patents affected the pace of technological change; there were parallel developments in taxation, banking, and finance, in science and education. Romer's model led directly to consideration of the institutions favorable to commerce—precisely the consideration that had been championed for years by Douglass North, Richard Nelson and Sidney Winter, Nathan Rosenberg and Paul David. The old-timers grumbled that they had known it all along. They lamented seeing the broad outlines of the work they had done restated in mathematical terms, especially since the new mathematical approach seemed to wash out precisely the details that were important to them.

Romer replied with his own version of the parable of mapping Africa, the metaphor of an hourglass. For much of its history, he said, economics has evolved in decentralized fashion, with its applied fields developing language and conceptual tools appropriate to their separate concerns. These were like so many dialects of a demotic tongue—labor economics, industrial organization, banking and finance, international trade, public finance, development economics, and so on. But with the coming of mathematics, field after field had gone through a process that could be thought of as resembling an hourglass resting on its side, with the vertical dimension representing the breadth and immediacy of its concerns, and the horizontal dimension representing the passage of time. As the younger generation turns to mathematics for its tools, a progressive narrowing takes place. For a while what its students have to say about the world is severely constricted by unfamiliarity with their newly acquired abstractions. But as they develop facility with their new vocabulary and new tools, these specialists' concerns gradually widen, until they are once again talking about a full range of issues—but now with a new and more precise understanding than before.*

What about the analysts who warned that humankind would soon be running out of the fossil fuels that had made possible the era of cheap and abundant light? It was one thing to recognize that prognosticators since Malthus and Ricardo had been forecasting imminent shortages for two centuries. It was another to note that human resourcefulness had intervened at every juncture to devise still cheaper and less environmentally disruptive alternatives. (Save the whales!) But just because alarmists were wrong in the past didn't mean they would always be wrong. Human ingenuity is very great, but, as Nordhaus himself has cautioned, "Sometimes the wolf is real."

No economist in the late 1990s thought more carefully about the three competing theories of growth than did Charles Jones, the Berkeley researcher who had raised the first questions about the *Star Trek* implications of Romer's model. At one point Jones obtained a National Science Foundation grant to develop teaching materials, and in 1998 he published *An Introduction to Economic Growth*. After carefully explicating each model, he concluded that each economist was preoccupied with a slightly different question. Why are we so rich and they so poor? Solow answered that it was because rich countries invested heavily in equipment and education and used these resources productively, and poor countries did not. Lucas asked how the rapid transformations known as economic "miracles," as in Japan or Germany or Korea, were to be understood. With a careful study of their transition dynamics, he declared. And Romer posed the question, What is the engine of economic growth? His model clearly demonstrated that the engine is invention, and that its drivers are entrepreneurs who, for one reason or another, create the stream of new ideas that, taken together, we call technological progress.

---

* David Kreps described Romer's hourglass in detail in his "Economics: The Current Version," in the winter 1997 issue of *Daedalus*.

To the most fundamental question of all—What does economics itself have to tell us about our the prospects for *our* lives?—the traditional answer, that economics is about scarcity and diminishing returns, surely can no longer seem adequate. The newest improvement in illumination is the solid-state white light–emitting diode (WLED), a fundamentally more efficient (and thus environmentally friendly) source of light than the cheapest fluorescent lighting now in use. WLEDs may transform Western nations' dependence on imported oil. But the new technology is of special interest to the 1.6 billion or so persons in the poorest regions of the world who still lack access to electricity today, for not only do WLEDs offer illumination comparable to the kerosene lanterns now most widely used, at a tenth to a hundredth of the cost; they also do not require an expensive electric power grid to do their work. Their AA batteries can be recharged by solar panels no bigger than a paperback book. They represent an advance as dramatic as did cell phones.

So what is economics all about? Land, labor, and capital, with technology considered as a force apart? Or people, ideas, and things, with the production and distribution of knowledge a matter of central concern? Scarcity? Or the countervailing forces of scarcity *and* abundance? For most people the story of the true cost of lighting is persuasive. It is the growth of knowledge that is the engine of economic growth. As the poet Blake put it, "Truth can never be told so as to be understood and not believed."

CHAPTER TWENTY-FIVE

The Ultimate
Pin Factory

ANOTHER EXAMPLE OF THE POWER of bits-and-atoms economics to make sense of the modern world was becoming apparent in the mid-1990s. This one was covered extensively in the newspapers. The rise of Microsoft demonstrated the possibilities open to a modern equivalent of the Pin Factory.

Thanks to its success in establishing its Windows operating system as "the universal" for personal computers, Microsoft enjoyed powerful increasing returns to scale, both internal and external. It was like the story of the QWERTY keyboard, except that in this instance Microsoft owned the design, and the market was truly global.

What, then, of the Invisible Hand? Might the forces of specialization win out over the countervailing forces of competition? Could a single firm take over a world market? Could it control the development of technology, crushing competitors when they arose? What about the bifocals of Adam Smith?

In the 1990s these were pressing questions of public policy, for the personal computer was, in fact, only one of two great information-processing technologies that appeared in the 1970s. A second industry made its appearance in those years, approaching many of the same tasks from a different direction—as differently as did, say, personal automobiles from railroads. The second system was, of course, the information highway—the Internet. So unexpected were its potentialities that they took Bill Gates himself by surprise.

What happened next was a battle for control of the basic machinery of the Internet—"the browser war," as it came to be known. It was as if central casting had dispatched two new rival technologies to act out the pageants that, years before, had been envisioned by Alfred Marshall, Allyn Young, and Joseph Schumpeter, "creative destruction" and all.

So well does the collision of the personal computer industry with the Internet illustrate the principles of endogenous technological change that it should be no surprise to discover that Romer was deeply involved in the story.

THE RISE OF the Microsoft Corporation from kids working in a college dormitory to the most highly valued company in the world in the course of barely twenty years is by now fairly well known. How in 1974 Gates and his high school friend Paul Allen learned from a hobby magazine about the appearance of a home computer for hobbyists, the Altair 8800—"Project Breakthrough! World's First Minicomputer Kit to Rival Commercial Models." How they offered to sell to its manufacturer, for 50 cents apiece, copies of an "interpreter" for its microprocessor chip, written in BASIC programming language and stored on perforated paper tape or cassettes or floppy disks, which would render the little computer operable by any fluent programmer—copies that they estimated he in turn could sell for between $75 and $100, so useful would the instruction set be to potential users. How, when he accepted, they then worked night and day for two months writing the program they had promised (and how Harvard hauled Gates before its administrative board and issued a stern warning against commercialism after an assistant professor discovered that he and an employee were using a university computer to write their code). How their software—the term itself was scarcely understood outside a narrow circle—proved to be an instant success.

In February 1976 Gates wrote a famous "Open Letter to Hobbyists." He was bursting with pride about the interpreter he and his friends had written for the Altair. But he complained that though he and two co-workers had toiled almost around the clock for sixty days to write the program, and most of a year thereafter debugging and documenting it, and though thousands of copies had changed hands, the royalties they had received up to that point amounted to something less than two dollars an hour. Why? Because people were "stealing" his software, Gates complained, making unauthorized copies and passing them around.

Until then, software had been for the most part either a friendly, cooperative enterprise among hobbyists or a gentlemanly business among corporations, handled by committees and billed the way a big law firm might bill clients—an invoice might read, "Software, $500,000." Now Gates was proposing a very different model, one much more like, say, book publishing. "Who can afford to do professional work for nothing?" he asked. "Nothing would please me more than being able to hire ten programmers and deluge the hobby market with good software," he said.

But to do that he would have to collect a royalty on each copy of his programs that was sold, as did writers and recording artists. And that meant, in this case, "shrink-wrapping" the software—creating a licensing mechanism that would place restraints on what buyers could do with their copies, and technical means of enforcing it, so as to exclude those who hadn't paid for a copy from possessing one. (Before long, code was incorporated into a program itself that kept software from running more than one machine at a time.) The extension of copyright protection to this new form of property would be hotly debated in hobby circles and university computer labs for many years, but its logic was quickly embraced in the marketplace. Soon Microsoft was offering customized versions of its BASIC interpreter (by now described as a "compiler") for nearly every new machine that tumbled out of the silicon cornucopia— Radio Shack, Apple, Commodore, and all the rest.

(Gates may even have known exactly what he was doing. The following autumn he took Mike Spence's famously difficult advanced microeconomics course—at the very dawn of the excitement about "bandwagon effects," monopolistic competition, and network economics. Enrolled in the course as well was Steve Ballmer, a fellow cardplayer with whom Gates had grown friendly. The two finished first and second in the course, but Gates didn't wait for his grade. He left Harvard one term short of graduation, to manage the business full-time in New Mexico. Ballmer joined him in 1980, after business school and a stint at Procter & Gamble.)

The personal computer industry in the 1970s was beginning to take off. It went from an indistinguishable speck in the industrial census known as the Standard Industrial Classification (SIC) code to a significant fraction of GNP in a quarter century. As microprocessor chips grew in power and complexity, the demand for software to harness them grew even faster. Gates understood full well (even if hardly anyone else did) that the kind of strategic investment he was making could create a barrier to entry into his obscure little market that, under the right circumstances, might become impregnable.

For software was the ultimate nonrival good. Computer programs, after all, are just a long string of numbers, arranged in bit strings consisting of nothing but 0s and 1s. At first, a piece of software required a medium for its delivery—a stack of punch cards, a paper tape, a magnetic tape cassette, a floppy disk, a compact disk. Nowadays it may be transmitted more easily, nearly instantaneously, over the Internet. But in most respects the information contained in a software program is like a book, a map, or a recording; the interesting thing is the content, not its physical package. Once it has been written, software may be copied endlessly with no diminution of its usefulness, and perhaps even a dramatic increase in its value, if the network effects are strong. Shrink-wrapping, creating a market in stores for new programs, and placing licensing restrictions on their subsequent use turned the software industry into the newest marvel of the division of labor.

Gates's crucial stroke of luck came in the fall of 1980. That was when IBM asked Microsoft to supply an operating system for IBM's new PC, the well-financed machine that would finally establish the market for personal computers. The complexity of computers had grown far beyond an individual's capacity to manage the sequence of tasks they performed. Developers had begun writing modular applications, spreadsheets, and word-processing programs; no longer would an interpreter suffice to harness the power of the underlying microprocessor; now a much more complicated "operating system" would be required. IBM sought out Microsoft because it thought Microsoft had more experience writing operating systems than any other firm; Gates had made it a point to write programs supporting any and all of the new microcomputers that entered the market. It helped that Gates's mother, Mary, knew IBM's chief executive, John Opel, from their membership in the national board of directors of United Way.

Why didn't IBM simply buy Gates's company? (Or, for that matter, buy QDOS, the company that Gates bought after undertaking the mission, since he didn't really have an operating system, either?) Or put a couple of hundred programmers to work writing its own proprietary operating system and put the brash young competitor out of business? Gates's opportunity in 1980 existed at least partly because of an antitrust action against IBM undertaken by the administration of President Lyndon B. Johnson on its last day in office in 1969. In those days IBM enjoyed a formidable lead in mainframe computing. The government sought to break it up. To avoid that eventuality, the company unbundled its software—that is, it agreed to sell it separately—and thereby implicitly agreed to let others write programs for its machines. Independent software publishing had been created at a stroke. (Probably the bourgeoning complexity of computers would have forced IBM to unbundle software eventually, even without the law—in accordance with the process of vertical disintegration that Allyn Young had described forty years earlier in Edinburgh.) In any event, IBM was still looking over its shoulder in 1980, and when Gates told IBM he wanted a royalty on each copy sold, not a fixed fee, IBM acquiesced. Gates would be free to sell the same software to other computer makers as well. There would be no exclusive license. IBM couldn't be bothered to haggle. After thirty years of unparalleled success in the mainframe computer business, the company was paying $1.04 for its business cards.

After that, Microsoft grew explosively. As he had from the beginning, Gates poured profits into extending his product line. He had seen Apple's MacIntosh: the mouse, the cursor, the icons, the way that its operating system could keep more than one program running at the same time and visible in separate sections of the screen. He set out to incorporate these features in an operating system that would compete with Apple's Mac and IBM's Topview system. He called it Windows. The first system shipped in 1985. He charged IBM next to nothing for using the new operating systems on its machines. He made his money collecting royalties from IBM clones, of which there was an ever-increasing number. Before long he had elbowed aside IBM's plans to build a new operating system of its own; users of its PCs had become hooked on his product instead. Next he needed a version of Windows that would run on minicomputers and mainframes as well. In 1988 he hired a top software architect from Digital Equipment to build it. Microsoft was practically printing money, earning twenty-five cents on every dollar of sales. Gates could afford to hire the best programmers in the industry—as many as he could think of ways to employ—and designers and marketers too.

Users were quickly figuring out that the operating system and its underlying Intel microprocessor had become "the universal," much as the QWERTY keyboard once had. It was the system they would have to know if they were to connect up smoothly with diverse employers, much as typists had concluded that they would be better off knowing the dominant system than any other.

It was as if Gates had received through use a copyright on a hugely more complicated version of the keyboard. The machines themselves, IBM's PC and DEC's vaunted line of "minis" among them, had become "commoditized," less important than the software with which they were controlled. By the time IBM figured out that it had lost its leverage, it was too late. The operating system, not the computer, had become the relevant standard. A complementary product was driving the market.

Microsoft was becoming the Pin Factory, the ultimate Pin Factory, because its market was, quite literally, the entire world. The process was little different from the description of internal increasing returns that Alfred Marshall had given a hundred years before: the able man, the strokes of good fortune, the hard work, the abundant credit, the talented subordinates, the systematic improvements, the expanding market, the falling prices, the growing specialization, as well as some tactics that Marshall hadn't described. Seldom did Microsoft create the best products on its own. Instead, it became expert at blocking others' innovations, buying time while developing its own alternative products. Gates understood that he would have to keep moving and extend his reach or be acquired by more powerful rivals, whether IBM or somebody else. Before long, Microsoft had surpassed mighty IBM in market valuation. In just twenty-five years, Gates had become the richest man in the world

THE INTERNET's history is less well known. Its underlying technology started out long ago in Cambridge, Massachusetts, and proceeded along very different lines.* The story begins with MIT's assignment during World War II to build a "universal trainer" for the Navy—a cockpit-like platform that could simulate the handling characteristics of any number of different aircraft, depending on the perforated tape program that was fed into the computer to which it was attached.

This was the advent of something called real-time computing—a great dissent, it turned out, from the computer tradition dominated by John von Neumann and emanating from Princeton, which conceived of computers mainly as very powerful adding machines, characterized by the principle of "batch processing." The first machines cost so much that it was thought to be crucial that they never remain idle; hence programs were fed into them sequentially, in batches, by technicians; persons whose computations these "mainframes" performed never got near the machine.

The MIT idea was to build a computer based on feedback principles. It would have to respond to events as quickly as they occurred, in "real" time, speeding up, slowing down, constantly staying ahead of what was happening, until it was switched off. Real-time comput-

---

* A highly readable general-interest history of the Internet exists, in the form of a biography of the Johnny Appleseed of computer networking: *The Dream Machine: J. C. R. Licklider and the Revolution That Made Computing Personal*, by M. Mitchell Waldrop.

ing was considered to be a pipe dream by the wizards in Princeton and Philadelphia. Before long, however, it became clear to the tinkers in Cambridge that not only could such a computer be built; it could also control things in real time. It could, for instance, replace the air defense clerks who calculated optimal intercept paths and pushed around model airplanes on plywood map tables. The hush-hush early warning and missile defense system known as Semi-Automatic Ground Environment (SAGE) initiative of 1952 was budgeted at around two billion dollars over fifteen years—about the cost of the Manhattan Project plus the expense of developing radar. And soon it was clear that the new real-time computers could control the operations of much more mundane tools than radars—machine tools, for example.

The men who designed and supervised these early projects were autonomous scientists, for the most part, working mainly for the government on projects having to do with defense. The SAGE project connected computers, radars, airplanes, and ships and put Nike missiles near the centers of American cities. It catapulted its principal contractor, the IBM Corporation, from its role as a punch card tabulator to a position of dominance in the digital computer industry. It also spawned IBM's most serious long-term competitor, the Digital Equipment Corporation, in the first of a long line of technological disagreements taken to the marketplace. (IBM stuck with batch-processing while DEC put its minicomputers in the hands of scientists and engineers—expensive as they were, the first really personal computers.) Most important of all, the SAGE project established the significance of applications software, subsidiary specialized programs that would permit computers to perform many different tasks, which to that point had been something of an afterthought. The dogma here was to "put control of the machine in the hands of its operator."

Much of the romance in those days had to do with computer memory—with the steady progress from paper tape and vacuum tubes to ferrite cores, transistors, silicon chips, and microprocessors. Storage capacity, and thus program complexity, advanced by rapid leaps and bounds. The Atlas program to build an intercontinental ballistic missile was under way. The space race was gathering speed. Many individuals grasped the possibilities inherent in a network of big machines dividing their time among many users, sharing capacity much as did interconnected electricity-generating stations. As early as 1961 a network visionary like John McCarthy wrote, "Computing may someday be organized as a public utility, just as the telephone system is organized as a public utility." But none of the scientists who conceived of these projects was more important in the long run than a psychologist-turned-technologist named J. C. R. Licklider. Lick, as he was called, had a vision of computers working together that he described as man-computer symbiosis. The Internet was created by a community rather than by a single individual, but if there is one man whose involvement can serve as a symbolic counterpart to that of Bill Gates, it is Licklider.

Today connecting computers together seems like an elementary task, but in the early 1960s creating the elementary protocols that would let computers talk to one another posed a formidable challenge. In order to turn his vision of a network into a reality, Licklider joined the Defense Department's Advanced Research Projects Agency (ARPA) in Washington. ARPA was newly established to direct long-term U.S. R&D in the wake of the Russian success with *Sputnik*. Time-sharing was a classic case of "market failure." That is, companies never could be counted upon to develop the new techniques, for the reasons that Kenneth Arrow was thinking of when he wrote about the production of knowledge in 1960: the fixed cost of the new technologies (their "indivisibility") was so great that no company could reasonably expect to recover it and go on to make money. Only the government could afford the risk. It undertook investments not in the name of creating externalities, though they certainly did, but because it wanted to call into being a series of highly specialized new goods: an atomic bomb, a powerful computer, an intercontinental ballistic missile, a moon rocket, a time-sharing network.

Another ARPA project pursued a will-o'-the-wisp known as packet switching. Here the government was shopping for a communications network that could survive a nuclear attack. The idea was to create a decentralized system of switches that would slice up any message into pieces, standardized little packets of information that could then be sent any which way among the nodes of a network before being eventually reassembled into whole messages when they reached their destinations. Today those switches are known as routers, and while most of us think of them as being just another species of computer, they are in fact highly specialized machines that form the basis for communications technology as different in its logic as are personal automobiles and trucks from passenger and freight trains. Indeed, the very idea is similar: instead of long message trains moving along a few main trunks through central switching points (where they can be metered in time of peace and disrupted in time of war), millions of little message vehicles find their way (at the speed of light) along whatever routes offer least resistance, until they join up again at journey's end. That is packet-switching. There were many other engineering triumphs.

From their beginnings the technologies that formed the basis for the Internet were developed by people who, generally speaking, were responding to a set of incentives very different from that of Gates when he started Microsoft. They were computer professors, government grant-makers, corporate bureaucrats, military planners. To train the scientists and engineers who would build the system, ARPA invested heavily in human capital; it established the first computer science Ph.D. programs in the country, at Berkeley, Stanford, MIT, and Carnegie Mellon in 1965. The professors who became the first faculty at these schools in turn produced a distinctive industrial culture and ethos—one of cooperation, sharing, and even a certain disdain for sharp elbows. It was one such, after all, who sought to throw Bill Gates out of school for converting a school computer to his own use.

Like Topsy, the ARPANET just grew and grew. Once the Defense Department resolved to privatize it, in the late 1980s (the enabling legislation being that which its author, Al Gore, had in mind when he remarked that he had "created" the Internet), the organization that took the helm, the Internet Engineering Task Force (IETF), was essentially the same user group that had been building it for the Pentagon all along. This committee of self-effacing engineers was so low-profile as to be nearly anonymous. The IETF's methods were for the most part diametrically opposed to Gates's customer-oriented business model: bottom up, open-access, its membership limited to individuals instead of companies. Few among the makers of the Internet were trying to get rich off these developments, at least not at first. It was not that they were immune to the prospects of personal gain; nor is it correct to say that none had an entrepreneurial bent. But most were of a genus very different from the two-guys-in-a-garage variety. They took their gains in compensation in the form of autonomy, perks, prestige, and security rather than stock options. Instead of tinkering alone in dorm rooms, they emphasized teamwork. Instead of proprietary secrets, they developed "open" standards. The design of the QWERTY keyboard is a good example of an open standard. It is available to all, but owned by no one in particular. The design of the magnetic tape cassette, developed in the 1960s by N. V. Philips and quickly made available to be copied free of charge, was a more recent example.

As an industrial presence, then, the Internet was as stealthy in its advance as the personal computer industry was unmistakable. To begin with, the Internet was free, at least to its end users. No Charlie Chaplin advertising campaigns introduced its appearance on the scene. When the government decided to privatize ARPANET in 1991, the leading trade journal's report of this step wasn't picked up by the newspapers for six months. As a result, the sudden emergence of the Internet took most people by surprise in 1993. The telephone companies didn't have a clue, for example, when the transmission-control protocol/Internet protocol (TCP/IP) was adopted, even though it ultimately threatened to destroy their business by enabling the Internet to expand over telephone lines. The architects of the Internet designed it in such a way that it was always easy to "build on top"— to engineer new features into the existing setup without undermining its earlier functionality. (Microsoft's engineers built in just the opposite way. With each new iteration, the system had to be completely replaced, the better to earn a return on the company's investment.)

No wonder then that by the time the Internet actually emerged, it was a paradise for geeks, and geeks alone. Although a stupendous technological achievement, it was hard to understand, and hard to use. Bulletin boards and discussion groups mushroomed. But unless you already knew exactly what you were looking for, there was almost no way to find it—or anything else. It was natural, therefore, for a computer scientist named Tim Berners-Lee, working at the CERN physics research center in Switzerland, to propose in 1989 a series of protocols designed to make it easy to search the Internet as a whole, as if each activity possessed an entry in a giant index, and each user possessed a software program specifically designed for the purposes of search—a "browser," Berners-Lee called it. Such was the efficiency of the IETF's way of working—"rough consensus and running code"—that by 1990 an early version of the World Wide Web was being tested. A couple of years later the National Center for Supercomputing Applications' prototype "Mosaic" browser was rapidly spreading from lab to lab.

The breakthrough came in 1993. That was when a graduate student named Marc Andreessen and some of his friends at the University of Illinois wrote a browser program of their own. They made two small changes. They added some graphics, so that it could be operated with a mouse instead of text-based instructions. And they wrote their code so that it could run on the Windows operating systems of personal computers, as well as the Unix system more common among users in universities. They formed a company and called it Netscape. They gave their browser away at first, in hopes that it would quickly become the preferred gateway to the Web, in which case subsequent copies of their software would bring substantial revenues. Suddenly people were talking about the New New Thing.

SOMETHING WAS WRONG, Ballmer realized, when he visited his old Harvard College haunts in the fall of 1993 and found that the same kids who twenty years before had been excited about hobby computing were now talking about nothing but the Internet. He returned to Seattle and circulated a memo among top Microsoft executives slugged "What Think?" Within days the company had begun to gear up to integrate at least some Internet capability into its operating system. Its programmers made rapid progress. Soon they under-stood exactly what those Illinois boys were doing.

The Netscape browser was "middleware," a class of software pro-grams defined as the "/" in client/server architecture. But the term was not coined, much less fully understood, when Berners-Lee invented the Web and Andreessen began giving Netscape away. All that was clear was that a really good "/" would consist of a layer of software sufficiently flexible to be able to work with any operating system, Windows, Unix, whatever was next. And therein lay the rub, as far as Microsoft was concerned. If the program was as versatile as that, it would no longer matter what operating system you were using—or whether you were using one at all. Before long, presum-ably, you would be able to surf the Web and send all the email you wanted with a device much cheaper than a Windows-based PC!

Netscape middleware, in other words, had the potential to wrest away control of the computer desktop, to "commoditize" the operat-ing system, in much the same way Microsoft had used the Windows operating system to commoditize the machines themselves and reduce IBM's ability to command premium prices for its PCs. About the same time, Sun Microsystems began promoting a new program-ming language for the Web called Java. It had had similar possibili-ties, for applications written in Java would be compatible with any operating system, even a cheap Windows knockoff. If Java were to become a universal language, anybody would be able to write network-based applications with it. No longer would the operating system be the important thing. The Windows monopoly would be broken. The Internet would trump the PC.

It was at this point that the old technology (if you can call twenty years old!) sought to take over the new—that, in effect, the railroad reached out and tried to take over the automobile. Gates was deter-mined not to be upended by an unexpected rival, as he had bested IBM. He now dramatically reconfigured his strategy.

The battle between Microsoft and Netscape and other middleware vendors for control of end users on the Internet—"the browser war"—lasted about two years. It began with Gates's famous Pearl Harbor Day speech to analysts, on December 7, 1995, in which he declared war on Netscape, painting Netscape as the author of a sneak attack. Netscape stock dropped 17 percent on the news. Next, Microsoft quietly offered to pay Netscape to divide up the market, with itself taking the lion's share. When that didn't work, the software giant bullied and threatened Netscape's customers. It told Compaq, for example, that it couldn't have Windows if it also supplied Netscape to its customers. It developed its own browser, quite a good program called Internet Explorer, to be bundled with its Windows operating system and given away for free.

At the same time, Microsoft began to expand into whatever niches it perceived as somehow threatening its franchise. It became a master of technology "blocking," mostly by fostering interoperability of its own systems and discouraging their use with those of everyone else. Microsoft licensed Java, for example, but immediately announced its intention to "extend" the language, meaning change the way it worked on Microsoft platforms until it had become, in effect, a different language, one that worked well only with dominant Microsoft software. Microsoft's mantra became Embrace (the application), Extend (its functionality), Extinguish (the rival).* In her book about America Online,† Kara Swisher described how Gates said to AOL's chief executive, Steve Case, what IBM fifteen years earlier had been unwilling to say to Gates: "I can buy 20 percent of you, or I can buy all of you. Or I can go into this business myself and bury you."

Microsoft's attack was brutally effective. Netscape, which had briefly soared into the stratosphere on the stock market, fell back and eventually was taken over by AOL. Microsoft's rivals complained bitterly that they were being unfairly abused. The Federal Trade Commission had begun investigating the firm in 1990, but its commissioners deadlocked, and so the Justice Department took over the case, hiring as its chief expert (on Kenneth Arrow's recommenda-

---

* A good description of life on the receiving end of this strategy can be found in Charles Ferguson's *High Stakes, No Prisoners: A Winner's Tale of Greed and Glory in the Internet Wars*.
† *AOL.COM: How Steve Case Beat Bill Gates, Nettled the Netheads, and Made Millions in the War for the Web.*

tion) Brian Arthur, a noneconomist who had been working on increasing returns at the Santa Fe Institute.* The government filed suit in 1994 and quickly obtained a consent decree that turned out to be entirely cosmetic. It had been powerless to alter Microsoft's behavior, especially in light of the looming Internet threat.

By 1996, however, the outbreak of the browser war had renewed the Justice Department's interest.

IT WILL BE YEARS before the story of the government intervention in Microsoft's battle in the 1990s with the middleware providers on the Internet is told. By its sorry conclusion, the episode had something of the flavor of a bad dream, part of the overheated decade that followed the end of the Cold War. But certain aspects of the story are already clear.

For one thing, the government fielded a first-rate team. Janet Reno was still attorney general—she would oversee the case throughout—but now a well-known former public-interest lawyer named Joel Klein had become deputy assistant for antitrust. He hired the celebrated attorney David Boies to serve as the government's lead trial lawyer. Boies in turn enlisted the MIT economist Frank Fisher to serve as his principal expert witness. Fisher's presence added heft; thirty years earlier he had been the lead economist in IBM's defense. In-house antitrust division economists were heavy hitters as well—Daniel Rubinfeld of Berkeley and Tim Bresnahan of Stanford in succession.

For another thing, the government this time had caught Microsoft red-handed. An avalanche of documentation obtained in discovery demonstrated that not just Netscape but also Sun's Java architecture and a number of other rivals had been the targets of illegal practices. Above all, the case came before a very different judge. When U.S. District Court Judge Stanley Sporkin declined to bless the earlier consent decree, the Washington Court of Appeals

---

* For a discussion, see M. Mitchell Waldrop's *Complexity: The Emerging Science at the Edge of Order and Chaos.*

had replaced him on the case with Thomas Penfield Jackson, a Reagan-appointed conservative.

Microsoft was caught flat-footed. The Seattle firm had almost no presence in Washington, no experienced lobbying arm, no access to good advice. It behaved like a spoiled adolescent. In one of its most embarrassing gaffes, the firm at one point actually lobbied Congress to cut the Department of Justice budget. No experienced corporation would ever do that. The *New York Times* columnist Thomas L. Friedman described Gates and Ballmer as "the Young and the Clueless." "How would you feel if the biggest company in your town tried to use its influence to slash the funding of your police department, at a time when the police department was bringing charges against the company?" Friedman asked. And in due course Judge Jackson found the company guilty of violating the Sherman Act, of having used illegal means to defend its monopoly. The trial proceeded to its remedy phase.

At this point the government asked for a breakup. To explain how the measure would work, it produced a surprise expert, all but unknown outside the economics profession, but their outside expert on the remedy all along. It was, of course, Paul Romer. He had been recruited, the government explained, because he had recently formalized a theory in which incentives in the marketplace determined the rate of technological change.

In his declaration to the court, Romer explained that the advantage of the theory was that it "lets one trace the effects that social institutions in general, and legal institutions in particular, have on incentives, and thereby the rate of technological change." The stakes were high. Over time, he continued, little differences in the growth rate have a big impact on the standard of living. As a result, decisions about the law, and especially about high-tech antitrust law, "can be among the most important policy decisions that a society makes."

The theory might be new, said Romer, but the principle was much the same as that underlying the decision some twenty years before to break up AT&T. At that time, the matter was largely one of common sense. There was no high theory, just the strong intuition that market competition would stimulate innovation where regulation had failed.

And so it had. The *Wall Street Journal* railed bitterly against the AT&T decision in 1982 (unlike Microsoft, AT&T had agreed to a breakup). But within months MCI placed a large order with Corning for fiber-optic cable, and the telecommunications revolution began.

The same considerations applied to Microsoft explained Romer. Historically, people working for other companies were responsible for the development and commercialization of the industry's most import innovations. The outsiders' ideas included email, the electronic spreadsheet, the word processor, the Windows-based graphical user interface, instant messaging. By limiting competition in computers, Microsoft had diminished incentives not just to Netscape and Java but to uncounted other potential developers as well. He wrote, "No system of comprehensive central planning, neither one controlled by a government, nor one controlled by the managers of a single firm, can hope to be as robust and reliable a mechanism as competition among many actual and potential firms for purchase by final users."

And so the government asked the court to break the company in to two parts, Op and Aps. It wanted to separate the groups that supported the Windows operating system (Ops) from those that pursued various applications (Aps), including the fabulously profitable Office suite. The Internet Explorer browser would go to Aps, with a license to Ops. The two could be expected to begin to compete with each other and all the others, almost immediately. Each new entity would have annual revenue of around $8 billion, profits of around $3 billion. Aps could confidently be expected to begin to try to undo Windows' chokehold on the PC desktop, just as had Netscape and Sun a few years before. The exact magnitudes were uncertain. But the expected benefits would overwhelm the costs. The breakup would raise the rate of innovation for the whole economy.

Gates's reaction to the government's petition: "Whoever said this doesn't understand the software industry." Microsoft would vigorously defend its business practices.

FOR ITS DEFENSE throughout the trial, Microsoft had relied on the MIT microeconomist Richard Schmalensee. Now, not surprisingly, it turned to Freshwater economics for its defense—to Chicago, in particular, and to Kevin Murphy. Murphy had grown in stature since his days as one of the three young authors of the trio who analyzed increasing returns in their "Big Push" paper in 1987. His testimony added an element of careful Chicago-style price theory to the argument against breakup, an issue known as double marginalization.

Perhaps as a potential monopolist, Microsoft had not been charging for its software all that the market would bear, Murphy argued. In not, and if the company was broken up, then each new company might abandon its parent's traditional restraint, and price its narrower products more aggressively. In that case, the same operating system and word-processing suite sold separately might cost consumers significantly more than when bundled together—two profit margins to pay instead of one. Better to leave the monopolist in charge of everything. It kept prices from getting too high.

Romer replied that this made sense only if high prices were dissuading people from buying PCs. But by skillfully exploiting techniques of price discrimination—offering cheaper versions of the operating system to original equipment manufacturers and non-business buyers (Windows XP Home Edition), and versions of Office software to students and teachers at a fraction of the cost of the corporate package—Microsoft had already solved the double marginalization problem, in a way that required no coordination of pricing between Ops and Aps. In fact they were charging as much as the market would bear.

Besides, no one seriously thought that the major issue was the price to the consumer. The key, the neglected effect of competition was on the incentives to people who developed new technologies like the browser. If they could deal with two firms, instead of a single monopolist ("I can buy 20 percent of you, or I can buy all of you. Or I can go into this business myself and bury you"), they would have a better chance to earn an appropriate return. It was ironic, Romer said, that Chicago had abandoned the idea that competition could be a powerful force supporting the discovering of new ideas. The problem was that they were prisoners of plenitude. Lacking the appropriate theory, they couldn't think clearly about the discovery of new ideas and the growth of knowledge, only about the price of the existing good.

Microsoft didn't leave its defense entirely in Chicago's hands, of course. It appealed to a medley of other professional opinions. The company added Lester Thurow to its prospective witness list. Its executives called on Treasury Secretary Lawrence Summers and the Council of Economic Advisers' Martin Baily to argue their case. ("The only incentive to produce anything is the possession of temporary monopoly power—because without that power the price will be bid down to marginal cost and the high initial fixed costs cannot be recouped," said Summers in a subsequent speech.) Chicago's Gary Becker cited Schumpeter's old argument that monopolies may innovate more freely because they don't have to worry about competitors who might copy their new products. The claim that breaking up the company would speed innovation was "unconvincing," Becker said. Paul Krugman, by now an influential columnist for the *New York Times*, explained double marginalization and came down pretty firmly against the Justice Department. The AT&T breakup had led to the fragmentation of the cellular phone system, hadn't it? And now the United States was "lagging behind Europe and Japan in mobile phone technology." (So much for the emergence of fiber optics and the Internet!) "Let's hope we're not about to cut off our noses to spite Microsoft's face."

Judge Jackson had badly wanted a negotiated settlement—never before had the government failed to obtain consent to a breakup—so he asked Circuit Court Judge Richard Posner, a preeminent authority on economics and antitrust law, to arbitrate the case. For two months lawyers trooped to the celebrated jurist's Chicago chambers, but in the end negotiations broke down. After all the years of argument, Gates and Ballmer were still giving high-profile interviews, seeking to overrule the judge themselves, asserting they had done nothing wrong. Clearly they had not learned enough about public relations and lobbying during the course of the trial; not to mention their civic obligation.

On May 24, 2000, Jackson held a one-day remedy hearing, and two weeks later he ruled that the company should be broken up. If he was going to be reversed, he explained, let it be sooner rather than later. Nor did he wish to impose himself on the industry and attempt to micromanage technological decisions, the way U.S. District Court Judge Harold Greene had done fifteen years earlier in the AT&T case. He preferred competition to administration. So, amid high drama, he ordered the Ops and Aps solution, and sought to close the case.

Unfortunately, however, Jackson, whose daughter was a news reporter, explained too much about his reasoning, and too well. He began giving (embargoed) interviews to the press even before he ordered the breakup. If he could pursue a remedy of his own devising, he told Ken Auletta of the *New Yorker*, in his chambers even before the trial was done, he would assign Gates to write a "book report" on a recent biography of Napoleon Bonaparte noting, "Because I think he has a Napoleonic concept of himself and his company, an arrogance which derives from power and unalloyed success, with no leavening hard experience, no reverses." Judge Jackson's willingness to explain himself was easy to understand and admire. But it also made him easy to overturn.

With the presidential election of 2000, the case dissolved in a frenzy of politics. Ballmer, a lifelong Democrat, conspicuously supported the candidacy of George W. Bush. Microsoft contributed heavily to the inauguration celebration. In June 2001 the Washington, D.C., appellate court, which Judge Jackson had sought to bypass by invoking a provision requiring that appeals go directly to the Supreme Court, found a way to reverse him anyway. To teach a lesson, its members removed him from the case and appointed a new judge, Colleen Kotar-Kotelly.

The rest is history. It was a University of Chicago–trained lawyer, Attorney General John Ashcroft, who told the court that the Justice Department had changed its mind. The Bush administration didn't want to break the company into Ops and Aps, after all, despite the Antitrust Division's victory the year before. So much for the rule of law! There was something humiliating about the government's retreat under pressure from a case its lawyers already had won before a Reagan-appointed judge. The very next week, Al Qaeda struck in New York and Washington, and the Microsoft case was all but forgotten in the United States. The theater of complaints against Microsoft now shifted to Brussels and the European union.

Microsoft had gotten off the hook a second time. It had learned a good deal about how to play by the rules, and how to avoid the appearance of impropriety. But clearly it hadn't lost its drive to extend its dominion. In mid-2000, barely a month after Judge Jackson had ordered its breakup, the company announced plans for "Windows.NET," a software cloud that would extend the Windows system from PCs to servers, televisions, game boxes, and cellular telephones. In moving into the market for server software, Microsoft was preparing to attempt to take over the software of the Internet itself.

BY THEN, HOWEVER, a new threat to Microsoft had emerged—one that might not require the intervention of a judge. Those hobbyists and other software sharers to whom Gates had addressed his memo in 1976 had not taken his shrink-wrapped revolution in software publishing lying down. They had, after all, created the Internet and the World Wide Web ("they" being a vast and disparate confederation of computer visionaries and enthusiasts spread all over the world and spiritually headquartered in Berkeley, California, and Cambridge, Massachusetts and Helsinki, Finland).

Going all the way back to the assistant professor who hounded the undergraduate Gates for using university property to create a business, these secrets sharers resented the entrepreneurial tilt. Enthusiasm for the culture of the market had affected every industry and every country in the world since the early 1970s ("It is glorious to get rich," said Deng Xiaoping as he led China onto "the capitalist road" in 1979). By the late 1990s, these secret-sharers—not all anticapitalists, by any means, but all of them critics of extreme forms of private property—were prepared to strike back directly at Windows' dominance, with an operating system known as Linux that was essentially being given away, the creature of a loose, but powerful, tradition known as the *open-source* software movement.

The carefully protected trade secrets of its source code had over the years become Microsoft's "inner shrink wrap." A black box was at the heart of all Windows operating systems—the program's "kernel."

It guaranteed that Windows couldn't be cloned or otherwise modified until it was "something else"—a product that some other vendor would be free to sell as an improved version of the original. Early on, Microsoft had won a crucial battle with Apple by letting anyone write programs to run on Windows, controlling access to its kernel with applications programming interfaces, or APIs, while Apple offered only applications it had developed itself. Not surprisingly, many more developers created software for Windows than for Apple. That didn't make Windows itself an open system, however. Those APIs were highly effective locks and keys.

In 1991 the open-source ideal acquired a highly visible champion. A twenty-one-year-old named Linus Torvalds was in many ways the anti-Gates, a single individual who personified the philosophy of this ideal. Disturbed by the inefficiencies of the proprietary model—the constant crashes, the resistance to modification—the young Finnish computer scientist resolved to build his own system, one that could be freely modified, that would therefore become more robust as time went by. As long as his fellowship covered his fixed costs of living, he could afford to write computer code and give away what he coded for free. It was little different from doing scientific research and publishing in journals, in the expectation that good results would lead to recognition through the etiquette of citation.

Torvalds's most important innovation was not technical but social. The journalist Eric Raymond explains, "Until the Linux development everyone believed that any software as complex as an operating system had to be developed in a carefully coordinated way by a relatively small, tightly knit group of people."* Torvalds developed his Linux quite differently, he says. "From the beginning, it was rather casually hacked on [improved upon] by huge numbers of volunteers coordinating only through the Internet." He achieved a bug-free program not by autocratically enforcing rigid standards but by

---

* For a marvelous description of this standard approach to creating a big new software product, see *Showstopper!: The Breakneck Race to Create Windows NT and the Next Generation at Microsoft*, by G. Pascal Zachary.

"the naively simple strategy of releasing every week and getting feed-back from hundreds of users within days, creating a sort of rapid Darwinian selection on the mutations introduced by developers" Linux, in other words, was developed along the same friendly and, more to the point, nonpecuniary lines as was the Internet itself: rough consensus and running code.

Anyone who uses a computer has firsthand experience of the way in which these different incentive systems have delivered very differ-ent experiences to their users. The PC itself today is a closed system, exorbitantly expensive relative to the tasks for which most people use it (email, Web access), prone to failure, hard to hybridize, difficult to use, and hard to fix. The Internet, on the other hand, and particu-larly the World Wide Web, is easy to use, robust, innovation friendly, priced very differently to its users. The two technologies embody very different values, imply different social norms.

And therein lay the real bombshell discovery that had been at the heart of "Endogenous Technological Change"—that the nonrivalry of knowledge meant that the crown jewels of economics, the Invisi-ble Hand theorems, could not stand. The market simply could not get the prices of these goods "right."

EVER SINCE ADAM SMITH the most important idea in economics has been the proposition that, left to their own devices, individuals will pursue courses that lead, as if arranged by an Invisible Hand, to the outcome that is "best overall." Economists have refined Smith's intu-ition to a very fine grain. The efficiency of decentralized competitive markets under certain conditions is what Kenneth Arrow and Ger-ard Debreu demonstrated mathematically in the early 1950s, leading to an eventual Nobel Prize. It was then that economists began to talk of the Invisible Hand theorems as propositions so well established as to have been *proved*.

True, departures from these idealized conditions were ubiquitous in any real economy, no matter how competitive it might be. Monopolies would cause distortions. So would external effects. But the policy against such "deadweight losses" was clear. It was to seek everywhere to reduce them, by assigning property rights and breaking up monopolies. Clear away the underbrush, and the magic of the market would take care of everything else.

To which Romer replied that assigning property rights was no problem when the resources were scarce and rival: a piece of land, the right to use a certain portion of the radio spectrum, permission to release pollutant emissions into the air. But when a new good was associated with a new idea, the striking reality was that there were no hard-and-fast rules for dealing with it—in fact, there *could* be no hard-and-fast rules. New goods are associated with fixed costs, and fixed costs, represented as "nonconvexities," pose inescapable dilemmas for decentralized markets.

The example that Romer liked best was oral rehydration therapy—a means of treating children suffering from diarrhea by giving them something like Gatorade to drink—water mixed with small quantities of salts and minerals. It saves their lives, it turns out, since untreated dehydration is often fatal. Oral rehydration therapy can be used anywhere in the world; the beverage costs next to nothing to prepare. And the property of reuse of the idea means that the treatment will raise livings standard for everyone, everywhere. So what is the "right" price for the development of oral rehydration therapy? On the one hand, the price on discoveries of this sort should be very high, since such a treatment can save millions of lives. You want a large incentive to discover an AIDS or a malaria vaccine. But as soon as the good exists, the "right" price drops to zero. The new good should be given away.

What about innovations that are less dramatic? The same considerations apply. The degree of protection to be conferred on new ideas was inevitably a social choice. Whatever rules were adopted would depend ultimately on the values not just of a few people doing the work, or those making the decisions about who should do the work, but of all the persons in a society.

After all, the same scientist (or a close substitute) might reasonably be expected to make the same discovery, whether he was working on salary in an industrial laboratory—Bell Labs, say—or in his own laboratory underwritten by a venture capitalist in California. The lab in question might then earn monopoly profits on the new invention (a microprocessor) or, alternatively, license it to corporate competitors for next to nothing (a transistor). Property protection could be strict, like ASCAP's, a nickel paid every time a song was played. Or it could be easy, like the Grateful Dead's laissez-faire attitude toward amateur recordings of their performances, with revenues coming mainly from concert tickets rather than from a tight hold on authorized recordings.

Or cash compensation might not be involved at all. There are all kinds of other ways of giving credit. Citations. Merit Badges. Team play. Family ethics. Religious considerations. As Romer says, The market is not everything. There are many other kinds of institutions that we construct.

The PC and the Internet—perhaps the easiest way to understand the opposition between these two very different styles of technological development is simply to visualize the circumstances in which their respective entrepreneurs-in-chief lived. Bill Gates's $97 million house on Lake Washington is famous—66,000 square feet under various roofs (though only a modest 11,500 square feet set aside for the family's inner sanctum); a grand staircase, a theater, a library, a formal dining room, a conference room, an exercise room, and a techno-playland family room. Licklider's longtime home in suburban Arlington, high on a hill overlooking Spy Pond and Boston, was a modest four-bedroom frame house built in the 1920s.

Both systems work, and probably work best together. Society gets the benefits either way. But for all the talk about the glories of capital allocation by the NASDAQ among individual entrepreneurs, the evolution of the Internet has shown that corporations and committees can work wonders, too.

WHAT *WILL* HAPPEN with Microsoft, a firm whose operating system can, in principle, still become "the universal" for the entire world market, thanks to its huge head start? Will it continue to trump the Invisible Hand? Or will George Stigler, George W. Bush, and all the others who put their faith in laissez-faire be proved correct? Will competition triumph eventually without their help?

Or was Romer right—that the occasional intervention could dramatically improve outcomes, both for consumers and, in this case, for the United States? Privately, he pointed out that foreign governments, whether European, Indian, or Chinese (or perhaps all three) could make large-scale investments in Linux, dramatically altering the incentives to write open-source applications around the world. In that case, consumers around the world would benefit from the appearance of cheaper machines, but leadership in software might then shift to another continent. In somewhat similar circumstances in the 1960s, American steel companies hid behind their government and delayed making investments in new technologies until it was too late.

Moreover, new middleware technologies will appear that will finally dissolve the Windows operating system's dominance of the desktop—the task at which the Netscape browser almost succeeded before it was crushed. The Google search engine is the most ambitious candidate. By offering email and Web-based storage, Google's middleware may become the primary interface with Web-based applications, rendering Microsoft's Office suite easy to bypass. In that case, too, the whip hand in development will shift to somebody else.

One way or another, the Microsoft story seems almost certain to turn out in the end like Alfred Marshall's parable of the trees of the forest. The company will finally lose ground to competitors after a lengthy run. It is common sense, not economic theory, to assert that no tree grows to the sky. Sure enough, in September 2005, Microsoft itself quietly embraced the government's logic of separating Ops and Aps. The company reorganized itself into three business groups (down from seven), each under a president of its own. A platform division would manage the Windows operating system. A business division would control the Office suite and myriad other applications. The company's Xbox game console was assigned to an entertainment unit.

The ostensible purpose was to reduce corporate bureaucracy and thereby "make fewer decisions faster." The more urgent need was to meet the growing competition from Google, EBay, and open-source software. Would spin-offs into autonomous companies follow, sooner or later? Perhaps. At that point, the Microsoft business units would go into competition with one another. Cut along the dotted lines: the government's antitrust experts and Judge Jackson, it turned out, had understood the software industry better than had Microsoft after all.

Already Gates has turned some part of his attention and his fortune to stimulating the creation of new ideas in global health, particularly the development of vaccines against a variety of Third World diseases and new ways of delivering them. The second half of his life could be as interesting as the first, but for different reasons. The irony is that, in its philanthropic activities, the Gates Foundation has routinely embraced the particulars of Romer's arguments, as refined in the subsequent discussion. Gates Foundation grant recipients are free to patent anything they invent, and sell as much as they please to the rich, but with the stipulation that new technologies be made available to poor countries for little or nothing. Gates, meanwhile, remained the richest man in the world. And all this Schumpeterian drama was rendered more visible, calculable, and, to some extent, manageable by the model introduced in "Endogenous Technological Change." Romer, however, did not linger long. Even before Judge Jackson's breakup order was overturned (and he was relieved of his responsibility as the chief expert for the remedy of separating Ops and Aps), he had moved on to something else. He had started a little software company of his own.

CHAPTER TWENTY-SIX

The Invisible Revolution

THE INCREASING-RETURNS revolution passed almost unnoticed in the press, its developments for a time overshadowed by events. The turn toward markets, the collapse of communism, the advances in information technology and molecular biology, the Internet bubble—what academic squabble could compete for attention with all this history in the making? Then, too, the new ideas stemmed directly from mathematical economics. Many people were reluctant to believe that sweeping changes in everyday perception and language could arise from a handful of equations.

Even inside technical economics, there was little to signal that anything resembling a major transformation had occurred. The *Journal of Economic Perspectives* was one place to look for recognition: it had been established in 1987 as a means of showcasing developments in economics for a lay audience. A symposium on new growth theory appeared at the end of 1994, with contributions by Romer, by Helpman and Grossman, and by Solow. It came close on the heels of a similar symposium on network externalities and was followed in turn by symposia devoted to the monetary transmission mechanism, the economics of voting, of crime, and of primary and secondary education, one group of invited papers after another, until it was all but impossible to distinguish one set of developments from the next.

The more cerebral Econometric Society, with its world congresses every five years designed to showcase new developments, was little different. And when various special issues on "economics at the millennium" rolled out in 2000—the *Quarterly Journal of Economics*, the *Economic Journal*, the *Journal of Economic Perspectives*—there was little indication that anything had changed very much.

The first draft of the recent history of economic thought apparently had been outsourced to the Swedes.

Meanwhile, a gold rush occurred among business consultants and other strategic thinkers. Peter Drucker in the early 1980s was the first to stress the significance of a "knowledge economy." In 1990 Michael Porter of the Harvard Business School reintroduced Marshallian ideas about clusters of related industries in *The Competitive Advantage of Nations*. Soon books like *Working Knowledge, Intellectual Capital, The Invisible Continent, The Work of Nations*, and *The Wealth of Cities* were streaming from the presses, and consulting and accounting firms boasted innovation centers and knowledge practices.

By the mid-1990s a "new economy" had been discovered. A central figure in the drama was the Federal Reserve Board chairman, Alan Greenspan. In December 1996, with the Dow Jones industrial average a little over 5000, he chided markets for their "irrational exuberance." The next year, stock prices roared to a Dow of nearly 7000 despite the warning, and Greenspan took his analysis back to the drawing board. Seven months later, a *Business Week* cover story declared "the triumph of the new economy" and reported that the chairman had concluded that the economy had entered a new era. The term exploded into use.

The Internet became a potent metaphor for the "new rules" said to be governing business. Globalization, technological change, the end of the Cold War, deregulation, the celebration of business culture, low inflation, and the end of the business cycle were some of the reasons given. (Little noticed was the way in which the Asian financial crisis had forced Greenspan to flood American capital markets with liquidity.) Economic journalists celebrated the "death of distance," the "frictionless economy," "the weightless society," the "flattened world." Romer appeared in some of these books, most notably in Michael Lewis's *The New New Thing* and Thomas Friedman's *The Earth Is Flat*. Eventually Greenspan himself described "a deep-seated, still-developing shift in our economy," the result, he said, of a "mostly exogenous" burst of technological innovation.

Even then there were very few appeals to the authority of economics couched in terms of *discovery* in those years, at statements of "what we know now"—nothing remotely like the "chasm between darkness and light" by which the Keynesian revolution had been characterized. Typical of the mainstream view was that of the Berkeley professor Hal Varian, a prominent microeconomist, writing in the *New York Times* in early 2002:

> There was never a new economics to go along with the new economy. Sure, there was a lot of talk about increasing returns, network effects, switching costs and so on. But these are hardly new concepts; they've been part of the economics literature for decades. Furthermore, though these are important ideas, they aren't Big Ideas. They explain certain phenomena well, but they have limited reach. Those in search of a really big idea had to look further back in economics literature . . . [to] "The Nature of the Firm," a 1937 paper written by Nobel laureate Ronald Coase [, which contributed the idea of transaction costs].

At the beginning of the twenty-first century, then, there was still almost no hint had of what had happened.

IN *THE STRUCTURE OF SCIENTIFIC REVOLUTIONS*, Kuhn devotes a chapter to what he describes as the "invisibility" of scientific revolutions. Scientists and laymen derive their ideas of how science proceeds from a source that systematically disguises the existence and significance of revolutions, namely textbooks and the popularizations based on them. That is, textbooks present only the most recent outcome. They are rewritten after each revolution to incorporate what earlier scientists had to say about the problems that are still considered relevant, and to leave out what they thought about problems now considered to be little or ill understood. Why dignify what brilliant science has made it possible to discard? Science thus is portrayed by the texts as cumulative, linear, as if scientists built their understanding one brick, one discovery at a time. The result, says Kuhn, is that the most important episodes of scientific change, when one way of understanding gives way quickly and completely to another, drop out of the story.

If economists themselves couldn't necessarily be counted on to give the news, and if American newspapers had cut back sharply on their coverage of the field, there was, at least, Stockholm. Economics now makes its progress October by October. If it hasn't won a Nobel Prize, it hasn't really happened, at any rate where outsiders are concerned.

Entering the Swedish spotlight in the 1990s were the men who had turned to rocket science at the end of the 1960s. It had taken a change in the generational leadership of the selection committee to make it so. Assar Lindbeck (born in 1930) stepped down as its permanent secretary, having served since the economics prize was begun. Torsten Persson (born in 1954) took over. Robert Lucas was honored in Stockholm in 1995 for his work on expectations. Robert Merton and Myron Scholes shared the prize for their options-pricing formula. George Akerlof, A. Michael Spence, and Joe Stiglitz won in 2001 for asymmetric information. Especially interesting was the prize was 1994, when John Nash, John Harsanyi, and Reinhard Selten were finally honored for creating the formal foundations of game theory—the real breakthrough having occurred forty-five years before.

The economists who went to Washington at the beginning of the 1990s also gained in visibility—among them Stanley Fischer, Joseph Stiglitz, and, especially, Larry Summers. During the administration of the first President Bush, Summers became chief economist at the World Bank, then, after Bill Clinton was elected, rose steadily through the Treasury Department ranks, eventually becoming the youngest treasury secretary since Alexander Hamilton, and finally president of Harvard University. His old friend Andrei Shleifer moved to Harvard from the University of Chicago in 1992 to lead a U.S. mission to Moscow on behalf of the U.S. Agency for International Development. His deputy, J. Bradford Delong, moved to Berkeley, wrote a textbook, and started a widely read blog.

The main figures in the increasing-returns revolution kept low profiles for the most part. Romer taught at the Stanford Business School, retaining his relative anonymity even in the midst of the Microsoft case. Elhanan Helpman, still splitting his time between Tel Aviv and Harvard, declined the presidency of the Bank of Israel in order to work with Grossman on a big research project on the international division of labor. Xiaokai Yang, the leader of the heterodox Australian school, died in 2005 at 55, not long after completing an introductory development text in collaboration with Jeffrey Sachs. Only Paul Krugman continued to soar, becoming a star columnist for the *New York Times* and a best-selling author.

The reception of new growth surely was complicated in this case by the legendary figure of John Maynard Keynes. The Keynesian revolution proved to be a powerful narrative device for at least two generations, and the appearance in the 1980s and 1990s of Robert Skidelsky's three-volume biography only lengthened the shadow of the great man. Comparisons to Sigmund Freud were sometimes made. Was it possible that, in the end, Keynes would be remembered more as a literary figure than a scientific one? It scarcely mattered. As Louis Menand wrote of Freud's *Civilization and Its Discontents*, "the grounds have entirely eroded for whatever authority it once enjoyed as an ultimate account of the way things are, but we can no longer understand the way things are without taking it into account." Arguments about the relative significance of macroeconomics and growth economics seemed destined to be carried on far into the future.

Bob Solow spent the decade squaring the old arguments with the new: he published a book of lectures on Arrow's learning-by-doing model, another on monopolistic competition and macroeconomics, and, finally, a second edition of his growth lectures of 1970, with six new chapters parsing the new models. "No one could have ever intended to deny" that technological progress is "at least partly" the result of economic forces, he wrote. "The question is whether one has anything useful to say about the process." His "manna from heaven" shorthand for technological change had been widely misunderstood. "'Exogenous' does not mean either 'unchanging' or 'mysterious' and certainly not 'unchanging and mysterious.' It is a temporary designation, meaning that we try to work out in detail how the rest of the model adjusts to the exogenous elements, but not the other way around."

Similarly, the economic historian Joel Mokyr concluded that nothing very significant had happened. It was Mokyr, remember, who in 1996 had convened the session of the San Francisco meetings at which Romer described the distinction between atoms and bits publicly for the first time. But in *The Gifts of Athena: Historical Origins of the Knowledge Economy*, a collection of otherwise penetrating articles on the development of the institutions of science and technology that he published in 2002, Mokyr traced back economists' interest in knowledge along every conceivable path *except* that of Romer, whom he left out of his account altogether.* It wasn't that Mokyr doubted that technological change was a thoroughly economic process. He quoted Abraham Lincoln: "The patent system added the fuel of interest to the fire of genius." But his descriptions never go beyond the literary realm. Readers looking for clues to the economics of knowledge will find mainly evidence of the lingering power of the Solow model to imprison nonmathematical economists. The history of technical change still lay where John Stuart Mill had placed it, *outside* of economics, where historians need to know no mathematics to discuss it.

The movement west to California of many powerful figures in the new economics of knowledge probably had something to do with its cool reception as well. The changes taking place in economics in the United States in the second half of the twentieth century roughly

---

* Mokyr's citations are a veritable Who's Who of the parallel universe of influential literary growth theorists. The book is dedicated to Eric L. Jones, David S. Landes, Douglass C. North, and Nathan Rosenberg. The topic of the economics of knowledge is said to date back to Simon Kuznets. G. L. S. Shackle recognized it as a glaring omission. Fritz Machlup is said to have faced up to it squarely, but incompletely. The entrepreneurial historian Jonathan Hughes, Mokyr's teacher, is warmly remembered. The "Stanford school" of Paul David and Nathan Rosenberg is praised. The evolutionary approach of Richard Nelson and Sidney Winter, like new growth theory, gets short shrift.

mirrored those taking place in baseball. Baseball in the 1950s consisted of two easily understood leagues with sixteen teams, all but one having its home east of the Mississippi River, and a World Series between the two pennant winners at the end of the season. A couple of decades later the game had thirty teams in six divisions and a very complicated system of playoffs—to say nothing of sea changes in player development and compensation. The game itself was pretty much the same, but its institutions were very different, and league play was harder to follow. The game's most lucrative markets remained in the East, as did its power center.

And then there was Romer himself. Over the years rivals had occasionally portrayed him as something of a publicity hound. In fact, he was quite the opposite, shying away from op-ed pages. He was not an avid member of any clan; he was a less than enthusiastic networker in a field that, for whatever reason, had grown increasingly dominated by cliques. He walked out of the two best departments in the discipline, Chicago's and MIT's, and presumably declined the private offer of an invitation from a third, that of Harvard. His subject, growth, was not quite macroeconomics; its policy prescriptions lacked the urgency of stabilization or monetary policy. He self-consciously tied up work on growth after fifteen years, and began to write about the preferences.

As a result, in the first years of the new century, Romer was something of a stealth presence in the economics profession. He had achieved enormous influence, but not yet much recognition. He eschewed invitations to give Yale lectures, Schwartz lectures. An editor described him as having started many things and finished few. A fellow economist complained that, like Chamberlin, he had only had one idea. Maybe. Maybe not. But, if so, like Chamberlin's, or like Ronald Coase's, what an idea it was!

AMONG THE YOUNGER GENERATION the great antagonist of knowledge-based models in the 1990s was Harvard's Greg Mankiw, who stuck by his augmented Solow model long after his coauthors, David Romer and David Weil, had bailed out. Something of a climax in the controversy occurred in March 1995 in Washington, D.C.

The occasion was meeting the twenty-fifth anniversary of the founding of the *Brookings Papers on Economic Activity*, a journal that had become perhaps the most important in its field of policy matters. The presenters included Jeff Sachs and Andrew Warner on globalization, Maurice Obstfeld on floating exchange rates, Robert Hall on lost jobs, and Paul Krugman on trade. Mankiw discussed "The Growth of Nations." Romer was invited to respond.

Mankiw was steadfast in his defense of Solow. True, if the goal was to explain why standards of living were higher today than a century ago, then the neoclassical model was not very illuminating, he allowed. But then, to explain the *existence* of economic growth was not really the puzzle. "That task is too easy," he said: "it is obvious that living standards rise over time because knowledge expands and production functions improve." A more challenging mission was to understand reasons for the *differences* among the wealth of nations. Why were we so rich and they so poor? To explain this, accumulation of capital in its broadest sense was enough.

After all, Mankiw said, knowledge was an essentially unmeasurable variable. Models employing various forms of intellectual property would be hard to test. Knowledge traveled around the world fairly quickly, as opposed to capital. State-of-the-art textbooks were to be found even in the poorest countries. Even when a firm had some monopoly power over an innovation, he continued, it could last only a short time, until the innovation became a worldwide public good. The best assumption, therefore, for a first approximation would be that all countries have access to the same pool of knowledge, and that nations differ mainly in the degree to which they take advantage of this free public good by investing in physical plant and human capability.

Romer countered that, even in the more recondite and obscure traditions of growth accounting, the recent history of the public good model in growth accounting was a story of obfuscation and strategic retreat. First, it was found that the model couldn't explain the portion of output ascribed to capital. Opening up the augmented Solow model to let capital flow freely meant that skilled workers in poor countries would have to earn two hundred times more than unskilled laborers. (The ratio in the United States was two to one.) How about modifying the elasticity of substitution between capital and labor, then? Improbable numbers there, too. "Fitting the public good model to these data is like squeezing a balloon. You can make it smaller in one place, but the problems always pop up somewhere else."

Besides, the evidence was overwhelming that knowledge was *not* a public good. That was what trade secrets, tacit knowledge, technological know-how, and intellectual property were all about. Romer cited the example of Mauritius, about which he had written a case study in 1993. For a century this isolated island in the Indian Ocean had followed standard development dogma, keeping tariffs high to encourage the development of import-substituting local industry, but with scant success. Its only exports were agricultural. Then, in 1970, its government created a low-tax enterprise zone. Hong Kong garment assembly firms moved to it with alacrity. Before 1970 the rag trade didn't exist on Mauritius. By 1990 it accounted for a third of all jobs.

The problem in Mauritius, said Romer, was not a low level of saving; the islanders could have afforded sewing machines. Nor was it that laborers were too ill educated to use them. It didn't matter whether the shelves of the national library held garment-manufacturing textbooks or not. The problem was that, until the entrepreneurs arrived from Hong Kong, no one on the island knew enough about the garment business to begin production. "This knowledge did not leak in from Hong Kong. It was brought in when entrepreneurs were presented with an opportunity that let them earn a profit on the knowledge they possessed," Romer wrote. So if the freely available public good model didn't apply to something as low-tech as garment assembly, where could it possibly make sense?

Mankiw's position, Romer told the Brookings conference, was that his augmented Solow model was "close enough" for macroeconomics. "What constitutes 'close enough,'" he continued, "depends on what one is trying to accomplish—getting the answers right, or catering to a target audience." The new Keynesians "may be paying too much attention to how their model will be received and used by outsiders, and too little attention to what they think is true"—a reference to their persistent fear that the new growth economics would somehow play into the hands of those who equated tax cutting with faster growth. The profession, he concluded, should not settle for that sort of scientific behavior.

After the Brookings meeting, there was the usual spirited discussion—and a growing sense that Romer had won the argument. The evidence couldn't be squared with Mankiw's assumption that the poorest countries with the worst policies had the same access to technology as every other. The models that included intellectual property and entrepreneurs and technology policy no longer could be resisted, at least not at the research frontier. The stream of articles and books on the mechanics of economic development grew into a torrent: on inventions, institutions, cities, legal systems, intellectual property regimes, colonialism, demographics, climate, globalization—all conceivable sources of the wealth and poverty of nations. Graduate schools kept teaching the augmented Solow model because it fit in so smoothly with all the rest of what the textbooks had to say. But the newest work increasingly undercut it, and gradually Mankiw stopped defending his model in the research community. He went into government instead, as chairman of the Council of Economic Advisers for two years under George W. Bush. Then he returned to Harvard University, where he replaced Martin Feldstein as the head teacher of introductory economics, the largest-enrollment course in the college.

Meanwhile, rumors swirled around Romer at Stanford. He had quit teaching. He had ceased publishing in technical journals. He was involved in some sort of a start-up venture, a software company. Many people concluded that he had left economics altogether.

MOST USEFUL, THEREFORE, was the appearance of a book by Elhanan Helpman in the autumn of 2004. In *The Mystery of Economic Growth*, he described in an elegant package of barely 220 pages where the developments in growth theory stood—"what we know, what we do not know, and what it is that we need to learn to improve our understanding of a subject that affects, in major ways, the well-

being of billions of people across the globe." Since the summer meeting on trade in 1980, Helpman had been a soldier of the increasing-
returns revolution; he had watched its complex developments
unfold. Now he presented a summary of what was known and what
was yet to be learned, designed to appeal to nonspecialist economists, other social scientists, policy makers, and anyone else interested in this important subject.

Economists have been studying the topic of the wealth of nations
without interruption since Adam Smith, wrote Helpman at the out-
set of the book, and two recent waves of research have "changed our
views"—one that started in the early 1950s and lasted until the early
1970s, another that started in the mid-1980s and continues to the
present. Much has been learned, he said. "But the subject has proved
elusive, and many mysteries remain." Indeed, the mystery of economic growth itself "has not been solved."

What makes some countries rich and others poor? The riddles
Helpman set forth were little different from what Romer had laid
out in his thesis in 1983, and what Lucas asked with such force in his
Marshall Lectures in 1985. Average world growth rates have been
accelerating since 1820, and sharply in the years since World War II.
Why? Meanwhile, the disparity among nations has increased. Why
has development been so uneven around the world? Helpman firmly
centered his book on the second question, the convergence controversy, instead of the much narrower question that Chad Jones had
identified in his text—what is the engine of economic growth?

The rest of *Mystery* was organized into six chapters, lucid
accounts of accumulation, productivity, innovation, interdependence, inequality, and institutions and politics. In the innovation
chapter, Helpman decomposed the work of the 1980s and 1990s into
two subwaves, an "aggregate" approach to growth employing
spillovers and a "disaggregated" approach from Romer '90. (He still
employed the old-fashioned term "'disembodied' knowledge"
instead of "nonrival goods." He avoided the phrase "intellectual
property" entirely.) He omitted the determinants of population
from his account for the most part, too, unable to fit it into his tale:
partly because it was not his field, he explained, partly because of

professional disagreements among those whose field it was. If he were to write the same book five years hence, he wrote, he expected he would have to change nothing more than the chapter on institutions and politics. That was where the work was still going forward at a brisk pace.

All in all, *The Mystery of Economic Growth* was a wonderful book. It had all the clarity and subtlety that had marked Helpman a leader in the first place. In a sense, it marked an end of the controversy, since he treated the theory explaining technical change as part of the established corpus of technical economics, not an upstart hypothesis. There may be no better place than Helpman's book for an outsider to see what it means to think like an economist, to think carefully. Certainly there is no better place for insiders to learn the broad outlines of current research consensus.

And yet, for all the new information it contains, the book seems to imply that nothing much has happened in the past twenty-five years. The behind-the-scenes excitement is carefully omitted. It is as though no one had ever so much as spoken a cross word about increasing returns, or nonconvexities, or the cost of lighting a room at night. The revolution is invisible. Economics has returned to normal. Much has been accomplished. There is much more to be done. The mystery has been conserved.

CHAPTER TWENTY-SEVEN

Teaching Economics

THERE IS ONE LAST PLACE in the economics profession to check for turbulence, the better to gauge the significance of what has happened since "Endogenous Technological Change" appeared in 1990—another sounding board of opinion, insulated from day-to-day notice and attention, and from the professional incentive system, and charged with responsibility for managing the stock of economic knowledge and additions to it. Let us return to the Meetings—this time to the exhibition hall.

Careful readers will recall that we paused in our narrative late in the afternoon of Friday, January 5, 1996, in Plaza Ballroom B of the San Francisco Hilton. Romer, Marty Weitzman, and Robert Solow were on the dais, the press in the audience, and Romer was saying, "Theory tells us where to carve the joints." Other interesting developments were occurring that day, too—in the exhibition hall, where a new introductory text by the Stanford University professor John Taylor was being presented.

At age forty-nine Taylor is on his way to becoming one of the fathers of the profession. He is a plausible candidate for an eventual Nobel Prize, for his work building expectations into monetary policy, developing the policy framework known as inflation targeting. He has been to Washington, first as a member of the president's Council of Economic Advisers and then as a governor and vice chairman of the Federal Reserve Board. On that day, however, Taylor was introducing the principles text on which he had spent many of his nights and weekends for the last three years.

Two years earlier Joe Stiglitz had done the same. Two years later Ben Bernanke and Robert Frank took their turn.

As we have noted, economists write texts for many reasons: because they want to make a lot of money, because they love to teach, because they want to influence the way the subject matter of economics is generally understood and therefore what everybody teaches. For many years Taylor has been an unusually enthusiastic teacher of elementary economics to freshmen. But this day he is hoping to achieve something more than to launch another clone.

It is a commonplace among students of the history of economics that each epoch must have its own text. In the two centuries since the very beginning of the field, only five textbooks have become dominating standards, the hold of each lasting for forty years or more: those of Adam Smith, David Ricardo, John Stuart Mill, Alfred Marshall and, since 1948, Paul Samuelson. Yet much has changed in economics since 1948.

At a certain point it became clear that the run of more than fifty years of Paul Samuelson's great text must soon be nearing an end. In San Francisco in 1996 the hunt for its successor is well under way.

TEXTBOOKS ARE A PART of the apparatus of economics that is hidden in plain sight. They are, of course, the point of entry of students into the field, something like a million of them of them in the United States alone, who each year enroll in introductory economics for the first time. Most students never pass beyond the introductory level, but there are intermediate and advanced versions for those continuing in the field as well, not just in broad fields such as microeconomics and macroeconomics but in specialties such as public finance, money, econometrics, trade, growth, and environmental economics. All textbooks work more or less the same way, whether they are communicating economics, organic chemistry, history, or Latin. They teach their subjects to their students as languages, each with a special vocabulary and syntax of its own.

It was from the literature of language acquisition and instruction, after all, that Thomas Kuhn borrowed the word "paradigm" to describe what he called "the standard set of examples, methods, beliefs, and phenomena that constitute a disciplinary core." Just as students learn grammar and syntax through a combination of drill and improvisation, so there are glossaries and exercises and problem sets at the end of every chapter of an economics text, the equivalent of language drill, whose purpose is to build fluency and check comprehension. All textbooks share an underlying purpose: to initiate students into a standard curriculum of currently accepted views. In a certain sense, for their particular subjects, textbooks provide operating systems for the human mind.

Practically overnight after it appeared in 1948, Paul Samuelson's textbook became the standard encapsulation of the new set of Keynesian neoclassical principles that had emerged from World War II. Once the authority of its interpretation of Keynesian doctrines was recognized in the late 1940s, Samuelson's introductory *Economics* quickly replaced Marshall's *Principles* as the "universal," the book from which all the best students wanted to learn. The result was a bonanza for publisher and author alike: eighteen editions over fifty-five years, millions of copies sold, translations into more than forty languages—in short, the very model of increasing returns. In the end, Samuelson said, the greatest joy was less the money than the opportunity to shape the agenda. "I don't care who writes a nation's laws—or crafts its advanced treaties—if I can write its economics textbooks," he wrote.

Samuelson's book quickly spawned imitators, much as the doctrine of monopolistic competition would lead you to expect. Slight variations on a successful theme are as attractive to college freshmen and their instructors as to anyone else. The most successful of these clones appeared in 1960. Professor Campbell McConnell of the University of Nebraska closely modeled his book on Samuelson's approach. But he wrote more simply, with less math, and was less demanding in his problem sets. Before long, McConnell's *Economics: Principles, Problems, and Policies* was outselling Samuelson's text by a significant margin. McConnell's publisher? The same as Samuelson's. McGraw-Hill was pursuing the classic strategy of product differentiation: a text for every taste and pocketbook.

Every couple of years thereafter, one or more new texts appeared, ordinarily preceded by an intermediate macro or microeconomics text, designed as a combination practice run/trial balloon. The trick to a successful entry was soon discovered. It was to change a little, but not so much that other professors wouldn't want to teach it. There should be nothing too idiosyncratic: just a mountain of plain vanilla with a little topping. Thus McConnell became Economics Easy. When Edmund Phelps sought to integrate game theory into an introductory text in 1985, the project was a succès d'estime but otherwise failed to meet expectations; the market's verdict was that the book was much too difficult. Publishers recruited economists of the next generation to gradually take over their best sellers: Samuelson became Samuelson/Nordhaus; McConnell became McConnell/Brue. And every couple of years now, there has been some new attempt to restate economics in light of what was learned, in hopes of adding something to the standard pattern on which most of the profession could agree.

By the very nature of science, there can be only one basic understanding, perhaps only one basic design among textbooks in a particular field at a particular time. By definition, that best practice example is its overarching paradigm. When the paradigm changes, then everything else must change as well. Until then, however, variations on the theme are just so many added flavors. And despite the constant changes in dogma, there was nothing yet resembling Samuelson's *Economics*, which, in retrospect, had been to Marshall's *Principles* as a railway car is to a carriage.

It would be picturesque to report that, while Romer explained new growth in the hall above, Taylor's text carried the day in the classroom on the floor below. Indeed, his text is the first to introduce some of the standard new growth themes. Nonrivalry and excludability are defined, but in the chapter on public goods, and they are not linked to intellectually property. The Solow model makes its appearance, but technology is treated as an input, though there is still confusion about what is rival and what nonrival about a can of

Coca-Cola. There is considerable emphasis on technology policy that was not to be found in most introductory texts.

But the appearance of Taylor's text in 1996 causes no big stir. Perhaps there is a little less excitement than the year before for ebullient Stiglitz's entry into the market with a Saltwater-flavored version. A little more than when Bernanke and Frank's text appeared in 2001, spiced with behavioral economics. To be sure, Taylor has built into his text several Freshwater innovations. (An earlier New Classical intermediate macro text by Robert Barro for Wiley scarcely made a dent.) But this is normal innovation, Samuelson served with a special sauce.

Each new text achieves some mind share in the intricate battle of opinion among leaders in the field. Each claims a profitable niche. But none is sufficient to displace the well-established market leaders. The market remains nicely carved up. There was nothing to write a news story about, nothing to contradict the judgment that there can't be a next Samuelson, because there is no new Keynes—no sharp discontinuity between the new generation and the old.

INSTEAD, THE TALK in San Francisco among the inner ring that year was about a young Harvard professor named Greg Mankiw, who had emerged as a leader of the next generation of the New Keynesian school. In 1992 Mankiw had startled the profession by publishing an intermediate text in which the topic of growth came first in the book, instead of at the back, the position to which it had been almost universally consigned for forty years. This reflected the excitement about new growth that was general in those days.

Ordinarily, the author of an intermediate text sticks with his publisher—in this case Worth, a unit of the German Holtzbrinck firm. With his book especially well received, however, Mankiw did the economic thing. He made headlines in 1995 by putting his plan to write a principles text up to auction. Some lively bidding followed. The publishing giant McGraw-Hill, looking for a template for the next generation of its texts, led the action for a time. It dropped out when Harcourt Brace Jovanovich, freshly returned from bankruptcy protection and determined to send an emphatic signal, offered $1.4 million, the biggest advance ever to that point.

All the better way of emphasizing to the outside world that Mankiw would be among the first of the leaders of the Perestroika generation to attempt the task that everyone agreed had to be performed—to integrate the insights of both New Classical and New Keynesian economics. That was the sword in the stone. Presumably the author whose text succeeded would replace Samuelson as educator of the next generation of the young.

Yet another contract to write a textbook was generating talk in San Francisco that year. Its author was none other than Paul Krugman. Having lost its front-line author Mankiw to the competition, Holtzbrinck's Worth Publishers unit sought out and signed Krugman instead, whose intermediate international text (with Maurice Obstfeld) had been a considerable success.

Already it was manifest that Krugman was a remarkably clear writer. *The Age of Diminished Expectations: U.S. Economic Policy in the 1990s*, a little primer on various policy issues originally written as a limited-distribution giveaway, turned into a best seller in 1990. He followed with a second popular book, *Peddling Prosperity: Economic Sense and Nonsense in the Age of Diminished Expectations*. Both authors identified as New Keynesians, but one habitually voted Democratic and the other Republican. Indeed, at a certain point, *Fortune* magazine had asked the liberal Krugman to write a bimonthly column opposite the more conservative Mankiw. So competing texts would simply take their natural opposition to the next level.

Mankiw had a big head start. His introductory text appeared in August 1997. It was accompanied by a memorable public relations campaign—including a cover story in the *Economist* (a man scratching his head in a maze full of texts). The book had a definite Saltwater flavor, though it dropped the familiar "Keynesian cross" diagram of actual demand plotted against effective demand, which had been the backbone of Samuelson's text, in favor of an aggregate supply/aggregate demand analysis. There was not much about the role of expectations in the book. Growth still came first, but Mankiw's boldest innovation was in fact a dramatic shrinking of the subject matter he sought to cover. His book was a third shorter than

most other introductory texts and much simpler. Mankiw summed
up freshman economics in fewer than 800 pages, with very few equations. "To explain this choice I must make a confession," wrote
Mankiw "I am a slow reader. . . . I groaned every time the professor
gave the class a 1,000 page tome to read."

By 2003, with the appearance of its third edition, Mankiw's *Principles of Economics* had vaulted to near the top of the charts in the
elementary market, selling roughly as many as McConnell/Brue,
something like a year in the United States and another worldwide.
Meanwhile, McGraw-Hill, worried about the threat, had signed the
new text with a behavioral slant by the Princeton macroeconomist
Bernanke and microeconomist Frank of Cornell University. The
book they wrote did well, was widely admired, but seemed unlikely
to displace the market leaders—at least not before Bernanke was
named chairman of the Federal Reserve Board. So in the first years of
the new century, everybody waited for Krugman. The feeling was that,
if any book had a chance of overtaking Mankiw's, it would be his.

For Krugman, however, the disruption had been substantial. His
move to Stanford hadn't worked out. After only two years in California, he returned to MIT (the need to care for his parents figured in
the decision; so did his itch to be near the action on the East Coast).
He left *Fortune* for *Slate*. In 1999 he surprised everyone by joining
the *New York Times* as an op-ed columnist. His fame grew. He moved
to Princeton's Woodrow Wilson School. He became the foremost
critic of the presidential administration of George W. Bush,
embroiled in constant controversy. He added his wife as coauthor
and together they labored away, passing drafts back and forth. And
by the summer of 2005 they had completed their task.

A VERY DIFFERENT STORY was unfolding all the while in California.
It commenced in the fall of 1996, when Paul Romer first began
teaching M.B.A. students at the Stanford Graduate School of Business. He had finished up his growth project. He was preparing to
enter the field of behavioral economics. The interesting problem of
the moment was getting his student to learn. These were some of the
brightest kid in the country. But they were having a hard time keeping up with the material.

This was no longer the long-haired, blue-jean-clad researcher who had begun his teaching career at the University of Rochester fifteen years before. After his first semester he even bought a suit—a source of merriment to those who had known him in Rochester. He was, however, frustrated. Teaching macroeconomics, even to highly motivated M.B.A.'s, was not much fun. Students came to class unprepared. Despite the intellectual excitement of Olivier Blanchard's intermediate macroeconomics text, their eyes glazed over. They wanted to understand the subject, but they weren't doing the work necessary to learn.

Romer had long recognized the interesting puzzle about what a good teacher really does—a puzzle at once intellectual and now suddenly highly practical. Why did his Stanford students pay him to force them to do something that they wanted to do anyway? There was something more to it than simply creating a forfeit device, binding themselves to a situation in which they had to either learn or fail. Even so, they still didn't do the work. He found out that much when he began cold-calling in class, to see who was prepared. He discovered, too, that it was a brutal process, resulting in much embarrassment.

What his students really needed he decided, was a *coach*. Learning was a lot like sports. In order to master the subject, they themselves would have to do the hard work, practicing daily, alone and in study groups. They also needed someone nearby, who knew shortcuts and techniques, the various ins and outs of the game, someone who wanted them to succeed at what they were doing, whose respect they craved—but whose job, they understood, was not to make things easy for them but rather to make the experience rewardingly hard. What *he* needed was the equivalent of a stopwatch, or a heart-rate monitor—some way of gauging their performance and discovering which areas needed work.

He knew what to do to elicit more effort from them—assign more homework. The trouble was that he didn't have time to grade it. Perhaps his assignments could be put on a machine. After a year he hired an inventive graduate student in computer science to code the exercises he developed in such a way that they could be put on a server, done online, and graded automatically.

Now Romer assigned his problem sets before class, not after. He gave frequent quizzes, and kept track of each student's performance. He stopped cold-calling in class, but participation in class discussions rose anyway, as students felt more a part of things. Before long, Romer was putting his course assignments, lecture notes, and Q&A sessions on the course's Website as well. He devised online experiments, double-blind auctions, and the like, of the sort that had been invented at Caltech and the University of Arizona and that were gradually becoming a staple of instruction in the better schools. He incorporated current affairs into his problem sets, asking students to estimate the possible cost of the war in Iraq, or to weigh the choices facing the Fed at the next meeting of its Open Market Committee.

He found that students not only came to class better prepared but enjoyed it more. They were more confident and, yes, more knowledgeable. The nature of the course had changed. And in his third year at Stanford, he won the distinguished teaching award that was voted annually by the business school students themselves.

After James Surowiecki, writing in Wired.com, noted the fact that the venture-capitalist John Doerr found the class interesting enough to sit in on it occasionally, Romer had to password-protect its Website. Rubberneckers were threatening to crash the site. But it was when other business professors began to ask to adapt his tools to their courses that Romer knew he had achieved a breakthrough

IN ANOTHER PART of California, Romer's father was undertaking a similar challenge. Education policy had been at the center of Roy Romer's twelve years as governor of Colorado, and as far back as the Bush education summit in 1989, he had taken an active interest in the use of standards and assessments in getting students to learn. He chaired the National Education Goals Panel that set early childhood education as the most fundamental challenge facing the nation.

Barred from seeking a fourth term Romer was the senior Democratic governor in the nation, ready for a new job. In 1997 he went to Washington, D.C., to cochair the Democratic National Committee, helping steer the party through the Clinton impeachment trial. Had Al

Gore won in 2000, Roy Romer might have become secretary of education. Had Gore stumbled, he might have run for president himself.

Instead, the three-term former governor sought the widely advertised position of superintendent of schools in LA. In July 2000 he got the job. He would be "the Donald Rumsfeld of education," as columnist George Will described him, too old to run for another elective office, but still ambitious, possessed of the impatience to do something rather than be someone. He and his son the professor talked frequently about the ins and outs of improving K–12 education.

Publishers were not meeting the needs of the children of Los Angeles any better than those of Stanford M.B.A.'s. Teaching materials were expensive and uninspiring. They worked well only in the hands of the most gifted teachers. But the supply of "master artisans" available to teach the teachers was shrinking. While the son wrote software to measure the performance of his students at Stanford, the father hired the Educational Testing Service in Princeton, New Jersey, to create a series of achievement-based tests in math so that his students would know what they needed to know. He gave them every ten weeks in order that teachers and supervisors could react quickly when students were not learning. Ever the politician, Roy Romer devised a good line to explain is mistrust of the usual "normed" tests, which were graded on a curve: "Which would you rather know— that your pilot's skills are in the top 50 percent? Or that she can land the plane?"

At Stanford, Paul Romer's thoughts turned to textbooks. He, too, had been approached in the 1990s by McGraw-Hill. He was as cognizant of the Samuelson problem as anybody else. Turning out another variation on the theme had been of little interest. "The main thing I learned from them is how hard it would be to do something really different." The plain-vanilla-with-a-little-topping strategy had become an industrywide business strategy. The trick was to publish a new edition every three years, incorporating just enough new material that the old book would seem out of date. Students, meanwhile, had gotten wise to the publishers' tricks and were rebelling in ever-increasing numbers. With prices soaring to over $120 a copy, surveys showed that more than half of those who enrolled in economics courses bought used books or no books at all. Hence the turned-off M.B.A. students who came to Romer's class.

So not long after his father took the job in Los Angeles, Paul Romer decided to start a publishing company to market the course management system and online teaching materials he had devised. The possibility had originally come up a year or two before, during a weekend trip to Sweden to speak to executives of the Skandia Life Insurance Company as part of their annual retreat. Romer's spiel about the implications of nonrivalry for global publishing had led the venture-minded Swedes to become interested in the possibility of backing some kind of start-up, one that might tie in to their retirement business. (This was the height of the dot-com mania, remember, a period in which several economists were concocting online "financial engines" of various sorts.)

Convinced that textbook publishers would find it difficult to abandon the business model that had made so much money for them, Romer and the Skandia venture capitalists sensed an opportunity. In November 2000, while he waited for the Microsoft damages trial to begin, he returned to Sweden to dicker. He came home with an $11.2 million commitment to a new firm. A search firm came up with the name Aplia. The new company's logo was a cheerful little face that could be construed either as the possessor of a bright idea or as a fuse-lit bomb.

THE APLIA PLAN had three prongs—one each for textbook publishers, teachers, and students. The first and most important emerged quickly. Romer would address the used-book problem. This he would do by selling his tools to any publisher that wanted them, building out the online teaching materials and course management tools that had proved so successful in his class in such a way that they could be adapted for use with any mainstream introductory text. Aplia's platform would remain textbook neutral.

After all, economics was full of concepts that were well illustrated by interactive computer graphics—change this and see what happens to that. It wasn't always easy to code these graphics in the form of exercises, much less integrate them seamlessly with the words necessary to explain them. But this was precisely what he had already learned to do. He had a good head start in devising the sorts of applications that textbook authors would find attractive. He knew where to find economics instructors to write new demonstrations. His head start would enable him to cover a considerable fixed cost.

With much of the time-sensitive window dressing that filled half of any text shifted to the Web—problem sets, illustrations drawn from current events, quizzes, and tests—publishers would need to update their texts far less frequently. They could offer an online version of the text for much less than a copy in paper and ink. The book itself could shrink.

The second selling point was the traction the new Web-based system offered the teacher. Once the instructor had chosen a text, he could select from a large library of Aplia-developed materials with which to teach it—all of them up to the moment, and more or less tailored to the text. Problem sets would be automatically graded and fed back daily to the teacher and student alike in the form of progress reports. Students would take tests by manipulating interactive graphs and data. They would grasp the concepts better than before—or, if they failed to understand, the instructor would know and be able to take remedial action. Thus the real pitch for adoption of Aplia's materials would be made to the teacher. Teaching would be both easier and more effective—and without taking any more of the instructor's time.

The third overture would be to the students themselves. Romer knew from his own experience that they were shrewd judges of educational software. The real test of the new materials would be whether the students who used them would learn the subject better than those who didn't. Certainly the students themselves understood the difference. Aplia would rely on word of mouth among students and their teachers. If it worked, their preferences could be expected to become part of the sale. It wouldn't be like the nineteenth century, when rival typewriter manufacturers ran typing contests in hopes of persuading bosses and their secretaries that they would type faster with their designs—not with such twenty-first century safeguards as large randomized trials and human experimentation boards. But the personal experience of efficacy would be a vital part of the competition.

Aplia was the third major gamble of Romer's career. Leaving MIT for the University of Chicago certainly involved a risk, but he was very young and not yet committed to economics. Quitting his Chicago professorship and moving to California without a job was perhaps even more surprising, but within a year Romer had landed on his feet. Going into business for himself was a still bolder move. Even inside the profession, he was far from famous. He was forty-five years old. Perhaps he would simply be ignored.

He took a two-year leave of absence from Stanford. He plowed his savings into payroll. He finished a course he was teaching with Tom Sargent and said good-bye to graduate students. After a paper on technical training at an innovation conference, he stopped doing research altogether. To many he seemed to retire from the field. He was brain-dead, snorted one economist. An editor who called on Romer found him excited to be running a business. It was kind of sad, he mused, to find him trying to prove his academic point through publishing.

But Romer turned out to have a knack for business. He recruited developers, editors, and field representatives; he hired, fired, and refinanced. For a couple of years he operated in near-total stealth, attending regional economic meetings around the country to gauge instructors' needs and scout for developer talent. He demonstrated his software to invited guests in private suites during the Meetings, instead of taking a booth in the exhibition hall.

His first customer was W. W. Norton & Company, publisher of Hal Varian's best-selling intermediate microeconomics textbook. Varian had been supported through six editions by one of the best workbooks ever written, *Workouts in Intermediate Microeconomics*, compiled jointly with Theodore Bergstrom of the University of California at Santa Barbara. Now Romer agreed to put paper-and-pencil problem sets online, offering instructors a chance to assign machine-graded homework requiring the same kinds of answers—equations, numbers, and graphs—that students would give in paper-and-pencil exercises. Happy to be able to give more homework without having to spend more time grading papers, teachers snapped it up.

Then, in November 2003, Aplia agreed to support the Krugman text. The publisher would offer the traditional 800-page textbook for around $100, or an electronic version for around $60, bundled with a subscription to the mandatory Aplia problem sets and periodic tests worth around $30—a subscription that all students enrolled in the course would be required to have, in order to do their course-work, whether they bought a hardcover edition, an e-text, or no book at all. The idea was to tip students into preferring the online edition. Romer and Krugman were "threatening to shake up the real life economics of the $3.9 billion a year US college textbook indus-try," reported Charles Goldsmith in the *Wall Street Journal*. "Few would dispute that the industry was in need of reform."

In early 2005 Mankiw's publisher quietly signed up Aplia to sup-port his text as well. The company's travelers had complained that, unable to offer it, they were losing out to the Krugman text in the market for new adoptions. As usual, Romer offered only a nonexclu-sive license, as had Bill Gates for his computer operating systems twenty years before.

And as he prepared for the Meetings in Boston in 2006, the course management and instruction system that he had first designed for his students at Stanford was supporting some large fraction of the cutting edge of the market for introductory college economics.

COULD A COMPLEMENTARY GOOD gain control of the market for col-lege economics instruction? That was, of course, the fundamental question behind Aplia's dash to market power. In much the same way, the QWERTY design had become standard among typewriter keyboards, and Microsoft's Windows operating system had turned the PC itself into a commodity, no matter who manufactured it. Might Aplia become "the universal" in online economics—the stan-dard tool by which students wanted to learn? That was the really interesting question at the meetings in Boston in 2006.

Certainly a tournament had heated up among authors of intro-ductory texts themselves. Krugman and Mankiw attracted the lion's share of the attention. But Romer had quietly agreed to turn his course lectures into an intermediate macroeconomics text for John Wiley and Sons, perhaps with an elementary text to follow, making it at least a three-way race. Meanwhile, Pearson signed Columbia's R. Glenn Hubbard (a senior advisor to George W. Bush) and Harvard's David Laibson (a prominent behavioral economist) to develop two more new approaches. Norton had Stiglitz and Houghton Mifflin had Taylor going forward. And McGraw-Hill had Bernanke and Frank. Its Samuelson/Nordhaus title was fading, though. What would the publishing giant do next?

More broadly, what pedagogical architecture would replace Samuelson in the twenty-first century, as Samuelsonian economics of the twentieth century replaced the Marshallian traditions of the nineteenth century? It was far too soon to tell. When the thirty-year-old Samuelson had taken a couple of years off after World War II to write a text—"for those who will never take more than one or two semesters of economics but who are interested in the subject as part of a general education"—both economics and publishing had been smaller and more decentralized businesses, cottage industries instead of multinational enterprises. The plain-vanilla plus-special-topping business model hadn't yet been discovered. Publishers could afford to take a flier. And Samuelson himself never expected the book to last so long.

Certainly in 2005, Web-based "supplementals" to the standard texts and course management tools had become all the rage since Aplia started its business. Higher education publishers had awak-ened to the importance of deadlines and graded homework. They were scrambling to put their old "self-assessment" and demonstra-tion tools online. Competition was forcing them, too, to become more complete service providers to higher education.

And precisely because the publishers were waking up, and because technology was ultimately nonrival, there was no guarantee that Aplia would join the big four international publishers as a durable business. Perhaps it would be absorbed by one of them instead. Said Romer, "It's not clear we'll make a killing. But I always said that it would be easier to change the industry than to make a profit. I've already had a bigger impact there than I ever could have had by just writing about it." Economics pedagogy was changing, along with the economic theory itself.

It was all a long way from that day ten years in San Francisco, when Romer had expounded new growth theory upstairs in the Hilton Hotel while John Taylor rolled out his text with the new material in the exhibition hall below. Would Romer return to research economics? He didn't know. The company's revenues were surging. Then Skandia pulled back from its investment in the United States. So, in 2005, Romer's father and brother provided a second round of funding, essentially diluting away the Swedes' interest in control. Aplia had become the newest Romer family company, along with the John Deere dealerships. His father's contract with the Los Angeles schools ran through 2007, when he would be seventy-nine. Paul Romer himself had turned fifty in 2005. He was teaching again. His children were grown. He and his wife had filed for divorce. His goals had changed. It wasn't clear what would happen next.

As usual, his gamble had stimulated a certain amount of resentment. He was definitely not part of the gang. But his enthusiasm was undimmed. "I'm right where I want to be," he said—"in the thick of the most important policy issue facing the United States—how to educate people for a world of global competition." Then too "there is the challenge of educating all the kids who will go to college in India and China. . . ."

CONCLUSION

We've come to the end of our story—the tale of how one paper in technical economics precipitated the redefinition of the basic factors of production, of how, during a few years in the 1980s, land, labor, and capital became people, ideas, and things, thanks to a useful new distinction between atoms and bits.

Along the way we've developed a pretty thorough picture of how things happen in university economics—and a deeper appreciation, perhaps, of how a new discovery triumphs not by making its opponents see the light but by being embraced by the next generation.

But our account would be incomplete without a summing up. So there is a new economics of knowledge. What has changed as a result? The answer, it seems to me, is not much—at least not yet. The really important changes are those in the world itself that have already occurred—the surge of discovery and innovation, the retreat of the state from top-down economic management and control, the opening of global markets. Professional economics has caught up with the significance of these developments in the nick of time. The hard work of assimilating the new understanding, and acting on it, is still ahead. Here I must put aside my role as a reporter of goings-on in the community of economists, a cat looking at kings, and write instead simply as a citizen and father.

At least since Henry the Navigator, governments have understood that it was in their interest to subsidize the production and diffusion of knowledge, to support the useful arts, to extend education, to protect intellectual property, and to promote free trade. After all, Bacon's dictum "knowledge itself is power" dates from early seventeenth-century England. The French Revolution and Napoleon stimulated learning and democratized it, from the calculus and the *grandes écoles* to the public schools. By the nineteenth century German universities set the global standard for scientific excellence, and Germany rose to become Europe's most powerful industrial nation in the years before World War I.

Americans, too, have had a technology policy from their earliest days, though they have rarely called it that. English colonists founded Harvard College in 1636. The law of patents was written into the U.S. Constitution. The beginning of the Civil War was accompanied by the passage of the Morrill Act, creating the land-grant universities, extending higher education to the farthest frontiers. A surge of immigration in the late nineteenth century led to widespread creation of high schools in the early twentieth century. The end of World War II brought the GI Bill, which opened the doors of college to all veterans. The Bayh-Dole Act, creating a slew of incentives for private development of the fruits of government-funded medical research, was passed by Congress in 1980, the same year that Romer began his thesis. The recognition that universities themselves play a major role in the economic system is the easy part. Take a look at any map. The places with universities are the ones that have remained on top or renewed themselves around the world. That knowledge is a powerful factor of production requires no more subtle proof than that.

That said, the ideas of economists really do have great force, once they are widely accepted. "Endogenous Technological Change" has begun to have its effect. Twenty years after new growth theory first made its appearance, Germany's chancellor, Gerhard Schroeder, made a surprising announcement in early 2004. The German central bank would sell much of its gold and invest the money in German universities; the French central bank quickly followed suit. The next year the British government offered a large contract to the successful developer of a successful malaria vaccine, much as once it had one offered a substantial prize for the invention of a reliable means of finding longitude at sea. The idea was not just to promote worldwide a cure for malaria, which caused around two million deaths and countless injuries per annum; the bounty was intended to stimulate British biotech capabilities as well. In Singapore higher education is practically a state religion. In India and China university systems are training engineers and Ph.D.'s at a furious rate and thinking rigorously about how to improve their universities to a point at which they, too, can compete for international students. In 2005 India's prime minister appointed an eight-member Knowledge Commission to propound ideas for radical reform.

Should the United States seek mechanisms by which to train more scientists and engineers? Robert Solow is surely right when he says we can't routinely double R&D spending and expect to get results, any more than we can routinely slash taxes and expect revenue to increase. Laboratories enjoy no special exemption to the principle of diminishing returns, even though sometimes the discoveries made there (and in the tinkerer's garage and the marketer's imagination) lead in the opposite direction, to increasing returns. Romer's preferred remedy is a somewhat more sophisticated version of the National Defense Education Act (NDEA) of 1958, which doubled federal aid to education, especially higher education. That Cold War measure, enacted after the Soviets put the world's first satellite in orbit, provided the most substantial stimulus to American research universities since the Morrill Act of 1862 established the land-grant public colleges in all the states. Virtually all those in the generation that made the revolutions in computers, telecommunications, and biotechnology went to school on the NDEA in one way or another. Its voucher-like apparatus seems to have been especially well suited to make a big investment in higher education pay off. Romer says the most important ideas of all may be such "meta-ideas"—ideas about how to support the production and transmission of other ideas.

What's a meta-idea? Some examples include the emergence of openness in scientific communication, the decline of prior restraint of newspapers, the rise of journals, the discovery of the patent system, the establishment of public education, the invention of the agricultural extension service, the implementation of best-practice planning initiatives (of the sort that put Japan on the road to industrialization in the 1870s), the advent of government funding of research universities, the introduction of the system of peer-reviewed competitive grants, of advanced study institutes, science talent searches, math camps, and the like. It will take years before the policy implications of the new economics of knowledge can be traced out in any detail. There is no reason to think we have it all figured out.

A meta-idea par excellence is openness and trade. Probably no story is more symbolic of the new realities than IBM's decision in 2004 to sell its $12 billion-a-year personal computer business to China's big computer manufacturer Lenovo, along with permission to use various IBM brands for five years while burnishing its own. Overnight, Lenovo thereby became the third-largest global PC producer; IBM got $1.75 billion with which to pursue more lucrative businesses, if it can develop them—mysterious long-lived batteries, for instance, or new and altogether faster means of computing. It is by now an old saw that Asian manufacturers can produce television sets and American producers can manufacture "content," and everyone will be better off. As much as anything, it was the speed with which IBM recognized that it could no longer manufacture personal computers profitably that was breathtaking—barely a quarter century after it virtually invented the market for them.

Compare IBM's quick reaction to the new realities of the twenty-first century with the generally uncomprehending and foot-dragging American response in the 1970s and 1980s to the rise of Japan. Consumers, of course, knew at once that better cars and cheaper television sets were good for them. How long did it take for American managers to adjust to the rise of the Japanese steel, automotive, and electronic industries? The sanction given by the new growth economics for IBM's sale of its PC business to China is important for two reasons. Efforts to keep China from becoming a low-cost producer of personal computers could no more succeed than earlier efforts to deny China the secrets of nuclear weapons or moon rockets. They could only delay the inevitable for a few years, whereas willing commercial integration fosters trust among trading partners. A vigorous Chinese economy broadens the market for successful American products, and the American economy gets an early warning that its costs are out of line.

For most of human history, well into the first half of the twentieth century, it was fairly easy to get a good job almost anywhere in the world on the basis of strength and endurance alone. Gradually machines and engines and assembly lines replaced muscle power, and a powerful build was no longer a ticket to a livelihood, except perhaps in professional sports. Now computers have transformed the world again, and this time traditional blue-collar jobs are the casualties. A striking example of what that means can be found in *The New Division of Labor: How Computers Are Creating the Next Job Market*, by Frank Levy and Richard Murnane.

When the Boeing 727, that great icon of the jet age, first rolled out in 1962, it was only after five thousand engineers had worked nearly seven years to develop it. They couldn't be certain that the blueprints were consistent, so their first step was to build a full-scale model. Only then could they translate blueprint specifications into settings for machine tools (skilled lathe operators already having been replaced by numerically controlled machines). Even then, the parts fit together imperfectly. Assembly workers therefore adjusted them by hand with metal shims to ensure that the plane was tight. (Shims, usually tapered, are used as a filler or leveler between components that otherwise wouldn't fit together smoothly.) Such was the complexity of manufacturing that a 727 weighing forty-four tons typically contained an estimated half a ton of shims. Of the nearly 1,800 planes delivered, 1,300 are still flying, shims and all.

Thirty years later, when the Boeing 777 model came along, barely five years were required to build it, even though it was much bigger and more complex. This time, there were no more paper blueprints. No mock-up was required. The 777 was the first airplane to be completely designed with computers, which guaranteed the internal consistency of its parts. Using computer-assisted design and manufacturing software purchased from a French engineering company, Dassault, Boeing engineers were able to take their numerically controlled machine tool settings directly from their plans. The plane fit together smoothly as a result. The manufacturer boasted, "The first 777 was just .023 of an inch—about the thickness of a playing card—within perfect alignment while most airplane parts line up within half an inch of each other." In other words, shims were no longer necessary—nor were the services required of those relatively highly skilled workers who were good with them.

Safer, cheaper, cleaner, and more comfortable planes have been the result. Airfares have declined. More people fly more often. Prices have fallen further as competitors entered the market, most notably the European Airbus syndicate, demonstrating that, thanks to the nonrivalry of knowledge, a head start conveys no insuperable advantage.

But the *composition* of employment changed dramatically. There were more high-paying jobs for CAD/CAM operators, software engineers, imaging device manufacturers, airport architects, and pilots, though flight captains no longer earned anything like the salaries they had when airlines were carefully regulated. There were more low-paying jobs for those who guided airplanes to their parking places, manufactured jetways, manned the imaging devices, swept the terminals. But there were many fewer jobs for blue-collar workers in machine shops, on production lines, in travel agencies, in the cockpit itself. Today, component-manufacturing plants can be located anywhere around the world, since airplane manufacturers know that the parts will fit together seamlessly wherever they are made. Competition between Boeing and Airbus has stiffened. Decisions about where to manufacture are made partly in response to political pressure from customers. Boeing even moved its headquarters from remote Seattle to Chicago. The city where three hundred years earlier French voyagers had carried their canoes over the dune from one watershed to the other had become a global crossroads. The company shed clerks and secretaries and added linguists and lobbyists in the process.

The globalization of the twenty-first century is just beginning. Tensions among the European nations, Japan, China, India, the United States, and the rest of the world are likely to become very great. The situation is vastly more complicated by the presence and number of "role player" nations—Scandinavians and eastern European nations, the Brazilians and the Russians, the Australians and the Turks. The growth challenges of greatest significance to the industrial democracies will have little to do with the issues that have dominated their politics for the last thirty years—tax cuts and depreciation allowances. Instead, the most important meta-ideas in the coming decades will have to do with making choices about how to map into the rapidly changing international division of labor. The goal today is market specialization and globalization, not colonization, but the importance of interlocking institutions— economic, legal, and political—is greater than ever. Not since the mid-nineteenth century has such a race among nations loomed.

How did nations fare in that global competition? Cut away the high emotions, the colonial smash and grab, the tragic wars of the twentieth century, the slow but certain advance of human rights, and we can see clearly that the nations that did best were those that did something fundamental about education. In *Scale and Scope: The Dynamics of Industrial Capitalism*, the great historian Alfred Chandler developed a very clear picture of how the differences played out among the industrial styles of Great Britain, Germany, and the United States.

Three varieties of managerial capitalism were on display, Chandler said—personal, cooperative, and competitive. He showed how in each case increasing returns to manufacturing led to economic strength: the first companies to invest in large-scale manufacturing plants obtained cost advantages, much as economics would lead you to expect. These manufacturing giants were the first multinational corporations. They created international marketing and distribution chains. They evolved the structures required to manage them. And they retained their superiority for decades.

In Great Britain, however, the system of personal capitalism by and large failed to keep up. In Germany close cooperation among political and business leaders built fortunes quickly and, for a time, the world's greatest universities, but somehow either led to war or failed to prevent it. So competitive American companies, many of them creatures of the Sherman Antitrust Act and subsequent legislation, emerged triumphant in the mid-twentieth century. The institutions of textbook capitalism—capital markets, management structures, regulatory regimes—are major parts of the story. Yet the institutions of greatest interest today may be those that lurk just beyond Chandler's focus—in the human capital policies that, quite visibly in the United States, extended education and training to ever greater portions of the citizenry and built the industrial workforce into a postindustrial powerhouse.

Obviously, it's not enough to send large numbers of kids to college to study alienation and folklore, only to graduate them into an economy for whose few opportunities they are ill suited. Higher education must be tied to market signals in some loose way that students can understand and accept. Some part of Europe's slowdown may stem from the vast expansion of education opportunities after 1968 when little thought was given to where the graduates might find work. This is part of the challenge of managing a national economy in an age of rapid globalization. It means paying closer attention to where the economy is headed, and devising new incentives for those who need more education and training—vouchers, apprenticeships, expanded forms of training and testing, national service opportunities, and so on. Early childhood interventions may be the most cost-effective policies of all, since they prepare children of the next generation to take care of themselves as citizens and workers who might otherwise become truculent political factions and wards of the state.

We've come a long way from the day when Adam Smith, offering what was probably the first meta-idea to be contributed by an economist, wrote that all that is required for economic growth is "peace, low taxes and a tolerable administration of justice." That's still not a bad recipe for the basics, but how much more complicated our understanding of the world has become since then! The most recent discovery, the one that has not been obvious all along, is that, in a rapidly converging global economy, capital will by and large take care of itself (with an occasional nudge from central banks), but human and technological resources require a degree of active management by the state.

The need for technology policy is the inescapable conclusion that emerges from "Endogenous Technological Change." It seems unlikely that government science managers and education secretaries will ever be thought of as ranking on a par with central bankers or finance ministers or even trade negotiators, but technology, training, and education policy will eventually come to be seen in countries all around the world as a necessary and legitimate responsibility of government, as important as monetary and fiscal policy, and even harder to execute well.

This, then, is the message of the new growth economics. Reform the patent system, by all means. Renegotiate the international intellectual property regime, with a view to creating better access for the poor to knowledge that already has paid for itself many times over in the West. Consider anew the institutions that call knowledge into being, in hopes of making them more efficient—there are other effective allocation mechanisms besides the capital markets, private foundations, and governmental agencies (ARPA, NASA, and the National Institutes of Health). And by all means, continue to innovate boldly in new industries.

But first, rebuild the education systems of the old industrial nations and create new ones for developing nations, in ways that emphasize the new realities of international competition. Either that or suffer steadily growing inequality as the newly industrializing nations, with their sharply lower costs, enter global markets.

Where's the money going to come from? The conventional wisdom is that the issues of the aging baby boomers will dominate politics in the industrial democracies for the next twenty or thirty years, that greedy geezers demanding benefits will leave no room for the kind of investment in human capital necessary to adjust successfully to the new global order. In that case immigrants willing to work hard for less will take over much of the middle of the economy, as they have in the United Kingdom. Romer himself is pessimistic, fearing that the United States won't be able to do in the twenty-first century what it did in the twentieth—build up its high schools dramatically, send millions of students to college for the first time, and boost research universities and graduate schools. Then again, who knows what direction politics will develop next? The wealth created by the greatly expanded global market will be enormous—enough, perhaps, to permit the boomers to enjoy improved living standards *and* create broader opportunities for the next generation. But the tensions will be very great. We are headed for a crisis of a highly complicated sort—and, as Romer says, "A crisis is a terrible thing to waste."

Meanwhile, there is technical economics—mathematical, empirical, free to make its own mistakes—and an indispensable guide to the modern world. It seems to me that you couldn't ask for a clearer demonstration than the one we have told here of how economics makes progress over time. Moreover, this story of economic discovery is only one of many that could be told. The theorist and historian Jürg Niehans once wrote that standard treatments of the history of economic thought convey the impression that the past was an age of giants, while a bunch of pygmies engage in agitated babble in the present day. Presumably the same could be said of physics or public health. But who seriously longs for the good old days of Isaac Newton and Louis Pasteur?

Certainly it is true that as various facets of life have come to be more fully understood, a diminution of romance has occurred. This flip side of the growth of knowledge is what Max Weber long ago called "the disenchantment of the world." Otherwise, nothing could be further from the truth. Economics has never been more exciting. Its greatest challenges lie ahead, to discover the *deeper* secrets of the wealth of nations, the faculties that Adam Smith called our moral sentiments—what it is about human nature that we call humane.

ACKNOWLEDGMENTS

The strong opinions of this book were come by honestly. Long before I read "Endogenous Technological Change," I had, like many others, read Allyn Young's "Economic Progress and Increasing Returns." Indeed, I had already spent a dozen years trying to pierce the mysteries of what economists had to say about specialization and the growth of knowledge, without conspicuous success, either on my part or, it seems to me (and this is precisely the point), on theirs. An account of that earlier adventure in journalism, centered on the work of the economist Peter Albin, was published in 1984 as *The Idea of Economic Complexity*. That book took eight years to write. This one took a dozen. Neither would have taken so long but for the merry competition with family life and daily newspapering.

Even though I heard an early version of Romer '90 presented as "Microfoundations for Aggregate Technical Change" in Buffalo in 1988, I didn't begin to comprehend its significance until I read Lucas's "Mechanics" later that year. It was Lucas who introduced me to Romer in Chicago ("The guy you want to talk to is Paul"). Even then it was not until Barbara L. Solow and F. M. Scherer each called my attention, in the kindest possible fashion, to a revealing mistake I made in 1992 that I finally understood the difference between the exogenous and endogenous approaches to the growth of knowledge. Truth emerges more readily from error than from confusion! My particular thanks to them.

My thanks, too, to Daniel C. Tosteson, who wrote a letter that led me see what I had written in that earlier book in a completely different light. Thanks also to Les Lenkowsky, for arranging for me to be invited to that Buffalo meeting. It was Mitchell Waldrop's account of developments at Santa Fe Institute in the increasing-returns revolution that persuaded me to write this parallax version.

Various important insights were shared along the way by Otto Eckstein, Gary Becker, Hendrik Houthakker, Karl Case, Richard Zeckhauser, Robert Lucas, Allison Green, Nan Stone, Eytan Sheshinski, Jürg Niehans, Howard Johnson, and Ernst Berndt. Aida Donald and Michael Aronson originally proposed that the book be written, after I dumped a version of the story into the newspaper, hoping to walk away from it. Those who read portions of the manuscript at early stages were Frank Levy, Bob Gibbons, Mark Feeney, and Robert Phelps. Drake McFeely took the project over when I got stuck, restarted it, and then encouraged me for six long years to completion. Robert Solow, Robert Lucas, Elhanan Helpman, and, of course, Paul Romer were helpful at every stage, though I must stress that Romer, in particular, bears no responsibility for the outcome.

This sort of an account never would have been possible but for the commitment to beat reporting of the old *Boston Globe*, where I was permitted to follow the field for twenty-three years, first as a reporter, then as a columnist. It was a wonderful newspaper, whose unique traditions, to all intents and purposes, have ceased to exist. No other news organization would have supported the reporting on which it is based. Thanks therefore to the memory of the late John I. Taylor and to Benjamin Taylor, in particular, and to the Taylor family, in general; and to all the men and women who made the *Boston Globe* the paper that it was before its sale.

The Sabre Foundation permitted EconomicPrincipals.com to find itself after the newspaper column was shut down. And the American Academy in Berlin provided a quiet office in which to write, a crowd of spirited and congenial colleagues around the breakfast table, and a *Monatskarte* for one of the world's great cities, just when I needed it most. To all in the extraordinary group of friends at the Hans Arnhold Center, my heartfelt thanks.

INDEX